RACE HORSE MEN

RACE HORSE MEN

HOW SLAVERY AND FREEDOM
WERE MADE AT THE RACETRACK

KATHERINE C. MOONEY

Harvard University Press

Cambridge, Massachusetts
London, England
2014

Library of Congress Cataloging-in-Publication Data

Mooney, Katherine Carmines.
Race horse men : how slavery and freedom were made at the
racetrack / Katherine C. Mooney
    pages cm
  Includes bibliographical references and index.
  ISBN 978-0-674-28142-4 (hardcover : alk. paper)
  1. Horse racing—Social aspects—United States—History—19th
century. 2. Horse racing—United States—History—19th century.
3. African American horsemen and horsewomen—United States—
History—19th century. 4. African American jockeys—History—
19th century. 5. Southern States—Race relations—History—19th
century. I. Title.
  SF335.U5M66 2014
  798.400896073—dc23   2013037080

For Mom, Dad, Anne, Morris, Adin,
and all the animals

Contents

RACE HORSE MEN

Prologue

The Loss of the Stirrup Has Won the Race

EVERYTHING DEPENDED ON the start. In a dash race of a quarter mile like the one North Carolina planter Willie Jones and his opponent had agreed to, the two horses circled and plunged beside the starter, as their jockeys tried desperately to keep their mounts calm. All strategy would be exhausted after the first moment. From then until the horses crossed the finish line, the contest would be one of main force, as the horses and riders jostled each other along the narrow track laid out amid the crowd. The ritual was a rough but much-beloved tradition of the colonial South, its tricks and subtleties as much to be savored as victory itself.

Jones and an old friend from Virginia had agreed to an intercolonial match race and staked a hundred hogsheads of tobacco each on the outcome. Jones had sent his entry, the delicate, nervous Paoli, ahead to the course and had arrived himself only shortly before the start. No sooner had he dismounted than Austin Curtis, the enslaved black man who was Jones's trusted jockey and groom and would later serve as his trainer and stable supervisor, delivered a nasty surprise. Their opponent was to be the mare that everyone knew as Bynum's Big Filly, though Jones and her owner had an agreement to the contrary.

Willie Jones preferred to be the man surprising rather than the man surprised when it came to the races. By the early 1770s, when

Paoli faced Bynum's Big Filly, he had firmly established himself as a crafty competitor. He and Austin Curtis had once disguised a pony-sized speedster aptly named Trick 'em as a packhorse and, with both men loudly professing their reluctance, entered him against a well-regarded racer. The odds had skyrocketed, and Jones and his friends had laughed all the way to the bank.[1] To pull off a victory for Paoli against a mare like Bynum's Big Filly, ridden by the cunning slave horseman Ned, would be more difficult, but Jones had the luxury of Austin Curtis in the saddle.

The size of the wager and the fame of the competitors had drawn a large crowd, a wall of bodies that lined the course. The jockeys began to circle their horses. Only when both were for the same fleeting moment roughly parallel to each other and the track would the starter send them off, and an experienced jockey could circle again and again, shouting "No!" to forestall the start, as he sought to gain a sendoff that would find his own mount ready and his opponent unprepared.[2] The experienced filly stayed quiet and alert as her rider turned her, but Paoli's nerves began to fray, just as Ned had hoped they would, and he kept the horses circling, his eyes on the other animal and on Austin Curtis. Suddenly Ned saw the weakness he had been waiting for and quickly lined his mare up. The two horses shot away from the post, the silence broken only by the rumbling, concussive rush of their passage. With horror, Willie Jones realized that his rider was galloping the narrow course at high speed, his opponent dangerously close, with only one stirrup. Without it to support his weight, his balance seemed impossible to maintain. The horses dueled at close quarters, locked together all the way to the finish. As the judges conferred, Jones rushed to Curtis to ask what mischance had caused such a potential calamity. "No chance at all," the jockey was said to have replied. "We made two turns, and could not start. I saw old Ned did not mean to start fair. . . . So I drew one foot, to induce Ned to think I was off my guard. . . . Away we came—both horses did their utmost, and the loss of the stirrup has won the race." It had, indeed. Austin Curtis had brought Paoli home a winner, the judges finally determined, by twenty-three inches.

Those inches lived on in legend, one of the early thrillers of America's first mass-audience sport. Fifty years later, Curtis's explanation of his daring ride was still being served up in print.[3] Americans before the twentieth century, dependent on equine transportation, lived in a world where horses' habits and peculiarities formed an integral part of daily living.[4] But they also followed the exotic world of Thoroughbred racing, where the equine verities they knew so intimately were transmuted into glorious power and speed. In the twenty-first century, when most Americans think of the racetrack only in the week before the Kentucky Derby, such a preoccupation can be difficult to grasp. Horse racing is usually regarded as a charming anachronism, a colorful survival—the sport Americans followed before baseball, football, basketball, ice hockey, and the countless other contests the country has adopted in its place. But in the eighteenth and nineteenth centuries, men from wildly varying walks of life—white and black, free and slave, young and old, rich and poor—felt deep passion for the world of the backstretch. For many Americans of earlier times, horse racing was not merely a leisure pastime but a practice to which they owed a powerful and tenacious allegiance; the racetrack was an institution that defined who they were or who they wished to become. This book tells the story of the American racetrack and the white and black men who made their lives on it for almost a century, from the Jacksonian period to the eve of World War I. The story is, in truth, a patchwork of many stories. It is less an attempt to answer a set of analytical questions about historical cause and effect than a portrait that seeks to reveal some complex and difficult realities in the lives of people in the past.

RACING WAS ALWAYS an indispensable part of life in colonial America. The English built the first racetrack in New York in the 1660s. By then, breeders in Britain had perfected the crosses between imported Arabian horses and older European stock that produced the Thoroughbred, a breed of horse designed to fly. Virginia and Carolina planters raided the great racing stables across the Atlantic and came away with stallions who would found their own dynasties in America.[5] In the eighteenth century, groups of men in towns and regions across the United States met and chartered themselves as jockey clubs, on the model of Britain's Jockey Club, headquartered at Newmarket, or on the model of the club in Charleston, South

Carolina, which claimed to predate it. In 1797, the Kentucky Jockey Club was formed in John Postlethwait's tavern in Lexington. The group agreed both to a set of rules and to the laying out of a course in Lee's Woods. The pattern was repeated at countless hotel bars and woodland tracts.[6]

Spectators pressed into colonial racetracks and gathered on market and court days to watch less formal races, like the one Austin Curtis won with one stirrup. Boys cherished glimpses of famous runners and stored up their memories of great contests to relive in old age.[7] They inherited the dramas and assumptions and argots of racing as a birthright that often extended into a lifetime commitment. Philip Fithian, who had come to Virginia as a tutor to the sons of Robert Carter III in 1773, sat across the dinner table from local beauty Sally Panton and hoped to get a chance to talk to her during the meal. But any tenuous efforts at flirtation were doomed, he informed his diary disgustedly later that night. The only dinner conversation consisted of "Loud disputes concerning the Excellence of each others Colts—Concerning their Fathers, Mothers . . . Brothers, Sisters, Uncles, Aunts, Nephews, Nieces, & Cousins to the fourth Degree!"[8] The Carters and their neighbors saw nothing odd in discussing horses with all the command of detail that they lavished on the human families about whom they cared the most. Indeed, they appear to have found horse gossip just as absorbing as the human variety.

Wealthy men like Willie Jones bankrolled and sometimes supervised the breeding, raising, training, feeding, shoeing, medicating, grooming, and running of Thoroughbreds. Why were they willing to put so much time and so many resources into racing? American historians have contended that what really stirred a Virginia or Carolina planter's blood was the chance to gamble impressively large sums. In doing so, a wealthy man demonstrated how reckless he could afford to be with his income and thus how richly he deserved to have the respect of his neighbors.[9] The pleasure of a wager may account for the magnate who enjoyed besting his friends aboard a talented animal or pointing out to them that his horse had just triumphed at the local race ground. But it seems an insufficient explanation for the sheer amount of time and effort such men devoted to thinking and arguing about the minute details and frequent disappointments that lay behind a single afternoon's racing. Scholars of British history, who have a longer record of national equine obsession to explicate, have given more emphasis to the horse itself, and the voices of their human subjects decisively support their choice. The British artist Benjamin Marshall, who painted the racehorses of the wealthy at the turn of the nineteenth century, observed of his clients in the shires: "I discover many a man who will pay me fifty guineas for painting his horse who thinks ten guineas too much to pay for painting his wife."[10]

The horsemen of the eighteenth-century British Empire and their nineteenth-century descendants were willing to pay good money for pictures of their horses because they genuinely found them beautiful. And, like the allure of most beautiful things, the horses' appeal did not lie solely in the aesthetics of their construction. They inspired such devotion because for their owners they evoked a sense of clarity about how the world worked or should work. Willie Jones was an Old Etonian, brought up to revere the sporting culture of the British Atlantic world.[11] What he inherited from his forebears he and his friends passed down to generations of wealthy white men who followed them to the track. For powerful cliques of upper-class men in the United States between the colonial period and the turn of the twentieth century, the track was about far more than the careless joy of ostentatiously splashing money around in symbolic moments of display. To justify weeks and months of worry and money put into the work of the office and the pasture, the barn and the breeding shed, affluent white men had to understand racing as more than one of many means to show off their wealth. Eighteenth-century racing enthusiasts coined the name "turfmen" for themselves, adopting it as a title of rightful authority both on and off the track. To be a turfman was not merely to be rich; it was to be a gentleman worthy of respect in the most select circles for savvy and judgment, grace and style. It was to be marked with the right to rule.

The nineteenth-century track became a proving ground for the powerful and the aspiring, an incubator of socially and politically useful alliances, a place in which men took practical realities and fashioned them into what they believed to be concrete evidence of the rightness of their ideologies. It helped to shape the political convictions of generations of elite white men. From the beginning of American racing, some of the nation's most prominent turfmen were Southerners, and at the track they practiced sophisticated and complex forms of human bondage and believed that they demonstrated how integral slavery was to building a powerful and prosperous United States, how richly they deserved Northern deference to their economic imperatives and social customs. Decades later, with the coming of emancipation, they joined with congenial Northerners to stifle the effects of Reconstruction and bring businessmen together across regional boundaries against working-class agitation. At the track, powerful men exhibited in a particularly revealing light how continuously and deeply they believed in the necessity of hierarchy to make a great and modern United States and how hard they were willing to work to protect social divisions and inequalities.

AMONG SOUTHERNERS, the mechanics of subordination were an issue of particular urgency, because the racetrack was not just a stage on which white men acted out the world they wanted to make. It was a place run on the labor and skill of black men. Everywhere Willie Jones went on the race grounds of colonial North Carolina, Austin Curtis went as well, familiar to knowledgeable men as a formidable opponent, as his one-stirruped victory attested. Grooms, trainers, jockeys, breeding supervisors—these men were absolutely necessary to a successful stable. A wealthy horse owner, proud of his competence, might know what had to be done around a barn; he might thoroughly enjoy ensuring that stable work was done up to his specifications; he might even pitch in and help on occasion, but he could not and did not wish to be everywhere and do everything necessary to a large operation. So much depended on subjective judgment grounded in long experience. How was one hoof disease to be distinguished from another in the early stages, when it might still be cured? What minute adjustment of saddle or bridle could magically cheer up an unhappy and recalcitrant animal? Most owners left such questions to specialized workers. The knowing ones understood that their stables, their little worlds in which they demonstrated their rightful authority, depended on such men. They would never be invited into drawing rooms, but at the racetrack they were to be acknowledged.[12]

Austin Curtis was not just a social inferior. He was an African American slave, both an individual and a commodity that belonged to Willie Jones. His situation was hardly an unusual one. Africans had a well-deserved reputation for equine expertise in the Atlantic world. The people of North Africa and the Middle East were world famous for their horses, and trans-Saharan caravans brought their animals and their equestrian practices to West Africa, just as trade with Europeans brought to Britain the Arabian foundation sires of the Thoroughbred.[13] Horsemanship became a signature accomplishment, especially for northern West Africans. By the seventeenth century, Malinke horsemen traveled throughout the region, selling their formidable services as cavalry to the highest bidder. The kings of the Yoruba and the Hausa boasted massive stable complexes, over which slaves presided.

Such slaves were valued members of the royal household, supervisors of large staffs, intimates of princes. Slaves like the Oyo king's chief horseman, the *Olokun Esin*, gave orders and received privileges. They were in charge of legions of other stable slaves, many of whom performed manual labor that carried no status and, indeed, was thought to embody the degradation inherent in servitude. But all equestrian slaves, whatever their privileges, were obliged to use their command of horses' speed and endurance to hunt down other bondsmen who had attempted to escape.[14] Horsemen's slavery was always a complicated institution that separated them from their fellow slaves and sometimes even drew lines among the men who worked in the stables.

Across the Atlantic, African and colonial-born slaves continued to bear the responsibility for the care of horses and other livestock. In French Saint Domingue, an epicenter of Caribbean sugar production, slaves were the primary caregivers and veterinarians for the work animals who kept plantations running smoothly. Men with such skills were among the most expensive slaves in island markets; white owners trusted them with extremely valuable four-footed assets, even as they kept a sharp eye out for the trouble that might

Illustration of African groom from William Cavendish's *A general system of horsemanship in all it's branches*, 1743 edition. By the nineteenth century, black men had been an accepted part of British and American stable workforces for more than a century. *Beinecke Rare Book and Manuscript Library, Yale University.*

come from according deference to slaves' specialized knowledge and granting them positions of relative autonomy.[15]

Slave owners readily accepted the presence of black horsemen in their stables, a natural result of lifetimes of owning bondsmen and reading the classic equine treatises of the seventeenth and eighteenth centuries, like those authored by William Cavendish, first Duke of Newcastle. Included in his tomes were engravings of the North African grooms who cared for his imported horses. The artist carefully stippled the faces of the men to an unrelieved black and gave them knotted hair; prominent foreheads; and thick, flat noses. These men were unmistakably alien, yet they were an acknowledged fact of life in the ducal stables.[16] Long habit and implied precept thus reinforced each other for American gentlemen like Willie Jones.

Until the turn of the twentieth century, black men like Austin Curtis would be a constant presence in American racing stables, their expertise necessary to the world white turfmen held so dear. Austin Curtis and those who followed him onto the track lived in highly unusual bondage, in which they wielded considerable authority and commanded autonomy and privilege beyond the wildest dreams of most slaves. But they were also subject to more subtle pressures than many of their contemporaries—the knowledge of their own difference, the fear of their privilege's fragility, and the tension of constantly calculating self-interest that often divided them sharply from loved ones and colleagues. They enjoyed many of the conventional signifiers of freedom—the ability to move without impediment, to exercise some control over their employment, to offer opinions that might well be heeded. In Carlyle Brown's *Pure Confidence*, a 2005 play about the relationship between white turfmen and their slaves, the black protagonist asserts his desire for freedom, and his owner scoffs, "Hell, I don't know no nigger more free than you." What does he want with a piece of paper, his owner asks, when he has experienced the thrill of driving a great racehorse for home, gathering himself and his mount at the top of the stretch and feeling the surge toward victory? "Boy, if that ain't freedom, then the damn thing don't exist," the turfman concludes.[17] Black horsemen had daily experiences that transcended the conventional restrictions of slavery, so they knew how flexible and clinging the coils of bondage could be, how many irregularities and potential threats it could absorb. They faced the likelihood that they would live out their lives knowing only very circumscribed forms of freedom, and some even buried their hopes for it and turned to forms of mastery over animals and people that seemed a negation of bondage easier to attain. The story of the slaves who worked American Thoroughbreds illuminates just how complex and insidious human bondage could be, how deeply and how differently it marked the disparate people who lived in it.

WILLIE JONES AND HIS BROTHER between them owned nearly 300 slaves, so many that they often did not recognize men and women who were legally their property.[18] And yet from the time Jones and Austin Curtis were both young men, they wandered together through the mid-Atlantic, matching races, running up the odds, sizing up their opponents, and seizing their chances at victory. Curtis was as well known as Jones; on Curtis's unerring eye would be built the mightiest empire in antebellum racing. In the 1790s, Marmaduke Johnson, a planter from Warrenton, North Carolina, forty miles to the west of Jones's Halifax County home, got bitten by the racing bug. Like rich men before and after him buying their way into the horse business, he took a fat roll of cash to an expert. He asked Austin Curtis to find him a prospect—a young, inexperienced mare that could be a successful racehorse and later, Johnson cannily calculated, a profitable broodmare. It was a tall order. It can take years of training to know whether a horse can be a good racer, and genetics and plain luck determine the horses that become important breeding stock. But, at the farm of a man named Jordan just across the border in Virginia, Curtis found a small gray mare that he liked, and he bought her for Johnson for fifty pounds Virginia currency. Usually called Johnson's Medley Mare, identified by owner and sire, she turned out to be a great success at the racetrack, but in the breeding shed she was an immortal. She was the mother of Reality, who became the mother of Bonnets o' Blue, who became the mother of Fashion, each of them in her turn considered the greatest mare in American racing.[19]

The Johnson stables, founded on the offspring of Curtis's purchase, dominated the Thoroughbred world for decades. Marmaduke Johnson's son William was nicknamed "the Napoleon of the Turf," and all his equine exploits were subject to critical scrutiny in the sporting press of the 1830s and 1840s. In 1833, the writers and subscribers of the *American Turf Register*, frustrated by the sparse records kept on American Thoroughbreds, sought to establish just what the little gray mare's bloodlines were. In the days before an official Thoroughbred registration process, a purchaser depended almost entirely on the seller to tell him the truth about a horse's pedigree. Especially famous horses' *real* breeding was inevitably the subject of rumor and speculation that could discomfit or enrage an owner or breeder. Vicious acrimony was always a pen stroke away when the topic of breeding came up, and, for a mare so important to the Johnson enterprise and to racing as a whole, the density of proof demanded was particularly high. Allen Jones Davie, the great-nephew of Willie Jones, was almost apologetic when he wrote to the editor that he did "not mean this as a *contradiction* to provoke contest," but he was quite sure his version of the pedigree was correct, "because the blood was so stated by Austin Curtis . . . who, though a man of color, was one on whom all who knew him relied."[20] Immediately, all debate in the columns of the *Turf Register* ceased. Austin Curtis had made his name one to conjure with. In life and in death, he was a man to be recognized and reckoned with, and he and the men of his generation paved the way for black horsemen of comparable skill and standing to follow them. Black horsemen fascinated white turfmen, who knew how they depended on the competence of men like Curtis in a sport that they used to define themselves and make sense of their world. In Austin Curtis's lifetime and long afterward, white turfmen told stories to themselves and each other that made the reality of that dependence seem commonplace and safe.

Indeed, much of what we know about black horsemen comes from the tales of white men. Throughout the nineteenth century, such stories circulated around the track, crossed the nation in letters, and came to homes and offices in a growing number of racing periodicals. How many of these stories were true? We cannot know. But it is true that they are stories—and as such they are worth examining, not necessarily for their factual content but for the facts that fictions tell us about the people who tell them. The stories white men told reveal how deeply white turfmen needed black horsemen's work, how complex were their efforts to ensure black men's subordination, and how tortuous and desperate the logic of those efforts could be.

Willie Jones left only a few sentences about Austin Curtis. They appear in the petition he filed with the North Carolina General Assembly in 1791 to free Curtis, who "by his attachment to his Country during the War by his fidelity to his Master (the said Willie Jones) and by his Honesty and good Behavior on all Occasions, has demonstrated that he deserves to be free."[21] Jones started with an affirmation of Curtis's loyalty to the American cause in the Revolution, a difficult choice for slaves in the Carolinas, torn between the hope that white Americans would grasp the implications of their own quest for freedom and the reality that the British government was promising emancipation to those who joined His Majesty's cause.[22] Something about his own situation—a concern about traveling safely to British lines, a disinclination to leave the familiar, a knowledge that Jones had promised he would be free, and a hope that their long and curious camaraderie might carry some weight—decided Austin Curtis's loyalties in the American Revolution. Throughout the Carolinas, the British and the Americans were on the hunt for top-notch bloodstock, and Curtis had a perilous job to protect the animals in his care. Major Isaac Harleston of South Carolina nearly lost the famous imported stallion Flimnap to a British raiding party, but his groom concealed the horse in a nearby swamp and then spirited him over the border to the safe haven of Willie Jones's place in Halifax—or, as the groom may have thought of it, Austin Curtis's place.[23]

When Jones drafted the manumission request for the state legislature, such memories were perhaps uppermost in his mind, and they were decidedly memories that would appeal to the men who had to vote on his petition. His language, too, was safely vague and reassuring, a formula designed to soothe legislators' fears and echo their customary usages. Curtis was faithful; he behaved well; he *deserved* to be free because he was so extraordinary and thus, by implication, would take his good fortune gratefully, not seek to undermine the institution of slavery. Jones may have crammed into the restricted vocabulary of faithful servitude decades of feelings about his long racetrack partnership with Curtis, or he may not have known how to think beyond the barren boilerplate phrases he used about their history together. The general assembly repeated Jones's language, granting Curtis his freedom because he had "demonstrated that he deserves to be free."[24]

In the hackneyed words of the petition there are indicators and foreshadowings of the tangle of necessity and fantasy that turfmen wove around black horsemen in the nineteenth century. Examining the confined world of the track, we can unpick those knots and see that white turfmen were often strikingly sincere in the ties they professed with black horsemen, with these particular privileged slaves. But as clear as their sincerity is their complete inability to see black horsemen as full human beings. They recognized these black men as competent professionals and often as congenial companions. But they only saw black horsemen in relation to themselves; they could hardly imagine them with lives and feelings in which white interests played no part. This view of human beings as useful instruments was smotheringly all-encompassing, far deeper than any individual affection or sentimentality, malice or hypocrisy.

Turfmen could thus speak of black horsemen in emotional terms and believe they were describing their feelings accurately. They entertained ideas of horsemen as the perfect slaves, precisely calibrated extensions of a master's will and living proof of the long-term viability, the cutting-edge power of a slave society. They dreamed of black men who could support them in their efforts as seamlessly as the black assistant of William Faulkner's mythical horse trader Pat Stamper, of a wordless bond like the one that the two men shared, "a kind of outrageous rapport like a single intelligence possessing the terrific advantage over common mortals of being able to be in two places at once and directing two separate sets of hands and fingers at the same time."[25] Black talent and black subordination were equally integral to turfmen's vision of a great American future. They created in their stories generations of slaves and freedmen whose skills furthered important and difficult work while their blackness dictated their every feeling and action. The world of the racetrack reveals a complicated and painful form of human bondage, in which turfmen simultaneously acknowledged black men's individual talents and integrated them into their conceptions of slavery and black inferiority.[26] These complex forms of recognition and justification survived slavery, and they continued to dictate much of white men's view of black horsemen into the twentieth century. In the small space of the stable, we can see how white men negotiated this balancing act so necessary to their view of hierarchical order, how daily interactions with individual human beings could be made to bolster and particularize theories of human servitude and subordination.

WILLIE JONES mentioned Austin Curtis in another document as well. In his 1798 will, Jones left Curtis $200 and the use of fifty acres and a house until one of Jones's sons came of age.[27] When he died in the winter of 1808, Curtis left over three hundred acres to his wife and provided for his eleven children. He had bought his son William and emancipated him, which meant that at least nine of his children were free at his death. His daughter Lucy's husband was strictly forbidden by the terms of the will to touch her portion.[28] Austin Curtis's authority held as good at home as it did in the barn.

We do not know what Austin Curtis felt about his experience of bondage or about what he achieved in freedom. He left no written record of his life, nor of what it felt like in his stomach and throat to draw his foot out of the stirrup and send his mount careening toward the finish line at top speed. But in the provisions of Curtis's will, in the few accounts by those who came after him, and in the other scraps of evidence they left, we can sometimes see not only the pain of black horsemen's lives, their sacrifices and frailties, but also their pride and determination and style. Enslaved horsemen struggled to make their way at the track, in a profession and a world that demanded minute calculations of status and self-interest. A few ultimately dared to use their work to benefit their families, friends, and communities. After emancipation, men made freedom for their families out of their racetrack lives, just as Austin Curtis had done. Black horsemen of the 1860s, 1870s, and 1880s had learned their trade in slavery or had been taught by men who had; their ties to bondage remained personal. The spotlight American newspapers shone on their careers illuminates how a particular group of former slaves and their sons experienced and tested the abstraction called freedom. Privately and publicly, they did the daily work of defining and displaying its multifarious meanings and the range of its consequences. Postbellum black horsemen achieved prosperity and respectability and commanded attention and admiration in the African American press. Curtis and his successors were subjects on which many black people exercised an old but unwritten American right—the right to tell a heroic story that promised a better future.

THERE WERE ALWAYS those who found the lives of black horsemen inadequate grounds for hope, who believed them too compromised to serve as a model for the future of African Americans. In 1931, the Harlem Renaissance writer Arna Bontemps recounted the life of a nineteenth-century black horseman in his novel *God Sends Sunday*. At first Little Augie, the novel's central character, glories in the sense of confidence that sitting on a horse gives him as a small, crippled child. As he grows up, those feelings evolve into a proud belief in his own independence. As Bontemps describes his thoughts, "He was no simpering pie-backed nigger. . . . He was a race-horse man." But Bontemps saw in those words only a fleeting conceit, not true autonomy. He believed that kind of pride pulled unwary young men into a degrading dependence on rich white horse owners and a consequent adoption of white standards of value and white-sanctioned forms of self-destruction. Augie shares a final scene with his nephew. The boy, standing with his uncle and a horse, realizes that they both take comfort in the animal's "warm unembarrassing presence." But Augie's life has taken him beyond the simplicity of that bond. "The tiny old man looked into the horse's face sadly, like one remembering love. And it seemed as if water would drop out of his eyes."[29] Augie's career at the track leads him to drinking, gambling, and, ultimately, murder. He ends the novel on a train, speeding away from the family that has disowned him. The track had been a snare for black men, Bontemps suggested, one that had taken their talents and diverted them from building their own communities and their own political and cultural future.

Bontemps's great-uncle had been a jockey, and the matter-of-fact harshness of his portrait of Augie's downfall has the grim certainty of pain felt close to home.[30] But white turfmen at the turn of the twentieth century did not share Bontemps's view of black horsemen as pathetic figures. Instead, they saw evidence of the emergence of a proud corps of black racehorse men poised to claim a freedom that entailed respectability and even equality. More unsettling still, they came to believe that those men's example inspired African Americans to resent the constraints placed on their freedom and to reject the codes that kept them subordinate. And so white men forced black ones out of the racetrack jobs that they had held since before Austin Curtis. They mobilized their personal power and the power of the state to make the fictions they advanced to justify the expulsion appear valid and true. As Jim Crow ended black men's decades of prestigious, widely recognized work in the Thoroughbred world, many of them simply could not bear it. Buried in the newspapers of the period are the records of the mental breakdowns, domestic assaults, and suicides that tore them and their families apart. The racetrack reminds us of how deeply Jim Crow wormed its way into daily life, into dreams and hopes. It was insidious, and it was deadly.

While the Thoroughbred industry was a confined sphere and black horsemen a tiny minority of slaves and freedmen, the unusual intimacy of the world of the track and the attention afforded it brings us into the heart of the personal consequences of some of the greatest political debates of nineteenth-century America. Examining the world of nineteenth-century turfmen shows us just how thoroughly political convictions were—and are—entangled with personal identifications, with beliefs about who and what is good and right, and with fidelities and passions without any direct connection to the legislative chamber or the ballot box. To follow the characters and events of the world of the racetrack reveals the complicated ways in which ideas about race have been moored in physical reality and vested with power, so that they have gained the strength to slaughter human beings.

RACING MEN of the nineteenth century were accustomed to thinking about horses and horsemen from earlier times. They reached back into the past for performance records, training tricks, jokes, and lessons. The dead were ever-present in American stables. Willie Jones, Austin Curtis, and the horses and men who came after them thus appear throughout this story, long after their natural lifespans, because the men of the nineteenth-century racetrack knew they lived always in the presence of the past, and they looked to it for precedents and answers. The horses and the men they carried in their minds have largely faded from our view, but the convictions that they held dear, the hopes and fears with which they lived, have shaped today's United States.

The privileges and loyalties of turfmen certainly did not die with the nineteenth century. In 1922, when Alfred Gwynne Vanderbilt Jr. was nine, his mother took him to his first race. He would go on to own the mighty gray Native Dancer, one of the greatest Thoroughbred runners and sires ever. As an old man, Vanderbilt explained the lure of the sport he had adored from that first childhood moment. "When I go to the track," he summed it up, "I know who I am."[31] Vanderbilt went to the racetrack the day he died at the age of eighty-seven.[32] American men of an earlier time would have understood the deep certainty Vanderbilt expressed. Those feelings have survived the centuries, as have the entrenched race and class hierarchies that white turfmen's careers show us with uncomfortable clarity. These are histories whose consequences we live with so intimately that we can overlook their presence. But we never escape them.

Just as much as the men of the nineteenth-century backstretch, we live with systems of inequality so enmeshed in daily life and reflex, so resilient in the face of challenge, that to eradicate them seems well-nigh impossible. And, like them, we are still in the presence of the dead: the African American men who sought to make lives under those constraints and who demonstrate for us the dignity and grace, the callousness and wretchedness with which human beings have lived with their history, which is also our history. Some of those men, far removed from Alfred Gwynne Vanderbilt, also knew who they were at the track. Like Bontemps's Little Augie, some of them followed that feeling into isolation and self-destruction, but others made of it the basis of lives of proud distinctiveness. They have left traces of their certainty for us to reckon with. In 1925, George Marshall, who had been born in Kentucky before emancipation, died in Rock Island, Illinois, at the age of about seventy. At some point in his final illness, he or a family member answered brief questions about the most basic details of his life. In the official record of his death, the state of Illinois noted his occupation as "Race Horse Man."[33]

1

The Glory of the Four-Mile Horse

HE WAS NOT a beautiful horse. A chestnut, with a white star and one white hind foot, he was only of average height and stockier than most Thoroughbreds. His flesh drooped on the underside of his head and neck, and his bones jutted out awkwardly. He got his first set of horseshoes, a necessary precursor to regular work, when he was three, an age at which many horses were already accomplished racers. And he was five before he caught the eye of the racehorse entrepreneur Cornelius Van Ranst, who purchased the stallion from his Queens County, New York, breeder. What Van Ranst saw was not the blocky head or stumpy neck, but the perfectly formed, tremendously powerful hindquarters, the twin engines that powered the horse's ground-shaking gallop. That gallop marked him as worthy to be called Eclipse, named for the greatest Thoroughbred in British racing history, his namesake's maternal great-great-grandfather.

In 1822, the skeleton of the British Eclipse appeared for sale in the pages of the *London Monthly Magazine* as a unique decorative accent for a sportsman's home or stable, intended to provide both a striking conversation piece and a ready reference. A man concerned about whether one of his horses had the proper build for first-class racing could compare the animal's frame to the bones of the greatest runner ever. Meanwhile, the American Eclipse, who had been respectably successful on New York tracks after his late start, had retired to stud, passing on his reasonable speed and remarkable endurance to his foals for a fee of $12.50 per breeding. Horsemen seldom put active breeding stallions back into regular training; to do so halts a valuable source of income and can also entail some risk, since hormonally charged stallions can be dangerous. So Eclipse had made only a few appearances since his retirement.[1]

But in September of 1822, the *New York Evening Post* published a letter from James J. Harrison of Virginia, the owner of Sir Charles, who had scored impressive victories in the South. Harrison addressed "THE OWNER OF THE AMERICAN ECLIPSE" and graciously offered Van Ranst the opportunity to put up either $5,000 or $10,000 to run his horse against Sir Charles to determine the best racer in America in a match that autumn in Washington, D.C. If he had hoped to overawe Van Ranst or to make him doubt his eight-year-old horse's chances against a younger challenger, he was soon disabused. An acceptance came quickly, and the Northern owner made clear his confidence. He chose to stake $10,000 rather than five, "that the object of the contest may correspond to the fame of the horses."[2]

American races for mature horses in the first half of the nineteenth century were grueling affairs. They were run in heats that, in the most prestigious races, were usually four miles apiece. The horse that took two out of three stages was the victor. The horses ran one heat, rested for a fixed time, ran another, then repeated the process if necessary. (In comparison, the mile and a half Belmont Stakes, the final jewel in today's American Triple Crown, is regarded as an unusual test of endurance for twenty first-century Thoroughbreds in the United States.) In front of a large crowd in Washington in November 1822, the feat was too much for Sir Charles, who broke down and couldn't finish the match race, leaving Eclipse the victor by default. A chagrined Southern contingent, led by the Virginia turfman William Ransom Johnson, made a daring proposal. Johnson would bring a horse of his choosing to the Union Course on Long Island in May 1823 and match the animal against Eclipse for national supremacy, with each side putting up $20,000. The Northerners at once accepted the challenge, with a consortium of prominent New Yorkers contributing to the cause. Steamboat heir John C. Stevens, the first winner of yachting's America's Cup, John Livingston of the New York political family, and most of Gotham's kingpins of public entertainment all contributed funds. They were so confident that they were willing to accept Johnson's terms, to make it, as the newspapers shouted, "Eclipse against the world!"[3]

James Harrison's offer was one thing. But a challenge from William Ransom Johnson—who had six months to train a handpicked horse—was another. Johnson's stables on the Appomattox River near Petersburg, Virginia, were the epicenter of racing in the South, and Johnson himself, with his dramatic shock of silver hair and his unerring eye for a horse, had earned his nickname, "The Napoleon of the Turf." The Johnson family investment in Thoroughbreds had begun with Johnson's Medley Mare, the horse Austin Curtis had selected out of the pasture for William Ransom Johnson's father, and the younger Johnson owned platoons of enslaved grooms, stable foremen, jockeys, and trainers, all skilled in their craft. After months of trials, Johnson settled on a formidable challenger named Henry, a young chestnut stallion an inch or two shorter than Eclipse. The two horses shared a blood tie to the great sire and first English Derby winner Diomed. Henry came originally, like Johnson himself, from the neighborhood of Halifax, North Carolina.[4]

It was said that sixty thousand people flocked to the Union Course to see the race and that twenty thousand of them had come from the South, including the slaves who traveled with the Johnson racing stable and with other Southern turfmen. Flags were to be raised in public places to signify the winner, and people who couldn't get to the race congregated within sight of the poles to catch the result.[5] New Yorkers were eager to put cash down on Eclipse against "the knowing ones of the Peedee, the Santee, the Waccamaw, and the Roanoke, who are all on the ground with their little negers, and appear to be up to a thing or two . . . [but] nothing from a slave holding state beats us liberty and equality boys."[6]

Josiah Quincy Jr., scion of the great Massachusetts family, was fortunate enough to have gotten a box seat ticket through a Harvard friend. The Long Island ferry was fully packed, and he walked most of the way from the landing to the race, since "an unbroken line of carriages" stretched from the water to the track gate. "On arriving," he recalled, "we found an assembly which was simply overpowering."[7] Two very important people were absent, however. William Ransom Johnson had contracted food poisoning the night before. And on the other side Samuel Purdy, Eclipse's usual, solidly experienced, white rider, had bowed out after a disagreement with the horse's owners, who had to settle for a lackluster substitute. In the first four-mile heat, Henry led from start to finish, and a despairing hush fell over Eclipse's backers.

Then suddenly a huge cheer filled the air. Purdy had appeared out of the crowd and agreed to get back on Eclipse. The horses were only a little over a mile into the second heat when Purdy made his move. Cadwallader Colden, a New York racing promoter and journalist, was watching the race from astride his own horse when he saw the runners through a break in the crowd at the rail, and the friend next to him shouted, "see Eclipse! look at Purdy! by heaven on the inside!" Purdy had taken Eclipse between Henry and the rail, saving ground and daring the other jockey to squeeze him into the fence. Josiah Quincy, seated behind the caustic Virginia orator John Randolph, heard the congressman's distinctively shrill cries, "You can't do it, Mr. Purdy! You can't do it, Mr. Purdy! You can't do it, Mr. Purdy!" But Purdy could. He got Eclipse's head to Henry's hindquarters, then pulled him even, then got his nose in front, and brought the horse home two lengths ahead. In the last quarter mile, the screams and applause "seemed to roll along the track as the horses advanced, resembling the loud and reiterated shout of contending armies." Josiah Quincy had not bet a single cent, but, when Eclipse finished in front, he was so overwhelmed that "I lost my breath, and felt as if a sword had passed through me."[8]

With the third heat to decide everything, Eclipse's stamina and Purdy's experience told, and this time they took and kept an early lead. The victorious Purdy rode Eclipse to the judges' stand as the band played "See the Conquering Hero Comes." Mail coaches set out on their rounds flying flags emblazoned "Eclipse forever." When he managed to get out of bed, William Ransom Johnson sent a challenge for a rematch that fall in Washington to John C. Stevens, the representative of the syndicate backing Eclipse. Stevens responded with a graceful demur; their horse had defied age and conditioning and won splendidly, and he, Van Ranst, and their associates did not propose to repay him by demanding more.[9] Both notes were couched in punctiliously respectful terms. The gentlemen of the opposing syndicates dined together, and the Southerners toasted New York, "unrivaled in her population and in her enterprise for internal improvement—so far victorious on the course." Not to be outdone, the Northerners raised their glasses to Virginia, "ambitious of being distinguished in all things useful to our common country."[10] The New York papers, previously vitriolic on the subject of Southern racegoers, were gracious in victory and inclined to give up on the idea of sectional competition. "[T]hese contests of North against South, lay the foundations of sectional jealousies, and create a spirit of rivalry when there should be union. The horses of Virginia, Carolina, and Long Island, are still the horses of the country."[11]

The partisan Southern Democrat John Randolph, who had staunchly supported Henry, had such a famously vicious tongue that, forty years after he was dead, men still flinched at the imagined sound of his voice.[12] But Randolph praised Purdy earnestly as "the last and only hope of the north in a struggle between it and the south, where pride and skill were at stake. I was opposed to him; I joined in the general wish of every true son of the South that his great knowledge of his vocation should fail him. But we were all doomed to sad disappointment. . . . The renown of the performance of that day, will go down with the history of civilized society, and transmit the name of Samuel Purdy . . . to the latest posterity."[13]

RANDOLPH HAD GOOD REASON to assume that American boys for centuries to come would learn about Samuel Purdy in their youth. He belonged to a generation of men who regarded the racetrack as an immutable part of their sons' heritage, an increasingly intricate system of institutions and practices and events that would shape them into the men they should be. Thoroughbreds ran through young men's conversations with one another, as they figured out who they were and what their place in the world was. James Gage, who had gone from South Carolina to Paris to study medicine in 1836, received an eagerly awaited letter from his brother that April full of news from home. The letter could have detailed the news from the Alamo, sent along family affection, asked what it was like to dissect French cadavers. Robert Gage instead gave James a detailed account of several horse races, then finished with, "I have given you all the news I can think of. Remember me to all and write often."[14] For the Gage brothers, passion for Thoroughbreds was part and parcel of their bond with each other, a marker of comfort and familiarity that made the pull of the sport all the stronger.

Young men like James and Robert Gage had grown up in a racing world with an organizational infrastructure substantial enough to support the national sensation of the Eclipse-Henry match race. Local jockey clubs had sprung up across America in the early decades of the nineteenth century. Small groups of locally prominent men gathered to elect officers, write racing rules usually borrowed from an established club, and schedule race meetings at a track that the club built and maintained, along with amenities like grandstands and box seats.[15] By 1830, there were tracks from New York to New Orleans, with at least one in virtually every state east of the Mississippi. Some states, like Virginia, boasted more than a dozen, located in cities and hamlets alike.[16] And at tracks all over the United States, affluent and aspiring young men learned to see in racing and its codes the pleasures and demands of mature manhood. This was a world whose rules they learned early to enjoy in the company of friends with whom they expected to share the sport until they grew old.

Most men still ran their stock locally, but more ambitious owners extended their reach regionally or even nationally. Clubs made an effort to avoid scheduling race meetings that overlapped with those elsewhere, and thus was born almost year-round racing. Northern tracks hosted meetings in the spring and fall, and, when temperatures began to drop, racing came south for the winter.[17] Owners shipped horses by train or steamboat, or a trusted groom walked them to a track that could be several states away. But no matter where he was, an experienced racehorse owner would find the rules of racing fairly similar. Jockey club members served as stewards on race days, checking entries, ensuring that no owner or trainer who had previously violated the rules had entered a horse, seeing that

jockeys were properly attired and met the standard weight requirements. Other club members, wearing red or white badges to distinguish them from the crowds, kept order, made sure that the horses
had a clear path from the barns to the track, and checked that only
members and their families or invited guests entered restricted
parts of the grandstand.[18]

Jockey club stewards welcomed into the members' area of the
grandstand not only their club colleagues but all the members of
their families except, by rule, young men over twenty-one.[19] By
then, youths were presumably expected to have taken up their own
club memberships as a sign that they had fully reached adulthood
and embraced its responsibilities. They inherited the obligations of
maintaining the rules of racing and upholding its significance as a
marker of what it meant to be an adult male. Thomas Porcher Ravenel of South Carolina thoroughly enjoyed staying in a "Bachelor
Lodge" with other young men at the Pineville races in the 1840s,
joining in the fun at the track and at jockey club-sponsored dances.
But when he reached the age of thirty and was elected a steward of
the course, his diary entries for the week of the races became exer-
cises in the description of responsibilities discharged.[20] When he
went to race week every year, the contrast between the sameness of
the place and the difference in himself, in what was expected of him,
must have been a constant reminder that he had become an adult.
He had become a man like his father, who had considered joining
the St. Stephen's Jockey Club a rite of passage important enough to
note in his own diary in 1809.[21]

Fathers made clear just how important horses were in what they
passed down to their sons and grandsons. The Virginia Thoroughbred breeder Thomas W. Doswell painstakingly handwrote a codicil to his will leaving his son not only his gold watch but his equine
paintings and books, along with the bookcase he kept them in.[22]
When John Minor of Mississippi became fatally ill while visiting
the North, he composed what turned out to be his final messages
home. He sent loving notes to his wife and poetry to his little girl.
His final letter to his father was about a horse. He could use the
conventions of Victorian sentiment with the women in his family,
but John and his father, even in moments of crisis, perhaps espe-

cially in such moments, talked about horses.[23] For horses stood, as the South Carolina turfman John B. Irving put it, for "a rich legacy that has descended . . . in trust from an honorable ancestry," a legacy that sons were obligated to keep for their fathers. "Let us hope, then," Irving wrote piously, "that we of the present generation will never feel less attachment than our fathers did, to the sports of the Turf; and that, whatever other changes may occur in our State, no change will ever take place in the celebrity of our horses."[24] Thoroughbreds and Thoroughbred racing stood for the standards that fathers wanted sons to meet and for the heights sons wanted to achieve to prove themselves to their fathers.

Among the lessons that the racetrack passed down were the codes of proper sporting behavior. John B. Irving was adamant that one of the proudest traditions of racing was that gentlemen raced their horses without a thought of the money involved, which meant, he insisted, that tracks like the one in Charleston were happily free of rigged racing or "vulgar clamor" if an unexpected horse passed the winning post first.[25] Gentlemen knew that cool acceptance of defeat and the loss of large wagers was a time-honored and respected way of demonstrating wealth and ease, self-mastery and fitness to exercise authority. The scrupulous graciousness of both sides in the Eclipse-Henry match proceeded according to established forms, long practiced by men concerned with their own honor.[26] Gentlemen paid their debts to other gentlemen, followed approved formulas in couching their challenges to each other, and carefully disclaimed any wish to label anybody a liar when they called a horse's bloodlines or past performances into question.[27]

They were correspondingly eager to heap scorn and vilification on professional gamblers, men who raced for money, or "blacklegs," as they were called. Such men were not entitled to be paid what they were owed or to be treated with politeness.[28] John Randolph, a passionately devoted turfman, vented his contempt for "men . . . who prowl about every public place for plunder with the most unblushing effrontery; assuming the airs of gentlemen and exchanging familiar salutations with men of honour."[29] Randolph was perhaps even more jealous of his personal honor than other men because he was small, smooth-chinned, and high-voiced in a culture in which gender difference was painfully important. He may have had particularly vehement feelings about men who seemed to assume easily a hard-won identity of which he was fiercely proud.[30] But Randolph did not see the boundaries of honor differently than other men; he only policed them more pedantically. And he knew very well what he shared with his peers and how to use their common feelings against his foes. In the disputed presidential election of 1824, Henry Clay, the Speaker of the House and Randolph's only serious rival as Congress's most enthusiastic turfman, arranged the victory of John Quincy Adams in exchange for a cabinet post. Randolph, speaking on the floor of the House, famously likened Clay to a blackleg. The term of opprobrium was not mere colorful character assassination; it was selected with surgical precision to signify Randolph's contempt in a fashion designed to be obvious to his victim and his audience. The two men fought a duel over the incident. Shots were exchanged, but no blood was spilled.[31]

Randolph had not only selected an insult that would sting Clay in a particularly personal way; he had spoken before an audience that would understand how cutting was the epithet he used. Racing was a perennially popular pastime in Washington, D.C., where the National Course was a favorite place for politicians of all stripes to meet and cheer on their favorites. Even presidents were not above the allure of the turf. Andrew Jackson, already a lion of the racing scene in Tennessee, brought his stable to Washington after he was elected to the White House.[32] The men in the nation's corridors of power, Northern or Southern, Democrat or Whig, spoke the language of the racetrack fluently or knew and respected men who did. When John Randolph wished to point out to his congressional colleagues that a good leader could delegate jobs to skilled subordinates without impairing his own authority, he used William Ransom Johnson and his army of grooms as an example, but he did not bother to explain who Johnson was.[33] His audience would have recognized the name of the South's most prominent turfman, the man who had prepared Henry for battle against Eclipse.

But racing was not merely a convenient source of popular shorthand for powerful American men. Watching a Thoroughbred in motion could, as novice racegoer Josiah Quincy had learned on

Long Island, induce breathless awe. John B. Irving used Biblical language to convey the majesty of a truly beautiful and athletic animal: "When we look at his neck, do we not see, as Job says, that '*He has clothed his neck with thunder!*' When we look at the fire in his eye, do we not remember this expressive language: '*He cannot be made afraid as a grasshopper; he mocketh at fear, and is not affrighted.*'"[34] In horses, men saw bravery, power, and nobility that humbled human frailty. The combination of mystical emotion and comfortable companions, of reaching for one's hopes and knowing one was fulfilling expectations—this was a mix of forces potent enough to foster powerful ideas about how the world should work. The racetrack was to become early and to remain late something that mattered deeply to many wealthy and powerful American men, particularly to Southerners. It was an institution open to the conflicts of the outside world, to debates over how a true democracy should allocate authority, how a slave society could both preserve itself and thrive. At the track, Southerners illustrated the answers they espoused to these questions and upheld racing as an institution that demonstrated the power of Jacksonian slaveholding society and justified the immunity it should enjoy from Northern interference. Racing, long acknowledged as a symbolic display of power, flourished as an institution precisely because it was far more than symbolic. It was a school, a showcase, and a testing ground—a political arena in the most literal sense. It gave concrete, compelling form to abstractions about the rightful workings of power.

In Old World aristocracies, great men had asserted their birthright to rule aboard warhorses and later racers and hunters. American democrats would demonstrate their authority in the saddle as well; they would wield power because they had earned the right to do so, their skills with an animal both an assertion of equality with any aristocrat and a reminder to ordinary voters of a commonly respected and well-understood skill mastered. Even as the United States embraced the ostensible belief that all white men were equal, Francis Blair wrote to his friend Andrew Jackson about a well-bred Thoroughbred mare he was fond of, "I think it worthy of the ambition of a Republican to ride '*booted* and *spurred*,' what the nobility abroad value almost as their own blood."[35] Thoroughbreds taught and represented important lessons about the hierarchies permissible within American democracy. John B. Irving saw in the perfect obedience of a powerful but well-trained animal a salutary lesson about the natural order. Some had been made to serve and some to be served, and a gentleman respected hierarchical structures and learned to hold gracefully his position in them, above some but below others.[36] How these hierarchies were to be shaped was the question.

Horses would have a role to play in their formation. In response to a letter to the editor of a sporting magazine, in which the author expressed concern about a racehorse stumbling, John Randolph scoffed, "When this is the case, it proceeds from his being trained very young to throw his whole weight on his shoulders. Put him in the riding house, and teach him to carry his chief weight on his haunches, and you will not find him to be a stumbler."[37] Here Randolph displayed his talent for wounding by implication as well as by accusation. A true gentleman would have at hand the great texts of classical horsemanship that explained how to strengthen a horse and teach it to balance itself evenly, usually through work in an indoor arena or riding house. (Randolph's own library included shelves of British-printed equine books and magazines.)[38] And more importantly a true horseman would think nothing of diagnosing the problem (probably without having to look it up, so intimately would he be acquainted with the texts) and hopping aboard to perform a rather delicate piece of horse training. In honing such knowledge and skills, attributes long associated with inherited wealth and power, democrats demonstrated that their system could produce men worthy to take places of national and international prominence, leaders their fellow citizens should respect and obey.

Southerners especially valued the role of horses in establishing an appearance of easy, uncontested power. The writer J. H. Ingraham, who visited the races in Natchez, remembered his own fascination at seeing Southern planters on horseback: "They appeared as much at home and at ease in their saddles, as in a well-stuffed arm-chair after dining generously. The Mississippian sits his horse gracefully, yet not, as the riding-master would say, scientifically. He never seems to think of himself, or the position of his limbs." The

Southern gentleman did not even have to consider the mechanics of his mastery, so graceful and intuitive was his control. Ingraham firmly believed that the way Southern planters rode, the way they strode the paddocks of racetracks, said something profound about the whole of their lives: "Home is, perhaps, the proper scene for studying the planter's character, but it will never be perfectly understood until he is seen, booted and spurred, with his pocket-book in one hand, and bank bills fluttering in the other, moving about upon the turf."[39]

THIS WORLD OF DEMOCRATIC MASTERY drew together white men across the divides of Jacksonian America. In the era of the Missouri Compromise, racing provided a welcome cohesive force for wealthy and prominent men from both North and South. Turfmen's personal ties bound them as firmly together across regions as they could have hoped. As William Ransom Johnson and John C. Stevens toasted one another's equestrian success and their respective sections' advancements, turfmen clearly regarded themselves as part of a national community based on mutual respect. Richard Singleton, the South Carolina cotton planter who was one of the great turfmen of his racing-obsessed state, corresponded amicably about a mare he had for sale with Cornelius Van Ranst, the breeder and trainer who had raced Eclipse.[40] New York's Cadwallader Colden, who had penned one of the definitive accounts of the Eclipse-Henry race, fancied himself a national clearinghouse for advice and information about Thoroughbreds. Colden, who had failed as a racing magazine proprietor and a racetrack promoter, was a visionary with a mind above the petty realities of budgetary constraint. But the sweeping scope of Colden's ideas was actually matched by the number of men who sought his grandiloquently phrased advice. When Henry Clay of Kentucky and William J. Minor of Mississippi prepared to go to England to buy stock for their growing stables, they consulted him.[41] Racing men kept in constant touch on paper, soliciting and giving opinions, offering thanks and compliments, sharing understandings about their own competence and a profound conviction of the personal and philosophical significance of "the glory of the Four-Mile horse."[42]

These common understandings could draw together unexpected comrades. When his speeches on the Missouri Compromise were printed in newspapers across America, Senator Rufus King of New York became a public voice for Northerners advocating the restriction of slavery's spread. Slaves imprisoned for their roles in Denmark Vesey's abortive 1822 revolt in Charleston supposedly reported that Vesey had much admired King. And Southerners already feared King because he was a former Federalist who might yet seek to revive the party and the political fortunes of New England. King's alleged role in inspiring the Vesey conspiracy seemed to prove conclusively that Southerners were right to insist that Northern attacks on slavery would inevitably produce servile insurrections. Ranged against King, voice sharpened to a lethal point, was always John Randolph, increasingly convinced that to strengthen national authority was to create a force that might destroy slavery and Southern power. The contrast between the two men reveals in microcosm what was at stake in the Missouri Compromise moment—two regions fearing the decline of their prestige in an evolving nation, one intent upon protecting and expanding human bondage, the other increasingly fearful of the potential of the three-fifths compromise to swell the political clout of slaveholders.[43]

But at the Eclipse-Henry meeting, only months after the Denmark Vesey revolt, only a few years after the Missouri Compromise had inflamed them both, King and Randolph were said to have stood shoulder to shoulder to watch the race.[44] So recalled the nationally circulated turf magazine, the *Spirit of the Times*. Whatever the truth of the story, its implication was clear. If King and Randolph could be reconciled on the backstretch, even if only momentarily, Southern slavery could not break the nation. Compromises could be hammered out to preserve both bondage and union, and the track was a prime place to bury personal and sectional animosity. A correspondent for the *American Turf Register*, a prominent racing magazine based in Baltimore, thought intersectional match racing would assuredly lead to "the promotion of that good feeling best calculated to cement, more strongly, the bonds of our glorious Union." Two months later, he explained himself further. Racing gave men with common interests but different regional backgrounds an opportunity to meet, "there being sufficient evidence of the friendships *thereby* produced—gentlemen of the two extremes liking each other the more they are brought together, prejudices dispelled, and the bonds of our union itself more strongly cemented."[45]

These personal relationships were all the more useful because at the track aspiring men, both Northern and Southern, could advance their social position through a safely familiar mechanism. The track eased the tensions of upward mobility for the newly wealthy and allowed more established men, sometimes uncomfortable with the pace at which money and status could be garnered in Jacksonian America, to judge and accept newcomers into circles of friendship and power. The ruthless steam transport baron and sometime racehorse owner Thomas Gibbons, who had benefited from the talents and drive of his young manager Cornelius Vanderbilt, wrote to his son in 1822 that Vanderbilt was becoming dangerously ambitious, building a new steamboat that would dwarf Gibbons's own and even starting "his brown colt in a match race. He is striking at every thing. I am afraid of this man."[46] Vanderbilt had signaled in terms he knew Gibbons would understand that he did not intend to remain anyone's subordinate for long. A decade later, Vanderbilt would start a horse sired by Henry, Eclipse's famous rival, in a heat race including an animal owned by Gibbons's son and two horses owned by the Stevens brothers.[47] In later years, Vanderbilt would confine his passion for equestrian contests to harness racing, where he often drove himself and took terrifying accidents in his stride, but he knew where coming men announced their arrival in the 1820s and 1830s, and that was with Thoroughbred runners.[48] Racing was a useful pastime for men who were inching their way up the social ladder, who had some spare cash but wanted to be more than affluent. They wanted to be trusted gentlemen, their parvenu status politely forgotten in the excitement of their turf successes.

The professional and small-time planting men of the South were as eager to use racing to establish themselves as the nascent tycoons of New York. Only two months after Vanderbilt's outing at the Union Course, James Henry Hammond turned to a new front in his relentless campaign to join the tightly knit South Carolina aristocracy. He had already married the sister-in-law of Wade

Hampton II, one of the most prominent scions of that class. And now he bought a part interest in several racehorses. He joined a jockey club, laid out a training track on his own plantation, and in 1835 put down the money for the distinguished Virginia-bred racer Argyle, who ran with great success in the Carolinas. The horse would go on to make Hammond a tidy sum in breeding fees, but "he could not measure in dollars and cents the satisfaction he had felt in attending the festivities of Charleston's race week as one of the inner circle of triumphant owners."[49] His brother-in-law, Wade Hampton II, would offer him a free breeding for one of his mares to the stallion Monarch, for whom Hampton had allegedly turned down an offer of $20,000. "I should feel but little satisfaction . . . if his services were not as much the property of my *particular* friends as my own," Hampton insisted, and Hammond must have rejoiced that the ties of the turf had accomplished exactly what he had set out to do. He was no longer a nobody, not even a suffered in-law, but a man worthy of the forms of regard and respect.[50]

The Hampton family doctor was an able young man named Josiah Nott, who would later move to the cotton trading city of Mobile. Growing rapidly and in need of polished professional men, Mobile fueled Nott's dreams of social advancement. The doctor hoped to cut an impressive figure in a place where "the mania for racing and stock . . . is tremendous, and as soon as they get out of debt every body will go into it."[51] He had a model for success in his old friend Hammond.[52] Nott turned to the breeding and racing of Thoroughbreds as a key to social advancement. Indeed, he used not only Hammond's strategy but his horse, breeding two mares to Argyle in 1836.[53] By 1838, Nott boldly assured his young relative, the medical student James Gage, that he could "show you how to make 200 per ct on an investment" in bloodstock.[54]

Hammond and Nott were fiercely loyal to the slave society in which they had succeeded, Hammond as a proslavery politician who spoke in blunt terms of the right of masters to rule over subordinates, and Nott as a doctor who gave scientific imprimatur to bigotry with his theories of biologically dictated black inferiority. Others joined them, like Austin Woolfolk, the noted Baltimore slave trader who had publicly assaulted abolitionist Benjamin Lundy.

Woolfolk documented himself as a gentleman when he provided a list of his Thoroughbreds, including a broodmare on her way to the prominent stallion Leviathan, in the exclusive columns of the nation's preeminent racing periodical the *Spirit of the Times*.[55] Slave-owning gentlemen might affect to disdain slave traders as greedy monsters who tore families apart and violated the contented relationships that masters maintained on their own plantations, but no one stopped Woolfolk from publishing a notice of the fruits of his trade alongside those of his customers. Slave traders and parvenus might be distasteful, but they were accepted in turf circles as men who helped support masters' authority in a slave society and eased the workings of a world based on human bondage.[56] Repugnant as many Northerners may have found such men, they knew well the tensions and benefits of economic mobility and joined with Southerners in viewing the racetrack as an acknowledged and useful site to display aspiration and police and reward successful advancement.

But racing was not merely for owners. It was also for spectators and tied the wealthy to the men in the crowds on the backstretch, men who, in the 1820s and 1830s, spoke with a louder voice in American politics than ever before. Thoroughbred owners always paid elaborate deference to the benefits of racing for the common man and to a nation built on sturdy agrarian virtue. John B. Irving insisted that the huge sums of money tossed around racetracks ultimately profited the farmer, who bred horses, supplied fodder to his neighbors, and produced sons to work as professional horsemen.[57] If small farmers saw the profits that accrued from horse racing, they did so in negligible sums. But one reality of racing was incontrovertible. Rich men did not and could not have a monopoly on fast horses, because talent was not always recognized and assigned its commensurate dollar value. Any man scrambling to make ends meet could look at a horse he had picked up cheap and hope that one day he would see a flash of speed and temper and beauty that was his very own. "And this it was," racing historian John Hervey would write a hundred years later, "that gave the turf its wide and irresistible appeal, forming a bond close and warm between it and ordinary life. It produced a community of interest impossible under other conditions."[58] The racetrack was supposed to paper over class distinctions with the joys of common aspiration.

At the races, lower-class men could cherish a pride in their own independence, a taste of equality as the crowd shouted in one voice when the leaders came to the top of the stretch. Racing was one of the masculine rituals that smoothed the edges of class difference in the raucous world of Jacksonian politics.[59] For Southerners, the racetrack not only eased class tension but strengthened the ties that bound free men in a slave society. Great planters were willing to indulge their lesser contemporaries, because their neighbors had to stand with them in defending slavery against abolitionists and policing potentially rebellious or runaway bondspeople. The fastidious and tough-minded Mary Chesnut, who married into a South Carolina family of turfmen politicians, grimaced at her menfolk's sharing an after dinner cigar with a local yeoman farmer. But her husband and father-in-law knew that the male camaraderie of tobacco would help to ensure political unity.[60] In Natchez, white artisans and farmers paid subscriptions to the local jockey club and raced their horses at the track against one another. Wade Hampton, who gave his brother-in-law Hammond free breedings to his famous stallion Monarch, regularly offered the horse's stud services at a reduced rate to area smallholders.[61] The pleasure of raising a good horse, knowing it was as well bred and athletic as those of the grandees of the turf, was as much appreciated as a fine cigar and a studied deference to a man's political opinions. As young yeomen learned how to talk to other men in the courthouse square, how to handle themselves in bar fights, how to explain their opinions to their elected representatives cogently and expect that they would be listened to, they were initiated into the ways in which free Southern white men expressed their independence and their capacity for mastery over other people.[62] The track, rich with memories and understandings of the rightful workings of democratic authority, could be theirs, too, to relish.

Racing, turfmen understood, served as a valuable institution of cohesion in a contentious democracy in which elites vied for power while voters, factions, and regions disputed how that power was to be allocated. At the races, debtors and creditors settled up. Planters, businessmen, and politicians made deals in the members-only section of the grandstand. John B. Irving, who had been a member of the South Carolina Jockey Club long enough to know, put it gracefully but matter-of-factly. The races were

> instituted, not solely for the enjoyment of the outward effect of the beautiful spectacle which a well contested race presents; nor even, altogether, to afford an arena on which, in honorable and gentlemanly rivalry, the speed and power, and value of our horses may be tested; but to have, in an especial manner, an important bearing upon *our social relations*—to link town and country together, and our State with her sister States, binding them to each other by mutual interests, and the promotion of a common object—to bring together those from all parts of our State, and from racing regions beyond our borders, who are, by unavoidable circumstances, separated throughout the rest of the year, that they may, at least once in twelve months, "smoke the calumet" of kind feeling and cheerful intercourse.[63]

The races could foster a feeling of unity in the owners' boxes and tolerant respect among the infield's yeomen that seemed indispensable to elite white men of the 1820s and 1830s.

Irving located the source of that valuable sense of social unity in "the marked absence of all *care* except the *care* of the horses."[64] He made a valiant effort to describe what the course was really like: "It is a subject that cannot well be pictured by words—though many attempt it, none can throw in, *truthfully*, all its shifting shapes and hues, for they are as varied and dazzling as are the changes in a kaleidoscope."[65] The crowds and the excitement swelled on race day as storekeepers hung closed signs, judges adjourned courts, and clergymen left their churches unattended. The races were "shared in by every one, from the Governor and ladies in the Grand Stand to the negroes who sat unmolested on the fence tops."[66]

Black faces were everywhere in the crowd, Irving remembered, so much so that the course had a "*Backgammon Board* appearance . . . during the running of the heats, *black* and *white* groups, dotting the Course here and there, and changing color with surprising regularity—chameleon-like—the *black* faces turning *white*, and the *white*

faces looking very *black*, from time to time, as their respective favorites fail to equal their anticipations."[67] The crowd was so mixed
that Irving made a heavy-handed joke about its fluidity, a dangerous
subject for humor in a society based on racial subordination and human bondage. But the hierarchy to which the races were meant to
give democratic imprimatur, the white unity on display, required a
black audience in the South. While the races served to tighten the
bonds and paper over the divides between North and South, established and aspiring, rich man and yeoman, for white masters they
performed a final and essential task. They displayed and strengthened a unified slave society. The making of mastery was a constant
process, and the racetrack was one of the crucial sites where it was
manufactured.[68]

At Southern tracks, people of color routinely watched the elaborate performances of mastery on view. In December 1835, Mississippi cotton and sugar planter William J. Minor brought home six
horses he had purchased in England. "They were led up main street
by six white men," a Natchez diarist recorded. The men "were imported too." The writer was free black barber William Johnson,
who preserved the incident for posterity because it seemed an important part of his world. Just the day before Johnson had "Bought
a Black Horse at the sale of Mr N. Gelespies property for the sum of
$30, Six months Credit."[69] In his own small way, William Johnson
could enjoy membership in the brotherhood of racing men, just as
William J. Minor did.

Johnson relished the track above all other public amusements
because there his freedom mattered more than his race. Instead of
sitting in a segregated section as he would in a theater, he exchanged
wagers and challenges with men like Samuel Gossin, the farm manager of the local planter Adam Bingaman, and St. Clair, a local car-
penter.[70] In his diary, Johnson meticulously recorded his equestrian
affairs, the bets he laid and the workouts he put his horses through
in preparation for competition at the track.[71] Just as smallholding
white farmers enjoyed privileges in breeding to Wade Hampton's
stallions, William Johnson "took a wride out to Col Bingamans and
I took my Big Sorrill mare and The Bob Tail mare. . . . I had The
Small mare put to Ruffin and the Big Sorril mare put to Grimes."[72]

Bingaman was perhaps the greatest racing man of the lower Mississippi Valley, but the services of his valuable stallions were available to a free black artisan. The races reminded some free black men like William Johnson of the pleasures of their sometimes precarious liberty and divided them from slaves, helping to stem a potential source of disruption to the order of bondage.[73]

Slaves were prominent in racing crowds because including them also bolstered the existing order. Masters used race days to demonstrate that their power was rightful or at least inevitable. But they also knew that the races could be a prized form of recreation for slaves, and the policing of the opportunity to participate in a community-wide event served as an extra reminder of their subordination. Going to the track was a ruthlessly regulated privilege. One Northerner visited the whipping house in Charleston, to see where men beat slaves to a master's specifications for a dollar. The whipping he saw, so the professionals assured him, fit a common pattern: "The boy was stripped naked, his feet fastened to the floor, his hands placed in a rope overhead, and then drawn straight by means of some blocks, then a cap drawn over his head and face. The boy I should think was not over 13 years of age. He was whipped very hard—*the skin flying at every blow*—After he was let down, and had gone out, I asked his master what he had been doing. He said he had run away the day before and gone to the races. . . . I was told that quite a number had been brought there that day to be punished for the same offence."[74]

Slaves had to seek permission to spend a day as part of the raucous, inclusive display of mastery that John B. Irving depicted. And slaves who were allowed to spend a day at the track were still subject to dangerous scrutiny. If J. H. Ingraham had seen planters as natural authority figures, the British visitor James Stuart saw in Charleston the violence that constantly underlay their power. Stuart had seen one of the jockey club stewards in action on race day. "[N]o sooner did a man of colour appear on the course, and within his reach, then he struck him with his horsewhip. . . . Here on the racecourse, there were at least two men of colour for every white person, yet they were obliged to submit to treatment which a white man dared not even to have threatened to a person of his own colour. The race turned out a very good one."[75] Planters wanted slaves to remember their vulnerability as they watched the performances of power on the backstretch or cheered on a long shot in a closely fought duel.

The track's violence could be more than physical. Another British visitor, Isaac Weld, reported with disgust of Virginia "that it is no uncommon thing there, to see gangs of negroes staked [wagered] at a horse race."[76] Andrew Jackson observed casually of a race to be run at the course he frequented at Clover Bottom near Nashville that the stake "was to be in cash or negroes as I understood."[77] Even if a slave was able to go to the races and enjoy himself with his friends, he always ran the risk of returning from his day out to the knowledge that he or a family member or a friend had been sold or lost in a wager.

The racetrack was thus a place that bound together Northerners and Southerners, aspiring and established freemen, in a fashion designed both to embrace the chaotic possibilities of Jacksonian America and reaffirm established hierarchies. Men in power demonstrated that they had earned their authority with skills and proficiencies long associated with social and political mastery. They found ways to judge and accept potential new partners whom Jacksonian democracy brought into their orbit. Perhaps most of all the track allowed Southern masters to solidify the bonds of their slave society and to illustrate for Northern comrades and hesitant political and economic partners that their system was a strong and secure one that should be left alone to function. The racetrack's rituals smoothed Southern social divides and secured Southern prominence within the Union. And like many places of ritual, the track was full of ghosts.

THERE WERE BLACK MEN who worked daily in barns and on backstretches haunted by those brutalized and sold away. Their lives and white men's efforts to explain them and fit them to the needs of mastery shaped the American racetrack more surely than any other set of factors. The entire performance of Thoroughbred racing in the South depended on black labor. Slaveholders understood that their whole existence depended on the work of millions of African Americans. But this smaller world's dependency was no socioeconomic commonplace, so ubiquitous as to be taken for granted. It was an immediate need for particular men with very specific skills. Racing might seem an ideal pastime for a dilettante, but such men could not last for long without expert assistance. In 1830, a young man wrote to the *American Turf Register* to congratulate the magazine on running a piece about the practical details of horse training. Such writing was a great public service, he pointed out, because many enthusiasts were inexperienced in putting a horse into racing condition, and thus "there are many persons, both north and south, who are . . . compelled to depend on ignorant negroes, or persons unworthy of confidence."[78]

Southern white men eager to assert their authority on the racetrack wanted an instruction manual because the everyday reality of the stables revealed that the whole performance of racetrack mastery, all the feelings of security and manhood bound up with it, often rested on the expertise of black men. Even when William J. Minor, the noted Mississippi Thoroughbred breeder and owner, published a pamphlet of his rules for training two year olds, the silences were as telling as the sentences. Minor went into typically fussy floods of detail over horses' diet, when they should be groomed and bathed, what kind of exercise was good for them. But between the rules were gaps in which judgments must be made, so habitual for men who knew how that they would hardly have noticed them, so alien for those who did not that they could easily founder on the first page. What were the reliable signs that a horse was cool enough to eat safely after exercise? How did the light play differently on the coats of healthy and sick animals? Minor offered sound instructions, but his book was written and meant to be read in full knowledge that in the stables were workers who, at a glance, could answer those questions.[79]

In the South, slaves usually did the myriad jobs of a nineteenth-century racing stable. The majority of slave horsemen were stable boys or grooms. They were in charge of the horses' daily needs, making sure they were clean, comfortable, and healthy. It was an exacting job, requiring long and anecdotal training for a young man, who would probably have been paired with a more experienced groom to learn how to spot a telling detail and do the hard work of maintaining a thousand-pound animal safely and efficiently. Riding a Thoroughbred in training or competition, by the time of the Eclipse-Henry race, was the job of a jockey, who might also have the skills of a groom but had to be remarkably small. For most of the nineteenth century, three-year-old Thoroughbreds, who were judged only just old enough to compete safely in grueling heat races, were usually allowed to carry about ninety pounds in competition, including jockey, saddle, bridle, and all other equipment. Four year olds could only carry a little over a hundred pounds.[80] Many jockeys were thus boys or very young men, prized even more for their slightness than their skill.

A rank above the jockey was the trainer or stable supervisor, an adult who had begun his career as a groom or a rider. The owner himself, like William J. Minor, might be knowledgeable, but he usually employed a professional for daily oversight. The man in charge was at least as often black as he was white. When Thoroughbreds were shipped to the track to race and the enslaved stable force went with them, the trainer supervised both horses and men.[81] He worked the horses, had the last word on their welfare, made sure the grooms did their jobs properly, gave instructions to the jockeys, took the brunt of the owner's wrath, and walked the tightrope of his trust. Enslaved trainers were highly valued and carried commensurately high price tags. Opportunities to acquire such expertise were to be seized, as the columns of the *American Turf Register* made clear when positions in the barn of William Alexander, a black man who had learned his trade in the Johnson stables, were advertised: "A few likely boys ... will be taken, and, under him, thoroughly instructed in the art of training horses for the turf. . . . The knowledge of training the racehorse thoroughly well is at this time a profitable trade; few others adding as much to the value of a slave, or to the productive capacity of a free laboring man."[82] The skills of men like William Alexander were valuable to turfmen in purely cash terms. But they were also significant because on those skills white men's whole racing world depended.

From conception through foaling, training, competition, and retirement, the champions of the South were in the hands of slave horsemen. While white horse owners advertised the services of breeding stallions and negotiated with mare owners over fees, they were unlikely to get involved with the often dangerous moment when a hormonally charged stallion mounted a mare who might attack him, depending on her temper and the timing of her own hormonal cycle. In the great Singleton breeding operation, the slave Cornelius, not Richard Singleton, was the man who supervised such risky occasions. James Chesnut wrote to Singleton about how pleased he was that his unpredictable mare was pregnant, due to Cornelius's careful judgment of her fertility.[83]

A successful racer made his or her sire a lucrative property, which enhanced the value of exact knowledge about which stallion had fathered which foal. Even men without a direct financial stake in a particular stallion might have strong convictions about the relative superiority or inferiority of an equine family, and the desire to have a cherished opinion upheld could be as strong as avarice. Thus the concentration of power and knowledge in the hands of the black men who did the actual work of breeding was remarkable. In the famous dispute over who had sired Sir Archy, the successful runner and sire of Henry, John Randolph, with typical cantankerousness, announced that a white groom who had taken care of the stallion Diomed had confessed to him that Diomed had not sired Sir Archy. J. M. Selden, whose father had managed Diomed's stud career, published a point-by-point refutation. Diomed, he pronounced, had always been in the care of a particular slave named Charles, so any white man who claimed otherwise was an unreliable source. Moreover, Nat, the slave who had brought Sir Archy's mother Castianira to be bred, was still in the neighborhood. Selden had checked with him, and Nat had assured him that he had been present when the mare had been bred to Diomed in the mating that had produced Sir Archy. Nat's word was immediately accepted as definitive.[84] The breeding shed was thus one of the sites in the American South where slave testimony held weight and slave expertise dictated the flow of events.

Slaves continued to supervise their charges throughout their careers. When John B. Irving sought to describe some of the most notable turf figures of his time, he could not omit Cornelius, the trainer of Richard Singleton's Thoroughbreds: "I presume no one in the habit for the last thirty-five years of attending the Charleston

Races, but recollects 'old Cornelius.' He was . . . a feature in the crowd upon a race field."[85] Cornelius was not like other slaves at the racetrack, part of an anonymous assemblage. Cornelius was a well-known individual, to be greeted by name, pointed out to visitors, spoken to, and listened to. Stewards wearing red ribbons did not use their whips to keep Cornelius back. Cornelius himself might carry a whip, as he led a fractious Thoroughbred through a crowd. In later years, jockeys would be great celebrities, as their craft came to be more generally recognized as a skilled and difficult one, but until the 1850s it was the trainer who was the celebrity. Both on and off the track, Cornelius and his contemporaries were men of authority.

Turfmen were constantly on the lookout for men whose skills might lend themselves to horsemen's specialized work. Theodore Stewart remembered the day his master saw his father ride a horse. "He said a nigger what could ride lak dat had no bizness in de fiel', so he made a stable boy outen pappy."[86] Sometimes masters seized on mere physical potential. William Green, whom his owner had traded to another man for a trotting horse, had his vocation summarily decided for him. His new master "kept a great number of fine noble horses, with a number of race horses; and being of the right size for a rider, he took me to ride races."[87] Size, in the case of jockeys, was absolutely paramount, while some rudimentary skills could be inculcated later. Wade Hampton, explaining to his old friend Andrew Jackson why he had not sent him two young slave boys to apprentice as jockeys, enjoyed his own benevolence for a sentence of explanation as he wrote, "they are family Negroes, & . . . the *distance* would create great affliction amongst their relations." Then he revealed a more pressing concern: "And when I found that neither of them could ride at less than 100 ls. I gave over the idea."[88]

Paternalism was in decidedly short supply in jockey training. Jacob Stroyer had harrowing memories of his beginnings in the trade. The white man in charge of the Singleton stables in South Carolina instructed the boy to bring him a whip each day and then forced him to lie in an empty stall for a flogging. After that initial period of brutality, the boy learned to ride under the direction of an older black man, who was supposed to beat him every time he fell. One day, Stroyer came off, and his bolting horse struck him in the face with a hoof; a horseshoe nail pierced his cheek and broke a tooth. His black supervisor cleaned him up and brought him home, but the white man put him back to work immediately, leaving his injury untreated. The boy confronted the stark truth that he had no one to turn to for protection. His father pleaded with his son not to fight back against the constant beatings, because, if he did, his parents would bear the consequences. "I know it is very hard, but what can we do?" he asked his distraught wife, "for if we try to keep this boy in the house it will cause us trouble." He could only assure his son that he believed that freedom would come, though they might not live to see it. Stroyer's stricken mother was vehement in her helplessness: "I wish they would take him out of the world, then he would be out of pain, and we should not have to fret about him for he would be in heaven."[89]

The physical battles continued, even after a boy had learned the basics of his trade. They took a new and terrible form, especially for jockeys, as it became more difficult for a skilled young man to maintain his size. A nineteenth-century jockey ate very little and regularly swathed himself in five or six layers of heavy clothing and walked ten or twenty miles to melt off pounds. When that failed, purgatives might make up the difference.[90] Men who had to torture themselves to keep their jobs obeyed a stern enough imperative. But the extra burden of bondage, of having no legal control over a body that another person wished so earnestly to shape to a particular end, was a heavy one.[91] Compounding slaves' common experience of malnutrition, jockeys endured additional debilitating practices in the name of weight loss.[92] The Virginia Whig politician and Thoroughbred owner John Minor Botts was in the habit of burying his well-known jockey Ben up to the neck in the manure pile to sweat off pounds, bringing the man a glass of water, and pouring himself a mint julep.[93] One sporting magazine printed a reader's letter with two pressing questions: How to stop someone from growing, and how to get a girl to go to a concert with you? The magazine's answer was casually forthright about both the realities of bondage and adolescent insecurities: "Negro jockies are stunted and reduced by burying them three times a week (four hours at a time) in stable manure, up to their chins. This steaming process is sure to be attended with the desired effect; we doubt, however, if you will like it. To your second question we would say that, if you wish a lady to accompany you to a concert, you had better oil your hair and ask her to go."[94] The violation of slaves' bodily autonomy was an omnipresent reality of antebellum racing. There was no need for the aspiring Romeo to pause over it as he debated over toiletry brands.

Slaves knew that danger only continued after their training ended. Working where the master watched closely could be a nightmare. Frederick Douglass knew that horsemen were spared the labor of the fields, but he disavowed any envy for the father and son who managed the stables of his master, Colonel Lloyd: "[N]o excuse could shield them, if the colonel only suspected any want of attention to his horses—a supposition which he frequently indulged, and one which, of course, made the office of old and young Barney a very trying one. They never knew when they were safe from punishment. . . . Every thing depended upon the looks of the horses, and the state of Colonel Lloyd's own mind when his horses were brought to him for use."[95] Douglass remembered floggings. William J. Minor was in the habit of punishing slaves who displeased him in their work with his horses by beating them and then sending them to the fields.[96] Privilege withdrawn easily became punishment.

But privilege attained was heady stuff, and the better known a horseman was, the less subject he was to the constant threat of violence. Men who made themselves individually indispensable and well known in racing circles lived in an orbit circumscribed by judiciously extended indulgences, the most immediately apparent of which was unusual mobility. A skilled horseman necessarily led an itinerant life—traveling with a mare to a stallion, with a string of runners to the races, to deliver a horse to a buyer, to examine an animal for sale, or to carry messages between white turfmen that might require knowledgeable explanation.[97]

The arrival of an enslaved man of expertise and wide experience could cause some uneasiness on a plantation. Such men, planters assumed, were more likely to have come into contact with abolitionist sentiment. John Randolph, when negotiating with a mare owner, admitted that, while he was happy to board visiting slaves, he was wary of men he did not know unless he had some assurance that "the politico-religious Fanatics have not been at work upon them."[98] But casual acceptance, rather than concern, was usually the order of the day when it came to horsemen. Thoroughbred owners wrote out passes for such men that might give some idea of their destination and then turned them loose on the roads and assumed they would be back.[99] When the Singletons needed a skillful trainer to replace Cornelius, they turned to the Virginia bloodstock importer A. T. B. Merritt to try to hire his well-known trainer, Hark.[100] But when Richard Singleton wrote, Merritt had already given Hark permission to find himself a job and thought vaguely that he might have gone to Norfolk. Merritt promised to write and find out if Hark were still available. If so, Hark would come to South Carolina as soon as possible. That turned out to be a bit later than expected, because Hark returned a month later after spending a few weeks in North Carolina "at his wife's house." The delay was regrettable, but Merritt finished cheerfully, "all things will turn out for the best."[101] If Hark had not found himself a job and instead had left the state to see his family, no one seemed concerned.

Hark's ability to travel so freely would have been extraordinary for most slaves but was reasonably common for men of his standing in his profession. Mobility was only one among many benefits for men like him. Slaves regularly participated in informal economies; legally, enslaved people could have no property, but white owners recognized in their customs that slaves often possessed various goods, including small sums of cash.[102] Slave horsemen had more opportunity than most of their contemporaries to make money for themselves. A stallion's breeding fee was typically advertised with the addition of a dollar for his groom.[103] Money flowed more freely at the races. Richard Singleton's accounts after a race meeting showed $1.75 for Levin, $7 for Jacob, and $16 for the stable boys as a group. A trainer or jockey might come in for a share of the purse if his owner were feeling generous and probably picked up tokens of gratitude from winning bettors. The same bill showed $62 for Cornelius.[104] When Hark went back and forth between the Merritt and Singleton stables, he usually got a very respectable sum for traveling expenses, and, amid confusion about whether owner or hirer had paid him, there was room to keep fifteen or twenty dollars for himself if he wished to do so.[105]

Hark would have had a very nice pocket in which to put his money. Men like Hark and Cornelius, when they appeared at the racetrack or in the paintings that white Thoroughbred owners commissioned of their prize animals, dressed in frock coats, dress shirts, and trousers. Richard Singleton understood that custom. In his papers, along with the records of the mass-produced clothes he issued to his field slaves, he kept the bill for tailored garments for a few men, including some of his horsemen.[106] A. T. B. Merritt apologized, when he packed Hark off to Singleton for the first time, that they had not had time to get Hark properly outfitted for the racing season. "If he should need clothes and I am sure he will, be good enough to let him have whatever he wants and charge them to me," Merritt requested. Hark was well aware of how his profession demanded he dress in public, as the trainer of the Singleton stables, and his wishes about his appearance were to be deferred to.[107]

Trainers' opinions on other matters were to be heeded as well. Merritt had been concerned about a filly with a small swelling on her leg that he was thinking of sending down to the Singleton stables. He had half-decided not to send her, but he said he would wait for Hark, who was away from home. If Hark thought it was all right, she would go. Merritt was the master, the owner, the man who paid the bills, but Hark, who was legally his property, was the man with the last word.[108] And that last word applied to matters beyond the minutiae of stable management. A man named Charles Redd wrote to Richard Singleton, hoping to secure a few of Singleton's highly regarded horses to bring to Natchez to sell. He admitted that it was an awkward proposition to make to a stranger, but he presented his credentials reassuringly: "My groom is Drummonds Old Peter from Virginia, who your man Cornelius, can tell you about." Only as an afterthought did Redd remember to add that he was also a bank president. What was important was the professional respect between two enslaved black men; on one's opinion of the other would a potentially lucrative business transaction between white men be based.[109] Such weighty authority in matters concerned with their work and deeply important to masters was a hard-won and cherished privilege.

If such respect among planters for the acumen of black men seems remarkable, it took root early in a young white boy's life. In his memoirs, Confederate naval officer James Morris Morgan began with his boyhood along the Mississippi River in Louisiana. He made sure to include Charloe, an elderly slave horseman whose growth had been stunted in childhood by being starved and buried in the manure pile in order to get his weight down. Charloe was at least trilingual and could play the violin. He traveled the area with his well-known mount Ben as a veterinarian and part-time specialist in schooling particularly tough horses. "Charloe was my hero," remembered Morgan of his boyhood self.[110] Young white men grew up across the South knowing slaves like Charloe, who excelled in work that Southern youths followed adoringly.

As adults they understood that some horsemen were not just neighborhood figures. They were celebrities to be handled with care. When A. T. B. Merritt offered Richard Singleton's son, Matthew, Hark's services for a mere fifty dollars a month, he emphasized that he had never before offered them for so little. He may have felt the need to reassure Singleton, since fifty dollars a month was a steep price in a market in which hirers grumbled about skyrocketing costs when they paid a hundred and fifty dollars a year to hire a slave.[111] Hark was not just any slave, as Merritt made clear when he reiterated their agreement that Hark would go nowhere near the South Carolina Lowcountry, famously rife with disease, until the end of malaria season. Unlike the slaves who stayed on plantations as whites fled the area, Hark was too valuable to risk.[112] Singleton was not merely paying for a slave or even a slave with specialized skills. Enjoying the usual forms of mastery was no treat for Singleton, who was one of the South's largest slaveholders. He was paying for the privilege of being temporarily associated with a man who was well known across America. Hark's name had appeared in the columns of the sporting press, along with those of up-and-coming white men, as the magazine praised the intelligence, integrity, and skill of the best of the younger generation of horse trainers. The master of such a man must be worthy of respect.[113]

IN WORKING WITH HORSES, then, black men could gain mobility, autonomy, opportunity, even deference. On them depended all the necessary and beloved details and purposes of racing. White men needed slaves like Hark, Cornelius, and their peers, but slave owners also kept a shrewd eye on the threat such men's position could pose to bondage. A small school of Southern turfmen proclaimed that all black horsemen were ignorant animals, capable only of taking direction and usually not even very good at that. Josiah Nott wrote to the *Spirit of the Times* that black jockeys "cannot recollect more than one direction at a time."[114] Nott built on an increasingly popular assumption that black people were biologically and quantifiably inferior to whites. This pseudoscience would help to earn him the place in Southern thought and society that he so craved.[115] But the doctor's sweeping generalizations were ill-suited to the world of horses. The frequent correspondent to the *Spirit* who wrote under the name "N. of Arkansas" complained in commenting on one particular runner, "[T]he trainer is a colored man, so was the rider, and if you can get a *negro rider* to disobey a negro *trainer*, you can get something I never could."[116] The jockey had chosen to follow the instructions of the black trainer instead of, presumably, the horse's white owners or backers. To a man accustomed to the power dynamics of the antebellum stable, the assertion of inherent black inferiority or stupidity was too simple to be an effective assurance of white mastery. Not when slaves persisted in following orders given by black men, rather than those given by white men, not when black expertise was so readily evident.

Most Southern turfmen did not seek to deny black men's competence or the privileges they held. Instead, they put their faith in those very privileges, the carefully calibrated system of security and reward that defined horsemen's bondage. They created a form of slavery all the more powerful and resilient because it allowed for and fed on the extraordinary accomplishments of black horsemen rather than seeking to suppress them. Turfmen's casual acceptance of slave horsemen's status reflects their belief that they had created a structure that would stop those men from using their privileges to kindle a revolt. But in addition to crafting a highly specialized form of slavery to serve their needs safely, turfmen broke ground on a narrative project that would span a century—telling themselves and each other why their horsemen were assets, and not threats, to racial order. If recalculating how likely it was that a privileged horseman would risk his position in an act of rebellion occasionally kept a turfman up at night, in the bright light of morning he could draw on an arsenal of soothing platitudes and assumptions that seemed to demonstrate just how unnecessary midnight fear was.

White men sought to define and understand slave horsemen as valuable commodities to be shaped into perfect complements to the horses over whom they labored. When James Henry Hammond purchased Argyle to aid in his social climbing, he also immediately sought to buy George, a slave groom and horse trainer. George was so much in demand for his skills that three men discussed whether they could each own a third of him, just as they each owned a third of a racehorse. George was understood as a human being of skill, but he was also a thing to be shared among friends.[117] This was a balance that most turfmen sought to strike and find comfortable. Instead of quickly dismissing black horsemen as inferior or fretting over the implications of their privileges, they cast them as the organic extensions of white men's will. Other slaves might fail them, but horsemen never would. Jockeys must have been a particularly seductive group for men who believed they could physically shape other human beings into faultless consumer commodities. Jockeys, after all, were positive proof that slaves could be physically shaped in accordance with white desire. Their very bodies could be evidence that every facet of their lives was subordinate to a white man's wish. A jockey could be starved down to an exact weight that suited his owner's purpose. He might have trouble doing his job, but centuries of racing history suggested that jockeys, when desperate and skilled, were extraordinarily resilient in the moment of competition. Jockeys were proof that torture *could* make a perfect slave.[118]

But horsemen were not merely bodies that could be shaped into submission. White people loved to believe that they had no independent desires of their own. John B. Irving could think of no greater compliment to a slave's fidelity, "integrity and character" than to compare him to Cornelius.[119] Slave horsemen were a comfort, because white men told themselves that black men in the stables truly could think of nothing better than to do a white man's bidding. In her recollections of antebellum Charleston, Mrs. St. Julien Ravenel summed up the world of the racetrack as the members of the city's jockey club wanted to imagine it: "Nothing could exceed the enthusiasm of the negro grooms and jockeys on these occasions. Identifying themselves with their masters, as they always did, it was 'my horse' to the trainer and rider, quite as much as to the owner."[120] A man who had been with a horse's mother at his birth, had broken him to saddle and bridle, had fed him every day, had treated his diseases, had conditioned him for strength and endurance, and only sometimes saw the white man who paid for the operation, might well and rightfully call the horse his own. But Ravenel, with generations of turf-loving Ravenels behind her, did not entertain that explanation. A black man could not consider a horse his own because he was the human being to whom the horse was closest; he must call the horse his own because he was so strongly invested in the interests and desires of white people.

White turfmen often expressed themselves affectionately to the horsemen they knew best. Horsemen talked face-to-face with masters, as few slaves were able to do, and they discussed topics that were of mutual concern. They were integral to a world of male camaraderie, in which men told jokes, traded opinions, and enjoyed feeling knowledgeable and certain. They were part of a system that assured white Southern turfmen that slave society could flourish in harmonious unity. And white men repaid these feelings of competence and security with gestures of genial indulgence. A. T. B. Merritt wrote to Hark when he was hired out to the Singletons to assure him that his wife and children were well and shortened the hiring contract he offered to allow Hark to spend more time with them.[121] James Chesnut, who had sent a slave named Abram to be instructed by Cornelius, asked if he were far enough along in his training as a horseman to come home to his enslaved wife for Christmas.[122] When Chesnut asked about Abram, he also asked Singleton to extend his thanks to "my old friend Cornelius." We do not know what Chesnut meant when he called Cornelius his friend. It may have meant that he appreciated Cornelius's skill with horses, like the difficult mare he had managed to breed, or that they exchanged congenial words when they met on the backstretch at the Washington

Course in Charleston. It was that sort of relationship that John James Audubon, watching the men who took care of horses and hunting dogs on Southern plantations, described: "These men, who are so important to the success of the chase . . . consider themselves privileged even to crack a joke with their masters."[123] There is no reason to believe that Chesnut was not completely sincere when he called Cornelius his friend. The real question is what that meant to each of them.

White men who could speak with affection of their slave horsemen and could express deference to their opinions were certainly not white men who had unusually beneficent attitudes toward all enslaved people. Matthew Singleton, Richard Singleton's son who followed him onto the racetrack, had corresponded with A. T. B. Merritt over the years about Hark's desires, his family, his thoughts on various subjects, and we have no indication that he did anything other than abide by the promises he made respecting those things. But Jacob Stroyer remembered Matthew Singleton whipping a man until the blood welled out of the slave's shoes. When the whipping was over, Singleton said only, "You will remember me now, sir, as long as you live." When Singleton died, the general opinion in the slave quarters was that he had gone to hell.[124] John Randolph, appealed to by a slave who said the overseer was going to kill him, told the overseer to go ahead, that he had enough slaves to kill one every other day. When the man substituted beating for murder, Randolph complained, "I told you to kill him."[125] But all his life Randolph called the old black man who had first taught him to ride "father," in a sign of respect markedly different from the generic "uncle" sometimes used for older male slaves.[126]

One way of looking at these contradictions—the indulgence extended to certain privileged slaves and the brutality meted out to others—is to dismiss the former as barely worth discussing, a tiny exception clung to by planters eager to claim virtues for themselves in the midst of daily abuse.[127] Another is to point out that extending some level of autonomy gave planters a hold over slaves deeper and more insidious than direct physical violence. If slaves had nothing, they could not be managed with the threat of having something they loved taken away, as horsemen were clearly manipulated when they were threatened with removal from their jobs and the privileges that accompanied them.[128] But what the lives of black horsemen reveal about their relationships with white men, at least from the perspective of the white men involved, is the degree to which violence and degradation, affection and dependence existed simultaneously and without self-conscious contradiction or cunning hypocrisy. These slaves were different, certainly, but their difference did not necessarily accord dignity to their status as human beings.[129] James Chesnut could call Cornelius his friend with complete earnestness, without needing to consider at all the crucial differences of power between them or the differences between his relationships with other white men he called friends and his relationship with Cornelius. What he shared with Cornelius was the closest thing to friendship he could imagine sharing with a black man, and so he called it friendship, probably without pausing to think about whether the word necessarily connoted a more equitable relationship.

We do not know what Cornelius thought of his relationship with James Chesnut or, indeed, what he thought of being a horseman. But there may be some illumination in considering the memories of Jacob Stroyer, who, after his traumatic training as a jockey, came to have strong feelings about his work. By the time his master died and the horsemen were sent to the fields, he "had become so attached to the horses that they could get no work out of me, so they began to whip me, but every time they whipped me I would leave the field and run home to the barnyard."[130] At the end of his account of the fall that drove a nail through his cheek, he proudly finished, "I am happy to say, that from the time I got hurt by that horse I was never thrown except through carelessness, neither was I afraid of a horse after that." It was a difficult achievement, bought with much pain, and both he and his parents were fiercely proud of it. Thirty years later, he could not resist naming and describing the horses he had ridden, adding that his readers might have heard of them, for they were famous.[131] While riding or training an athletic horse was a skill that was difficult to achieve and often came with physical costs, it was also an accomplishment to be proud of. Victory in competition belonged not only to the man who owned the horse. It surely belonged as well to the trainer because of his intimacy with the animal, the rider because he had felt the exhilaration of sitting astride it as it pounded for home. A white man might legally own the bodies of both man and animal, but ownership might not have been the first feeling of a black man in the winner's circle.[132] A white man could enjoy the control of a great horse by proxy, but the black man still enjoyed it in fact.[133]

There were black horsemen who ran away, who took advantage of the mobility of their jobs to make a break for freedom.[134] But the vast majority of black horsemen stayed where they were. They had their moments of glory and pleasure. They may have had moments when the children of the slave quarters looked at them with awe, as Henry Clay Bruce remembered gazing up at the itinerant slave teamsters of his youth, whom everyone regarded as "uncrowned king[s]."[135] They were, after all, men who had managed to undo the usual equation between white masters and horses, whose size, speed, and power could be ruthlessly deployed to hunt down escaped bondspeople or simply to remind them of their subordination.[136] They may have suffered the consequences of rejection by other slaves, who knew that the delicate balance horsemen maintained was a world away from their own lives. But solitude might also mean security. And for a man who had suffered a hard apprenticeship, had seen what he could lose, it might have seemed safer to keep what he had, difficult as it was, because he knew it and enjoyed some of it, than to risk it in the unknown thing called freedom. As a free man, he might be unable to practice the profession that was an integral part of his life, the job that made him a man of importance. As a returned fugitive, he would lose all his hard-won privileges. What horsemen had was not freedom, but it was closer to it than any other life they could see readily available to them or those around them. That calculus may help to explain how A. T. B. Merritt managed to secure for Matthew Singleton the services of a young slave jockey in North Carolina: "If you desire to hire him let Hark know through me your wishes, and how much you will give, and he will see if he can be procured."[137] Far from striking out on his own toward freedom, Hark was offering to enter the slave market as a hirer, to bring a boy further into the itinerant world of the racetrack. Perhaps he saw nothing wrong with that. It was a world that he had learned

how to navigate, and, for a man who had learned to prefer circumscribed certainty to hope, it had merit.

Men like Hark were figures of authority, perhaps even figures to
be admired or to be emulated, but their abilities and privileges were
deeply rooted in the world of their work. They were not community
leaders.[138] They were racehorse men, who bore the burden of their
humanity under extraordinarily testing circumstances.

2

Knowed a Horse When He Seed Him

IN THE JUNE cane fields along Bayou Teche, humidity could seem to suck away the air, leaving only enervating damp. But Annie Porter had other worries. She and her sister could not live indefinitely on their connections to their late uncle, sugar planter and Whig politician Alexander Porter of Louisiana. It was 1884. Slavery was dead and Southern Whiggery even deader. The Porter sisters were still living at the family estate, but they were now renters, leasing the property from new owners.[1] But Annie still clung to the remnants of the past. Northern magazines avidly published tales of happy former slaves, and Annie decided to send to *Harper's New Monthly Magazine* her transcription, fulsomely dialect-laden, of the recollections of "Uncle Charles," who had, decades before, supervised her uncle's stables. His full name was Charles Stewart, but Porter never acknowledged his surname.

Charles had eagerly anticipated the interview, she noted affectionately, and, when they sat down together, he was "arrayed in his Sunday clothes, and it being a warm night in June, the feeling of self-respect must have been genuine indeed which compelled him to put on a plush waistcoat reaching nearly to his knees, heavy white velveteen trousers ending in a pair of shooting gaiters, the whole surmounted by a long black frock-coat, a spotted silk cravat of vast size, and a small jockey's cap."[2] Porter so meticulously described Stewart's clothes for comic effect; she apparently believed that no former slave, not even an elderly man like him, had a claim to gravitas, so his efforts at dressing up could only be buffoonish. If he spoke or acted self-importantly, that was merely evidence of the laughable eccentricities endemic to black men of his age. Annie Porter, both because she was female and because she had been a child at the time of her uncle's death, had not learned the codes that had governed Stewart's career. She entirely failed to recognize a version of the formal clothes of the antebellum stable supervisor.[3] Porter did not understand, but Stewart told her he had been a powerful man.

Porter wrote up and mailed off her account, which appeared in *Harper's* in the autumn of 1884. She transcribed a life story that spoke volumes about the privileges of a slave horseman of the 1830s and 1840s, as the South assumed preeminence in racing and a new axis of power ran between the cotton and sugar turfmen of the Deep South and the Bluegrass breeders of Kentucky and Tennessee. It was also a story of the terrible costs of that privilege, of how autonomous and talented slaves made slavery itself stronger, how the institution was designed to bear their weight and use it to shore itself up. But Annie Porter seems never to have noticed the complexities of her tale. She saw what she expected to see, a man who was an integral and comfortable part of her home. She might not have known Charles's world, but she was its child—the product of a Southern cadre of racing-mad Whig politicians who built themselves a community based on common views and stories, economic policies and infrastructural agendas, assumptions and truisms. They wrote and painted their world so vividly that they believed they had called it into being, and they believed, too, that, with Henry Clay to lead them, their vision would transform the nation itself. And slaves like Charles Stewart were, both in daily detail and in ideological abstraction, at the heart of the vision that many Southern Whigs ardently espoused for the United States.

In his narrative, Stewart was quick to note that he had been distinctive from birth. His mother was a slave, but his father was a free man of color, a Virginia seaman who had served on whalers in the

Illustration of an elderly Charles Stewart from the 1884 story "My Life as a Slave." Stewart's clothes are similar to those he would have worn as a prominent Thoroughbred trainer. *Harper's New Monthly Magazine,* October 1884.

Atlantic. In eastern Virginia, the water was an accepted place of respectable employment for free black men, and the young Stewart would have known that his father's job instantly identified him as a man of some consequence.[4] He was careful to tell Annie Porter that his father, too, had been named Charles Stewart, that, even though his father had a free family, he bore that independent man's name. His father, he remembered, had repeatedly tried to buy him, but the family that owned his mother had ultimately sold young Charles, at the age of about twelve, to William Ransom Johnson. His new owner sized the skinny child up as a potential jockey with a single glance. "Do you know a horse when you see one, boy?" he asked. Stewart's "Yes, sir," dictated his future.

Stewart began his career as a groom, rubbing Reality, a talented runner and a daughter of Johnson's Medley Mare, the founding matriarch of the Johnson stables. He rode his first race as a seventy-pound thirteen year old. In 1823, he was a junior member of the team that saddled Henry for his match with Eclipse. Later in the same race meeting, he rode a colt for the New York sportsman John C. Stevens and made $300 for his efforts. Once Stewart had established himself as a groom and then as a jockey, trainer, and stable foreman, Johnson put him in charge of several of the finest horses in his stable near the track at Petersburg. The young man supervised with a free hand the animals and a staff of both black and white men and boys. "I had plenty o' money," he remembered, "an' nobody to say nothin' to me. I jes' had to train an' exercise my horses, an' send 'em up when dey was wanted."

In 1832, Stewart took charge of the gray stallion Medley, a son of Reality.[5] William Ransom Johnson sent the stallion, under Stewart's supervision, to stand at stud at the Pennsylvania home of J. C. Craig, the brother-in-law of Nicholas Biddle, president of the Second Bank of the United States. Stewart's job was a difficult one, since he had to walk the horse all the way from Petersburg to Pennsylvania without assistance; five years later, he rode and walked Medley and another Johnson star stallion, Monsieur Tonson, to Kentucky. There he supervised the Johnson stable's satellite breeding operation.[6]

Stewart's headquarters were in Paris, Kentucky, a few miles east of Lexington, and he was well acquainted with Henry Clay and other luminaries of the Kentucky turf, many of whom sought to purchase him from Johnson. In 1841, Stewart was sold to Alexander Porter to be the head trainer of his recently expanded stable in Louisiana.[7] Most slaves who arrived at New Orleans, the great slave mart of the cotton and sugar South, experienced it as a fearful succession of pens and yards. Stewart came down the river on a steamboat from Kentucky, observed that New Orleans was not as large as New York, and continued on to Porter's Oaklawn estate in St. Mary Parish, where he took charge of all the horses on the place.

Stewart was eager to enumerate the privileges his skills had earned him over the course of his career. Not only did he travel virtually at will, but William Ransom Johnson gave him a free hand with expenses and allowed him money for himself. Johnson's business agent banked Stewart's cash for him, and his balance ran into hundreds of dollars. That arrangement stood him in good stead when he went out to an area farm, on which a local slave speculator had settled men and women he had recently brought in from South Carolina. There Stewart saw the girl he wanted to marry. Her name was Betsey Dandridge, and her father gave permission for their wedding, elated that his daughter would be tied to a man who could purchase her, thus essentially securing her freedom and that of her children in one of the only ways open to slaves. Stewart, however, quickly ran into a problem, since the speculator, whom he knew, had already sold the Dandridges to another man with whom he was not acquainted.

But such a situation was no real obstacle to a man as assured as Stewart. He located the new owner, standing on the steps of the courthouse in Richmond surrounded by a group of prominent white men, and made his request successfully. He recounted the incident with pride to Annie Porter: "Jes' as soon as I steps up to him . . . an' interjuces myself as being 'Colonel Johnson's Charles,' he was . . . affable. . . . I seed two or three gen'lemen I knowed well a-standin' by, but I didn't ax nobody to speak fur me; I up an' speaks for myself, an' jes' as soon as I had sensed him wid what I was sayin', he laughs an' says, 'Why, Charley, you can have her jes' as she stands fur three hundred and fifty dollars.'" He may have enjoyed the opportunity to ensure the future of his family. But more than that he savored the fact that he had strolled up to a group of white men in a public place, a site of civic power, and had spoken without being spoken to first. He explicitly noted that he had not asked for any

white man's intercession, apparently because he enjoyed conjuring
with his own name. Stewart, when he remembered the incidents of
his life, was quick to emphasize the status his profession gave him
with white men whom other slaves feared. He spoke of Henry Clay
as a valued comrade when he described him as "mighty . . . perlite . . .
an' knowed a horse when he seed him, I tell you." As a boy, he had
told William Ransom Johnson that he knew a horse when he saw
one. Now his work allowed him to use the same language to speak
of one of the nation's most powerful politicians—one knowledgeable man indicating his respect for another.

Perhaps the most emotionally satisfying experience his job
brought Stewart was the purchase of his son Johnny, "sech a fine
boy it was a picter to see him . . . an' jes' as like his daddy, what was
me, you know, as a ole rabbit is like a young one." Johnny was the
child of his second wife, named for her father and brother. After her
death in Kentucky, Charles, who was on his way to Louisiana as the
property of Alexander Porter, went to her owner and asked to buy
the boy. For $150, his son became his property. Perhaps Charles
Stewart thought of his own father, for whom he was named, who
had wanted to buy him but never had. His son did not bear his
name, as he bore his own father's, but Johnny wore his face. And
Stewart's job, the income and status it brought him, had allowed
him to do something that the man he had loved and honored had
never been able to do. In the end, his success was short-lived; the
child never made the trip to Louisiana, perhaps because, as Stewart
explained, "An' some folks is so cur'ous dat I wa'n't sho dey would let
a free nigger, or rader a nigger dat belonged to his own daddy, stay
on de place. . . . An' de eend of de mahter was I lef' him, an' I ain't
never seed dat chile sence." He left his son with his dead wife's
mother and sister; his mother-in-law was a slave, and his sister-in-
law was likely one as well. Stewart promised to send for Johnny as
soon as he was settled and could take care of him, but he never did.
So while Johnny was theoretically Stewart's property, the child may
have lived on in bondage to white people. The father left the son as
he had been left, to make a life in the shadow of slavery after a
childhood of relative security and affection, because, while he could

purchase the boy, his much-valued position was not necessarily secure enough to keep him.

Stewart's choice of language in the story of Johnny suggests that he was quite aware of his audience, as aware as one would expect in a man so experienced. He called Johnny free only once, then carefully identified the child as his property. Perhaps he did not want Annie Porter to think that he would ever have dreamed of using his status to change his lot in life or his family's or to undermine bondage itself. He had learned in a hard school that a horseman's privileges were usually his alone. Sharing them threatened to end them. Johnny seems to have been the one person—the son in whom he saw himself—for whom he considered even momentarily breaking that rule and a lifetime's habit of cautious self-preservation. For Stewart had no hesitancy in speaking of purchasing other family members and obviously continued to think of them as property. He knew that a man who did not seek to extend or pass down his privileges, a man who fit his life to white needs and desires, could enjoy those privileges securely. He could experience in his own way what it meant to be a success in the antebellum South. Stewart's ultimate achievement was not freedom. It was mastery.

Stewart's decision to purchase his first wife was not born out of a romantic passion for her but of a sense that something was missing from his life: "I says to myself dat I was lonesome en dat big harnsome cabin, dat I was well off fur eberything 'ceptin' a good nigger to cook an' wash fur me." A wife was thus a fitting addition to the comfortable life his skills had earned him. Purchasing Betsey was no effort to secure her freedom and that of their children. It was a step toward ensuring that, in his own house, he was the master of a woman who belonged "to me, hide an' hyar." Just as the act of negotiating with Betsey's white owner was a welcome opportunity for Stewart to test and enjoy his own intimately understood and carefully judged privilege among white men, the purchase was also a chance of relishing his power in the presence of his fellow slaves. His prospective father-in-law immediately and respectfully called him "Colonel Stewart," in deference to his intimacy with Colonel Johnson, and was quickly made to understand that Stewart had no chivalrous feelings for Betsey Dandridge. When the older man openly expressed his concern that Stewart appeared to be hesitating over the purchase, Stewart bluntly informed him, "let me tell you, sir, dar is a heap o' difference 'twixt axin' a lady fur to be your spouse, an' buyin' a gal dat you don't know de price of." Not for Stewart the niceties of the first if the realities of the second could not be negotiated. His career as a horseman had made him a man with a cash income and a fine home, a man who, like other aspirants to status in the nineteenth-century South, wished to mark his social success by becoming a master. Betsey was to be both his wife, with the patina of respectability that implied, and his slave and possession, the crowning mark of his success.

Betsey Dandridge Stewart kept house with great skill and competence and had three children in the short time of her marriage. But she profoundly disappointed her husband in ways he only vaguely summed up with, "she couldn't seem to tell de trufe to save her life." What Betsey lied about, Charles never specified. He sought a variety of ways to cure her, including requesting prayers from family members at camp meetings. But his most frequent solution to the problem appears to have been beatings with "birch rods split fine, an' a light hickory stick 'bout as thick as my littlest finger." As much as any master, Stewart was discerning about the instrument with which he caused pain, as he tried to shape his possession to fit his desires.

Betsey had never set eyes on Charles Stewart before he appeared one day, in the midst of her fear that her family would be separated forever on the auction block. She may well have lied to her husband, and we have no way of knowing what she thought of him. Like anyone being abused by a domestic partner, she was certainly not unique in her community, though those around her may or may not have exhibited their own scars to her.[8] Despite the inequities and tensions within the slave community, most of Betsey's peers shared with their spouses and lovers that they were the slaves of a third person, a white person. Some of them may have taken out their frustrations with their situation on one another, and others may have clung more tightly together against its pain, but they shared that reality in common. Betsey was her husband's property. Whether his ownership would have been upheld in a court or not, the white men of Petersburg and Richmond had recognized Charles Stewart informally as her owner and were willing to treat her as his possession.[9] When her husband decided that he no longer wanted to deal with her supposed inadequacies, he elected to sell her back to her original owner for the same price he had paid. To compensate for "de war an' tar of de four year I had done kep' her," Charles volunteered to throw the family's three children into the bargain. Almost immediately, he left for his new assignment in Kentucky and "was jes' as happy as a king."

Part of his happiness in Kentucky was a second wife, named Mary Jane, whom he remembered as the great love of his life. He recounted his terrible grief at her death to Annie Porter and explained that, without her, he had not wanted to stay in Kentucky, where they had been so happy together. Nor did he want to go back to Virginia, where he had planned to return with her and their son Johnny. Instead, he asked William Ransom Johnson to sell him and stage-managed his own sale to Alexander Porter, hoping that the unfamiliar bayous of Louisiana would help to assuage his sorrow. But he also betrayed other feelings he had about Mary Jane and her death. "She was jes' as fond o' me as I was of her, an' it did 'pear hard luck to lose her jes' as I was makin' up my mind to buy her out an' out, only en course it was a fortunate thing I hadn't bought her, as long as she had to die, kase den I would ha' lost her an' da money too," he consoled himself. Charles Stewart might sometimes be a sentimental husband, but he was also a hardheaded slave market dealmaker. And Stewart himself was always subject to the slave market's realities as well. The papers of the white men involved suggest that Johnson sold Stewart not because he had lost his wife but because he had acquired one. Perhaps Johnson had no interest in a slave horseman tied to a family.[10] Charles chose to remember his sale as a generous gesture of respect from his former owner, but it may actually have been an indication of just how fragile Stewart's privilege was.[11] It may also have been an attempt on Johnson's part to stave off financial collapse with the cash Charles's sale would bring; in 1845, he sold most of his slaves at public auction, and at his death his heirs inherited an estate in complete disarray.[12]

For most of his life, Charles Stewart was valued principally as a possession, and he seems to have had difficulty in seeing the people he was closest to as anything but objects. In the end, the creatures that he understood best, that made him feel like himself, that gave him a way to comprehend the world, were horses, not other people. When he sold Betsey Dandridge Stewart and their children, he took his profit to a horse dealer in Petersburg and bought an animal named Brown Jim. Not only had he decided that he preferred having a horse to having a wife, he explained his decision to sell his children in the terms of a man intimately familiar with the conventional wisdom of equine breeding. Horsemen believe that the mother, who teaches the foal how to relate to human beings, has a profound effect on it that far outweighs her genetic contribution.[13] In considering whether to keep his children, even if he sold their mother, he decided, "No, she must ha' come of a bad breed, an' a colt is mos' apt to take arter de dam, anyhow; I better git shet of de whole gang of 'em, an' try a new cross." In the end, Charles Stewart had become too good at being who he was, too skilled as a privileged slave and horseman, to be a loving husband or father.

Stewart had learned to cope with his reality, to adjust his expectations to fit the heights he thought they could reach. He was quick to tell Annie Porter that he was proud he had been sold to her uncle for $3,500. "I bet dar ain't many folks wuf dat' mount o' money Norf or South." Certainly, he was unlikely to have told her about any secret desires for freedom, but he may also have decided that, instead of seeking to become free, he would work hard and succeed in becoming a master, because that was the greatest negation of slavery available to him. That was what he had learned from living as a slave in the highest stratum of bondage. But that quest did not leave much room for the love of a family that did double duty as tokens of his success. So he turned to the animals with whom he had a less complicated relationship, the horses who had made him, for good or ill, what he was, who had taken him from an uncertain childhood to a secure and skilled adulthood. "How I did love dem horses!" he recalled to Annie Porter. "It 'peared like dey loved me, too, an' when dey turned deir rainbow necks, all slick an' shinin', around sarchin' fur me to come an' give 'em deir gallops, whew-e-e!

how we did spin along dat old New Market course, right arter sunrise in de cool summer mornings!" That was a love and a joy he understood and trusted.

IN THE 1830s AND 1840s, the young Charles Stewart shared that joy with a rising generation of men, his white contemporaries on the turf, whose lives and ideas were shaped in accordance with the world of the track and the extraordinary men and animals encountered there. These men helped to move the richest contests in racing westward, as slavery's epicenter itself shifted to the estates of the Old Southwest. When Charles Stewart went from Virginia to Kentucky to Louisiana in the course of his career, he was part of a network of men, money, knowledge, and devotion that defined the boundaries of a new home for Southern—indeed, American—racing.

The king of Southern tracks in the 1830s and 1840s was still a product of the Eastern Seaboard. He was a Virginia stallion named Boston, so vicious that no one even attempted to put a bridle on him until he was two years old. He came by his temper honestly. His mother's sire was the famously evil stallion Ball's Florizel. (The trainer Green Berry Williams, explaining why he had not accepted a lucrative offer to work exclusively for John Randolph, had couched his decision in language his contemporaries could understand when he admitted that he would rather be in a stall with Ball's Florizel than on a farm with John Randolph.[14]) Training Boston was a nightmare; "he could bite, plunge, and kick, in the most scientific and efficient manner possible, frequently kicking out twice before touching the ground." When such tricks failed, Boston liked to lie down and roll, trying to crush his rider underneath him. The horse bounced around among trainers, most of whom concluded that the best solution to his intransigence would be "either to castrate or shoot him—the latter operation preferred." Finally, he was given to a black horseman named Ned, who worked for the white trainer John Belcher, to break. Ned rode Boston everywhere for months and ultimately tamed him. Under the supervision of William Ransom Johnson, Boston carried the banner for the South on Long Island in 1842 against the Northern star Fashion, in front of a huge crowd that included forty members of Congress. Fashion's victory that day did nothing to detract from Boston's celebrity. Racetrack aficionados delighted in telling tales of his temper, his seemingly impossible ascent to greatness. But Boston was one of the last of the great stars of the Virginia track that made his name there and in intersectional competition with Northern horses.[15]

The centers of power in American racing had slowly been shifting westward and southward for years. As early as 1829, the *American Turf Register* had observed that great stallions were migrating from the East to sire successful racers in the trans-Appalachian West. "Old Virginia, ever high minded, always generous, 'like the mother of the Gracchii, when asked for her treasures, she pointed to her sons'—and with them we send *our horses*."[16] As Southern planters' sons migrated into the rich new country of Kentucky, Tennessee, Alabama, and Mississippi, expanding the reach of slaveholding America, they brought with them the values that their fathers had inculcated in them in their youth. Part of remaking the world they had grown up in, with themselves in the roles of the patriarchs, was hewing racetracks out of the wilderness, matching their horses, and learning what men they trusted and admired in the heat of equine competition. Thoroughbred raising and racing helped to create an expanded South that might grow different crops but in the end felt the same allegiances to slavery as a political and economic institution and to its defense and customs.[17]

The flourishing economy of the lower South allowed such men to transplant the infrastructure necessary for highly successful Thoroughbred racing, and increasingly Southerners refused to travel north or east to prove their champions' mettle. Now men from New York, Richmond, and Charleston, the epicenters of early nineteenth-century American racing, came to Nashville, Louisville, and New Orleans to see nationally significant races, rather than staying closer to home. As Southerners felt themselves more arbiters of their own success and less inclined to assume New York as the proving ground of superiority in the Thoroughbred world, New York racing perceptibly slowed down. The Union Course continued to be a destination for national match races into the 1840s, but it was no longer the only or even the preferred site for such contests. The financial crisis of the late 1830s, which shook New York's banks, damaged local racing that already depended heavily on about a dozen major owners. New Yorkers continued to own famous horses, and crowds continued to enjoy the racing at the Union Course, but prospective buyers with slightly less cash to spend were drawn to the popular sport of harness racing, which took off in New York in the antebellum period.[18] Southern interest remained firmly with the running horse, but the planters of Virginia and South Carolina could not always keep up with their western competitors. Even after the Panic of 1837, cotton belt and Bluegrass Thoroughbred enthusiasts continued to find the cash they needed to race first-class horses. In Tennessee, Kentucky, Mississippi, Alabama, and Louisiana, it seemed entirely appropriate that any man with the discretionary income to do so should put his money into a Thoroughbred.[19]

Indeed, in 1838, the *Spirit of the Times* reported, "The great reduction in the price of cotton and sugar has not prevented many gentlemen in the South-west from engaging in breeding and importing fine stock."[20] The West, particularly the famously fertile horse country of Kentucky, Tennessee, and northern Alabama, now produced its own animals, rather than relying on horses brought from the hallowed racing stables of the East. Imported British stallions Luzborough and Glencoe stood at stud at Franklin, Tennessee, and Forks of Cypress, Alabama, respectively. And when the towering Glencoe daughter Peytona soared to victory at Nashville, a *Spirit of the Times* correspondent, trying to describe the noise for his readers in the East, marveled, "[I had] never . . . heard a good old-fashioned Tennessee yell. You ought to have your measure taken for one, and have it shipped by first conveyance."[21] This was a dispatch from a new frontier of racing, of a quality to match or surpass anything that had come before. Breeding and racing networks now tied the Deep South to Kentucky and Tennessee. Mare owners in Mississippi and Louisiana sent their animals to be bred in the Bluegrass.[22] And when their homebreds were not as successful as they wished, the same planters eagerly bought up the stars of the Bluegrass tracks with high rolling abandon.[23]

Turfmen in the lower Mississippi Valley also turned to their friends in Kentucky and Tennessee when it came time for their horses to run. Mississippi and Louisiana planters were members of

Kentucky jockey clubs and nominated their horses to the expensive stakes races run on the tracks in Nashville, Louisville, and Lexington.[24] But by the 1850s everyone admitted that the most lavishly run track in America was at New Orleans, where the planters of the Mississippi Valley brokered their crops and spent their money. The Metairie Course, located only a few miles from the banks and merchants of Canal Street and the neighboring slave pens on Baronne, first hosted races in 1838. The Metairie regularly offered thousands of dollars in prize money and pulled in runners from all over the new Thoroughbred heartland, as well as competitors from the older centers in Virginia and South Carolina.[25] Great planters came from all over the South to New Orleans just as men ten and twenty years before had gone to Charleston to watch the races, to talk business and politics, to meet one another's sons, and to consider the future of their world. When the running ended at the Metairie, they adjourned to the palatial St. Charles Hotel. The Metairie Jockey Club met at the St. Charles, and planters and political parties did serious business there. On the weekends, temporary auction blocks were set up at each end of the hotel bar, and slaves from the pens near the hotel were sold to the highest bidder.[26] The hotel, as much as the track, was a place where mastery was made, where men expressed who they were as horsemen, politicians, planters, and owners of human property.

When the grandees of the Virginia and South Carolina turf came west, they faced a formidable group of adversaries in a new generation of turfmen. The *American Turf Register* observed of the prospects for the New Orleans races in the spring of 1842, "There are only two stables from Mississippi,—'but oh Lord!' Beating the cracks from Natchez isn't quite as easy as slipping off a slippery log. Did you ever see a cat-fish trying to climb a lightning rod?"[27] The writer referred to the great stables of William J. Minor and his old friend Adam Bingaman. Bingaman and Minor were names that were virtually always said together in racing circles. Both men descended from families that had settled in Natchez before it was American territory, and both commanded formidable wealth and slave labor, Bingaman at his Fatherland Plantation and Minor at his Concord, Waterloo, and Southdown estates. They were among the

founders of the Natchez Jockey Club and the most prominent owners at the city's Pharsalia track, where some of the most competitive
races in the lower Mississippi Valley were run from the time of its
founding in 1835.[28]

Before he was thirty, William J. Minor earned a reputation as a
man whose opinion of a horse was worth having. The most famous
bloodstock agent in the world, Richard Tattersall of London, wrote
to him, "[C]andour is what I like from every one, particularly such
gentlemen as yourself, you being in my opinion a very good judge."[29]
To have the respect of so prominent a man only confirmed William
J. Minor's constant conviction that he knew best. Throughout his
life, he wrote a lordly scrawl with a heavy pen and eschewed the
period as a useful punctuation mark; the very look of his letters
pronounced him a man disinclined to pause and second-guess himself.[30] He supervised his own stables, which he ran at a consistent
profit, an unusual feat in as risky a business as horse racing. Horse
owners from all over the United States sent him their prizes to train
and race, paying him expenses or cutting him in for a share of the
purses the horses won. He even trained a filly named Crescent for
the family of Samuel Purdy, the jockey of American Eclipse himself.[31] When Minor started out in the horse business in 1835, he paid
$15,000 for the imported beauties who were the foundation of his
stable and another $15,000 for slaves with the necessary equine ex-
pertise to work them.[32] Ben Watson, who trained in Minor's stables,
Antony or Anthony Hall, his lead assistant, and George Moore, the
head groom, were black men but also well-known equine experts,
whose conversations merited write-ups in national turf magazines.[33]

The racing magazines welcomed Minor's letters and dubbed him
"the first breeder and turfman of the South West" and a "worthy
example for all gentlemen who have a fancy for, and a disposition to
indulge in the sports of the Turf."[34] His stature gave Minor a platform from which to trumpet his unshakeable opinion that Eastern
horsemen prided themselves on their achievements without sufficient cause and that Northern racing was the paltry business of
vulgarians.[35] Minor, like John Randolph before him, was often the
man in racing circles who expressed commonly held feelings more
loudly and pointedly than anyone else. Minor was a voluminous

writer of racing reportage and opinion, appearing most often with
the nom de plume "Young Turfman" in every racing magazine
from the 1830s until his death after the Civil War.[36] Indeed, his passionate commitment to his position as a turf correspondent and to
his own opinions and loyalties can be gauged by the fact that racing
historian John Hervey judged him more vitriolic than Randolph
himself: "His pen while brilliant was bitter, not with the abstract,
almost uncanny acerbity and barbed wit of Randolph . . . but the
burning animosity of a man who was giving battle to opponents
that he despised and desired to destroy—this including not only
men and horses but lines of blood and breeding theories. Intensely
sectional . . . he was the spokesman of his own homeland [the Deep
South], the champion of its champions and, in his championship of
them, went to extremes."[37] Minor explicitly made every expression
of his opinions an assertion of his status as a horseman and a gentleman and an opportunity to demonstrate his opponents' equestrian
and personal failings.[38]

No one was more likely to incur Minor's contempt than Richard
Ten Broeck, the track manager and entrepreneur who had become a
leading light of New Orleans racing. The bitterest dispute between
the two men was about a horse's mouth. Judging the age of a horse
was a tricky proposition in nineteenth-century America, because, in
the absence of a Thoroughbred registry that recorded the horse's
birth date, the best method for doing so was to examine the horse's
teeth. Equine teeth have grooves and hollows that evolve in pre-
dictable patterns as an animal grows older, and an experienced
horseman can lift a horse's lip, examine his jaw, and discern his ap-
proximate age. A wary horse buyer, reluctant to take the word of a
fast-talking seller, could purchase one of the numerous books and
periodicals that described in words and pictures the dental patterns
that marked a horse of a particular age.[39] But such manuals were
both imprecise and impractical. The final word on a horse's age was
still reserved for a man with the confidence and long experience to
walk up to a strange animal of uncertain temper, jam a thumb into
its mouth, and examine teeth that, in the hot, wet cavern of powerful jaws, probably bore little or no resemblance to an antiseptic
drawing. Minor was such a man and was inalterably convinced both

that Ten Broeck was not and that this difference said something profound about both of them.

Ten Broeck was the proud owner of an up and coming racer named Pryor, in honor of the well-respected white trainer John Benjamin Pryor, who worked Adam Bingaman's horses. At the New Orleans races, Ten Broeck entered his horse as a four year old, entitling the animal to carry the weight allotted to a horse of that age, and Pryor defeated the champion Lecomte, who belonged to Minor's good friend Thomas J. Wells. Minor insisted that Pryor was not four years old but five and had thus received an unfair advantage. If he had been entered as a five year old, he would have had to carry ten more pounds, equivalent to a two hundred and fifty yard disadvantage, according to the oddsmakers.[40] As the horses had rested between heats, Pryor's groom had squeezed water out of a sponge into the horse's mouth, and Minor claimed to have gotten a glimpse of his teeth. At a glance, he informed anyone who would listen, he had seen that the horse was older than advertised. Minor was quick to point out that he made no claim that Ten Broeck had knowingly cheated, implying that in this singular case the man's ignorance had surpassed his dishonesty.

The controversy exploded all over the sporting press. Ten Broeck, who had already sent Pryor to Kentucky to race, produced a veterinary certificate, attesting to the horse's age, that Minor scoffed at. He would be satisfied, he said, if Ten Broeck would consent to have the question decided by competent men in Kentucky, whom they would settle on together. Many of the great turfmen of the Bluegrass had their opinions on the matter printed and their ability to judge a horse's teeth called into question.[41] But to Minor's sputtering amazement, Ten Broeck elected to ignore the dispute and send the horse across the Atlantic to challenge English runners. Minor stubbornly continued drafting and redrafting fragments of letters, articles, and personal memoranda on the topic and preserved them in his papers. For him, the issue far transcended the dental peculiarities of a particular horse. Fueling his implacable rage was the outrageous fact that a man he could not respect had dismissed his opinion in a matter integral to his vision of himself as a man of competence and honor. The affair of Pryor's mouth was only the

bitterest and most minutely detailed of a series of such disputes in
the pages of the sporting press in the antebellum period. The men
involved were not merely arguing about equine minutia but about
who had a right to respect, prominence, mastery, and power.

THE SPORTING PRESS that covered the Pryor's mouth controversy
grew steadily in the 1830s and 1840s. Its stories and pictures created
a paper racetrack to be shared among friends, debated in barbershops, or examined in solitary concentration. These representations
of racing offered to a national subscription base a view of Southern
turfmen as preeminent figures in a beloved American institution, as
voices of authority, acuity, and benevolence, possessed of an established right to order their stables and their slave system as they saw
fit and to expect Northerners' respectful assent. The sporting men
of the Mississippi Valley avidly supported the new form of journalism. William J. Minor became one of the ardent patrons of the
sporting press, from the summer of 1833, when he paid Cadwallader
Colden ten dollars for an annual subscription to Colden's abortive
attempt at a national racing magazine.[42] Colden's publication, which
consisted mostly of reprinted stories from British periodicals,
foundered, but *The American Turf Register and Sporting Magazine*,
first published in 1829, established itself firmly as a national authority in equine matters. Its editor, Baltimore native John S. Skinner,
secured for himself a small place in American history when he
shared Francis Scott Key's captivity during the bombardment of
Fort McHenry and then became the first to print and distribute the
poem Key wrote on the subject. When the words were set to music
shortly thereafter, the resulting song became "The Star Spangled
Banner." But in turf circles Skinner was revered as the publisher of
The American Farmer and then of *The American Turf Register*, the
first attempts at an "authentic record" of the progress of livestock
and Thoroughbred horses in the United States.[43]

But for racing men of the 1840s, Skinner's successor overshad-
owed him both literally and figuratively. William T. Porter loomed
at a gangling six feet four inches when he came to New York from
New England as a journeyman printer. In 1831, still in his midtwenties, he and a young Horace Greeley were working on a new weekly

sports magazine called *The Spirit of the Times*. By 1832, Greeley had moved on to other papers en route to a nationally famous editorial and political career, but Porter had found his niche in writing about horses, fishing, and the theater.[44] Porter offered his readers something new in the way of American sports journalism. While Skinner's *Turf Register* provided sound, accurate records of race results, breeding, veterinary questions, and similar issues, Porter's *Spirit of the Times* put the spotlight on his writers, on the sporting opinions, gossip, and anecdotes they included with their reportage. Some of his correspondents even wrote fiction for the paper.[45] By 1839, the superiority of Porter's model was assured, as he bought out his Baltimore competition and assumed complete editorial control of the *American Turf Register*.[46] That same year, Porter increased the size of the *Spirit* from eight to twelve pages and doubled the price of a subscription from five to ten dollars. His magazine now cost more than many of the polished literary monthlies of the era, and his circulation still climbed past the 40,000 mark.[47]

Men all over America subscribed to the *Spirit of the Times*. Porter liked to boast that he numbered no less than eighteen members of Congress among his correspondents, and many more probably subscribed.[48] But many of his tens of thousands of subscribers lived in the South and particularly in the areas of the South where racing had its new centers. Bennet Barrow, on his plantation in Louisiana, noted in May 1840 that he had paid his ten-dollar fee for the magazine.[49] William Johnson, the free black man who made his living as a Natchez barber and raced horses on the side, got in three years ahead of Barrow, when the price was still five dollars, and secured his annual subscription.[50] The prominent breeder Robert Alexander, who found mail delivery slow to his farm in Spring Station, Kentucky, preferred to have Lees and Waller, the New York firm that handled his business interests, receive the weekly issues and forward them to him. Lees and Waller seem to have found it perfectly reasonable to add the *Spirit of the Times* to the services they performed for their client.[51] In towns all over the South and Southwest, men were getting their hands on the *Spirit of the Times* any way they could in the 1830s and 1840s. The mail simply could not come quickly enough for many subscribers, who waited eagerly for the next weekly installment. "Another ten days 'out and gone' and yet no Spirit of the Times," complained one far-flung correspondent. "If old friend Job had have lived in these times, I verily believe he would say, damn it."[52]

Porter's paper succeeded so overwhelmingly because he understood just how much was required of him as an editor. The job was simple, he reflected ruefully. A man in his position must know every detail about every horse competing in America; must understand all the peculiarities of every racing rule at every track in the nation; and must be well acquainted with every owner, breeder, trainer, jockey, and groom on the turf, with a shrewd idea of their talents and shortcomings. He should be able to use all that knowledge to predict the outcome of virtually every contest with minute accuracy: "With all these gifts . . . grant him good health, good nature, indomitable perseverance and assiduity, and one would think he might hope to become reasonably popular as a Sporting editor."[53] Further complicating the job was Porter's position as a New Englander, editing a New York-based paper, with large numbers of devoted subscribers living in the South and increasingly defensive about their role in racing and about the sacrosanct status of slavery. Porter insisted that the problem could be neatly circumvented by the magazine's adamant policy, summed up in its offices with the admonition, "No Smoking (Nor Politics) Allowed Here!"[54] The offices of the Spirit (and Frank's saloon a few doors down where writers and visitors adjourned after hours) served as neutral territory in the midst of Manhattan, right off of Broadway, opposite the Astor House. Sportsmen from all over the United States looked forward to dropping in on Porter when they came to New York.[55]

But determined bonhomie could not solve Porter's problem entirely. Charles Stewart's owner, Alexander Porter, speaking as an old friend to the editor but also as a slaveholding politician of considerable savvy, summed up William Porter's situation neatly:

You are in some respects the arbiter of horse reputation. . . . Your reasoning and your remarks must, if you expect to give satisfaction, *take a judicial tone.* That in a conflict of pride and opinion between the North and the South you should, *uncon-*

sciously to yourself, feel enlisted in favor of the former, is inevitable. You live there, you hear those around you continually dwelling on the perfections of a noble animal; you see her— you witness her generous exertions, and you end *by being in love with her.* All this is as it should be. . . . But then, my good namesake, *true wisdom consists in watching our strong qualities, and preventing them running into excess.* And there is this additional reason for your standing sentinel on your thoughts, that your paper is national, that it is meant by you for the whole country, and the topics of which it treats belong more to the South than to the North.[56]

Alexander Porter wrote in sentimental, even romantic, terms of the ties that bound men of a particular region to their own equine champions. But he was not only talking about horses; both men understood that to discuss a Thoroughbred was also to speak of a man's deepest allegiances and understandings of himself. The emotional bond Porter sketched was also one of loyalty to dreams of personal and national advancement accreted from childhood on. Southern men did not merely demand respect for their horses. They wanted slavery, the institution at the very heart of their racing world and their political and economic lives, held inviolate. In his editorial policy, William Porter took the advice to heart. To compose a national magazine covering topics so absorbing to Southerners, he had to create a determinedly apolitical publication that still managed to defer judiciously to Southern opinion.

Porter famously filled his pages with stories like "The Big Bear of Arkansas" and "A Quarter Race in Kentucky," tales that celebrated the sharp dealings and linguistic elasticity of men from the South and Old Southwest. Turfmen probably turned first to the racing results included on interior pages, but they read the fiction, too, and some of them even became successful writers in the genre of folk humor that Porter nourished into a mainstay of American literary history. Men who spent their time around stables could well appreciate the all-male world of the stories, in which inside knowledge of a horse or a situation could win the day. At the racetrack, they lived in such a world, where Southern men of different classes shared a camaraderie that bolstered and made comfortable a rapidly expanding hierarchical society.[57] The stories confirmed in the crafting of fiction what the rest of the paper was meant to confirm in the representing of fact—that the South was a distinctive and flourishing culture that the rest of what William Porter liked to call "the universal Yankee nation" enjoyed and respected.[58]

Porter's magazine handled the Southern economy and its basis in human bondage with the sensitivity necessary to the issue over which Southerners were most likely to take offense. Slavery was very seldom discussed in its pages; there was safety in silence. But when it appeared, it did so in reassuring terms. One Northern visitor writing of his travels in the South remembered discussing the death of a slave with a white planter, who eulogized the black man, impressing his listener. "I hail from a colder clime, where it is our proud boast that all men are equal. I shall return to my northern home deeply impressed with the belief, that dispensing with the name of freedom the negroes of the South are the happiest and most contented people on the face of the earth," he solemnly concluded.[59] Slaves were objects of vague pity, sentimental recollection, or demeaning humor in Porter's magazine. Slave horsemen were largely invisible in the *Spirit*'s columns, their labor concealed in the disputes of their owners. But Southern turfmen did not want such men erased everywhere. Indeed, they were central figures in turfmen's vision of the harmony of a slave society. They had to be displayed.

While Charles Stewart cared for William Johnson's stallion Medley in Pennsylvania, the Austrian expatriate Edward Troye painted the animal and his handler. The almost-white horse, muscled haunches gleaming and tail flowing, stands in profile. Stewart, clad in a vest, white shirt, and dress trousers and boots, keeps his eyes firmly on his charge. His right arm is raised to hold the reins near the horse's mouth, the gesture graceful and confident. Troye's portrait of Medley and Stewart was the first of many of his works to be engraved and published on a full page in the *American Turf Register*. Troye's success with the hauntingly beautiful pair served in part to establish him as the favored painter of Southern planters eager to immortalize their champions.[60] Troye enjoyed tremendous popularity with Southern turfmen. They paid him to come to their

The artist Edward Troye's portrait of a young Charles Stewart, at the head of Johnson's Medley. Stewart's fame as a horseman would allow him to travel around the United States and to buy and sell his wife and children. From the private collection of Catherine Woodford Clay. *Photo by Mary Rezny.*

homes and paint their horses, as generations of racing men had commissioned earlier painters. His Thoroughbred portraits were depictions of the world that white horsemen wished to imagine—a bustling agricultural and manufacturing paradise, regulated and capitalized to perfection, run by men of authority, intelligence, and foresight like themselves, full of athletic, well-tended horses poised to carry their colors to victory. Equine portraits joined a flourishing genre of plantation painting that depicted the world of slavery as planters wished to see it.[61]

Troye's paintings of black horsemen were strikingly individual portraits of particular professional men caught at work. Such pictures generally followed a formula. The groom held the horse, the trainer prepared to saddle the animal, and the jockey waited to mount.[62] In Troye's portrait of the champion runner Richard

Singleton, the horse appears nervous, eyes wide. His trainer, Harry Lewis, stands at his head, impeccably clad in a top hat and frock coat, the kind of clothes in which Charles Stewart demonstrated his past to Annie Porter. Both Harry and the groom who stands behind him glance at us. Harry's long, dark face is impatient, that of a busy man rudely interrupted. Already, he seems to remind us, the jockey, Lew, is strolling toward his mount. Harry has no time to waste on gawkers; he has to saddle his charge and prepare him to run. In the portrait of Robert Alexander's Asteroid, however, the gray-bearded trainer, Ansel Williamson, knows we are there and welcomes us to look at length. He is only now beginning the saddling process. From the other side of the frame, the jockey, Edward Brown, gazes at us inquisitively, as does the groom holding the horse. Brown crouches down, ready to leap aboard the undefeated champion as soon as Williamson gives the word. But right now they are content to take it slow. Their horse is a national star, and they are used to public attention.

Troye's portraits depicted men imbued with the authority of their own labor and mindful of their own dignity.[63] In most cases, they are the only portraits we have of men integral to the history of the American Thoroughbred. Frederick Douglass believed that such individual depictions of bondspeople, portrayals that allowed them to express their own personalities, were a crucial step toward slaves' recognition of themselves and viewers' recognition of them as people worthy of respect and thus entitled to freedom.[64] Charles Stewart and his contemporaries, the men in these portraits, left behind at least some remnant of the lives they lived and the privileges that came at such a terrible price. But the white men who commissioned and lived with these pictures, who raised Annie Porter to record Stewart's memories unblinkingly, saw in them none of the vital possibilities Douglass imagined, nor the painful ambiguities of these men's lives. They saw highly skilled men—acknowledged as individuals because their skills were not interchangeable and extended unusual privileges because they were supremely useful. They saw the perfect slaves necessary to strengthen racing and the slave South in which racing did invaluable work of self-definition, conflict resolution, and the justification of power. Horsemen like Charles Stewart were not a threat to slavery. They were living proof that a slave society could produce supremely competent professionals to labor in white interests at the complex and difficult jobs of modern agriculture and industry. They proved the strength of bondage and thus had to be exhibited in pictures that prefigured a glorious imagined future.

THE TURFMEN of the Bluegrass and the Deep South had made images of their world; now, they would remake the world in their image. What stories and pictures could make coherent, politics could make real. Turfmen of the 1820s had understood and experienced racing as an institution that drew together men of wealth and power in mutual respect. In the 1830s and 1840s, as Southern slaveholders asserted their preeminence at the track, Democrats continued to hold the sport dear. But Southern Whigs in particular embraced the world of the Thoroughbred as a stage on which they enacted and saw enshrined their most cherished convictions and visions of the future. And they believed that the man to realize their visions was one of their own—Kentucky's Henry Clay. When Clay died, the dignitaries of Washington gathered around his coffin in the Senate chamber, which he had ruled for so long, and Senate chaplain Charles M. Butler proclaimed, "Bury the records of your country's history—bury the hearts of the living millions—bury the mountains, the rivers, the lakes, and the spreading lands from sea to sea, with which his name is inseparably associated, and even then you would not bury HENRY CLAY—for he lives in other lands, and speaks in other tongues, and to other times than our's."[65] It seemed impossible to the men who had known Clay that he would ever be anything but a figure of national, even international, importance. But he was not only larger than life; he was an object of great personal devotion. "I have admired and trusted many statesmen," New York editor Horace Greeley reflected. "I profoundly loved Henry Clay."[66] Clay had the gift of inspiring love over and above loyalty, a talent that separates the great politician from the merely good.

Turfmen had ample reason to admire Clay, for he was proudly one of them. Clay was an active member of Lexington's jockey club and a well-known figure on racetracks around the South. In 1843, when William Ransom Johnson attended the New Orleans races, the *Spirit of the Times* paid him the compliment of saying that "[t]he arrival of no gentleman but Mr. Clay could excite such a sensation in town as Col. Johnson's."[67] But it was as a breeder that Clay would make his lasting mark on the racing world. Clay's first foray into Thoroughbred breeding on his Ashland estate near Lexington, Kentucky, came in 1806, when he joined a syndicate that purchased the English stallion Buzzard, who went on to a successful stud career.[68]

As an aspiring horse breeder, Clay found his political connections extremely useful. Certainly Nicholas Biddle, the head of the Second Bank of the United States, had cause to value Clay as his indispensable ally in the battle against those who thought a national bank an indefensible consolidation of power in a democracy. Clay may have been relying on the banker's gratitude when he wrote to him in 1838, "It is possible that I may have occasion for the use in England of from five to ten thousand dollars. Can I get from your Bank a credit. . . . And what shall I do to entitle myself to the credit? Must I give other guarantys than my own name? . . . Should I have occasion to use the credit, it will be in the purchase of a stud horse—a fact which I hope you will consider in the nature of a Bank secret."[69] Biddle cheerfully offered Clay as much cash as he required, with a signature the only necessary collateral, and enthusiastically endorsed the idea of importing a fine stallion. Clay evidently later decided that his request had been ill-advised for a man positioning himself for a presidential candidacy in 1840 and informed Biddle that he "thought it expedient to open a new source of Revenue" for the purchase.[70]

But, if a loan were risky, gifts were another matter entirely. In the summer of 1845, Clay's old friend Wade Hampton sent him a mare named Margaret Wood. "This filly seemed to strike your fancy," he wrote, "and I have ventured to send her to you, and earnestly hope you will accept her, as a token of my regard."[71] That November, William N. Mercer, a prominent Mississippi Whig, sent Clay the mare Magnolia as a sign of political allegiance and personal friendship.[72] Those two mares ensured the immortality of Ashland in the annals of the American Thoroughbred. Their descendants included more than a dozen Kentucky Derby winners and Iroquois, the first American-bred horse to win the English Derby at Epsom.[73]

The Ashland stud owed its sterling record to racing men's deep affection for Henry Clay and devotion to his ideas. Racing men of the 1830s and 1840s were accustomed to look for leaders they respected in the owner's box at the track, and they adored Clay's combination of politician's dash and sportsman's swagger. Such men delighted in repeating the story of the dinner at E. M. Blackburn's farm in Versailles, Kentucky, the final home of American Eclipse, where Blackburn had raised his glass to his friend, with the toast, *"Eclipse among horses as Henry Clay is amongst men!"* The guests erupted into applause.[74]

Southern Whigs, Clay's most loyal followers in the political party he led until his death, were prominent both in politics and on the turf in the 1830s and 1840s. By the late 1830s, a list of the nation's most committed and celebrated turfmen might have doubled as a list of staunch Clay Whigs. Southern Whig turfmen regarded their passion for racing and their convictions about electoral politics as inextricably intertwined, indivisible aspects of their lives and selves. When William Ransom Johnson won a seat in the Virginia state legislature, the *Spirit of the Times* reported gleefully, "The election resulted in favor of Johnson—every body expected it. . . . The Democratic nag . . . contested three miles and three quarters of the race 'neck and neck'—but . . . considerably dropped behind some forty or fifty paces in *the quarter stretch.*"[75] Robert Alexander, the master of Kentucky's Woodburn Farm, and his friends worried that without a Whig president, it would be impossible "to right the ship."[76] The Tennessee turfman Balie Peyton was famous outside of racing circles as the mainstay of the Tennessee Whig Party, the man responsible for denying the state's votes to Democrat Martin Van Buren in 1836.[77] In 1837, he wrote indignantly to the *Spirit of the Times* to complain that a horse he had raised and named Livingston had been renamed in honor of Andrew Jackson's political ally and longtime friend, Senator Thomas Hart Benton of Missouri.[78] Louisiana racing enthusiast Duncan Kenner named his sugar plantation Ashland after Henry Clay's own estate. Mississippi Whig

Adam Bingaman's horses proclaimed his sympathies with their names—his sorrel colt Henry Clay and his chestnut Nick Biddle.[79] In 1840, he provided the wagon on which local Whigs constructed a log cabin as a prop for the presidential campaign of William Henry Harrison.[80] Bingaman served the Whigs as a powerbroker in the Mississippi legislature throughout the 1830s.[81] And Bingaman's old friend, William J. Minor, was never shy about trumpeting his inveterate Whig convictions to the newspapers.[82] Even Minor, however, was not more vehement than Charles Stewart's owner, Louisiana's Alexander Porter, who served as president of the New Orleans Jockey Club and embarked in 1841 on an ambitious program of importing English Thoroughbreds.[83] When Henry Clay visited Louisiana, he was an honored guest at Porter's Oaklawn estate.[84] Porter bemoaned the Democrats' nominations to the Supreme Court in a letter to a friend, "I am doomed I suppose to see the mantle of Marshall fall on the shoulders of some fellow who in place of . . . integrity can cry 'hurrah for Jackson and damn the Whigs.'"[85]

The convictions of Clay's Whiggery were ideally suited to the leading horsemen of the Mississippi Valley. Clay's policies, dubbed his American System, which were the cornerstones of the Whig platform for the duration of the party's effective political life, were geared to promoting a protected, diversified, well-integrated economy. Such policies were predicated on the idea of a government eager to use its influence and central authority to partner with private initiative and enterprise. There would be national tariffs to protect agriculture and industry and thus create domestic jobs and markets; there would be infrastructure developments like publicly financed roads and canals that would connect those markets; and there would be a national bank that would facilitate the movement of credit and capital along those routes.[86]

The paramount importance of efficient physical and economic connections was most apparent to cosmopolitan Southerners accustomed to traveling often and to keeping up with diverse economic interests. Adam Bingaman had gone to Harvard and William J. Minor to the University of Pennsylvania. They and their friends sent their boys to Northern schools, spent their summers at Northern resorts, did business through agents with offices in New York.[87] And tariffs were obviously most appealing to men like the hemp-growing Clay, who raised crops also grown in other countries and thus depended on government-enforced import restrictions. Unsurprisingly, men like Minor and Alexander Porter, whose great plantations produced sugarcane, devoted themselves to protectionist Whig policy in the face of Caribbean competition.[88] Such men saw the need for and the productive capacity of advantageous partnerships between manufacturing and agriculture. Duncan Kenner's sugar estate depended on cutting-edge industrial technology. Slaves on Ashland loaded cane onto a small railroad that carried the cuttings to the steam-powered boilers in which they were processed.[89] Such enterprises demanded a free flow of credit, anchored by a sound financial system capable of backing extensive projects. The Bank of the United States had good reason to be popular around the Pharsalia Track; Natchez racing men served as directors of several different banks and knew firsthand the benefits to a landowner of having access to well-secured credit to improve crop acreage. They battled fiercely against Jacksonian incursions on the financial institutions they headed.[90] Minor observed, as dogmatically as he ever did on the subject of Pryor's mouth, "we never shall get right until we get a National Bank."[91]

The combination of Whig political leanings and equine obsession was no coincidence. The intellectual historian Michael O'Brien observes incisively, "Clay made his theory out of his circumstances."[92] Uninterested in economic abstractions, Clay looked at his own situation and extrapolated. If he, as O'Brien suggests, seems to have gotten most of his economics from the political columns of *Niles's Weekly Register*, he also got a good portion of his thought from the *Spirit of the Times*. Clay always insisted that Ashland was as good a farm as any Moses could have had if he had reached the Promised Land.[93] On his estate, he grew hemp with studious attention to the latest agricultural techniques, and his livestock included, in addition to his Thoroughbreds, purebred imported cattle, sheep, jackasses, pigs, and fowl. Clay found his animals as fascinating as the crops and votes he was always harvesting. "I never go out of my house, without meeting with some of them to engage agreeably my attention," he wrote happily.[94] Clay's attentive love for his farm was not a distraction from his legislative career; his feelings stemmed from the depth of his personal commitment to his vision of political economy. Clay could see in Ashland the proper workings of the American economy writ small. American agriculture, protected by tariffs from foreign competition, could fill American coffers, just as his own hemp crop, immune from cheaper Russian imports, flourished. Alongside agriculture worked industry, both run with a sharp eye for ways in which improved technology and infrastructure could aid their productivity.[95]

Whig powerbrokers saw in their own farms and their own lives what they believed to be hard evidence that their ideas were not only workable but were the best possible basis for future American prosperity and domestic peace.[96] The whole nation could be run as they ran their own stock farms. When William Ransom Johnson looked at Oakland, when William J. Minor looked at Concord, when Adam Bingaman looked at Fatherland, they saw what Clay himself saw at Ashland—a smoothly interlocking, robust little world of varied and extensive enterprises, which a man of vision, acuity, and expertise kept running perfectly. For men of earlier generations, stables full of Thoroughbreds and slaves had meant that the master of the estate was a man of substance and power. For the Whig racing men of the Mississippi Valley, the residents of their stables were also living proof that men of authority and vision could create a dynamic, harmonious community in which everyone flourished. A man intelligent and well organized enough to own a successful racing and breeding operation should and would be inevitably recognized as a natural leader. In a perfect Whig world, such men's estates and enterprises would be connected and supported so that their skills could be harnessed for the service of the country and the gratitude of the masses.[97] Their personal pastime and political convictions reinforced one another, imbuing Southern Whig turfmen with a sense of their own fundamental rightness, the coherence and efficacy of their party's vision of the future.

At the heart of that world, powering its institutions, would be slavery, the labor that made possible Whig turfmen's belief in their own self-assured competence. The world of Henry Clay and the world of Charles Stewart—the places and people they knew, the language they spoke, the stories they told—were coterminous. And as Clay and his allies constructed a national political program, their convictions were grounded in the extraordinary, painful lives of men like Charles Stewart. As a young man, Henry Clay had publicly agonized over the plight of slaves and pressed for gradual emancipation to be written into the Kentucky state constitution. Older politicians had admired his grit and acuity, one praising him in the language that Clay already spoke fluently as "the best three-year old he had ever seen on turf."[98] But gradual emancipation went down to decisive defeat in the Kentucky legislature. Even in the first flush of youth, Clay was no dewy-eyed idealist. His plans for the amelioration of slavery remained cautiously vague, careful of owners' and states' authority to regulate bondage. He might feel aversion for slavery, but he feared and disliked abolitionists, who threatened not only his personal finances but his vision of social order, with the prospect of immediate freedom for black men and women, without compensation for their owners. He became a leader in the colonization movement, arguing for the emigration of free blacks to Africa, in part because he simply could not imagine a substantial population of free people of color as part of his vision for modern America.[99]

By the time Clay led the Whig Party he was no three year old but a seasoned runner. In the American Colonization Society, he had worked with men with a wide variety of motives, including his fellow turfman John Randolph, who pushed for the colonization of free people of color because he believed them an imminent threat to slavery.[100] Early in his career, Clay had seen just how entrenched slavery was in the South, how impassioned its defenders were, and he came to accept human bondage as a regrettable inevitability, especially for a man aspiring to wield national political power.[101] He could not imagine his life, his career, or his country without it. Slavery thus never came between Clay's Deep Southern disciples, who assumed the absolute necessity of human bondage, and their leader.[102] They shared with him the conviction that slavery must be part of any viable plan for the nation's future. When Clay congratulated himself on his care for his most highly skilled slaves and boasted of the value of their labor, his allies saw their own faith in their slave horsemen and the fitness of bondage as a basis for a flourishing modern state.[103]

Many Southern Whigs feared, however, that their counterparts in the North would refuse to understand that bondage could and should hold such a place in the United States. To reassure themselves of party solidarity, they turned to common agricultural and sporting allegiances, the shorthand used among themselves to indicate shared personal and political convictions. They judged their political compatibility with Northern Whigs on the basis of commitments to farms and stables. The sporting papers featured admiring coverage of a speech Pennsylvania's Nicholas Biddle gave to the Agricultural Society of Philadelphia on American efforts to bring domestic Thoroughbreds up to the standards of imported English animals.[104] Biddle and his brother-in-law J. C. Craig were established Thoroughbred breeders. Charles Stewart had brought Medley to them in 1832.[105] One correspondent did call Biddle's credentials into question when he reported that Biddle had turned down the writer's offer for two royally bred foals. Biddle admitted that he had the "hobby-horse notion" that he would keep them around his farm because he liked the way they made the place look. The disappointed purchaser was bitterly indignant—why waste horses like that when they could go into training to be successful runners? But Biddle knew how the farm of a Whig gentleman should appear in order to properly display his convictions, and he was determined to keep the young horses to make the picture complete.[106] The sporting papers were also generous in their assessment of Daniel Webster, who was constantly complimented on his devotion to farming, the prosperity of his acres, the beauty of his imported sheep, and his passion for fishing[107] If Southern Whigs were wary of Webster as a Northerner, such stories soothed their fears. A Yankee he surely was, but his farm revealed him as one of them, committed to their favorite symbols of their ideals of political and economic authority's proper workings.

But Southerners continued to fear that common allegiance to a political vision grounded in agricultural, industrial, and sporting enterprises did not necessarily encompass deference to slavery. And they adamantly insisted that human bondage was the heart of a well-regulated United States. In 1832, Alexander Porter received a Massachusetts abolitionist newspaper from an indignant friend, examined it, and then burned it so it would not come to the eyes of his slaves. In allowing such sentiments to be published, he snarled to fellow Clay supporter Josiah Johnston, Northerners knowingly participated in inciting slave uprisings against fellow white Americans. If abolitionists hoped to free the slaves with their polemics, they were fools: "Is there no real, and enlightened friend of Philanthropy that will instruct these people that they are defeating their own object. They will only compel us to draw the cord tighter." To a committed slaveholder the connection between abolitionist efforts and servile insurrection was inescapable, and it could be met with only one response.[108] Slaveholders, if they were to preserve bondage, must use force to protect their authority. Porter evinced no particular pleasure in the thought of violence, nor did he expend any time in deploring it. It was an inevitability. Slaves who were the victims of violence were certainly not injured people. They were cogs in a large and necessary economic and political system, and the system must run smoothly.

Abolitionists, Porter told Johnston impatiently, wished to catechize men like him about the workings of bondage, when he and other slave owners knew its subtleties intimately: "Do they suppose we are ignorant of the lesson that all history teaches, that it is easier to retain men in abject and complete servitude, no matter how cruel it is, than to hold them slaves and extend to them a portion of the indulgencies of free men. If they do, they are mistaken, we are well aware of it. But we have weighed the risk, and are willing to run it, if they will let us alone."[109]

As the man who purchased Charles Stewart, Porter lived with the risk he bluntly pointed out. But men like Porter, as he said, were willing to run that risk because their ideas demanded it. Their vision of powerful, established Whig gentlemen running the nation like a complex of connected farms and factories depended on the labor of highly skilled slaves, like the slave horsemen who proved human bondage a precision instrument, fit to tackle modern economic realities. But Southern Whigs also ran the risk because they lived in the world of Charles Stewart as well as the world of Henry Clay and knew it was safer to do so than it might appear. Stewart had experienced a virtually unparalleled number of the "indulgencies of free men," but doing so had cut him off from his family, from any hope of passing on those privileges and thus attenuating slavery's power. Southern Whig turfmen believed they had created a slavery that could encompass and benefit from the skills of a man like Stewart—no wonder they confidently expected to rule the future.

3

A Storm Is Approaching

HARRY LEWIS had been sizing up horses for a long time. Edward Troye had immortalized Lewis's brusque professionalism in his portrait of the horseman at the head of the Thoroughbred Richard Singleton. By 1846, when the *Spirit of the Times* listed the runners stabled at the Lexington track, "old Harry" was one of the few trainers who merited mention.[1] Lewis had a discerning eye for young talent, and he liked the looks of Elisha Warfield's bay colt, a son of Boston delivered by the racing mare Alice Carneal in 1850.[2]

Warfield was over seventy, and his wife and his doctor thought it might be time for him to slow down. He had been a charter member of the Kentucky Association for the Improvement of the Breeds of Stock and had helped to select the site of Lexington's racetrack in the 1820s. He had in his library the first complete edition of the English Stud Book west of the Alleghenies and extensive back files of the *American Turf Register* and the *Spirit of the Times*.[3] Warfield, like Lewis, knew a promising runner when he saw one and hoped that Alice Carneal's colt, whom he named Darley, would be special. But, as the horse entered his three-year-old year, Warfield heeded the pleas of his family and friends and relinquished primary responsibility for the animal's training and racing.

Edward Troye's portrait of the Thoroughbred Richard Singleton with his
trainer Harry Lewis. Lewis would go on to be the first trainer of Lexington,
the most famous racehorse in nineteenth-century America. Virginia Museum
of Fine Arts, Richmond. Paul Mellon Collection. *Photo by Katherine Wetzel.*

Though Darley would run in Warfield's colors and under his official ownership, Warfield leased the horse's "racing qualities" to
Harry Lewis, who may have been a free man by 1853.[4] The two
men split the cost of entering Darley in his first race at Lexington
and arranged to share the prize money. The horse romped home,
catching the eye of the visiting Richard Ten Broeck, the impresario
of the Metairie Course in New Orleans, who had conceived the idea
of what he called the Great Post Stakes for his track. Each state
would enter a horse, and, with a $5,000 entrance fee, the field would
run for the richest purse ever offered in America. Ten Broeck, head-
ing a syndicate of Kentucky turfmen, offered to purchase Darley
from Warfield, intending to enter the colt as Kentucky's contestant
in the Great Post Stakes. The horse would be renamed Lexington
for the occasion in a gesture of Bluegrass pride.

Warfield only sold "all his interest" in the colt, but the technicality did not matter. The new consortium of owners did not intend to honor any standing arrangement with Harry Lewis. One owner's personal copy of the 1853 bylaws of the Lexington racetrack shows only one annotation—a check mark next to the rule that forbid a "negro or mulatto . . . to make a nomination in any stake, to be run over this course." The new owners armored themselves in regulations to ensure that Lewis was in no position to argue that he had any true right to dictate the horse's sale. In the end, Lewis was able to lay claim to the prize money the horse had won while in his charge, but he had to watch the greatest runner of his career leave his barn.[5]

The Great Post Stakes was scheduled to be run at New Orleans in the spring of 1854. Though invited to do so, New York, Virginia, and the Carolinas failed to offer entries to contest state supremacy on the track. The race clearly represented the new alignment of power in American racing after 1840, in which the Bluegrass and the Deep South held sway. Lexington would run for Kentucky and the four-year-old star Highlander for Alabama. Duncan Kenner's Arrow was the official entrant for Louisiana, but Rapides Parish planter Thomas Jefferson Wells so wanted his undefeated Lecomte to run that he arranged for him to represent Mississippi.

Visitors poured into the hotels of New Orleans. Young Eliza Ripley remembered sharing rooms in the servants' quarters at the very top of the St. Charles Hotel with Kentucky visitors like future Confederate general John Hunt Morgan and his wife.[6] Twenty thousand people packed themselves into the Metairie Course on the April afternoon of the race. The business district of New Orleans fell almost completely silent, for "everybody who was anybody, or wanted to be deemed anybody, had gone to the race."[7]

Lexington fairly easily won the first heat, slogging over a heavy track in a little over eight minutes. The Kentucky contingent roared their approval. But, in the second heat, Lecomte, another son of Boston, snatched the lead and held it until the last mile, when Lexington came charging up to challenge him. The two horses came into the homestretch neck and neck, amid the shrieks of the crowd and the thudding and slapping of the mud under their powerful strides. Lexington doggedly pushed forward and won by four lengths, taking the second heat and victory in the Great Post Stakes with a time of eight minutes and four seconds. One genteel Kentucky lady stood up on her seat and screamed with joy, Eliza Ripley remembered, "and never did I hear the full compass of the female voice before, nor since."[8]

Kentuckians exulted, but Lecomte's backers wanted another chance at Lexington. If the two horses met again, they were convinced, the Deep Southern horse would prove his superiority. Lexington's owners scoffed at the animal whose name Kentuckians drawled "Lee Count" with derisive ostentation.[9] The syndicate ordered Lexington to be put out to pasture for a well-deserved rest. But the call of cash sounded sweet to Richard Ten Broeck, who, as a shareholder in the Metairie Course, stood to gain a hefty sum in gate receipts from a rematch. Ten Broeck immediately bought out his partners and had Lexington reshod in racing plates and put back to work.[10]

Lexington had suffered a significant interruption in training, and it was not a good time to be at a disadvantage. Lecomte had inherited from Boston the same speed and power that Lexington had. And while Lexington's mother had been a perfectly good racehorse, Lecomte's dam had been legendary. A gray daughter of Glencoe bred by James Jackson of Alabama, Reel had been sold to Louisiana planter Thomas Jefferson Wells as a yearling. At three and then at four, she raced to seven consecutive victories, many of them against older horses. She so dominated the competition that Wells dreamed of a match race with Boston himself, but instead he retired her to the broodmare ranks and bred her to the Virginia champion, producing Lecomte, named for an old friend of the Wells family.[11] The colt blossomed into an outstandingly tough horse, with a blazing first burst of speed.[12]

Thomas Jefferson Wells did his best to avenge Lecomte's loss to Lexington by drawing on the expertise of his old friend William J. Minor and hiring the best men available for his stables. Like South Carolina racing grandee Richard Singleton before him, he turned to the Merritt family in Virginia and hired the great enslaved trainer Hark. In the days when the southern Atlantic coast had dominated the racing scene, Hark had moved between the Carolinas and Virginia; now, as an older man, he smoothly adapted to the sport's new geographical orientation. Hark, like Charles Stewart, came as a well-known, high-priced expert into the cotton and sugar country of the Deep South, which claimed black lives and families with a voracious appetite.[13] Hark thought a change of rider might be all the help Lecomte needed to win a rematch. The Louisiana sugar planter and turfman Duncan Kenner had recently purchased from Adam Bingaman a jockey named Abe, who had earned a reputation for fierce, even reckless, competitiveness on the tracks at New Orleans and Natchez.[14] With Abe aboard, Hark assured Thomas J. Wells, Lecomte could not lose.[15] Wells negotiated with Kenner to put the jockey aboard his horse, despite the fact that Abe weighed in at eighty-nine pounds, three pounds over what the handicappers obliged the horse to carry. Abe's skill and daring, Wells figured, were worth more than three pounds.[16]

Ten thousand people crowded into the Metairie Course to see the rematch. In the first heat, Abe took advantage of the dry track and Lecomte's blistering speed, got the horse to the front, and kept him there, despite Lexington's brave efforts to catch him. When Lecomte swept to victory by six lengths, the crowd yelled, and the clockers gaped at their watches. When the official time for the four miles was announced, the crowd roared louder. Lecomte had set a world record, going the distance in seven minutes and twenty-six seconds. In the second heat, Abe let Lexington keep the lead for the first two miles, bringing Lecomte up to challenge a few times to test how much speed his opponent could muster. When he was satisfied that he had the stronger horse, he pushed Lecomte into the lead at the beginning of the third mile and kept him just out of Lexington's reach for the rest of the race. When he brought Lecomte to the finish, he was riding with one hand and waving to the delirious crowd with the other. The time for the second heat was only a few seconds off the record Lecomte had already set that afternoon.[17]

Ten Broeck quickly challenged Lecomte to another match, designed to establish ultimate supremacy for the victor of two out of three. Each side would put up $10,000 to sweeten the pot for the champion. At first Wells refused.[18] But, in 1855, Ten Broeck discovered how to draw Wells out once and for all. Lexington needed no opponent. He would run against the clock. Ten Broeck brought in the famous white jockey Gilbert Patrick, nationally known by the nickname Gilpatrick, for the occasion.[19] The pair took the track in New Orleans that April and smashed Lecomte's record for four miles by more than six seconds. The *Spirit of the Times* reported gleefully that the news had been posted on the message board of the Astor House in New York as soon as it had come off the telegraph wire. Now the Louisianans must agree to a rematch.[20] Two weeks later, the rivals met again. "Lexington and Lecomte were the great lions of the day," reported the sporting press, and news of them merited "the same interest and avidity" as "the probable fate of a nation."[21] Thomas J. Wells's friends from the Red River district of Louisiana had descended on the city en masse. To his sister it seemed half of Rapides Parish was going to New Orleans for the occasion.[22] They rolled into town eager to lay their money down on Lecomte, "not only because they considered him the best horse in the world, but because he was Jeff. Wells's horse."[23] Abe would be back aboard, and Wells had also secured Anthony Hall, William J. Minor's African American assistant trainer, to help Hark for the occasion.[24]

In the days before the race, however, the men closest to the horse guarded a grim secret. Lecomte was sluggish and only picked at his food. In the end, Wells decided to start him anyway, relying on rumors that Lexington was also not at his best. But two miles into the first heat, Lecomte was clearly laboring, and Abe eased him, finishing well behind Lexington. When the horse did not recover in the rest period between heats, Wells received permission to withdraw him from the contest. In the first heat, Lexington had once again broken Lecomte's record for four miles. Lexington's backers pointed to the time as clear evidence of his superiority. Lecomte's supporters insisted that their horse had been drugged in a clear case of sabotage.[25]

Shortly after his victory, Lexington's sight began to fail, the result of an infection that ultimately made him completely blind.[26] Despite his condition, Thoroughbred breeder Robert Alexander paid $15,000 for him, at the time a stratospheric price, in the hope that he would pass his speed and stamina on in the breeding shed.[27] Alexander was widely regarded as uncannily prescient in such matters, but even he could not have predicted what was to come. Starting in 1861, Lexington would lead the American sire rankings every year until he died in 1875, as his sons and daughters won more money than those of any other stallion. His skeleton was then shipped to the Smithsonian for preservation as a national treasure.[28] His offspring made him America's leading sire twice more after his death. In 1905, the racing historian Charles Trevathan tried to convey that Lexington had been more than a horse. He had been an American icon: "There came a day when any little child . . . could have told you the story of Lexington. . . . Lexington belonged not alone to the turfmen. He was the heritage of the nation. He was Lexington in the minds of the people, and after him there were merely other horses."[29]

The popularity of the Lexington-Lecomte rivalry and Lexington's subsequent success as a sire reassured Southern turfmen that their vision of a powerful modern nation founded on slavery was secure. To them, because they weighted Thoroughbreds and black horsemen with their dreams of a future of perfect bondage and cutting-edge progress, an America that venerated Lexington must be a nation that recognized the viability of their conception of the United States as a slaveholders' republic. But as the 1850s wore on, as they embraced the popularity of racing and sought to use it to advance their ideas, the sport's increasing size and scope confronted them with realities that threatened their idealized vision. Both from within and without came suggestions that the racetrack could encompass a multitude of personal and political goals and that Southern turfmen could not reliably control its meanings and limit them to serve their own conception of the seamless alliance between slavery and progress. Indeed, they would soon be forced to watch as the future of slavery and the future of the United States diverged dramatically. But at the time of Lexington and Lecomte, they still pointed to their own fame and that of their stables as a sure sign of guaranteed stability and future success. Indeed, no one seems to have been anything but pleased when the match races helped produce a celebrity whose name appeared repeatedly in print.

ABE'S NAME LURKED in the reams of paper necessary to keep the bondage of Duncan Kenner's more than five hundred slaves functioning with maximum efficiency.[30] In Kenner's slave rosters, name followed name in alphabetical order on one side of the page, with columns on the other side carefully marked to record each hand's job in the field and rations allocated. Crouching at the bottom of the A's was the single word Abe, with no identifying notations of any kind. He needed none. He was probably too small to make a good field worker. He was diminutive enough to wear a coat cut to fit a child, as other paperwork recorded.[31] But some time in the year before the Great Post Stakes, Duncan Kenner had paid Adam Bingaman more than $2,300 for him. In 1853, the *Spirit of the Times* had trumpeted gleefully that the prices of all good bloodstock had gone up because of the great race and published a small list of horses and the sums they had brought. At the bottom of the list came "the Jockey Abe" and the amount given for him.[32] Abe lived in a delicate balance, as he was simultaneously an item of property and a high-priced professional, a piece of livestock and a man who needed no introduction but his name.[33]

Abe quickly became the most famous horseman of his generation, a beneficiary of a new technology congressional Whigs had staunchly supported.[34] By the time of Lexington and Lecomte, the telegraph brought racing news to the farthest corners of the country faster than ever before. A sporting magazine described a race meeting and told its readers that the coverage would skip directly to the details, since the "lightning has, doubtless, informed you" already of the order of finish.[35] Merely reporting the news, now that the telegraph made torrents of information instantly available, was no longer enough. Readers craved heroes. And Abe became one. He was a telegraph celebrity.

William J. Minor himself helped to establish Abe as a nationally notable figure, lauding his "great coolness and judgment" in pulling off a come-from-behind victory in 1853.[36] Sporting journals that had seldom if ever mentioned a black man's name and newspapers hungry for expanded racing coverage followed his career. Abe brought out the best even in recalcitrant horses, like the notoriously bad-tempered Whale. Before a race, Abe moved him away from the other entries, and the two stood quietly together on the track, though the horse would bolt if anyone but Abe tried to touch him.

At the start, horse and rider would surge forward, on their way to another victory.[37]

For the first time in American racing, bettors acknowledged that they put their money down out of faith in the prowess of the jockey, rather than in the particular talent of the horse, and newspapers across America reported it. The *Picayune* in New Orleans mourned for his opponents that "everybody can't have Abe," and the *Tribune* in New York informed its readers that Panic, the long shot from the Kenner stable, had taken a significant jump in the betting because of "the prestige of Abe."[38] For decades, racing summaries had listed only the horse and his owner; now, when Abe rode, the paper listed his name next to that of his mount. Usually he was the only jockey, white or black, mentioned by name in a story, whether he rode the winner or not.[39] His only close rival was Lexington's jockey, Gilpatrick. Abe was a slave and Gilpatrick a respected white professional, but on the track and in the columns of the racing press they battled as equals.[40] Abe was nothing less than a national figure. In the autumn of 1855, the *Spirit of the Times* called him "the famous Abe," and in the spring of 1856 they promoted him to "the world-renowned Abe." When he pushed a horse for home, the crowd screamed his name instead of his mount's.[41]

The cognoscenti of the courthouse steps in Richmond had known Charles Stewart. Men who bought a newspaper as far away as New York knew who Abe was. But Southern turfmen remained undisturbed about his fame. The prominence of one of their slaves seemed to reaffirm the power of both their horses and their political convictions and potentially bolstered the chances for national support of their vision of hierarchical order and harmonious bondage. They did not consider the lessons a man like Abe had learned in slavery that had nothing to do with their personal and ideological preoccupations.

Like other horsemen of his generation who came of age professionally in the 1850s, Abe worked with older men who intimately understood the world of racing, their role in its thrall over white turfmen, and the complexities and dangers of their position. Charles Stewart might no longer make the annual pilgrimage to the races, but Abe worked in close company with Hark, whose career had moved along the expanding boundaries of the world of the Thoroughbred. The Bluegrass stable boys with Lexington probably retold stories of Kentucky's great enslaved horsemen, like Harry Lewis, who was said to have gone to see his owner on his deathbed only to have the man pull a knife on him, so that Lewis could accompany him into the afterlife, "as he expected to train and run his horses in the next world," just as he had in this one.[42] When black men reached the professional heights Abe and a few others had attained, white men's dependency on them gave them the privileges that had shaped their lives. But those privileges and the constraints they entailed could be deeply hurtful to families like Charles Stewart's or potentially lethal, as Harry Lewis's rumored escape starkly demonstrated. Freighted with white men's requirements and expectations, understanding the benefits of their position and the pain and danger of their isolation, horsemen taught each other by example that each man had to calculate his own interests and painstakingly assess the subtle differences of status that might influence his situation. These lessons benefited turfmen in often separating black horsemen and their autonomous success from their fellow slaves, minimizing the threat such a specialized corps of bondsmen posed to slavery as an institution. But turfmen were disconcerted when Abe, Hark, and Lecomte confronted them with the complex realities of black horsemen's enclosed world.

When Thomas J. Wells decided that someone had drugged Lecomte in his last race against Lexington, his suspicions fixed first on Abe. Duncan Kenner, Abe's owner, and Graves, the white man who trained for Kenner, indignantly denied the charge and defended Abe. Hark, Lecomte's trainer, could easily have slipped the horse something, they pointed out. A furious three-cornered correspondence ensued among Wells, Kenner, and William J. Minor, always eager to dispense information and offer opinions. All three men lived comfortably surrounded by black horsemen, usually serenely confident that such men would never betray them. They had the pictures to prove it, in which men like Charles Stewart and Harry Lewis appeared as invaluable figures in a bustling, orderly world, washed with the lambent light of Edward Troye's canvases.[43] But incidents like Lecomte's drugging revealed that the light sometimes did not penetrate into the depths of the racing world they loved so much. In the shadows of a stall, things could happen that no white man saw or knew about. Men whom they were pridefully convinced posed them no risk could act according to imperatives turfmen only dimly suspected.

Wells started his investigations based on the testimony of one of his grooms. He reported that Hark had been overheard bemoaning Abe's treachery: "I can't help thinking about that boy . . . the trick he has played me, after the confidence I put in him, and the way I trusted him."[44] Meanwhile, Minor turned to Russ, "a fine boy," who was supposed to be a friend of Abe's and would presumably know if the jockey had drugged his mount. But the information broker par excellence in this instance was a man named Sam, probably Sam Page. Page appears in the slave lists at Ashland; he was a horseman in Duncan Kenner's stables. He traveled to New Orleans with the racing string and to Thomas J. Wells's place on Red River with mares to be bred. And he had a tale to tell. He poured it out to Graves, who immediately, as Sam must have known he would, passed it on to Kenner and William J. Minor. Sam claimed that Hark had hidden eighteen runaway slaves and pretended to be a magician who could protect them and drive away the slave catchers. For this service, he charged a fee. When he was sure the fugitives had given him everything they could, Hark "betrayed them and had them caught."[45] Sam's implication, conveyed through Graves, was clear: How could such a man be trusted?

Sam Page's story may have been true. Hark had carved out a life for himself that depended on keeping an eye on the main chance. His background as a horseman was not one that necessarily valorized solidarity over solitary gain.[46] But Sam Page was a horseman, too; he had learned how to talk to white men, how to position himself to appear worthy of their trust. He may have concocted the story; he certainly must have carefully calibrated the way he told it. Sam knew that revealing such secrets of the slave community—its hopes of freedom and its cruel betrayals—would bolster his status as an informer. Both he and Hark came out of the tale as men loyal to white interests, Hark because he had ultimately turned in the runaways and Sam because he was willing to tell the story. But Sam must have known that Hark's trickery, the degree of finely honed talent for playing both sides that the story revealed, would have worried a white man. If Sam's goal were to cast suspicion on Hark, he could not have selected his weapon with more precision. For he showed Hark to the planters as a man who could play the role of the faithful servant in an Edward Troye painting but who could also retreat into the quarters and look after his own interests.[47]

But Sam was not the only informant. One of Minor's sources claimed to have looked over Abe's shoulder on the boat home from New Orleans and seen that the jockey had a $100 bill. Others reported that Abe had been wary of letting anyone near his suitcase. The only man he trusted to keep an eye on it for him was Sam Page. If Sam were Abe's friend or even accomplice, he had a compelling reason to seek to throw suspicion on someone else. But the other grooms, who were treated as reliable sources, may also have had angles to play and grudges to pay out. We cannot know who, if anyone, in these contradictory testimonies was telling the truth. But we can see the remnants of the subtle, dangerous games that horsemen from grooms to trainers had learned to play.[48] They were too convoluted for the white men involved, who finally let the matter drop.

Minor, Kenner, and Wells could not hope to get to the bottom of the incident, nor could they punish the men involved in typical ways, because they were too valuable and well known to be treated as disposable. They were not accustomed, in any case, to disciplining prominent slave horsemen with anything but the subtlest pressures of privilege extended or withheld, with the weight of expectations made clear. That was what made these men their imagined perfect slaves. But the drugging incident amply demonstrated that there were things they would never know, places in which only black men worked, arithmetics of self-interest they could never add up. Perfect slaves were a chimera, and so was their dream of a harmonious slaveholders' republic. But they preferred to ignore the evidence that stared them in the face. Instead, they would display their vision to a wider world.

AMERICAN AUDIENCES might remember Lecomte's inglorious defeat. But Richard Ten Broeck still bought the horse and took him to

England to test him against British runners. He retained Gilpatrick and ultimately gained the services of Lexington's trainer, John Benjamin Pryor, who departed with the exhortations of the press ringing in his ears: "Go, Ben, and defeat them on their own soil, for the honor of our country!"[49] British turfmen admired Lecomte's size and the collected power of his gallop.[50] But the horse had little time to soothe the sting of his New Orleans loss. He died of colic soon after his arrival in England. (William J. Minor, despite his loathing for Ten Broeck, had advised Thomas J. Wells to sell, because horses were too fragile an investment to hold on to in the face of a good offer. He may well have felt a certain grim satisfaction at the news of the death.[51]) But Lecomte was not alone. A number of American turfmen aspired to take British racing by storm in the 1850s. Lecomte's half-sister Prioress, a daughter of Reel, actually managed a victory in the prestigious Cesarewitch Handicap at Newmarket, winning by a length and a half a hard-fought deciding heat after a three-way tie.[52] John Davis, trying to describe the noise of the occasion, could only say that the shouting from the small group of Americans present was "such as one hears on the Fourth of July at home."[53] But Americans had very little to shout about in their venture into British racing. They staunchly refused to admit defeat, but that refusal rang hollow as it stretched on into years of mediocrity.

What was at stake was not merely the pride of men enamored of American horses and eager to prove their mettle against the internationally preeminent British standard. The prestige of the United States itself and its potential as a global power seemed tied to these contests. The McCormick reaper, its powers demonstrated at London's Great Exhibition of 1851, had proven to skeptical European observers the vast potential of American technology and American crop acreage. Horace Greeley, who had seen the reaper tested before an audience, had reported of the skeptical men around him, "There was a moment . . . of suspense; then human prejudice could hold out no longer; and burst after burst of involuntary cheers from the whole crowd proclaimed the triumph of the Yankee Reaper."[54] Southern Whig turfmen, accustomed to seeing their horses as standard bearers for their convictions of American progress and social order, believed the next logical step would be similarly spontaneous cheers for American Thoroughbreds. They had already demonstrated this conviction with an attempt to expand American racing to Cuba, in the hope that Havana's "wealthy men of commerce" might fall in with their ideas. A few judicious words on the back turn, they believed, could strengthen the weave of the web of slave-powered Atlantic capitalism.[55] Great Britain, prime market for Southern cotton, must not only be impressed with the productivity of American agriculture and technology but be reminded of the vigor and flexibility of human bondage, its capacity to guarantee the vitality of a great trading partner. William J. Minor, as usual, articulated his contemporaries' feelings, their unquestioning faith in the ties between their horses and their dreams of international respect. "To make the English our fast friends for a century to come," he declared, "we must go over and win the Goodwood Cup with an American-bred horse; and then beat all England, heats of four miles, weight for age."[56] Only then would the English respect American power and American interests. But like the Lexington-Lecomte contests, this attempt to display the power of Southern turfmen and their plans for the future confronted men like Minor with realities of bondage that imperiled their serene assumptions.

With slavery acknowledged as a necessary and inevitable part of Southern racing and of the beliefs of its adherents, truly exporting American racing would have meant bringing slaves to England. But, though Gilpatrick made the trip, his rival Abe did not. American turf writers loftily assured their readers that, in the face of British skepticism about "Yankees at Goodwood, with their nigger jockies," the American owners had committed to a lily-white riding corps for the proposed campaign.[57] The whole purpose of bringing American horses to compete on English tracks was to demonstrate that American racing was no longer a provincial imitation of the original. Americans looked to the British to acknowledge them as worthy rivals, which meant bowing to British practices and prejudices. If the British used only white jockeys, Americans must do so as well or reveal themselves as colonial second-raters. Racing men kept silent about the other and more pressing reason for eliminating black expertise from their stables for the duration. They feared bringing slaves to Britain, where slavery had already been abolished.[58]

The status of one black man who came with the American stables signaled the awkwardness of turfmen's situation. Only in his twenties, the free man of color William Bird had already worked some of the best horses in the Thoroughbred country of Tennessee. Richard Ten Broeck employed a succession of head trainers, many of them selected more for their ostensible suitability as national representatives than for their talent with a horse. Bird labored on in an assistant's position and tried to make up for his bosses' shortcomings, though he and an interviewer later agreed "that steadiness and sobriety are very good things, but a man might be as steady as the Rocky Mountains and as sober as a bishop when he is asleep, and still lack the capacity to train horses." Bird's skill only served to throw light on American turfmen's difficulty. They desperately needed black men's expert labor, but they could not risk bringing slaves with them.[59]

Even men who chose not to be concerned about the problem William Bird exemplified might have looked askance at Robert Harlan, the owner of one of the racing strings brought to Britain.[60] Harlan bore an impeccable turfman's pedigree as a close relative—either a brother or a son—of James Harlan of Kentucky.[61] The elder Harlan was a Henry Clay man to the bone and, as his son John Marshall Harlan remembered, "gloried in being a Whig." In 1848, when the national Whig convention determined that the expedient choice for a presidential candidate was Mexican War hero Zachary Taylor, Harlan refused to cast his ballot for any man but the master of Ashland, "preferring to go down to defeat with the Clay flag still flying."[62] Robert Harlan had been born to Whig aristocracy, and he displayed the acumen on which Clay Whigs prided themselves. Educated with John Marshall Harlan and his brothers, he later went into business and succeeded handily. Moving to Cincinnati, he became an investor in real estate. He and John Marshall Harlan, later a United States Supreme Court justice, remained political allies all their lives.

But Robert Harlan's mother had been a slave woman, and he had purchased his own freedom from the Harlan family.[63] The sporting press, embracing Harlan as a representative of America overseas, dealt with a dilemma: here was a man who was a Harlan, but he was not white. The *Spirit of the Times* noted that Harlan was "a colored man in good circumstances, an excellent judge of horses, and a first rate trainer" but made no mention of the Harlans of Kentucky.[64] *Porter's Spirit of the Times* identified him with the family but said of his background only that "[h]e is regarded in the West and South as certainly the equal, to say no more, of Mr. Ten Broeck, as a Turfman, though there exists a somewhat extensive prejudice against him."[65] Readers who understood why there might be prejudice against Harlan would not be made to read the facts in print. Others could remain in happy ignorance. Harlan literally embodied the complexities that bondage entailed. He represented the dangerous possibility that, even sustained by a judicious mix of violence and incentive, the extension of privilege and the assumption of shared interest and subordinated will, racial slavery was not an institution of seamless and stratified perfection. The hierarchies and connections that slaveholding turfmen relied on to function under their supervision could founder not only on the possibility of escape but on the spectacle of a free and authoritative black man in the midst of their cherished world.

IN SEEKING TO ESTABLISH their political convictions as the guiding precepts of a powerful United States, turfmen opened their world to the voices of outsiders, men who called attention to just how tenuous their beloved myths of themselves and their world were. In reaching for new heights of national and international success, turfmen had ensured that sporting magazines would be a more lucrative investment than ever before. Racing journalism, pioneered by John S. Skinner and William T. Porter, attracted in the 1850s the attention of George Wilkes, who had an acute eye for a moneymaking proposition. He took over the *Spirit of the Times*, renaming it *Porter's Spirit of the Times* to pacify his subscribers, and three years later triumphantly proclaimed himself on the masthead of *Wilkes's Spirit of the Times*.[66] Wilkes was an entirely new kind of turf journalist.

The New York–born son of a cabinetmaker and an immigrant mother, Wilkes grew up among men who divided their lives among the polling place, the saloon, and the jail. His first arrest—for vandalism to a brothel—came in 1836, when he was still a teenager. In his early twenties, he began writing for papers like the *Sunday Flash* and *New York As It Is*, short-lived, racy sheets that thrived on frank discussions of sex and violence and ringing endorsements of workingmen's political views.[67] His writing ultimately bought Wilkes an indictment for libel and a short stretch in Manhattan's downtown jail, popularly known as The Tombs.

Almost immediately after Wilkes left prison, he came out with the luridly titled pamphlet, *The Mysteries of the Tombs*. In it, he chronicled his time in jail and provided pen portraits of various con artists and murderers he had met while incarcerated.[68] The pamphlet sold at a brisk pace, and Wilkes took his newfound success to the editorial desk of the *National Police Gazette*. The *Gazette* claimed to assist the police and the courts by detailing the appearance and behavior of criminals and the locations of their hangouts and hideouts. But it was transparently intended for voyeuristic readers, who ravenously consumed the details of the most sensational crimes and relished "Lives of the Felons" and other Wilkes features. Wilkes did his job very capably, in part because he was covering his own neighborhoods. In the late 1840s, he was reportedly still living with a notorious madam named Kate Ridgely.[69] But in the 1850s, he ventured into the sporting press, setting his foot on the first rung of the ladder to respectability.

Wilkes came from a new publishing world mapped by James Gordon Bennett of the *New York Herald*, who titillated his readers ceaselessly with sex scandals, mutilated corpses, and other staples of what would become tabloid journalism.[70] Walt Whitman magnificently dubbed Bennett "[a] reptile marking his path with slime wherever he goes . . . a midnight ghoul, preying on rottenness and repulsive filth; a creature, hated by his nearest intimates, and bearing the consciousness thereof upon his distorted features, and upon his despicable soul; one whom . . . all despise, and whom no one blesses—*all this* is James Gordon Bennett."[71] Wilkes did not like Bennett either—indeed, he once complained that one of the costs of living in a free democracy was that no public-spirited citizen had murdered the editor of the *Herald*.[72] But Wilkes's loathing was born of the jealousy of an aspiring rival.

Wilkes's *Spirit* ventured into new territory for a national sporting magazine. One of his first major stories was the match he had helped set up between England's boxing champion, Tom Sayers, and a Troy, New York, blacksmith named John C. Heenan, who had learned to box while working at California's Benicia navy yard. The old *Spirit* considered boxing déclassé. Wilkes chronicled every drop of blood and sweat spattered in the twenty-seven times Heenan knocked Sayers down in their world championship match in London.[73] With his gaudy sentences and sharp eye for the arresting and sordid, Wilkes was a strange new arrival in the literary imaginations and compilations of Southern sportsmen. But he was not just unsettling because men like him seemed to have no place in the serene and hierarchical structure of slaveholding turfmen's Whiggish visions of modernity. His political connections were deeply personal and openly dangerous.

In his youth, Wilkes had befriended David Broderick, the Washington-born son of a stonecutter who had moved to New York. The two young men had been comrades from the time they discovered a mutual affection for liquor and stylish prose. Broderick had begun as a volunteer-fire-company leader and Washington Square saloon owner, both occupations that led a man naturally to a career in politics in 1840s Manhattan.[74] In the 1850s, he headed to California and the gold rush. There he joyfully discovered electoral fields ripe for harvesting by a man educated in the hard school of New York municipal politics. He cabled to Wilkes, who arrived in 1852 to act as campaign speechwriter, vote securer, and fount of cynical wisdom.[75] In 1856, Broderick, champion of small farmers and laboring men, was elected as a staunchly antislavery Democrat to the United States Senate.[76]

Broderick differed sharply from some of his Senate colleagues, including turfman James Henry Hammond, who had used the racetrack so efficiently to bolster his social position. Long a committed slavery advocate and recently elected to the Senate, Hammond was determined to draw the line between gentlemen and those God had intended to serve. Laborers, Hammond cried in his 1858 speech in support of the admission of Kansas as a slave state, were the "mudsill" of the world, best used for wiping one's boots on. Slavery was not a distasteful reality, to be tolerated in the interests of national unity; it was the only logical response to the indisputable reality that all men had not been created equal.[77] Rising to respond, the new senator from California elaborately assured the chamber that he was certain the gentleman from South Carolina had meant no personal insult: "But, sir, the class of society to whose toil I was born, under our form of government, will control the destinies of this nation. If I were inclined to forget my connection with them, or to deny that I sprung from them, this chamber would not be the place in which I could do either. While I hold a seat here, I have but to look at the beautiful capitals adorning the pilasters that support this roof, to be reminded of my father's talent, and to see his handiwork."[78]

Senators might well be descended from men who had worked in the Capitol; Broderick now threw in their faces that he was the son of a man who had worked *on* it. He made clear that he had been born of and now represented free workers. Slaveholders were his enemies, who would use their sprawling, strangling economic power to deny men like him a chance to succeed. He wanted the fundamental dispute between their interests and his own out in the open. He rejoiced that the repeal of the Missouri Compromise "made the territories a common battle-field in which the conflicting rights of free and slave labor must struggle for supremacy."[79] Broderick's vehemence outraged proslavery politicians, including David S. Terry, the chief justice of the state of California, who killed Broderick in a politically motivated duel in the autumn of 1859.

Wilkes extravagantly eulogized his friend and inherited his $300,000 estate.[80] His legions of enemies took it as an article of faith that he had forged Broderick's will for his own gain.[81] (Technical examination later established that someone had apparently practiced Broderick's signature several times, then settled on the best attempt and copied the provisions of the will on the sheet above the forged name. The writer began to run out of room toward the bottom of the page and cramped his handwriting to fit the remaining space.[82]) But the money poured into Wilkes's periodicals and reminded his readers that the *Spirit* was the editorial property of a man deeply tied to a politics of white workingmen's rights and free

labor in the territories. Alabama Whig Johnson Jones Hooper explained that many Southerners had "been accustomed to regard the
'Old Spirit' as the single remaining link which bound us in kindly
feeling and sympathy to New York—as the sole relic of an era of
cordial association and genuine mutual esteem."[83] George Wilkes
seemed to put paid to that. Wilkes was no publicly avowed abolitionist; that kind of idealism had gotten his old friend Broderick
shot. But subscribers accustomed to only the most circumspect and
bland mentions of politics found Wilkes's blunt and irreverent
reportage disconcerting. He repeatedly joked about the crisis in
Kansas, which slaveholders considered no matter for mirth, but a
struggle that would decide the future of human bondage and of
their world.[84] Wilkes was an unapologetic outsider who had taken
over the loudest editorial voice of the turf world and mocked verities
that many of the *Spirit*'s subscribers took with grave seriousness.
Southern Whig turfmen deeply regretted the absence of the *Spirit*'s
reassuring platitudes in their bookshelves and at their clubs, just as
their party itself foundered on the issue Hammond and Broderick
had debated.

IT WAS THE TERRITORIES that posed the greatest threat to the
Whigs, not just as a like-minded coalition but as a viable political
party. As the 1850s began and unrest over slavery threatened the
progress of westward expansion, Henry Clay and his great Whig
ally Daniel Webster helped to piece together the Compromise of
1850, the group of bills that sought to resolve the slavery question
and keep the country at peace. The Compromise admitted California to the Union as a free state, while New Mexico and Utah would
ultimately decide the status of slavery by popular vote. Law enforcement officials outside of slave states were to be compelled by federal
statute to assist in capturing and returning fugitive slaves to their
owners. And the slave trade was banned in Washington, D.C., in a
sop to antislavery sentiment.[85] The various provisions of the compromise passed with the support of disparate coalitions, assembled
by the emerging Democratic powerbroker Stephen Douglas of Illinois. Neither the legalities nor the practicalities of the legislation
held out inspiring hopes for the enduring power of the Whigs and

their convictions. But the Whigs hailed the Compromise's passage as yet another victory in Henry Clay's storied career, the most recent and telling proof of the Great Compromiser's brilliance and his followers' right to rule.[86] The track at New Orleans welcomed Clay and Webster as guests and stewards of the course, in celebration of their victory.[87]

The following year, Clay wrote to his son, John Morrison Clay, in the midst of a marathon session of Congress, to give advice on which Ashland stock should be sold. The Clays should definitely keep a son of Boston, he insisted, because the value of those stallions had only increased with Boston's death.[88] When Clay himself died the following year, he left John much-valued black horsemen, like his slave Harvey, along with the great broodmares Margaret Wood and Magnolia.[89] He died convinced that the Southern Whig faith in progress and mastery would not be disappointed, that his son's life would be much like his own. But that faith, his followers quickly realized, might be misplaced. In 1851, the *Spirit* published a fictional account of the Natchez races in which a horse named States-Rights defeated the favorite, Union, much to the dismay of the Whiggish crowd.[90]

Clay's death left the Whigs, particularly the Southern Whigs who followed the turf, without a natural leader, but they were determined to hold true to his convictions and their own. "As a Southern man, a Union man, and as an American," William J. Minor knew his own mind, and he was determined that he would allow none of his allegiances to overwhelm the others, an increasingly difficult balancing act in an era of national tension. He still believed that the Whig Party was the only political institution capable of accommodating him and his principles, his faith in slavery and modernity. He stood firm behind Winfield Scott, the 1852 Whig presidential nominee, and defended him from the allegations of other Southerners that Scott had been seduced by the Northern wing of the party to make concessions on slavery.[91] But Scott went down to defeat in 1852, and the party itself imploded, never again fielding a presidential candidate. Montgomery Jockey Club secretary Johnson Jones Hooper pronounced the party's obituary with the cogency he had honed as a humorous correspondent for the *Spirit of the Times*. The

Whigs, he summed up, were "as dead as a mackerel."[92] In 1854, the Kansas-Nebraska Act superseded the provisions of the Missouri Compromise that had designated the 36′ 30″ line as a boundary between slave and free states. The new law opened the question of slavery in the territories to popular vote, delighting many Southerners and enraging many Northerners. Amid terrible bloodshed in the Kansas territory, national politics fractured on decidedly sectional lines and seemed unlikely to recover. The verbal duel between David Broderick and James Henry Hammond was only a faint echo of the desperate, gory battles that tore apart the territories.

The Whigs as an official party might have dissolved, but former Whigs resolutely joined up with the rising Know Nothing Party, previously a one-issue coalition devoted to nativism, to defeat their ancient enemies the Democrats. The choice was a simple one, fervent Virginia Whig and turfman John Minor Botts summed up, between the Know Nothings and the Good-for Nothings.[93] Hooper, convinced that the South must be protected from Northern incursions on its rights, embraced the Know Nothings as *the Only True Southern Party.*[94] Whigs across the South in 1856 looked to the Know Nothings and their candidate, former president Millard Fillmore, to return them to national prominence.[95] Fillmore had attended the Great Post Stakes in the spring of 1854, simultaneously enjoying the track and trawling for support among the Southern Whigs gathered at the Metairie Course, in true Henry Clay fashion. His deference to their ways paid dividends. Southern Whigs mourned Clay deeply, but many of them respected Fillmore for the decisive role they thought he had played as president in securing the Compromise of 1850. They believed him committed to national stability and the maintenance of the Southern right to protect slavery.[96] William J. Minor, reluctant to let old grudges go, might be most eager to grumble to Thomas J. Wells that he could not believe "Alexander was fool enough to pay $15,000 for Lexington." But he was just as stubbornly devoted to Whig principles as he had always been to Lecomte, and he adjured Wells, "You <u>must</u> carry Louisiana for Fillmore."[97]

The optimism of Minor and other racing Whigs was deeply misplaced. Minor might airily recount his allegiances as a Southern slaveholder and an American committed to national unity and claim to see no conflict between them, but other men saw them as diametrically opposed. Men who had committed themselves to a government with strong powers to help bind together public and private interests into a national economic and political community now eyed that government warily. They wondered if its authority could be made to extend to restricting or even eradicating slavery. The Whig Party had boasted a proudly national platform, intended to join together the whole Union in complementary forms of commerce and prosperity. The new coalition, full of disparate political groups from North and South, offered little of that kind of coherence or confidence. Southerners less forcefully committed than Minor were deeply wary of Fillmore, a New Yorker with a perceived history of willingness to compromise on the issue of slavery.[98] In 1856, Fillmore carried only a little more than 20 percent of the popular vote. Such a performance must have driven to doubt and fear even a man like William J. Minor, so obstinately and loudly devoted to his convictions.

The brawny, towering John Minor Botts, an old racetrack friend of William Ransom Johnson and a mainstay of Southern Whig principles, knew exactly where to place the blame.[99] Southern Democrats, he roared, had sought to move beyond the provisions of the Missouri Compromise and the Compromise of 1850 and had grabbed for more than they were entitled to. Most of his family's assets were in slave property, he loudly averred, and perhaps he thought of all those hot days he had spent drinking and watching his black jockey Ben steaming off weight in the manure pile. But in pushing for the Kansas-Nebraska Act, that "misshapen and ill-gotten monster," and other attempts to extend the reach of slavery, misguided Southern politicians had imperiled the balance of the entire nation. Instead of calmly abiding by existing practices, which would have allowed slavery to expand peacefully below the Missouri Compromise line, Southerners, with their insistence on more and more concessions, would drive the two sections apart so that no national politics was possible. He cried out again and again, in language with which Minor would have fully sympathized, that he spoke "as a Southern man and as a national man." But he saw more clearly than Minor did that fewer and fewer people were listening. There were dark times ahead, he predicted: "A storm is approaching, the violence and fury of which threatens to sweep over the face of the country. . . . [T]here will no longer be men of the North and the South, the East and the West, meeting in National Councils, under the style of a National Democracy or a National Whiggery; but it will be a meeting of the Free States against the Slave, and the Slave States against the Free. . . . It needs no ghost from the grave . . . to calculate the duration of the Union when that happens. . . . Its days will have been numbered."[100]

By 1857, Southern Whig turfmen were essentially men without a party. They had no electoral apparatus to promote or enact their vision on a national scale. So, unsurprisingly, some of them turned to another form of political institution—an association for displaying and ordering forms of power and connection, an organization that would reassert the bonds between union and slavery. In 1858, the *Spirit of the Times* called for a national jockey club for just such a purpose. "These individual gatherings of the National Club would bring together thousands of people from every section of the Union, and thus would North and South, East and West, become better acquainted with each other, and consequently forget their sectional feelings, and join in one general annual jubilee at a week's racing," the newspaper imagined.[101] But where was such a national club to hold its race meeting? A strong faction argued for Washington, D.C. Only "when it shall come to pass that the Congress of the United States, like the Parliament of Great Britain, shall *adjourn to go to the races*," would a racetrack be truly national, one correspondent argued, so the course must necessarily be headquartered in the nation's capital. Moreover, horses could easily be shipped to Washington from New Orleans, Louisville, and New York, and no one would have cause to feel that his horse was at a disadvantage because he had come significantly farther than his opponents.[102] And there were other reasons as well, another writer circumspectly suggested. Washington easily ranked as the best choice because "owners from the South can have here such riders and trainers as have handled their horses *at home*, the advantages from which are incalculable. The reason *why* such riders and trainers cannot go further North is foreign to our topic, and therefore not necessary to be spoken of. Still such good and sufficient reasons (lamentably to be said) do exist."[103] The magazine maintained careful discretion, but its meaning was clear. In Washington, slavery, the basis on which Southern racing rested, would be safe.

The jockey club proposal came to nothing precisely because nation and slavery, once seemingly so effortlessly integrated in Southern turfmen's farms and formulations, now seemed impossible to unite. F. M. Hutchinson of Liberty, Missouri, eager to sell his hulking gray racer, purchased space on the first page of *Porter's Spirit*. In screamingly large type, the paper proclaimed him "THE CELEBRATED BLOOD-HORSE BORDER RUFFIAN."[104] Those opposed to slavery in the territories had given that name to proslavery men, who crossed the border into Kansas to attack antislavery settlers with vicious abandon and vote illegally in territorial elections. Hutchinson, like other proslavery Missourians, took the name as a point of pride, a marker of resolute commitment to human bondage. Like generations of racing men before him, Hutchinson named his horse for men he admired and regarded as like himself, heroes he wished to honor on the field of competition. Turfmen began to consider whether, if it came to the choice, they would value slavery or union as paramount. Some had apparently made their choice already.

But many still struggled to remain loyal to both and continued to follow the old customs of racetrack bondage as if to assert the practical power of their visions of slavery in the face of circumstances that seemed poised to destroy them. Dimms, a black groom belonging to Robert Alexander, met the boat containing the imported British stallion Scythian in New York in the autumn of 1856. Dimms presented himself to Alexander's agents and examined the horse on a Saturday. He then consulted with the white groom who had made the trip with Scythian and announced that the horse could not possibly be moved until the following Monday evening.[105] He spent the weekend on the free soil of New York and returned to Spring Station, Kentucky, just as Charles Stewart or one of his contemporaries might have done twenty years earlier. Even in the midst of agitation over fugitive slaves, turfmen held to long-established practices. In 1859, Hark was off again on his travels, advertised as a "celebrated trainer" for hire just as he had always been.[106] His owners saw no need to change the patterns in which they and he had lived for so long. Surely, they insisted, slavery could somehow be preserved and along with it the Union. And for men like Dimms and Hark, continuing in the old ways may have seemed safest. Best to take the privileges offered unless and until they had clear indication of what was to come.

Turfmen may have initially found cause to hope in the case of the famous returned fugitive Anthony Burns, hope, even as their dreams faltered, that the future might still look much like the past. Burns had escaped from Virginia slavery to Boston in 1854, only to be captured and returned to the South under the provisions of the Fugitive Slave Act. After dragging Burns back from Massachusetts, his master sold him at auction to David McDaniel, a "planter, slave-trader, and horse-dealer" headquartered in North Carolina.[107] Historians have only noted McDaniel briefly as an incidental character in the saga of Anthony Burns, but to horsemen of his time David McDaniel was well known. He had operated racetracks in Raleigh and Waynesboro, North Carolina, and had owned some fine racehorses of his own, including the famous Hard Heart, a product of the Bingaman stables in Natchez.[108] A few years after his encounter with Anthony Burns, McDaniel would gain a prominent place in the slave trade in Richmond and take over the local track where William Ransom Johnson's horses had reigned supreme.[109]

Specialists cared for McDaniel's racehorses, but he put Burns in charge of his carriage and personal riding horses.[110] The former fugitive moved into the privileged world of the slave horseman; he lived separately from other slaves, and McDaniel upheld his authority in disputes with the overseer. Slaveholding turfmen could look at Burns's fate and feel assured that such a man could be used as befit his talents, his dangerous desire for freedom sublimated in a form of slavery in which they had learned to accommodate men of skill and drive so that their attributes actually strengthened the system of human bondage. But McDaniel, a hardheaded professional slave dealer, was first and foremost a businessman, and he never concealed that profit was his consistent motive. When abolitionists offered him the price he wanted for Burns, he took it and, somewhat to Burns's surprise, stood firm against a mob that tried to prevent the slave from being taken to the North and freedom.[111] Sectional conflict over slavery had disrupted bondage in the stables, the servitude in which Southern Whig turfmen saw embodied the power of slavery as the engine of a modern society.

In 1859, those disruptive voices penetrated the racetrack itself. The planter Pierce Butler, disastrously in debt, used the facilities of the Savannah racecourse to stage the largest single sale of human beings ever held in the United States. Slaves awaiting purchase were kept in the track's stables, then herded into the grandstand for examination. Just as William J. Minor had scrutinized the horse Pryor's teeth, prospective purchasers examined those of black men and women. They prodded them in the ribs and felt along their sides, just as Thomas J. Wells had done to see whether Lecomte was well enough to run against Lexington. A *New York Tribune* reporter, watching in horror for days as family after family went on the block, wrote angrily that he felt his stomach turn most at how comfortable the buyers were. They were looking at human beings in a place and a manner in which they were accustomed to look at animals, and they saw nothing incongruous in it.[112] Slaveholders had enacted their mastery, their ownership of animal and human bodies, at the racetrack for decades and used those experiences as a foundation for their beliefs about who they were and what America should be. Some remembered Horace Greeley as a journeyman printer who had helped set the type on the very first issue of the *Spirit of the Times*.[113] Now more people read his newspaper than any other in the United States.[114] And the trumpeting, national voice of the *Tribune* had called slaveholders barbarians.

By 1860, slavery threatened to tear the country apart in a four-way presidential contest in which voters divided sharply by section and position on slavery. Southern Unionists struggled desperately to dissuade their neighbors from responding rashly to the likelihood of victory for Republican Abraham Lincoln. During the 1860 campaign, John Minor Botts spoke vigorously from the stump throughout Virginia against disunion. "I did not make the Constitution, I am only reading it as I find it," he assured his listeners. He believed firmly that the founding documents guaranteed that slaves should be treated as a unique kind of property, for which special provision must be made. With that assurance, Southerners and slaveholders must be prepared to assert their rights in the Union and hammer out some reasonable solution, rather than stalking out, leaving behind a proud heritage. If South Carolina seceded, he had no intention of helping Virginia to follow her, he snorted. "I am not a slave to Slavery, and I will not make a fool of myself to please fools."[115] He still firmly believed that his allegiances to slavery and to the Union could be simultaneously maintained, that the election of Lincoln might necessitate discussion and compromise but not the end of bondage or even its great peril. Botts clung fiercely to Lincoln's personal promise to him: "I have always been an Old-line Henry-Clay Whig, and if your Southern people will let me alone, I will administer this government as nearly upon the principles that he would have administered it as it is possible for one man to follow in the path of another."[116]

Turfmen like Botts might still find comfort in the idea that they shared their reverence for their hero with Lincoln. But others looked at their glittering sport and desperately feared what was to come. In 1860, George Wilkes printed in *Wilkes's Spirit of the Times* a letter from England, in which the writer announced that, having seen all the horses of Europe, he firmly believed that "the American race-horse possesse[s] greater powers of endurance than any I have seen in the whole world." Turfmen could look at a ringing endorsement like that and wonder how it was possible for such a world as they had built, so beautifully ordered and maintained, to crumble. But the letter was signed by Robert Harlan and printed by George Wilkes. Harlan had once been a slave, and Wilkes mixed with radicals and free labor ideologues. The territories had exploded into bloodshed, the abolitionists had organized as a vocal force, and slavery itself and the world that it had created were threatened. Turfmen might hope that Botts was right and that Lincoln would honor the ideas and principles of Henry Clay, with whom so many of them had voted, to whom so many of them had looked as a model, for whom so many of them had named horses as a gesture of respect. But they must also have noticed that Robert Harlan had made his own gesture of respect and that one of his horses in England in 1860 was named Lincoln.[117] Running in the colors of a former slave, a horse with such a name only confirmed their fears of the Republican from Illinois. This man would surely destroy them if he could.

4

These Are the Verities

Thomas Doswell and his son Thomas W. Doswell were Virginians, but before that they were horsemen. They kept a wary eye on the disintegrating political situation, but they devoted their real attention to the racer who might be the best they had ever owned. The horse was the product of the finest Virginia Thoroughbred breeding; his sire was John Minor Botts's Revenue, whom William Ransom Johnson himself had taken to the racetrack. His dam was Nina, whose foals ultimately earned her owner $150,000. When she died, Thomas W. Doswell buried her with a full funeral, which everyone on his estate attended. "The old mare was as well known in Virginia," remembered one writer, "as if she had been one of her greatest statesmen."[1] The Doswells and Phil Thompson, the black horseman who had overseen the careers of many of the stable's champions, had watched eagerly as Nina approached her 1855 foaling date. Thompson was the first human being to set eyes on Nina's Revenue colt. He went and woke Thomas Doswell, because he believed immediately that the horse would be a special one. They called the colt Planet, and, in 1860, election or no election, the Doswells were ready to take him anywhere to run.[2]

The owners of the racecourse on Long Island invited Planet to their track in the autumn of 1860 for a race that carried a $5,000 entry fee and a $20,000 purse.[3] Running against Planet, who had never been defeated at a distance over two miles, would be the young South Carolina champion Congaree and Kentucky's Daniel Boone, who had bested Planet at two miles and boasted as his mother Henry Clay's great broodmare Magnolia.[4] National excitement stirred at the prospect. New York might not have an entry, but it would host the great champions of the nation, just as it had in the days of Eclipse and Henry. Perhaps the disputes over the national jockey club and, more ambitiously, the whole debate over the place of slavery in American life could be resolved peaceably if camaraderie rather than animosity were the order of the day. "The prospect of these horses meeting upon the Turf in October creates a great deal of talk among all persons who take an interest in racing," reported the *Spirit of the Times*. "[T]he Presidential election, will only come in and divide public talk, with, 'who'll win on the great race day.'" With electoral politics looking grimly divided, it seemed "of vast national importance, just at the time being, to bring twenty-five or thirty thousand noble-hearted Southern and Western men into the North to mingle freely with the people of this part of the country . . . try their favorite horses, and thus infuse by their presence a great deal of good feeling between the North and the South. . . . [T]here are good things and good fellows everywhere throughout our broad land, and although differing on unimportant points, yet taken as a whole we are a great people, and mean to remain so." Tiffany and Company designed a trophy for the winner.[5] Such a contest had brought Americans together before; surely it could do so again.

Assessing such superior horses and their power to unite the nation, sporting papers judged the presidential candidates "under the best circumstances . . . neither as honest or useful to the welfare of the country" as the animals preparing to compete on Long Island.[6] But all the hopes turfmen had cherished for a return to the feelings of earlier times were dashed when Daniel Boone broke down before the race and never made it to the post. Planet ran away from Congaree. The whole contest ended as a disappointment that attracted little attention and certainly did nothing to stem the tide of national events.[7] In November, Abraham Lincoln emerged out of a field of four candidates to take the presidency without carrying a single Southern electoral vote. In December, South Carolina, home of Congaree, became the first state to proclaim its secession from the Union.

But Thomas Doswell did not forget that he had a superior race-horse. Planet had traveled all the way to New York and still easily defeated Congaree, and his supporters believed he would have had revenge on Daniel Boone for his earlier defeat as well. Doswell was not going to let secession and the possibility of civil war prevent him from matching Planet against the best competition he could find, even if that competition was now, in some people's estimation, in a foreign country. In February 1861, as the Virginia secession convention met in Richmond, Doswell brought Planet to Charleston's Washington Course to prepare for what looked like a sure victory against the South Carolina mare Albine, owned by Jack Cantey.[8] Sired by the well-regarded racer Jeff Davis, Albine had not overwhelmed anyone in her early racing career. But the enslaved trainer Hercules, owned by the Sinkler family and hired by Cantey to work in his stables, had found the key to her.[9] As one writer later described her debut at Charleston in 1860, after a few months with the old black man, "[W]hat she would do for no white man she did for old Hercules. At the roll of the drum she lifted her nose out of his . . . gentling palm, gave a soft, confident whinny and romped away with one of the biggest events of the meet."[10]

The writer who sought to describe Hercules's relationship with his charge was DuBose Heyward. Best known as the author of *Porgy*, the novel that became the basis for George and Ira Gershwin's op-era *Porgy and Bess*, he was a son of Charleston and a descendant of generations who had enjoyed the Washington Course. In his 1932 novel *Peter Ashley*, Heyward creates a South Carolina-born protag-onist who has left his parents' plantation to seek a life of the mind in Europe and the North. Peter Ashley returns to Charleston deter-mined to live differently from his family and their friends. The central set piece of Heyward's novel is the Planet-Albine race, and Heyward paints with a sure touch the scene inside the grandstand as the minutes tick down to post time.[11] Peter stands at the bar with his male relatives and their friends and literally breathes in the scent of camaraderie, "leather, spirits . . . and the faint, not unpleasant, tang of the stable." Among the men lurks the specter of secession;

Peter knows that, once the race is over, the South Carolinians will once again curse the Virginians for their delay in exiting the Union: "But for this week—no politics, no war. Two score gentlemen from the two great commonwealths, speaking the same language, swearing by the same gods, feet on the same rail, and glasses touching. Eyes that met and seemed to say over the glasses: 'These are the verities. These gestures that express the life that we have brought to full flower, these moments of clean sport, of chivalry, out of the past, and by God's help, on down beyond us into the future.'"[12]

Little by little, during his day at the races, young Peter Ashley gives in to the seductive comforts of behaving in accordance with the tenets of his upbringing. Horses and racing become for him, as he reflects on his situation, shorthand for everything it means to live as a planter's son in a long-established slave society, a marker of how impossible it is to shed that life. A young man might leave, Peter muses, but then what? "His filly would become a mare, the mare would foal, and the colt in time would as likely as not capture the Pineville sweepstakes. The winnings would go halfway across the world to the rightful owner. There was no such thing as escape."[13] Slavery cannot merely be renounced. It is far too powerful for that. Peter Ashley slowly and ineluctably, in the course of the afternoon, changes all his plans and elects to become a tractable scion of the South Carolina aristocracy. Heyward reconstructs with lyrical power the match race's demonstration of turfmen's unwavering commitment to all the verities—Thoroughbreds, competition, and their own racial and social authority, with slavery as the foundation of all these venerated customs.

The race itself had all the drama of a thrilling fiction. The Virginia men were confident in Planet's chances against the less experienced mare in a race of four-mile heats. Thomas Doswell even warned Jack Cantey that his stallion would be too strong for Albine; he planned to have Planet set a scorching pace and exhaust her quickly. When they went to the post, Planet, with the slave jockey Jesse aboard, shot forward to take the lead, followed by Albine, with the slave Bedo up. Bedo had instructions to hold her a length or so off the pace, and she stalked Planet until the third mile, when Bedo brought her up to see if she still had the speed and stamina to challenge the leader.

The mare began to wring her tail, usually an indication of exhaustion, and wagers changed hands frenziedly. Bedo dropped her back once again, and Virginia bettors started counting the money they were sure to win. Albine stayed where she was, a length behind, until the last quarter of the fourth mile. At the top of the home stretch, Bedo turned her loose, and she surged forward, skipping over the track and soaring past Planet to win by several lengths. The official time recorded was seven minutes and thirty-six and a half seconds, the fastest four-mile heat run over the Charleston course in years.

Planet's supporters were stunned but assured themselves that the mare could not possibly repeat her victory. But when the two horses came out for the second heat, there was Albine, striding along at Planet's shoulder all the way until the final furlongs, when she pulled away again, in the fastest time ever for a second heat in Charleston.[14] Hercules, Albine's trainer, was ecstatic and asked the mare's owner to order champagne. Hercules wanted to treat all the gentlemen present to a celebratory drink because "he was willing to die, now that he had defeated . . . Planet." The champagne, for which Cantey paid, although Hercules had made the offer, flowed freely. Under its influence, the South Carolinians began teasing the Doswells about the ease of their victory. Thomas Doswell handled it good-humoredly but finally, pride wounded, offered to match Planet the next day against any horse they cared to name for $10,000.[15] These were the important things—the giving and accepting of challenges, the presence of a man like Hercules, accustomed to the privileges of his horseman's life, his talent safely subordinated in mutual celebration and allegiance to the world of the racetrack. These were the pillars of a slaveholding society, surely too powerful to be overturned.

The moment flew by quickly. Virginia followed South Carolina out of the Union, the nation went to war, and thousands of young men left their homes and families behind. DuBose Heyward gives us an evocative glimpse of the thoughts of Peter Ashley, so recently determined to carve out a different life for himself and now so firmly committed to the politics and society of South Carolina that he prepares to ride off to the Confederate army. As he stares at the ceiling in the night, he considers his future and can think no farther than the Charleston races of 1862. It never occurs to him that they will not be run, and he toys with the idea of entering his horse Starling, for surely, with Hercules to train her, "she'd be good for the Hutchinson stakes at least."[16] There were young men across the South who were unable to imagine a future without races like the one just run at Charleston. They were going to war to protect a society and make a nation in which the labor of men like Hercules supported white men's dreams. Ultimately, they had decided that their allegiance to the United States was secondary. First and foremost, they were slave-owning Southerners. And, as men like them always had, they turned to the racetrack as a display and emblem of their fundamental understandings of their lives and their nation.

SOME OF THE RACING WHIGS of earlier years had continued to cling to hope and to union long after others had given them up. In 1860, Thomas J. Wells of Louisiana resolutely supported the Constitutional Union ticket of John Bell of Tennessee and Edward Everett of Massachusetts, committed to no platform but the preservation of the Union.[17] From his farm in Kentucky, Robert Alexander eagerly monitored the progress of the Crittenden Compromise, the package of constitutional amendments and congressional resolutions designed to protect slavery permanently that fellow turfman John J. Crittenden had proposed. He kept close at hand his copy of a Kentucky petition in support of the Compromise, absently noting credits and debits related to his horses on the back of the sheet.[18] The national turf magazines added their calls for unity to those of Southerners loyal to the old Union. "To be a Carolinian may be a glory, but to be an American, is a superadded glory," one Northern correspondent reminded his readers in December 1860, as South Carolina threatened to become the first state to secede.[19] They did not want to report Southern racing results as foreign news, New York-based editors protested gloomily.[20] But many Southerners were now convinced that they must have an independent nation in which slavery would remain an integral part of the social order. One writer bluntly summed up the South's position to the *Spirit of the Times* in early 1861. Lincoln's Republicans "were a hostile and deluded people about 'niggers,' and would do great harm, even in Heaven itself, by their notions. I'm certain they'll contend for equality of rights among the angels themselves, they are so blind to the inevitable inherent differences in nature. . . . We'll make the cotton, and if you are friendly, we'll buy some of your fabrics and manufactures; but if you concern yourselves about our 'niggers' any more, we'll shut you out entirely and buy from Old England, duty free. There; thar, by thunder! who's beat now?"[21] By then turf magazine editors were reduced to pleading, "Gentlemen of the South, *'spur your proud horses hard, but do not ride in blood!'*"[22]

Henry Clay's visions of order and progress, enacted in politics and in his stables, had irrevocably collapsed beneath the weight of the struggle between nation and slavery. In December 1860, the equine enthusiast John Ryan wrote to his New York friend A. F. Giraud, "At 1 ½ Clock P.M. this day, the Sovereign State of South Carolina, in which I live, and where I hope to die, by solemn ordnance through a unanimous vote of her Convention Seceded from the United States. . . . We feel, we have done right, and are prepared to defend our act . . . [T]hen the Southern United States . . . will be . . . a great, free and glorious people."[23] South Carolina and her sister states in the Deep South, who shortly followed her out of the Union, preferred to leave peacefully, but they were intent on having an independent nation in which slavery would prevail, whatever the cost. As the spring wore on, hope for the preservation of old ways and the old Union flickered. The *New York Tribune* reported on the New Orleans spring races and lauded the jockey Abe's stylish victory aboard Duncan Kenner's Panic, the star of the meet.[24] But the continuation of racing held out no hope for national amity. Instead, Southern turfmen took their passion for secession with them to the track. Virginia horses had not run particularly well at New Orleans, Louisiana's Louis Bringier wrote to his sister, and he, for one, was pleased to see the state punished for her tardiness in leaving the Union: "They deserve something of the sort, for nothing else than hailing from such a miserable subservient state as Old Virginia."[25] But even in Virginia things had begun to move. The die-hard Whig John Minor Botts, called to meet with the president as Lincoln plotted the resupply or rescue of the federal troops still garrisoned at Fort Sumter, looked around in despair at the fulfillment of his own dire prophecies of the 1850s. War now seemed to him inevitable.[26]

Finally, after months of increasingly divisive news, *Porter's Spirit of the Times* announced, "The cloud that has for months darkened our prosperity and cast a gloom over the land has at length burst, and as we go to press the guns of the Confederate batteries are raining hot shot on Sumter." It was Henry Clay's birthday, the newspaper noted mournfully: "We cannot forebear exclaiming, '*Would he were here!*'"[27]

In Alabama, Johnson Jones Hooper, who had written pages of popular humor for the *Spirit of the Times* and praised the paper as the last tie many Southerners felt to the North, became the clerk of the Confederate Congress.[28] In Tennessee, Balie Peyton Jr., the son of one of Clay's Whig allies, left his law practice and entered the Confederate army. His father, bitterly opposed to his going and appalled by the dissolution of the Union he loved, gave him his own sword, which he had carried in the Mexican War.[29] In Virginia, John Minor Botts had no qualms about announcing that he believed that those who had supported secession and thus bore responsibility for the war would "answer hereafter, both in this world and in the world to come, for the most atrocious and stupendous crime that has been committed since the crucifixion of our Lord and Savior Jesus Christ."[30] The Confederate government locked Botts up as a dissident in a slave jail belonging to his old racing acquaintance David McDaniel.[31] And in New York, George Wilkes, immediately grasping that war journalism was the most dramatic and lucrative sports reporting of all, boarded a troop ship, where the chorus of "Dixie" "would frequently ring throughout the ship. . . . This song is also so popular among the Southern volunteers that it has become almost national with them. . . . The Northern volunteer is no less inspired by its notes, but he chants them with a different sentiment. . . . With him its words are a challenge of invasion, and I saw many an eye blaze . . . as its owner burst forth with a yearning note, 'I wish I was in Dixie!'"[32]

Wilkes followed Northern troops to Manassas, where he described both the glory of General Irvin McDowell, urging his soldiers on "like a splendid dream," and the beginnings of the unprecedented carnage that the war was to bring to American soil. The dead "lay about in the most fantastic shapes, some absolutely headless, some represented by a gory trunk alone, some with smiles, and some with rage upon their lips, as they grasped their bent and curiously twisted weapons, and some actually rolled up like a ball. Whoever would study the eccentricities of carnage, might here have graduated through all the degrees of horror, to a full experience at once."[33] Among the wounded lay Private James Jackson of the Fourth Alabama, who had come to the war from Forks of Cypress, where his father had bred the immortal Reel, the dam of Lecomte, and innumerable other great champions. Private Jackson, shot through the lungs, traded his watch to a Northern soldier for a full canteen of water and urged the new owner, if he ever wanted to put his horse in a match race, to use that watch for timing. It had been specially designed to meet a turfman's exacting standards for split-second precision. Months later, Jackson reported that the water he had gotten for that watch had probably saved his life.[34] He served in most of the major engagements in the western theater and survived the war.

WITH WAR A BLOODY REALITY, even formerly stubborn Whigs turned their attention to making the Confederate States of America the prosperous, slaveholding nation they had always hoped for. By November 1861, William J. Minor was already writing to Thomas J. Wells, soliciting his help in coordinating Duncan Kenner's campaign for a seat in the Confederate Senate. Kenner could be trusted to represent the interests of sugar planters, who wanted tariffs and other forms of state support as much as ever.[35] The institutions and centers of power might have changed, but the need to protect the interests that had united Southern Whigs still held good, as did a passionate commitment to the racehorses that sustained Southern dreams of prowess and progress. The *Charleston Courier* reported happily in 1862 that there would soon be a Southern sporting paper, a Confederate *Spirit of the Times* published in Nashville or another major Southern city. Such a paper would "be much needed at the South, as soon as we achieve our independence," the reporter reminded his readers.[36] It would be the necessary voice of a nation in which turfmen would be proud to live. In the same front-page story, the writer mourned the death of Hercules, the trainer of Albine, praising him as a man "busy in his vocation, always receiving from the passing crowd the notice and respect due to him from all who knew his worth as a faithful, upright, civil, humble man." Slaves like Hercules were indispensable to the creation of a new Southern nation.

Though Hercules had died, men like him would continue to be rewarded and celebrated for their role in a nationally significant pastime. The paper promised a review of Hercules's career for the benefit of younger men. That pledge suggested how intent Southerners were on passing down the hierarchies of bondage and the structures of privilege and self-interest that sustained them. They hoped that the relationships of the racetrack, both personal and political, would help found a new Southern nation.[37] The lessons learned in the stables would, they firmly believed, also constitute a crucial and militarily significant advantage in the fight to attain their independence. Those looking had already seen evidence of that advantage in perhaps the most prominent Southern family on the turf, the Johnsons of Petersburg, Virginia.

William Ransom Johnson Pegram, the grandson and namesake of the Napoleon of the Turf and the great-grandson of Marmaduke Johnson, the owner of Austin Curtis's Medley Mare, had been left fatherless at a young age. Young Willie Pegram and his mother had lived with his grandfather at his plantation, where William Ransom Johnson trained and traded Thoroughbreds and passed on his love for horses to his grandson.[38] W. R. J. Pegram grew into a staunch and daring officer, one of the most prominent of the young men who followed Robert E. Lee with unwavering devotion. He fought in every major battle in the eastern theater from his enlistment at the beginning of the war until his mortal wounding at the Battle of Five Forks less than two weeks before the ceasefire at Appomattox. He was only twenty-three when he died. But, young as he was, he inspired officers and enlisted men alike to feats of courage and endurance. With examples like Pegram, an officer who served under him wrote, the men "will go with Genl. Lee as long as the Battle-Cross floats on the field."[39] Pegram's fidelity to the Confederate cause was not merely born of romantic nationalism but out of a bone-deep commitment to slavery and black inferiority. He was fiercely glad when the Union put black troops into the field because it gave new energy to Confederate enlisted men, who saw before them the threatening prospect of a world of racial integration. He wrote with pleasure to his sister of the Battle of the Crater, near their childhood home in Petersburg, where he had watched black soldiers massacred in cold blood after they had surrendered.[40] They had to die to preserve his country, the one he had learned to love at his grandfather's plantation, surrounded by black horsemen. Such an upbringing, his countrymen proudly noted, had molded a remarkable officer. With such men as these, mounted on the best the South had to offer, the Confederacy must be victorious.

Horses were at the very heart of the Confederate army's idea of itself as a fighting force of dominant power and style. South Carolina horseman Preston Burch liked to remember that his father had been hauled up on multiple occasions for violating regulations by racing horses inside the army's lines. But time after time, his commanding officer, Wade Hampton, himself descended from a long line of turfmen, had only sighed that he ought to have the young man shot and asked him if he had won.[41] Even allowing for a large dose of family folklore, the story revealed the common understanding between senior officers and their subordinates that horse racing, which honed the power and endurance of men and their mounts, was too valuable to be sacrificed to the exigencies of war. Confederate cavalrymen embodied the idea that Southerners' skill with horses would inevitably defeat any enemy.[42] Long after the war, Virginians delighted in remembering the Fourth Virginia Cavalry, which had been mounted almost entirely on descendants of Boston, through his son, the famous racer Red Eye. Only horsemen worthy of the South, they believed, would have gone into battle on such beautifully pedigreed Thoroughbreds and handled so competently horses with such famously terrible tempers. The animals were so badly behaved, one man remembered, that trying to sleep near the Fourth was "as bad as camping next door to the Yankees."[43]

Southerners, who prided themselves on being born and bred to work with Thoroughbreds, clung tightly to their dreams of victory for long months and years. Traveller, Robert E. Lee's personal mount, embodied their hopes in his strong frame. Lee himself wrote that a painter or poet could describe the horse as he deserved, "his endurance of toil, hunger, thirst, heat & cold; & the dangers & sufferings through which he has passed. . . . But I am no artist . . . & can therefore only say that he is a Confederate *grey*."[44] Southern turfmen quickly took up the horse's somewhat vague pedigree and announced that, without doubt, Traveller was descended from the splendid runner Grey Eagle, from the English Derby winner Diomed. He could not be anything but a Thoroughbred, for he stood for the South itself.[45]

THE PRACTICAL BUSINESS of keeping and running Thoroughbreds, however, suffered disastrously during the war years. Though horses took on great significance as Confederate symbols, regular horse racing was suspended across the South. Lexington proudly continued to hold its races, but even it was forced to break with tradition in the spring of 1862, when Confederate General Kirby Smith camped his troops at the track during their campaigns against Union forces in the area.[46] Charleston's Washington Course, where Albine had won her unexpected victory, became the site of a camp in which Union soldiers were imprisoned. But Southern-owned Thoroughbreds were not merely denied the chance to run; they became spoils of war, with devastating results for the stables that had bred and cherished them. One later turfman would romantically attribute the blanks in postbellum Thoroughbred pedigrees to the turmoil of war, when the details of a treasured horse's family background, locked in its owner's memory, were lost "when a Minnie ball stretched him on the bloody soil of Antietam."[47]

Confederate guerrillas and regular Confederate cavalry stole and impressed horses with abandon, often with no regard for the loyalties of their owners. William J. Minor and many others sent valuable animals to Robert Alexander, whose British citizenship was thought to offer some protection to horses in his care.[48] The animals were indeed safe for several months, until the night Bill Quantrill rode up to the gate. Quantrill, who led the most bloodthirsty set of mounted Confederate guerrillas in Missouri, had made a long foray into Kentucky. At Quantrill's shoulder rode a lieutenant who had been with him since the beginning, the hard-bitten, hard-riding

Frank James, who had left his brother Jesse at home.[49] The raiders knew that they had attacked no ordinary farm; they wanted prime Thoroughbreds and asked for particular horses by name. Only the darkness and a quick and clever tongue allowed the brave black horseman Ansel Williamson, Alexander's trainer and stable manager, to substitute an athletic but unproven young animal for the already-famous racer Asteroid.[50] Quantrill's raid and another smaller one cost Alexander more than fifteen horses, some of them among the best he had. Alexander could take only cold comfort in the fact that he was not alone in his losses. Henry Clay's son and successor in the horse business, John M. Clay, lost more than $25,000 worth of horses to Confederate cavalry commander John Hunt Morgan. And when Morgan went looking for the horses of Lexington Unionist and prominent horseman James Grinstead and could not find them, he ordered the stables burned in revenge.[51]

Southerners under Union occupation were just as likely to have their Thoroughbreds stolen or confiscated. Elizabeth Harding, running the Belle Meade stock farm in Tennessee as her husband sat in a federal prison camp in Michigan, had to appeal personally to Union general George H. Thomas to protect her animals from soldiers who attempted to take her valuable breeding stallions.[52] Albine herself, the heroine of the Charleston races of 1861, fell into the hands of Union forces.[53] General Benjamin Butler, in command of occupied New Orleans, ordered the stables of William J. Minor and Duncan Kenner confiscated and sold to the highest bidder. Hopeful Northern buyers sent agents to New Orleans to pick up the expensive Thoroughbreds at rock-bottom prices. Panic, the star of the New Orleans races of 1861, ended up as the property of George Wilkes, who quickly assured his readers that the purchase had been made in the public interest. A better quality of Thoroughbred in the North would inspire more involvement in racing and in horse breeding, which would in turn produce Northern cavalry that could battle on equal terms with mounted Southerners, who had so often insisted on their legendary prowess that their opponents had reluctantly accepted it as fact.[54]

WITH THE HORSES so critical to Southern identity often dispersed, the black horsemen crucial to powerful men's views of slavery also began behaving in ways that unsettled their masters. *Wilkes's Spirit of the Times* could lyrically describe the slaves who gathered at the race-course in Sherwood, South Carolina, in 1861 as "reveling in blissful ignorance of the storm their complexions had raised in this 'Glorious Union.'"[55] But slaves all over the South were soon well aware of what the war might mean for them. The conflict brought confusion and difficulty for white slave owners and increased opportunity for escape. And it might bring at long last armed forces to guarantee freedom.[56] Slave horsemen, for years more mobile and more intimate with white people than most of their contemporaries, were quick to grasp that the war had changed everything.

In addition to having his horses confiscated, William J. Minor had personal experience of how planters could lose slave horsemen. In the autumn of 1861, eighteen Natchez slaves, many of them horsemen, were imprisoned at a local racetrack because planters believed that they had plotted an insurrection. From their positions close to white men and families, horsemen had heard the comments of worried masters. The Union commander, white men feared, would soon "eat his breakfast in New Orleans," and black men re-joiced and made plans to mount a rebellion, confident of military support on the way.[57] The details of the plot emerged in the close and long-familiar confines of the racecourse, where the suspected rebels were tortured until they talked. One man later claimed that he was beaten on and off for three weeks by a group of prominent Natchez men, who took turns with the whip. The planters brought in a doctor to determine when the blows were about to kill their victim. After a brief respite to pull him back from the brink of death, the torture would begin again. The leader of the inquiry and one of the men wielding the whip was Alexander K. Farrar, William J. Minor's and Adam Bingaman's old Mississippi Whig comrade.[58] Beside him every day was William J. Minor himself.

Minor's wife and daughter-in-law would later say that their husbands had gone armed to the racetrack, intending to intervene on behalf of the accused slaves if they could. Once there, they stayed. The slaves present remembered that they had questioned the accused and acquiesced in the violence, even if they did not participate. The Minor women recalled that John Minor had kept clear of most of the proceedings, while his father stayed resolutely through the whole process, though he insisted it turned his stomach. He later told his wife that, if such practices were necessary to preserve slavery, he would never own a slave again. He was an important man, and his neighbors were accustomed to hearing his opinions aired at excruciating length. But he did not lend his voice against the violence he supposedly abhorred. In the end, he decided that, for the crime of attempting revolt, the men accused must die, and he kept silence and went along with the rest.[59] Forty men were executed, several hanged in the confines of the racetrack, where Minor's horses had so often emerged victorious.[60] Natchez planters carried out the executions in that particular place to assert their continuing power at the racetrack, their determined mastery over men and horses on which they based their ideas of themselves and their self-proclaimed nation. But they could not change what their victims had already done. After generations in which horsemen had studiously sought to use their skills to make themselves safer, to make their bondage more bearable, these men had hazarded their lives in the belief that they could exploit their privileges to plan and carry out a successful insurrection to free themselves and those around them. The war brought the possibility that their standing would no longer isolate slave horsemen but would instead make them figures of community importance.

Duncan Kenner lost his horses just as William J. Minor did, and he had cause to note black horsemen's more typical ways of disrupting Confederate turfmen's hopes. Instead of revolting, they disappeared. Kenner's horses had come to the auction block from Ashland, his sugar plantation upriver from New Orleans, where the 111th Indiana had surprised the Confederate congressman in July 1862. Since Northern forces had occupied New Orleans a few months earlier, Kenner had been making preparations to foil any attempt to take him prisoner. He had retired the winning Thoroughbred Sid Story from the track and made him into his personal mount for use around the plantation. When Kenner, aboard his horse in his fields, got word that Union troops had tied up a boat at his river dock, he turned Sid Story and escaped at a speed no cavalry horse could have matched.[61] His wife and children, including his teenage daughter Rosella, were left behind. The Federals went through the plantation house, destroying and confiscating expensive items, including several of Kenner's prized equine paintings. They then rounded up every white man they could find in the area and took them as prisoners to New Orleans, along with all the horses in Kenner's stables, including the children's ponies.

The confiscation had not proceeded exactly according to plan, however. Whale, one of Kenner's most successful racers, obviously had to go with the others, but the horse was so evil-tempered that even getting him out of the stall was a battle. The Indiana boys cursed him, but they got no help from the one man famously able to handle the difficult animal. Abe was nowhere to be found. Once the raiding party finally got Whale under control and departed with their prizes, including several slave horsemen, they proceeded to William J. Minor's Waterloo Plantation, where they seized both horses and stable boys.[62] At Ashland, Mrs. Kenner turned to a few of her husband's slave horsemen for help. She kept a pistol and gave another to Henry Hammond, who had been a jockey in the Kenner racing stable. They stood guard together overnight, alert for slaves intent on revenge or marauders ready to attack a vulnerable household. The next morning mother and children traveled downriver. Driving the wagon in which the Kenner family departed was Sam Page, Kenner's racing groom and Abe's old friend, who had given significant testimony years earlier in the affair of Lecomte's drugging. Page knew what to say and what not to say, what compromises to make or appear to make, to preserve his own safety and privilege. If he knew where Abe had been during the struggle with Whale, he seems to have said nothing.[63]

If Abe took advantage of the chaos at Ashland to disappear from his previous life, he was not alone. The racing world of the South collapsed in wartime not only because so many of its precious horses were lost but also because the men who had worked the horses left their old lives behind. Some, like Sam Page, were wary and chose to continue as they always had until they saw clearly what the war would bring. But others, to the dismay of white men who had regarded them as the best examples of slavery's efficiency and beneficence, seized their chance. Parson Dick, the stud groom at James Jackson's Forks of Cypress estate in Alabama, rode off on one of his well-bred charges in early 1865 and was never seen again. His owners assumed that he had taken his mount and skills to a Union cavalry company forming only a few miles away.[64] Willis Jones's slave Durastus, who had been trusted to transport the valuable stallions Gaines's Denmark and Mambrino Chief out of harm's way, delivered his charges but did not return home.[65] And Abe, as he always had, followed the racetrack. He was among the first and most famous black horsemen to exert the privileges of his profession as a free man.

RACING IN THE DEEP SOUTH had ground to a halt, but it went on, at least intermittently, in Louisville, Lexington, Cincinnati, and St. Louis in the Midwest and in New Jersey and on Long Island in the East. Men like Abe still had a place to practice their profession. Border state men like Robert Alexander, whose British citizenship gave him a degree of distance from the conflict, and John M. Clay, who was too much the son of Henry Clay to do anything else, continued to run their horses, even on New York courses, throughout the war.[66] On June 25, 1863, less than a fortnight before the Union victory at Gettysburg and the fall of the Confederate stronghold at Vicksburg, the Lexington daughter Idlewild, trained by the free black horseman William Bird, "made a terrible example" of her competition in a much-heralded event on Long Island.[67] She ran down the colt Jerome Edgar in the final mile of the race. John M. Clay cheered Jerome Edgar on at the top of his lungs, using his considerable inherited vocal power, but to no avail. Idlewild came up even with him and then, as they turned into the backstretch, extended herself and soared under the wire alone.[68] The country still had an appetite for equine heroes, even, or perhaps especially, in the midst of carnage. One turf historian remembered, "What she did on that battle-day in June in her own private warfare makes good reading to the man who knows a race-horse. . . . [W]hen the . . . news of Idlewild's accomplishment reached the two armies it was camp-fire talk and trench tattle even when the minie balls were singing a death song over the heads of the men in the ditches."[69]

Northern men and wartime money had moved to fill the gap left by Southerners unable to compete during the conflict. A new coterie of powerful turfmen, some completely alien to antebellum racing

men, was emerging. One man in particular embodied that new generation's difference from the old. His name was John Morrissey, and
his journey to sporting leisure had been a circuitous one. Born in
Tipperary, he came to the United States with his parents as a tod-
dler in the early 1830s. Growing up in Troy, New York, Morrissey
worked in several local factories and then as a deckhand on cargo
ships. In his spare time, he fought with his friends and his enemies,
gaining a reputation as a tough man to take down, which was saying
something, since one of Morrissey's opponents was probably his
contemporary John Heenan, later to fight for a world title.[70] Em-
boldened by local success, Morrissey decided to take his talents to a
larger stage. As a young man, he instantly made a reputation in New
York City by strolling into the Empire Club on Park Row, the hang-
out of Isaiah Rynders, New York's most prominent political bruiser,
and offering to lick any man in the place. Rynders, impressed with
Morrissey's gall and his skill in a fight, took him up as a protégé.[71]

The Empire Club was Rynders's business headquarters, where he
arranged the deals that made him a valuable political asset to the
Democrats who ran New York. Rynders controlled street gangs and
toughs, who could be hired to break up the conclaves of political
opponents, to guard the meetings of friends, to keep opposition
voters from the polls, or to hustle in those who would vote right.
The men who carried weight in city politics were often the small
businessmen and volunteer firemen George Wilkes and David Broderick had grown up among. Like Broderick, many of the men affiliated with Tammany Hall and other Democratic organizations
worked in occupations that brought them into regular contact with
fairly rough customers. The best way to empty a Tammany Hall
meeting, so said their opponents, was to shout, "Your saloon's on
fire!" Such men did not hesitate to turn street gangs into political
weapons, and the crews that carved out territory in New York's
toughest neighborhoods regularly supplemented their income with
political fixing. Morrissey quickly became a leader of the famous
Dead Rabbits gang.[72]

Morrissey's new career as a freelance enforcer with political connections did not preclude engaging in more formal prizefighting. He
fought some of the greatest American champions of the era, including

his old acquaintance John Heenan and the formidable Yankee Sullivan, and was acclaimed American champion in the 1850s.[73] His success in the ring and his service to Tammany Hall made him a prominent figure in New York's Irish neighborhoods, where young men gathered around him, admired his brawn, and did his bidding. In 1854, his long rivalry with the nativist gang leader William Poole culminated publicly and violently. Poole was tolerated in more affluent corners of New York for his efforts to keep the immigrant Irish in check but feared and hated in Irish enclaves for his gusto and skill with a blade. Morrissey and Poole had confronted each other many times. Their last encounter took place in a saloon on Broadway, where they exchanged taunts. Morrissey grew so enraged at Poole's anti-Catholic slurs that he snatched up a gun and tried to shoot him, but the weapon refused to fire, and Morrissey stalked out. A few hours later, two of Morrissey's friends murdered Poole in the street. Morrissey himself was conspicuously absent, and no charges were ever brought against him. But his reputation was secured for good or for ill.[74]

Being a folk hero was steady if not necessarily lucrative work. And it led to other job opportunities. Morrissey's connections in Tammany Hall and city politics helped him to establish his own business, a gambling club called the Gem, where he welcomed both his tougher acquaintances and the wealthy men who had followed his career in the ring and liked the frisson that came from mixing with Morrissey's street friends.[75] Successful in one establishment, he branched out and became an owner of other clubs. He would never again make his living as a fighter. Instead, he learned to turn his wide variety of acquaintances to his social and pecuniary advantage. He could chat comfortably with a Vanderbilt or a Belmont, chewing on his large cigar all the while, and then he could go out into the street and get done the questionable things they wanted but did not wish to undertake themselves. It was a career for which Morrissey had trained all his life.

Morrissey shared his pathway to ease with his old friend George Wilkes, whom he had known well before the war. When Wilkes began publishing *Wilkes's Spirit of the Times*, he and Morrissey went to England to look over English prizefighters and the runners at Newmarket, and Morrissey penned an article for the paper detailing his opinions of the state of English sport and the look of English Thoroughbreds.[76] Morrissey and Wilkes had become sportsmen and men of considerable but comfortable notoriety. In the summer of 1863, as his old neighborhoods exploded in the New York draft riots, Morrissey sponsored a race meeting in the resort town of Saratoga, adding a new track to a depleted national racing schedule and giving a new destination to wealthy Northern sportsmen eager to spend wartime money far away from the front.[77]

Saratoga took off like a rocket that year. Union general Daniel Sickles arrived in town for the festivities only a few weeks after losing his leg at Gettysburg.[78] Prominent men flocked to Saratoga, including several of the land's highest elected officials. The telegraph wires between Saratoga and Washington buzzed with discussion of national policy, and President Lincoln himself delighted in telling jokes about Morrissey.[79] By 1864, Morrissey was serving as the on-the-ground supervisor for a consortium of partners behind the new racetrack. They included Cornelius Vanderbilt, as well as the stockbroker William R. Travers, the railroad and newspaper magnate Leonard Jerome, the New York racing enthusiast John Hunter, and John Purdy, the nephew of the jockey of American Eclipse himself.[80] The men who would dictate America's economic future in the postwar years were those in the grandstand at Saratoga, merchants and industrial kings who had already gifted Morrissey with stock tips that would keep him solvent for the rest of his life.[81]

Such men would rule postbellum racing. The Southern Whigs who had dominated the tracks of the United States for twenty-five years would never again command the kind of authority they once had. Southern racing and its accompanying vision of modernity and human bondage had died. As one turf writer put it at the close of the war, " 'Hark! what sound is it that bursts like a thunderbolt on the ear, reverberating through and through the length and breadth of the land . . . ? 'Tis the first gun at Sumter . . . and it sounds the death-knell of racing and of slavery in the South.' "[82] But some of the old verities remained. Racing as a consuming passion for powerful and wealthy men and as a means of imagining and constructing a national and racial order survived the cataclysm of the war. And the racetrack remained a place where black men's knowledge and authority traditionally commanded acceptance. The horsemen who rode and trained during the war years provided a foreshadowing of what that acceptance might entail in a free nation, what freedom itself could look like.

Black horsemen, even inexperienced ones, continued to believe that in a war-ravaged and uncertain world, horses were still their ticket to security and possibility. Mary Logan, wife of Union general John A. Logan, despaired over a former slave, trained as a jockey, named Boston, perhaps after the great racer. He had come into Northern lines in the area around Louisville. Taking him as her project, she attempted to mold him into an upright, respectable, deferential youth, in keeping with her understanding of what a young black man should be. He was polite but clearly had no particular interest in religious conversion or in the sort of employment she thought appropriate. Finally, she sighed, "he ran away and the last we heard of him he was engaged as a jockey at St. Louis."[83] Boston probably made a better living in the profession he was trained for than he would have in the ones Mary Logan thought suitable. And he certainly got a chance to see men in his calling succeed in ways that must have driven him to dreaming. At St. Louis, he could have caught a glimpse of—or even rubbed shoulders in the jockeys' room with—one of the most famous former slaves on the racetrack. Abe had reappeared, and he was as good as ever.

Abe had somehow made his way upriver from Louisiana to St. Louis, where he rode in the spring races of 1864. *Wilkes's Spirit of the Times* reported his appearance blandly, reminding its readers that Rhinodine's rider was "the able and veteran jockey Abe, who used to ride for Duncan F. Kenner in the South."[84] Between the rails of the track, at least, not much had changed. Abe's closest competitor in his first race was his old rival Gilpatrick, and the black man's skill convinced several different owners to give him mounts. Robert Alexander had watched many jockeys, but he had never seen Abe in person and was unprepared. As he and a friend stood on the rail at the end of a race, "as Abe rushed by so close to us that an outstretched hand would have touched him, Mr. Alexander exclaimed: 'I have seen all the best jockeys of Europe; not one of them is nearly the equal of that old darkey.' "[85] If Alexander were surprised, Ansel Williamson, the black horseman who trained his runners and had saved several of them from Quantrill's raiders, could not have been. He had put Abe up on horses he had trained for other Kentucky breeders at the New Orleans races in the spring of 1861.[86] *Wilkes's Spirit of the Times* was lavish in its praise of the jockey: "To extraordinary experience and judgment, Abe adds marvelous strength and skill. With a clip of the knees and thighs that incorporates him with the horse, and arms that never tire, he always has his colt right by the head, and directs unremitting observation to what the others are doing. His sagacity is greatly relied on by the gentlemen who know him."[87] He rode the favorite for the Travers Stakes at Saratoga in 1864, making his debut on John Morrissey's track in the first running of one of the greatest annual fixtures of American racing. Abe, along with a small cadre of other former slaves, was well on his way to becoming a legend in Northern racing circles. Turf writers poured prose over him, calling him a "little necromancer" and "that dark master of the equestrian art." Here was the real power on the turf, they insisted. "The magnates . . . fill the public eye, but to us, Abe, albeit small and shrivelled, is a mighty man."[88]

Abe and his contemporaries lived in the shadow of slavery, both with the skills that their past had given them and with the legacy of its hierarchies. In racing results, white jockeys were listed by their last names, while men like Abe were still listed only by the first. Sewell, the winner of the first race ever at the new Saratoga track, aboard the mare Lizzie W., trained by William Bird, carried only that one name into history. The sporting press further identified him only as a "contraband," the term given to slaves confiscated or freed by virtue of their owners' allegiance to the Confederacy.[89] Of course, the practice of using only first names divided white and black riders. But, as racing historian Edward Hotaling has argued, the names they had carried in bondage were, for former slave horsemen, one word resumes. They had lived their whole professional lives under them, and white men were now willing to pay them for the expertise that they associated with those names.[90]

Northern admiration for the exploits of freedmen like Abe at the track did not, of course, translate readily into any commitment to treating such men as equals. The *New York Tribune*, Horace Greeley's staunchly Republican paper, praised the black horsemen at

Saratoga and pointed out that "[o]ne of them, who passes by the soubriquet of Old Abe, is highly spoken of as a judicious jockey. The same democracy of feeling does not extend to the spectator's galleries, for an addendum to the Programme says: 'Colored persons not admitted to the stand.'"[91] At the racetrack, a national audience could see enacted the distance between freedom and equality, as black horsemen lived out in public the complex debate over what it would mean in practice for slaves to be free.

In the summer of 1864, as Abe prepared to ride successful runners at Saratoga, the *Daily Saratogian* inveighed against those who would support a Democratic candidate against Lincoln in the election that fall. A new president and his advisors would only *"help their rebel friends hold on to the institution of Slavery!"* Such a disaster must be carefully guarded against, especially now that the Emancipation Proclamation, long anticipated, had finally come into effect, to the glee of good Saratoga Republicans. They were grimly determined to destroy slavery, for the men who stood for it had already killed too many of their sons. The paper reported that Captain Charles F. Carter of nearby Pittsfield, Massachusetts, the latest on "that long list of martyrs who have gallantly laid down their lives for their country," had died of wounds received in the Red River campaign in Louisiana.[92] Perhaps the only person in Saratoga that summer who had seen the country where Charles Carter had died was Abe, who had spent a good portion of his professional life before the war working with the horses of Thomas J. Wells, including Lecomte, the most famous mount of his career. Did he stop and remember that place and those years of his life? Did he ponder what it meant that he now worked in a town that sent its sons to root out bondage on the Red River? Or did he tighten his saddle, adjust his stirrups, and eye the competition as his mount stepped delicately under him on the way to the start?

5

The Only Practical Means of Reunion

LONGFELLOW HAD NOT RACED as a two year old, and he lost his first start at three in the Phoenix Hotel Stakes at Lexington in 1870. But his owner, John Harper of Nantura Farm, in the heart of Kentucky's Woodford County, knew to be patient. The horse needed time to grow into his towering height and experience to ease his gawkiness into grace. After that first loss, he went undefeated at three. As a four year old, he set foot on Northern tracks for the first time and swept away the competition. Longtime Saratoga track manager Charles Wheatly remembered watching Longfellow start against New York and New Jersey champions. "As long as I live," he said, "I shall never forget it. When the flag fell . . . the big brown horse wheeled and gathered himself for a spring. He seemed to rise to an awful height, then he sprang forward, and in a twinkling he was in front."[1] Longfellow covered distance in tremendous bounds, his hooves sweeping along in strides twenty-six feet long. As he went by, a *Spirit of the Times* correspondent reported, "he le[ft] a rumbling sound, not unlike that of a storm cloud rattling along the ridges of a mountain."[2]

There was only one horse that could match him, knowledgeable racing men believed. That was Harry Bassett, a son of Lexington a year younger than Longfellow, the property of the horse trader and former slave dealer David McDaniel. McDaniel's stables led the nation in winnings in the early 1870s, but the old man particularly treasured his athletic young champion. His son, Henry McDaniel, who trained 1918 Kentucky Derby winner Exterminator, recounted his father's opinion of the animal succinctly: "My father thought there was no horse in the world like Harry Bassett."[3] Bassett's rider was the teenage James Rowe, a white boy born in Richmond, Virginia, whom the sharp-eyed McDaniel had allegedly pulled out of a job at a hotel newsstand. When he stepped aboard Harry Bassett, the fourteen-year-old Rowe already reigned as America's leading rider. At twenty-four, he would become the youngest trainer ever to win the Kentucky Derby, and he would go on to condition more American champions than any other trainer in the history of the sport.[4]

Racing fans waited eagerly to see if the two horses would meet in a clash of giants. George Armstrong Custer, writing as a special correspondent for the new racing magazine *Turf, Field and Farm*, visited John Harper's farm in the winter of 1871 and asked the question in the minds of thousands of people. Would the old man bring his champion east during the racing season of 1872? Would he match him against Harry Bassett? Harper answered confidently. "I don't say I am agoin to run agin any particular horse," he cautioned, "but I do say that I am goin to git my horse ready, and when the time comes I am agoin to the races at Long Branch and will run Longfellow agin any horse what wants to run agin him, and, gentlemen, thar's no livin horse can run with my horse if he is in fix to run."[5] Custer, who rode a son of Lexington in the Battle of Little Big Horn, was an enthusiastic horseman, and he thoroughly enjoyed discussing Longfellow with his owner.[6] But his affectionately folksy rendering of the old man was hardly unique. Magazines and newspapers across America delighted in depicting John Harper, the crude but canny old man in the white suit who went by "Uncle John."

The Northern press painted Harper's Nantura Farm as an interracial utopia for men who adored horses. Custer professed himself unsurprised to discover during his visit that "the youngest boy, white or black, can correctly trace the pedigree of every prominent horse, and give the time of each prominent race, with the place of each horse. He would not be a Kentuckian of the Blue Grass region if unable to do this."[7] Many Northerners liked to imagine that such mutual interests tightened bonds of long affection that drew former masters and freedpeople together. A *New York Times* correspondent at New Jersey's Monmouth Park, who had come to view Longfellow, reported that "I spoke with admiration, and the colored grooms listened with delight to my praise of their favorite. They love the horses of Mr. Harper as much as he does, and they love him as much as they do the horses."[8]

Only a few months before Custer's article went to press, Harper's brother and sister had been brutally murdered in the farmhouse at Nantura. As local law enforcement searched for the killers, Harper condoned the nighttime work of vigilantes, who tortured a black woman and boy as they interrogated them about the crime.[9] Northern journalists and racing enthusiasts largely ignored the episode and embraced Harper as a tender and sentimental old man, with a devotion to Longfellow that excited sympathy over and above all else. "We heard the remark made by one gentleman," a *Spirit of the Times* writer noted, "that it would kill old John if his horse was beaten, while being struck by lightning would not kill Col. McDaniel."[10]

David McDaniel carried a hard-edged reputation, which he had more than earned in his prewar career as a Richmond slave trader. He had lived in New Jersey since 1868, when he took over the management of a racetrack in Secaucus.[11] But moving north had not altered McDaniel's ideas about the best and most convenient stable help.[12] Black men were indispensable to dealing with the hot-tempered Harry Bassett. McDaniel firmly warned a Saratoga reporter that Bassett was one of the meanest animals the longtime horseman had ever dealt with. The writer warily eyed the champion, only to see a fourteen-year-old groom stroll into his stall and go to work with no difficulty. McDaniel's black stablemen handled his high-spirited horses "in a manner that would involve coroner's fees in the case of an outsider," the reporter wryly observed.[13]

McDaniel's riders were often former slaves as well. Most notable was Albert, described as "black as the ace of spades," whom McDaniel had purchased as a three-month-old baby. New York reporter Melville Landon asked the boy how long he had been with his present employer and was surprised when Albert casually responded that it had been about twenty years. Landon pointed out that Albert wasn't yet twenty years old, only to have Albert reply, "Wal, I'ze done been with Major Mac all my life. Sometimes down in Virgin, and sometimes up at the Patterson track—then over to Nashville and Memphis." Slavery might have ended legally, but it lived on in spirit in David McDaniel's stables, even if they were now headquartered firmly north of the Mason-Dixon line. Bondage, especially the itinerant, highly skilled life of a horseman, the story suggested, had not been about coercion but about long-cherished affection between master and slave. "McDaniel, who is a plain, blunt old Virginian," Landon rhapsodized, "fairly worships the boy, who, in turn, looks upon the Major as the very Caesar of the track."[14] Mark Twain, scrawling in the margin of his copy of Landon's work, called it "The Droolings of an Idiot," but not everyone had Twain's unblinking intolerance for the saccharine and self-satisfied.[15]

In the summer of 1872, the wait to see Longfellow and Harry Bassett do battle finally ended when both entered the Monmouth Cup at the racetrack at Long Branch. Longfellow rode the Pennsylvania Central railroad from Kentucky to New Jersey for the race, in a special car marked with a sign that read, "Longfellow going to Long Branch to meet his friend Harry Bassett." Wherever the train stopped, crowds gathered to gawk at him.[16] On the day of the race, a crowd of between 25,000 and 40,000 thronged to the course, despite the blazing heat. The spectators "were of all classes," the *New York Times* reported. "There was the rough . . . there was the sturdy laborer, there was the intelligent mechanic. . . . There were tradesmen, bankers, brokers, railway men, oil men." The ferries carrying passengers to New Jersey from New York sank so low in the water that the decks were awash.[17] The crowds packed in so tightly that the *Spirit of the Times* compared them to "the negroes from Guinea in the holds of the ancient slave ships over the charnel-house of the sea, the accursed middle passage."[18]

That it seemed appropriate to compare the horrors of the slave trade to a briefly unpleasant summer ferry trip suggested just how

little many white Americans wanted to confront the realities of human bondage. Instead, racing fans turned for a softly reassuring
portrait of slavery and its legacies to the stables of Longfellow and
Harry Bassett. The two racing stars were surrounded by "their true
and trusty bands of dusky retainers," grooms, trainers, and jockeys,
who worked with well-chronicled diligence and loyalty.[19] "Mr.
Harper has been in the habit of raising his own riders as well as
horses and corn," *Turf, Field and Farm* informed its readers.[20]
Harper was said to have rejected the urgings of his friends to put a
prominent white jockey in the saddle for the Monmouth Cup. "I
will ride my own nigger and . . . gentlemen, if he is beaten I will be
satisfied, as I will know that I got an honest ride," he explained his
reasoning.[21] Lifelong subordination produced a mystical bond of
unbreakable fidelity between master and laborer, an unshakable
guarantee of honesty, no less a source than the *New York Times* insisted. On the way to the post, their racing correspondent reported,
he had seen one bettor offer John Sample, Longfellow's black jockey,
a $50 bill if he won, adding, "The darkey smiled pleasantly and
showed his white teeth as he looked at his master, John Harper, as if
to say, 'I'll take it, but I win for massa's sake.'"[22]

The race was a close one. Sample kept his towering horse under
wraps until the homestretch, when he let Longfellow sail away from
Harry Bassett.[23] Two weeks later, the horses met again at Saratoga,
and this time Bassett took victory by a narrow margin. "Hats and
sticks literally darkened the air," an observer reported, "and I am
not sure that many a colored stable-boy was not tossed aloft for
joy."[24] But there would be no third race to decide ultimate supremacy, as there had been between Lexington and Lecomte. During
the contest, one of Longfellow's immense shoes had twisted and
bent in half, bruising and tearing his foot as he continued to run to
the finish with all the will of his tremendous heart. The injury
ended his racing career.[25] Visitors crowded around his stall, watching the great horse holding his lame hoof up and John Harper
weeping quietly as he looked at him.[26] The young black horseman
Andrew Jackson, who had come from the Bluegrass, remembered as
an old man that the whole state of Kentucky "mourned an' wore
crepe."[27]

But Longfellow's loss only increased his fascination. A Kentuckian who visited the horse in retirement in 1874 found him even more awesome in repose than he had been as a winning runner and proffered a telling comparison to illustrate his point: "There always seemed to me to be a kinship between Robert E. Lee and Longfellow; there is the same noble kindliness, the same gentle grandeur and the same look of quiet, unassuming heroism about them. I was never more struck with it than on this occasion." There had been two Northern men visiting to examine Longfellow, he noted, but they had no idea of the importance of what they were seeing. To them, he was a "fine horse" and nothing more.[28] A week later, the *New York Times* reprinted the account of the visit verbatim, with no comment on the story's appeal to Southern loyalties or disdain of Northerners' supposed inability to understand Longfellow's true claims to glory.[29]

The *Times* reprint was a dispatch from a new racing world, the home of a growing coalition of powerful men who knew the outcome of the Civil War but believed they could still shape what its result would mean. Northern turfmen would allow their Southern comrades to trumpet the grandeur of the Confederacy, because they shared with them a fear of the consequences of emancipation and of the larger question of what a free America would look like.

In the years of Reconstruction, the wealthy and politically influential turned to the track as generations of men before them had—as a place that could prove the right to rule, a site for modeling and displaying hierarchies, a meeting ground for potential allies. The leaders of the American racetrack in the 1860s and 1870s hoped to give postbellum freedom a set of meanings congenial to themselves and their political and economic associates. Their close attention to the black men who worked with Longfellow and Harry Bassett, their eager ascription of feelings of happy fidelity and self-abnegation, suggested just how much they feared the potentially revolutionary consequences of freedom. They had cause to fear, because the men who worked the great stars of the track were former slaves, who performed in the public eye and shaped daily the meaning of a free life. Even as a reunited coalition of wealthy turfmen used the racetrack to imagine and further a deeply conservative vision of postwar

America, they depended on black men who reminded them constantly of the potential threats to that conservatism.

Longfellow and Harry Bassett's duels on Northern tracks were landmarks in a new epoch in American racing. The era began with the founding of a new track. The prominent trainer Sam Hildreth, who grew up in Missouri, remembered that his father reminded him every year on his birthday, "In the year 1866 two big things happened in these here United States. In Independence, Missouri, Samuel C. Hildreth was born; in New York, they started racing at Jerome Park." His upbringing, Hildreth conceded, had been such that, in his youth, he had vaguely imagined that the Battle of Lexington had taken place in New Orleans in 1855, when Lexington defeated Lecomte for the second time.[30] But Jerome Park made an impression even on Americans less horse-obsessed than the Hildreths.

Wealthy New Yorker Leonard Jerome, already a Saratoga shareholder, had purchased a large piece of land in the still-rural Fordham neighborhood of the Bronx in 1865. By the time Jerome finished building the racetrack he thought New York deserved, it boasted an elaborate clubhouse, equipped with a ballroom, facilities for shooting and sleighing, and a variety of opulent amenities that impressed even Jerome's friends. Jerome Park was expressly designed as a playground for the rich, and its exclusivity appealed to New Yorkers with money to spend and those who wished to emulate them. "Society had pronounced in favor of racing and Jerome Park became the Mecca of fashion," summed up Walter Vosburgh, the turn-of-the-century handicapper and turf historian.[31] Jerome Park's success led to the construction of the Monmouth Park track at Long Branch, New Jersey, in 1870, and Jerome himself invested in a sprawling and lucrative track at Sheepshead Bay, Long Island, in 1879.[32] The surge in popularity of New York racing also benefited John Morrissey's established track at Saratoga, where hoteliers prepared for more guests than ever. In 1874, the new Grand Union Hotel unveiled more than eight hundred rooms and over two miles of hallways.[33]

"Racing . . . is the native sport of the South, and we hope that her turf associations will soon become as prosperous and flourishing as they were in days of yore," proclaimed the new Kentucky-edited magazine *Turf, Field and Farm* in November 1865, only months after Appomattox.[34] But five years of devastating war and the emancipation of millions of people had taken an irrevocable toll on Southern racing. The Washington Course in Charleston was unavailable to its former owners because it had been taken over by the Freedmen's Bureau.[35] In December 1865, the Metairie Jockey Club announced that it would start holding race meetings again, but the races only continued until 1872, when the owners of the Metairie Course sold the track to a local businessman, who turned the area into a cemetery.[36] Southern racing would never completely recover its absolute power. The centers of influence in the world of the American Thoroughbred had moved North.

So Southerners no longer had the luxury of waiting for the best horses in America to come to them. But they were undeterred. Only a month after Joseph E. Johnston had surrendered to William Tecumseh Sherman in North Carolina, William J. Minor, John M. Clay, and Robert Alexander served as official timers for the races at St. Louis.[37] Minor visited the site of Jerome Park while it was under construction and expressed the hope that "the completion of the Park would inaugurate a brighter era of the Turf."[38] Minor's old friend Duncan Kenner often appeared in impeccable formal attire for the races at Jerome Park and so impressed Northern racing men that the Saratoga track named the Kenner Stakes for him in 1870.[39] John B. Irving, for many years the secretary of the South Carolina Jockey Club, left his war-torn home in 1865 and moved to the New York area, where he promptly became the secretary of the American Jockey Club, the governing body of the races at Jerome Park.[40] Indeed, Southerners were disproportionately represented in the upper echelon of the American Jockey Club.[41] They might mourn the passing of many of their own tracks, but they still loved the Thoroughbred. New York racing brought them eagerly forward "to march upon the Northern route as they used to do when Planet was king . . . of Long Island."[42]

But the turf-lovers who held sway in racing's very highest circles were now Wall Street men, who loved speed and risk. Membership in the American Jockey Club was a social necessity for New York's stock market kings, steel and tobacco magnates, and railroad barons—Vanderbilts, Roosevelts, Carnegies, Lorillards, and Harrimans.[43] "When a new animal is to be brought out and shown off, whose time is remarkable," Matthew Hale Smith reported, "Wall Street is as excited . . . as if a great 'corner' was pending."[44]

Such news was eagerly awaited in the counting house of August Belmont, the president of the American Jockey Club.[45] Belmont had owned no racehorses at the time he took office, but he had maroon and red officially listed as his stable colors, and he promptly began purchasing good runners to wear his silks.[46] Belmont wanted to win, and he generally got what he wanted. In his midtwenties, he had arrived in New York under his birth name of Schonberg as a representative of the European financial giant, the House of Rothschild. The bankers had ordered him to New York to make a rapid assessment of the American economic crisis of the late 1830s; he was then to proceed to Havana. Disregarding his orders completely, he took an office on Wall Street and announced himself the agent of the Rothschilds in the United States. He then promptly went to work at climbing into the American upper crust, changing his name to Belmont and marrying Caroline Slidell Perry, the daughter of Commodore Matthew Perry and the niece of John Slidell, prominent Southern Democrat and former diplomat for the Confederate government.[47]

Racing news was welcome in rougher circles as well. Tammany Hall sachem William Marcy Tweed and his rival in machine politics John Morrissey, who was elected to Congress in 1866, remained prominent New York turfmen throughout the 1870s.[48] Tweed's Americus Club, Tammany's exclusive insiders' organization, limited to a hundred of the most influential of the boss's colleagues and subordinates, held jubilant clambakes to the sound of brass bands at the Monmouth Park races.[49] Tweed had spent some of the profits garnered in a long career in graft on a palatial stable at his home. "In some respects it is better to be one of Mr. Tweed's horses than a poor tax-payer of this City," the *New York Times* opined caustically.[50]

The track was a great solvent of social divides, as wealth provided a common denominator in the owners' boxes.

But no one felt the track's fascination more strongly than the man who founded Jerome Park. Leonard Jerome had started out as a newspaper owner in Rochester and had made his fortune on Wall Street in New York railroad stock.[51] He personally drove a four-in-hand of looming matched bays, each nearly six feet high at the shoulder, and he owned some of the prominent runners of the 1860s and 1870s, like Kentucky, perhaps the greatest racer of all Lexington's sons.[52] In a moment of glee, he once lifted his daughter Jenny onto the horse's back, an experience she remembered all her life.[53] When Jenny married Lord Randolph Churchill and gave birth to her first son, Winston Leonard Spencer Churchill, one old racing friend wrote to the proud grandfather, "Interesting breeding. Stamina always goes through the dam, and pace through the sire." Mrs. Jerome was said to have been appalled. Her husband, as comfortable with equine comparisons as he was uncomfortable with sentimentality, thoroughly approved and hoped for great things.[54]

Jerome proudly presided over Jerome Park's grand opening in the autumn of 1866. The track featured the new dash races, which had overtaken old-style heat racing. In dash racing, the horses ran only a single set distance, as modern Thoroughbreds do. Antebellum jockeys had made their careers in heat racing, in which a rider had to conserve his horse's energy jealously. In dash racing, a jockey's strategic decisions had to come with split-second precision, as he pushed his horse for the ultimate effort at the right moment, knowing there would be no second chances. In the first contest on opening day, before a crowd of thousands, including special guest Ulysses S. Grant, Abe let Robert Alexander's Bayswater swoop past the early leaders for the win. Jerome was so impressed that he put Abe in the saddle on his own Fleetwing later in the afternoon.[55] Abe's victories helped to propel Jerome Park to success and secure the patronage of wealthy Northerners for the new style of Thoroughbred racing. But his much-publicized presence and continued dominance also suggested how deeply the track was enmeshed in the greatest question to emerge out of the Civil War—in a new nation, where slaves had been emancipated and the national government had taken on a new role as guarantor of the rights of citizenship, what would freedom mean for Americans, both black and white?

Horses had been an integral part of the war for the men in the field. In his lyrical description of the final review of the Army of the Potomac, General Joshua Lawrence Chamberlain mourned that "we shall see them no more together,—these men, these horses, these colors afield."[56] To include the animals in his awe for his troops and their banners came naturally to Chamberlain, who recalled long night marches like the ones late in the Virginia campaigns of 1864 and 1865, when men had slid from their saddles exhausted, arms looped through their reins to tether their mounts in place: "Horses stood with drooping heads just above their masters' faces. All dreaming—one knows not what, of past or coming, possible or fated."[57] Only those who had been there could understand some dreams of war, some nightmares, and soldiers did not forget the animals who had marched and dozed alongside them. After Appomattox, horses easily became emotionally charged symbols, as some men used them to express how bitterly they still felt their differences, how strong their loyalty still was to old allegiances, how much they feared the changes that peace would bring.

No symbol more completely embodied the stubborn commitment of the defeated South to its heroes and its slave society than Robert E. Lee on horseback. Defeated Confederate soldiers had brought home strands of Traveller's tail as keepsakes of their lost cause.[58] When a projected design for a Lee monument in Richmond mounted the general on a horse with a bobbed tail, many Southerners were furious. The notoriously choleric ex-Confederate Jubal Early wrote to the governor of Virginia that if the design were selected, he would "feel like collecting the survivors of the 2nd Corps, and going . . . to blow up the thing with dynamite."[59] They wanted their beloved leader enshrined in stone aboard a mighty warhorse, with a sweeping flag of a tail, the only suitable mount for a man who still commanded their allegiance. They delighted in a story told of Traveller that, after Lee died in 1870, one of the general's daughters directed a young black stable hand to exercise the horse. But, though he had always been docile for Lee, Traveller refused even to allow the boy to mount. Finally, a white college student from Texas climbed aboard the horse, and Traveller behaved perfectly. In telling and retelling the story, Southerners, of course, completely ignored the realities of the equine world; black men would have worked with Traveller throughout his life. But they did not love the story for its accuracy; they insisted on it because it seemed to demonstrate that horses knew instinctively who was meant to master and who was not.[60] Traveller, revered as a Confederate symbol, still clung to the immutable codes of racial hierarchy.

Northerners had their own equestrian hero to venerate. Ulysses S. Grant loved a spirited horse. During his tour of duty in Mexico as a young officer, he had ended up with the one mount available, a three-year-old wild mustang only recently captured. The beginning of the day's march, Grant admitted, "was the first time the horse had ever been under saddle. I had, however, but little difficulty in breaking him, though for the first day there were frequent disagreements between us as to which way we should go, and sometimes whether we should go at all. . . . [B]ut after that, I had as tractable a horse as any with the army, and there was none that stood the trip better."[61] Grant's taciturnity does not mask his astonishing equestrian feat, nor does it conceal his affection for the animal that carried him. Northerners after the war were fond of pointing to his warhorse throughout the crushing, endless battles of 1864 and 1865. Lee might have had Traveller, but Grant had ridden Cincinnati, a son of Lexington himself. Union veterans liked to recall that when President Lincoln visited the lines, Grant loaned him Cincinnati.[62] Their leaders were amply qualified for the pantheon of mounted heroes; they, too, excelled at one of the essential skills of powerful men. Such men had proved themselves eminently worthy to lead a postwar nation, to preside over a reconstructed and free United States.

Racing men saw in their own ranks the divisions wrought by the war and most deeply by the central questions that it had opened: If blacks were no longer slaves, what would be their place in the America the war had made? What shape would freedom take? What would be the texture of its daily reality? Former Whig stalwart John Minor Botts scoffed at white Southern fears that emancipated blacks would wreak havoc on the South. If there were a race war, he announced, it would be the fault of white vigilantes.[63] Robert Harlan served as a member of Ohio's Republican leadership and as a delegate at large at the Republican convention of 1872.[64] Such men were intent on playing a leading role in laying firm foundations for a new world. On the other side of the divide were men like William J. Minor. He assured his old friend Stephen Duncan that Louisiana sugar could still compete with Caribbean imports, even if the fields were worked with free labor: "If we could get rid of Northern interference with the freedmen, I think we could arrange matters so as to obtain at least one half as much labor as we did before. . . . The expenses in time will not be greater, and if we can get a proportionate income and price, we may do, in a pecuniary sense, as well as ever. But the satisfaction of planting on a well regulated plantation is gone."[65] Emancipation had killed the vision of a perfectly structured, productive United States, a meticulously ordered slave plantation writ large, that had long inspired Minor. But with authority in the right hands, some vestiges of security, hierarchy, and productivity could be maintained.

Racing's disputes and the conflicts of the outside world were inextricably intertwined. In 1867, Southern racing men sought to form what they called a Turf Congress, in which they could meet and decide a unified regional policy on racing matters. It was an absolutely necessary step, one of its organizers insisted, because Southerners needed to make clear that they were "sufficiently strong to manage our own affairs in every department and the sooner we convince some people east of the Alleghenies of this fact, the sooner will we occupy our true positions."[66] If Reconstruction and its federal intervention into questions of African American labor and citizenship were to be thwarted, the racetrack would be one place where the battle would be joined.

Indeed, the demands of black citizenship had invaded the space of the racetrack itself. In May 1865, a huge procession of black Charlestonians honored the Union prisoners of war who had been buried in hastily dug and unmarked graves at the Washington Course. Thousands of black schoolchildren marched around the track singing

"John Brown's Body," followed by their elders. They deposited flowers ceremoniously on the graves, then watched as several regiments of black troops drilled in the track's infield. The celebration is now widely recognized as the first Memorial Day. The Charleston racetrack, so long haunted by slaves lost and sold away, had been consecrated to the dream of African American freedom.[67] In New Orleans, black men made the racetrack a place in which to stretch the boundaries of that freedom. When white authorities instituted segregation in the track grandstand, black racing enthusiasts sued the Louisiana Jockey Club for the right to integrated facilities at the course, and the black press applauded their efforts. "It should be remembered," the *Weekly Louisianian* noted, "that cases of this kind are not mere personal issues, but, that in a correct solution of them lies the settlement of the vexed question of Civil Rights, which is a matter of vital importance to every colored man in the State of Louisiana."[68]

IN THE RACING PRESS, buckets of ink were spent on the political legacies of the war. George Wilkes's *Spirit* enthusiastically endorsed Grant over Democrat Horatio Seymour in the 1868 presidential contest. "If you believe," Wilkes's editorial column trumpeted, ". . . that Wilkes Booth was a hero and Lincoln a gorilla, and that the dagger of Brutus should be again unsheathed . . . then vote as you believe. But we do *not* believe in these things, and, holding the firm faith that the election of Grant would be a blessing to the whole country . . . we give him our earnest and undivided support."[69] The gains of the war must be jealously guarded. Southern oligarchy had been humbled, but it must not be allowed to grasp again for its former power.

Wilkes particularly despised Southerners who threatened his business interests, and the Bruce brothers seemed poised to do just that. The Bruces were Kentuckians, the brothers-in-law of Confederate raider John Hunt Morgan. They thus had impeccable Southern credentials, and Benjamin Gratz Bruce, the younger brother, had been a Confederate sympathizer during the war.[70] In contrast, Sanders Deweese Bruce had risen to the rank of colonel in the

Union Army. But immediately after the war he and Benjamin made their peace and turned to their first allegiance, their passion for Thoroughbreds. In August 1865, with the dust of battle not yet settled, they began publishing the magazine *Turf, Field and Farm*. In 1868, Sanders Bruce, after a lifetime obsessed with equine pedigrees, brought out the first volume of his *American Stud Book*, in an attempt to chronicle definitively the heritage of every American Thoroughbred.[71] The Bruce brothers' new periodical was designed to provide Southern subscribers with a turf magazine that more assiduously reported on their local tracks and addressed their regional concerns. *Turf, Field and Farm*'s allegiance to Southern racial hierarchy was complete and bluntly expressed. "We believe that the pure Caucasian represents the species as God created it. It is the fountainhead, and the other varieties are modifications of it. These modifications have been established by time, and now they are as separate and distinct as the first ancestral character itself," the magazine proclaimed. Science established that black equality was a ludicrous political fantasy.[72]

Wilkes responded to the presence of rivals with his usual vituperation, pillorying *Turf, Field and Farm*'s editorial staff with gusto. The middle-aged Sanders Bruce, Wilkes assured his readers, "is the boy on whom the most grave responsibilities of the concern depend. He trades the horses, sells the dogs, buys the game chickens, and does the drinking."[73] But the Bruces' unapologetically Southern biases armored them against such barbs, and they retained a loyal Southern following and an increasingly tolerant Northern one.

"It would be an unjust reflection upon the gallantry of the Federal troops to attempt to disparage the bravery of the Confederate soldiers," *Turf, Field and Farm* announced in a laudatory article on Stonewall Jackson in 1866. "The grass is growing upon the graves of thousands of fallen braves, and to the mind of the soldier, they are heroes alike."[74] *Turf, Field and Farm*'s subscribers applauded this new voice on the scene, with its appeal for Northern recognition of the South's martial valor, without reference to her war aims. Here was a view of the war that did honor to all white combatants and elided the debate over causes and consequences. This sort of rhetoric and its burgeoning appeal to a national audience reflected the personal and political reunion that took hold at the track and strengthened its grip in the owners' boxes.[75]

The racetrack of the late 1860s was full of stories of happy reunion. William Cottrill of Alabama, at ease on the terrace of a hotel near Monmouth Park in New Jersey, was said to have met up with a man against whom he had fought at Mobile Bay. Both were delighted and "washed out all the lines and bridged the 'bloody chasm' with champagne. . . . They were fast friends after."[76] Racing men still spoke the same language about the things they treasured. When Fairman Rogers, a prominent Northern racing enthusiast, secured his copy of the first volume of Sanders Bruce's *American Stud Book*, in which each entry included the horse's pedigree for seven generations, he annotated the reference with exquisite care. Next to the entry for the mare Idlewild, he carefully corrected the date of birth for a foal she had delivered that had not survived. He meticulously noted that he knew his date was the right one, because he remembered a conversation with Robert Alexander at Jerome Park in 1866 on the subject.[77] When that level of care united two men, other loyalties tended to recede at least temporarily into the background, even so soon after the war. In 1870, Hamilton Busbey summed up the racetrack of the postwar period, "It was a theatre on which men of all political opinions could meet in social enjoyment. . . . It was the only practical means of reunion at the time. Men who, a few months before, had faced each other on the battle-field, stood side by side on the race-course, enthusiastically applauding the silken-coated thorough-breds."[78]

No wonder, then, that the *Spirit of the Times* touted the turf, as one headline put it in 1868, "as a Means of Restoring Cordial Relations." "Neither legislative enactments, nor the operations of commerce, nor the dealings of finance, are, in our opinion, as effective towards the restoration of real, frank, cordial, good feeling as the gathering together of many able and influential men from most of the States at the great race meetings," it proclaimed.[79] The government, it suggested, could make no better investment in national reunion than to provide prize money to the sport. John B. Irving, secretary at Jerome Park as he had been for so many years at the Washington Course, saw in the New York races the same cohesive power he had seen on race day in Charleston thirty years earlier. He even used the same tobacco-scented metaphor to describe the blossoming friendships he envisioned. Competition on the track, he wrote in 1866, "will do much to unite the people of the North and South—soften any asperities that may remain, draw long separated friends and a large influential class once more together, to smoke the calumet of peace, and to feel, by a warm grasping of hands, they are now one and indivisible, in a common brotherhood of affection and interest."[80]

THAT "LARGE INFLUENTIAL CLASS" made its home in both North and South and its money in a diverse array of fields, including agriculture, merchant banking, railroad building, and manufacturing. The Civil War had created a new American economy, which the wealthy were determined to protect. Growing companies expanded horizontally and vertically into conglomerates of unprecedented size for which thousands of men labored with only limited possibility of advancement. The free labor dream of so many Republicans and working-class Democrats like George Wilkes foundered in the face of postwar economic consolidation. Laborers could barely hope for promotion within the hierarchy of the shop floor, while their dreams of saving to become independent proprietors on land or in commerce faded into impossibility. Meanwhile, staunch Republicans and indignant Democrats insisted that it was not the business of the government to intervene in labor arrangements; to do so would be grossly unfair. The only guarantee the United States offered was a free chance, not an equal one. Those disadvantaged to begin with must redouble their efforts to succeed, if they wished to catch up with the industrial princes who controlled their workplaces. Government support for railroads and manufacturers should not be mistaken for interference; it was instead an appropriate investment in national prosperity and progress.[81]

Owners and proprietors held up the idea of contract as a universal solvent. Their idealized vision of free labor depicted a man with a contract as a man who had entered freely into a codified arrangement with his employer; the contract employee was the new embodiment of postbellum freedom. Both parties to a contract were expected to bargain shrewdly to gain advantages. A man with a contract thus had no standing to complain about his treatment. It was, however, usually the voices of men who were not contract workers that sounded loudest in praise of the system, because contract workers knew all too well just how much benefit they could secure out of a contract negotiated when they had no leverage. Men who worked under contract in railroad yards, coal mines, and manufacturing plants had no guarantee that their wages would feed their families, no restrictions on hours or conditions of work, no assistance provided if they were injured or killed on the job, and no hope for anything better than another equally wretched arrangement at the end of the stipulated term of employment.[82]

Contract had gained particular prominence through its use as a means of regulating free labor by ex-slaves under the auspices of the Freedmen's Bureau. To a growing and vocal group of wealthy white men, the great American divide was now not one between North and South or between black and white, but between affluent men who deserved to be left unfettered and laborers who sought to disrupt American industry for their own selfish ends. Once the Constitution technically guaranteed the abolition of slavery, equality before national law, and suffrage for black men, any further governmental assistance to former slaves would amount to unjustifiable special treatment that would, in turn, inspire white working-class agitation.

Many Northern Democrats decried Reconstruction in a calculated effort to secure white Southern support and rebuild a national coalition en route to a return to power. But other wealthy Northerners, too, were coming to see white Southerners as useful junior partners in an expanding national economy and valuable allies against the dangerous potential of unified workers.[83] Southerners must be left alone to manage their own affairs, as Northerners wished to be when confronted with strikers and other dissidents.[84] James Gordon Bennett Jr.'s *New York Herald* blamed the rise of crime and violence in the South on Reconstruction governments and on black corruption and lawlessness. The actions of reformers and former slaves, the *Herald* announced, "half justify the acts of the Ku Klux Klan and other illegal secret societies."[85] If white

Southerners felt the need to murder, rape, burn, and pillage to enforce their authority, it was a regrettable necessity forced upon them
by their former slaves.

The coterie of racing men affiliated with the American Jockey
Club turned to the track to shape a free nation to their own ends,
tightening the bonds that drew them together and made them a political force to be reckoned with.[86] "They suggest to my fancy the
swarming vastness—the multifarious possibilities of activities—of
our young civilization," Henry James wrote of the wealthy horsemen
gathered at Saratoga in 1870. "They come from the utmost ends of
the Union. . . . As they sit with their white hats tilted forward, and
their chairs tilted back, and their feet tilted up, and their cigars and
toothpicks forming various angles with these various lines, I seem
to see in their faces a tacit reference to the affairs of a continent."[87]
The amenities of racetrack areas like Saratoga appealed to people
from across the nation, including the South, as much as they had
before the war, and amity rather than animosity was the order of
the day.[88] "At other watering places, they *talked* stocks; at Saratoga
they *bought* and *sold* them," William Worthington Fowler explained.[89]
The track was one of the sites where real cash and real power were
allocated and exchanged. Sportsmen, enjoying the comfortable ter-
races of the Saratoga hotels or the Louis Quatorze-furnished clubhouse at Jerome Park, preferred to ignore sectional divides when
they could.[90] They had other business to do.

The most prominent political man on the turf was undoubtedly
August Belmont, now securely established as an American representative of the Rothschilds. Belmont had culminated his social
climbing as chairman of the Democratic National Committee and
president of the American Jockey Club.[91] In wartime, he had helped
to recruit German American regiments, had given large sums to
soldiers' charities, and had offered his assistance to the Lincoln administration in negotiating with foreign powers.[92] But he remained
willing to defer to the South on the subject of slavery, and his support for former Union commander and Democratic candidate
George B. McClellan, who proposed making peace with the South
in 1864, disgusted some of his neighbors. The always-acerbic George
Templeton Strong reported gleefully that he had seen Belmont

turned away at a polling place in the election of 1864, on the grounds that he was known to have laid a bet on the election. "Very few men would have been challenged on that ground," Strong admitted, "but this foreign money-dealer has made himself uncommonly odious, and the bystanders, mostly of the Union persuasion, chuckled over his discomfiture."[93] Belmont's opinions might render him anathema to stern Republican New Yorkers, but his flamboyance and his tolerance of Southerners made him a powerful leader in Reconstruction-era racing. While many of Belmont's fellow turfmen did not embrace the Democratic Party, they shared a broader commitment to a postbellum entrepreneurial conservatism, a belief in the sanctity of rich men's power to order their own business and the nation's, an antipathy toward government intervention in questions of civic equality and economic justice.[94] As turfmen in the 1860s and 1870s enjoyed the warmth of racetrack reunion, they felt their convictions take solid and stubborn form.

As generations of prominent men had before them, racing men of the 1870s created in miniature at the track the political and economic structures they favored, and they strengthened the bonds of camaraderie and common interest that could give their models formative power on a national scale. In the world of the racetrack at Jerome Park, governed by American Jockey Club rules, a jockey or groom could not switch employers without receiving written permission from the owner or trainer whom he was leaving. If he secured no such permission, his new employer would be forbidden from running horses at the track. In effect, if a racetrack laborer tried to change the conditions of his employment in one of the only ways open to him—by withdrawing his labor—he destroyed his chances to work at all, since no one would hire him. The corresponding rule protecting stable help from their employers stipulated that, *if* an employer had not paid one of his workers for three months, and *if* the worker complained in person, imperiling his continued employment, and *if* the secretary of the Jockey Club decided that the claim was justified, the employer would be disciplined.[95] In the world that they controlled, the wealthy men of the American Jockey Club had their labor problem worked out to their satisfaction. They demonstrated their abiding faith in contract's capacity to ensure the continuing authority of employers and the necessary subordination of laborers.

At the track rich men could demonstrate how different their money made them from the rest of the crowd in the infield, "people who didn't know a Thoroughbred from a jackass," men who were there to bet more than they could afford of the four or five hundred dollars a year a skilled worker earned in New York in 1870.[96] Just as Southern planters had demonstrated their right to rule at tracks in Charleston and New Orleans, the emergent elite of the new post-bellum nation demonstrated their presumed superiority. A working-man could pray that good fortune would visit him in the betting ring. The men who paid his salary did not need luck; their leisure to study the horses gave them a significant advantage in assessing the odds. They could afford to regard the sport as an amusement; they could pride themselves on their stoicism and resigned bonhomie when their entries were defeated. "Racing," August Belmont famously summed up, "is for the rich."[97] It illustrated for their own peace of mind and for public consumption how much more like each other they were than like the rest of the crowds.

The racetrack in New York drew men of power together—from railroad barons and manufacturers and bankers to politicians and planters eager to assert their continued power and significance. "Between the races," longtime jockey club official Walter Vosburgh remembered, "gentlemen met on the quarter stretch in earnest and often intense discussion on the topics of the hour . . . so intense that, sometimes, each would hold the other by the sleeve, and pound each other's shoulder in disputes over the stamina of the Eclipse colts or the relative stud merits of Lexington and Leamington."[98] Questions like the qualities of America's greatest Thoroughbred stallions drew them together and fueled their shoulder-pounding intimacy. But the topics of the hour on the backstretch were not always or exclusively equine. Racing men spoke, too, of the most pressing issues of the day, including what the legacies of the Civil War should be. Indeed, at Jerome Park in 1871, August Belmont left the grandstand in the middle of a heated discussion about Republican Senator Charles Sumner's powers in Congress in order to berate his jockey for losing the Westchester Cup with his racer

Glenelg.[99] In his capacity as Democratic National Committee chairman, Belmont hoped to find a man who could successfully carry the banner of Northern capitalists and their Southern allies to national power. And he knew where to find such a man—at the track.

At Saratoga in 1871, Senator Thomas Bayard Jr. of Delaware had served as a race day judge, but he had carefully solicited the assistance of Duncan Kenner and Paul Hebert of Louisiana.[100] Belmont had seen in his fellow turfman's racetrack behavior the model for the statesmanship he thought should lead the country. Bayard behaved in the halls of Congress precisely as he did at the track. He had spoken strongly on behalf of the readmission of Mississippi's delegation to Congress in 1870, arguing that the state's wealthy whites would best govern it. Echoing the fears of other Northern turfmen, he warned in 1872 that a powerful federal government, mandated to intervene in state affairs, could turn its attention from the South to the North with potentially disastrous consequences.[101] The argument that black civil rights must be protected left him wholly unmoved. He sat through the testimony of the congressional hearings on white vigilante violence in the Reconstruction South, heard firsthand accounts of men and women destroyed economically, assaulted, or murdered for daring to try to assert their worth as human beings. He signed the committee's minority report, deploring the violence but denying that much of it had even happened and suggesting that, if it had happened, it was justified by the manifest injustice of giving former slaves power over former slave masters.[102] When Charles Sumner proposed the integration of schools in Washington, D.C., in 1872, Bayard grandiloquently professed himself appalled and prayed on the Senate floor that "no blue-eyed, fair-haired child of any Senator on this floor, no little grandchild at that time of life when children are so open to impression and especially to evil impression, will ever be permitted to suffer by this proposed contact."[103]

A man who spoke in such terms was exactly the man Belmont thought he needed to advance the cause of the Democracy, as it courted Southerner planters and Northern industrialists. He and his turf associate and Democratic colleague, Saratoga track investor

John Hunter, eagerly supported Bayard's presidential hopes in the 1870s.[104] Meanwhile, Belmont wooed Boss Tweed, scrupulously treating him with the courtesy due a fellow turfman, rather than with the wariness of a carefully refined man of influence approaching a notorious political fixer.[105] The new Democracy would rely in part on the camaraderie of the turf to solidify the bonds of interest that united white Southerners infuriated by Reconstruction, wealthy Northerners who feared government interference in business, and city immigrants who relied on Democratic machines for patronage and power. Bayard's presidential hopes came to nothing, but the desires and fears that fueled his supporters helped to bring together a coalition behind the unlikely figure of Horace Greeley in the presidential election of 1872. The *Tribune* editor, formerly identified as a staunch advocate of Republican orthodoxy and black civil rights, had emerged since the war as a voice for reunion and indulgence toward white Southerners.[106]

George Wilkes spoke for the new faction in ringing tones. The war was over, he pronounced, and the questions over which it had been fought were settled once and for all. He was impatient with those white Southern Democrats "who are still howling about slavery and whether a negro shall be permitted to marry their sisters."[107] But he believed firmly that such men had become a tiresome and unimportant minority, that the Democratic Party could now stand for a powerful coalition of Americans who could not "comprehend why the Republican party must be made . . . a galvanized malignant corpse forever kicking at the unresisting South."[108] In the years since Wilkes had entered the racing world, the racetrack had brought him into elbow-rubbing proximity with entrenched privilege. He had even joined August Belmont, whom he had once condemned as an oligarch intent on disenfranchising the common man, in investment consortia.[109] Men like Wilkes looked at the industrial working class of the North, which seemed doomed to permanent subordination, and turned away from it and toward the employing class. They would stand with those they wished to emulate rather than those they feared they could once again become. As Wilkes rose in his profession, "his circle narrowed, step by step excluding those whom individual opportunity had neglected to humanize with wealth and power."[110] And Wilkes's fellow Gree-leyites similarly limited their own concerns. George Wilkes bet $20,000 on Greeley in the summer of 1872, though he insisted he seldom made any sort of wager. He had never bet on a horse race, he claimed, before he backed Longfellow in the Monmouth Cup that year.[111]

SOME READERS NO DOUBT GUFFAWED in disbelief at George Wilkes's declaration of probity, while others may have snorted their lack of surprise that he watched the odds too closely to take risks. But in laying bets on Greeley and Longfellow, Wilkes demonstrated his fidelity to a unified political vision. The Longfellow match dis-played the relations between former masters and former slaves as many prominent Northern men wanted to imagine them. In work-ing to elect Greeley, Wilkes and his allies sought to make national policy modeled on the world they believed they had created at the track, a world of skilled and loyal black men, of hierarchy and har-mony. Thomas Bayard, August Belmont, and their supporters feared what freedom would mean, how it would make itself felt in schools, churches, omnibuses, and children's minds. Postwar turf-men hoped that the track would help to limit freedom's revolution-ary possibilities.

"One of the best points in the character of the colored men is their strong love and devotion to the racehorse," one *Spirit of the Times* correspondent opined. "If you reconstruct the turf, all the whining hypocrites who are robbing your States and impoverishing your people cannot keep the negroes from going to the races; and by this means, among others, they will finally come to understand what the real good of the country demands, and what their fran-chises really mean."[112] The track had once fostered a conception of a highly skilled, precise, modern form of bondage governed by grada-tions of influence and manipulation, in which violence remained a largely unspoken but potent and omnipresent threat. Now turfmen hoped that the track could help form a similarly powerful vision of freedom. Black men might vote, but that would not necessarily over-turn established forms of hierarchy if they could be made to unite with former masters and masters' allies against the idea of racial equality. Making slavery had been a daily process. So, too, would be the making of freedom, and at the racetrack black men could display for others what it would "really mean."[113]

But in the places white turfmen hoped to affirm the limited freedom they had depicted with comfortable condescension at the Longfellow and Harry Bassett races, former slaves labored diligently to make their free lives according to their own understandings of what that meant. Black horsemen had continued in the same profession they had learned in slavery. They often worked for their former masters or acquaintances of their former masters, but they were no one's property. Their past in bondage had given them skills and reputations that the whole nation acknowledged, and they would now use those resources for their own benefit and that of their families and friends.[114]

The great names of the antebellum period were in evidence almost as soon as the war had ended. At Saratoga in August 1865, Hark appeared with a string of horses.[115] Anthony Hall, who had worked for William J. Minor as an assistant trainer, now supervised a barn full of African American boys and men. Hall was equally at home in Saratoga, where reporters found him "urbane and dignified," and in Mobile, where he conditioned a colt fathered by Voucher, one of Minor's stallions, a horse Hall had worked long before emancipation.[116] Slavery was at an end, but Anthony Hall could still apply the lessons he had learned from the sire to the son.

But the man who made the most decisive mark in Reconstruction racing was decidedly Ansel Williamson, who had impressed Southern owners for years before the war. Even the perpetually carping William J. Minor admitted that Williamson was "the best Negro trainer in the world and in truth a pretty fair hand with a horse."[117] In 1856, Robert Alexander had raced a colt named Ansel as a gesture of respect.[118] Both before freedom and after, Williamson worked in some of the most prominent stables on the American turf, including Alexander's famous Woodburn Farm. And in 1875 Williamson and the African American jockey Oliver Lewis assured themselves immortality as the trainer and rider of Aristides, the first Kentucky Derby winner. They were not alone in the history books. At least a dozen of the riders in the first Derby were African Americans, and black jockeys and trainers regularly won the Derby, as well as the other great fixtures of the period's racing calendar.[119] In 1870, Edward Brown, who had been born a slave on Woodburn Farm, where he was generally known as Alexander's Dick or Brown Dick, won the Belmont Stakes with Kingfisher, trained by the black horseman Raleigh Colston.[120]

Men like Abe, Ansel Williamson, and Edward Brown demonstrated publicly how all-encompassing freedom was, how many daily changes it entailed. Williamson was identified in the press with his full name, as white trainers were, in official lists of entries.[121] Abe, too, had adopted the surname Hawkins, though no contemporary periodical acknowledged it.[122] Even if they did not print his full name, when a *Wilkes's Spirit of the Times* correspondent ran into Hawkins in the crowd at the Jersey Derby, the two men shook hands. Abe had been a well-known figure in racing for over a decade. But only in a new world of freedom would a white man have extended his hand when he met the famous jockey.[123] Freedom was a daily series of tiny revolutions. The world had fundamentally changed, as the *Spirit of the Times* impatiently reminded its readers, after the magazine received a few letters from racing enthusiasts uncomfortable with black competitors. Their scruples were ridiculous, the *Spirit* scoffed. "Does any man with a pennyweight of brains think the less of Charles Littlefield or Gilpatrick because they ride against Abe or Albert or Alexander's Dick?"[124] Between the rails of the racetrack, at least, black men were to be the acknowledged equals of white ones.

In freedom, older men could pass on their skills to younger ones and hope to see privilege and experience accrue increasing rewards over the generations. Free men could afford to think of themselves as friends, colleagues, and mentors, as members of a group governed by more than individual interest. Ansel Williamson's most notable protégé was Edward Brown, whom he molded into a successful young jockey. Brown had his first famous mount with Asteroid, the mighty son of Lexington, when he was still an enslaved teenager in 1864, and went on to successfully ride stars like Kingfisher in freedom. In 1877, Brown saddled Kentucky Derby winner Baden Baden, becoming one of the youngest winning trainers in the history of the race. Brown, in turn, mentored William Walker, Baden Baden's teenage jockey, who had been born a slave and died in 1933 as one of the acknowledged experts on Thoroughbred breeding in the United States.[125] Williamson and others with insider knowledge also tried to take care of black horsemen outside their own immediate circle. Black men laid their money down at the betting windows with assurance, because they had inside information that had come from African American trainers and jockeys. The bookmakers at the Belmont Stakes of 1875 complained bitterly that they had taken huge losses because "Old Ansel, Lewis, and the western 'colored capitalists' in general came down, like the wolf on the fold, with heavy investments."[126] In freedom, black employment and information networks propagated the benefits that came from skilled work; they gave promise of economic and social mobility.

White Southern turfmen and their Northern comrades, hoping to create a reunified nation based on hierarchy and subordination, thus confronted black freedom not as an abstraction but as a set of daily experiences with men they knew personally. The changes in black men's status sparked an inevitable backlash. Southern owners had been long accustomed to shaping, threatening, and assaulting the bodies of their slave horsemen. They worried that emancipation had undermined their control of men they had always thought of as reliable tools and surrogates.[127] Without the endemic threat of slavery's legally sanctioned violence, it seemed impracticable to govern the track with subtle twists of fear or hope for personal advancement. Violence instead became public and loud with frustration at power and mastery attenuated or lost.

When Kentucky turfman Abe Buford started a race at the Lexington track, he found himself the victim of a crowd of wily jockeys eager to take advantage of an inexperienced starter. Before the days of the electric starting gate, trying to sneak into a superior position without alerting the starter was an ancient and honorable custom among jockeys; a really savvy rider, as the famous racing reporter Red Smith once observed, was "capable of removing a starter's coat and vest without getting caught."[128] But Buford, a white Southerner in the midst of Reconstruction, did not see professional cunning.

Edward Troye's 1864 painting of the undefeated racing star Asteroid with his trainer Ansel Williamson and his jockey Edward Brown. Williamson and Brown dominated postbellum racing and mentored many of the young black horsemen of the freedom generation. Virginia Museum of Fine Arts, Richmond. Paul Mellon Collection. *Photo by Katherine Wetzel.*

He saw a wall of black men, all determinedly insubordinate, and he responded with uncontrollable fury. He stepped out into the middle of the track and began throwing clods of hard mud at the riders and then yelled at William Walker, riding for the Harper stables, "Walker, you black scoundrel, I am going over to Mr. Harper's after this meeting, and if I catch you I'll lay fifty on your bare back."[129] It was a cry from the past, a vicious insistence that freedom meant something only in the technicalities of legislators and lawyers, a frenzied denial of all that Walker and his mentors and peers had made of emancipation.

William Walker had been born a slave on the Harper farm in 1860. He had rapidly become an integral part of the Harpers' winning team of horsemen, under the command first of Uncle John Harper himself and then, after his death, of his nephew Frank Harper. By the time he was thirteen years old, Walker had already ridden winners at Jerome Park, in the fastest company in America.[130] Still a teenager, he rode Baden Baden to victory for Edward Brown in the 1877 Kentucky Derby. But Walker knew that his skills could not protect him. When Walker rode in a match race at Louisville in 1878, local racing promoter M. Lewis Clark met him at the post. Clark had a notoriously nasty and impulsive temper and a penchant for threatening or assaulting even prominent white men who got in his way.[131] He snarled at Walker, "I hear there are suspicions that you are going to throw this race. You will be watched the whole way, and if you do not ride to win, a rope will be put about your neck and you will be hung to that tree yonder (pointing to a tree just opposite the Judges' stand), and *I will help to do it.*" With the threat of lynching ringing in his ears, Walker rode for his life and won.[132] Freedom meant that Walker could tell his story to the press, but it could not ensure his safety or even his credibility. Benjamin Gratz Bruce's *Kentucky Live Stock Record* insisted indignantly that Walker had made up the whole lynching story. "It is disgusting," the paper complained, "that a gentleman like Mr. Clark . . . should . . . be misrepresented and placed in a false light by such creatures as the negro jockey Walker."[133] Violence was the first tool to hand when it came to controlling the possibilities of freedom at the racetrack, and the unfolding of Reconstruction did not reliably ensure its condemnation or cushion its force.

But the antebellum track and the slavery that powered it had not been made by violence alone but by imagination, by the stories white men told themselves about black horsemen and the kind of bondage they lived in. So after emancipation they turned again to storytelling to define what they wanted freedom to mean. Their embrace of stories about Longfellow and Harry Bassett was part of a larger project of creating narratives of racial subordination and working to make them come true. As white Americans moved toward reunion, they turned also to writers who penned treacly tales of the Old South, always complete with the requisite faithful slaves or former slaves who never dreamed of embracing the benefits of their freedom. Instead, such slaves subordinated their desires and free will to the comfort of the white families for whom they worked.[134] Fictional horsemen appeared in such tales on occasion.[135] But most popular in racing circles were stories of the loyalty and submission of real black horsemen, who seemed to prove that the examples of free lives lived in public were not so dangerous.

The greatest jockey of the years immediately after the Civil War and thus the one potentially most threatening to racial order was certainly Abe Hawkins. Along with his last name, Abe had acquired some choice in the mounts he took. He could refuse to get on a bad-tempered, dangerous horse or demand more money for doing so, as he did in the case of the hardheaded Climax, about whom Abe observed that "he valued his arms enough to want $100 for the mount."[136] No one questioned his right to set his own price or to take the mount he wanted, because he was the country's best jockey "by long odds." The elderly jockey John McDonald, who had ridden in England, presented him with his riding jacket and cap, because he wanted the best rider in America to have them, and no one protested that such a gift should not go to a black man or that giving it demeaned a white one.[137]

Abe died in 1867 after a long bout with consumption, an illness common among jockeys debilitated by the struggle to keep weight off. In his death notices, his skills shared equal space with stories of his final months of life and his reconciliation with his former master Duncan Kenner.[138] For years afterward, racing men loved to tell how Abe had approached an old friend of Kenner's in the paddock at Saratoga and asked him if his former owner had suffered financial reverses in war and Reconstruction. "When you see Marse Duncan," Abe was said to have asked Kenner's friend, "will you please give him a message from me. Tell him I have ridden a great many races here in the North and have made right smart of money. It is all in the bank and it is his if he wants it because I am just as much his servant as I ever was."[139] All of Abe's prestige, all the money he had made, was rendered unthreatening, because he believed everything he had acquired was still Kenner's by right. And when Abe became ill for the last time, as turf periodicals delighted in reminding their readers, he returned to Ashland, where Kenner "attended with parental care to the wants" of his former slave. When Abe died, he was buried not in the plantation's slave cemetery like other former bondsmen but overlooking the Ashland training track, where he had worked so many champions.[140]

The incident of the offered gift may never have occurred at all; even if it did, it has reached us through a lens shaped by what whites wanted to believe about former slaves, rather than as a document of a real moment in time. Perhaps Abe offered money to Duncan Kenner because he knew that he still worked among Southerners who craved the reassurance of such a gesture, and he knew as well that he could afford it. Or perhaps he enjoyed extending a boon from a position of affluence to a former master now potentially in need. He could relish the delicious self-congratulation of generosity and know that Kenner would have to recognize his success. As for why he returned to the place he had been enslaved to die, he may still have had friends there, like his old confidante Sam Page. Ashland was a place he knew well, a place that had given him a skill that had made him a famous man. Perhaps he felt the power of his freedom in choosing to return when he did not have to. Perhaps it felt reassuring to go where his celebrity was a long-accepted truth. In 1866, the New Orleans papers had reported that he had returned to the track that spring with great success. "He is probably the best rider on the continent," they opined. ". . . We make these remarks for the benefit of strangers, for all frequenters of the Southern turf know Abe."[141] Whatever his motives or feelings, Southerners eager to establish that freedmen and their former masters were best left alone to re-create slavery's happy hierarchies readily embraced the story of one of the most famous black men in America and turned it into an illustration of their case against Reconstruction. Northerners could accept the story as proof that white Southerners would deal affectionately with self-subordinating ex-slaves, that Reconstruction was unnecessary as well as unwise.

By 1876, bipartisan aversion to racial equality and other possible consequences of black freedom had won out.[142] In 1877, Robert Harlan wrote to his half brother and political comrade John Marshall Harlan, "I write these lines with tears in my eyes—that the great Republican Party, hero of many battles and author of National Sovereignty, American Freedom, Civil and Political rights is being slaughtered in the house of its friends."[143] Grant had defeated Greeley in 1872, but those steadfast Republicans still committed to Reconstruction fought a losing battle in the next presidential election. The two major candidates of 1876 both eagerly indicated their support for the South. Ohio governor Rutherford B. Hayes captured the Republican nomination but made clear that the real divide he saw in the United States was between property holders and those workers who might "make war on property."[144] Hayes's opponent was New York Democrat Samuel Tilden, who had deferred so scrupulously to Southern and business interests that even August Belmont, long estranged from him in internecine party warfare, sent $10,000 in cash to the candidate for use in battleground states.[145]

Belmont was thus enraged when Tilden won the popular vote but faced the possibility of defeat in the Electoral College over disputed returns in Florida, Louisiana, and South Carolina. If victory were to be secured, it would require all the connections staunch Democrats could call into service, and turfmen like Belmont and his Southern counterparts knew immediately that the track could be a valuable source of such connections. The governor of Louisiana, one of the disputed states, was none other than James Madison Wells, younger brother of the late Thomas Jefferson Wells, the great racing stalwart of Rapides Parish. Duncan Kenner, now active in Louisiana Democratic politics and prepared to bring the state firmly into the Redeemers' camp, knew the best way to approach the notoriously iconoclastic Wells, who had been a staunch Unionist and Republican in wartime. Later, when a congressional investigating committee asked probing questions about whether Wells had solicited a $200,000 bribe from Kenner for delivering Louisiana's electoral votes to the Democrats, the questioners found the long relationship between the two political enemies confusing, especially since their homes were 150 miles apart. They had known each other through racing, Kenner patiently explained, and it was as a fellow turfman and in the name of old loyalties that Kenner had sought to influence Wells.[146] Kenner denied having paid Wells a bribe, though he admitted that he had also reached out to another old racetrack friend, D. D. Withers, formerly a Louisiana cotton broker and now comfortably ensconced with the racing set in New

York and New Jersey. He had vaguely told Withers that he might need money "to assist in promoting our material interests . . . and that I wanted him to do what he could."[147] Kenner insisted that he had not asked Withers to solicit money from any of his New York Democratic acquaintances.

Wells's family, however, always claimed that Kenner had handed over a check "from a Mr. Morrissey of New York."[148] John Morrissey would have been an ideal choice for Democratic chiefs poised to siphon their money to a useful but dubious recipient. He was their man for dirty work, both in the gambling rooms at Saratoga and in the back corridors of Washington. He gave more fastidious politicians the latitude to insist that they would not have anything to do with such corruption.[149] Alleged graft notwithstanding, the electoral votes ended up delivered, along with the presidency, to Hayes.

White Democratic horsemen had done their best to elect Tilden and failed. But, despite their disappointment, they had secured a national consensus about how the past was to be discussed and the future to be addressed. Hayes had promised the South patronage, internal improvements, and troop withdrawals in exchange for his disputed victory. When the new president kicked off a tour of the South in Louisville, he exchanged civilities with noted Kentucky turfman and ex-Confederate Basil Wilson Duke, at the head of ranks of gray-uniformed veterans.[150] The same year, a reader requested the *Spirit of the Times* to decide a bet over whether the North or the South had started the war and whether the war had been fought over slavery or to preserve the Union. The magazine cannily responded that it could not give a definitive answer: "It involves a point upon which our readers, unfortunately, have decided opinions, and, should we assume to give an *ex cathedra* decision upon it, we should expect a shrinkage in our subscription list, either north or south of Mason and Dixon's line, to follow promptly." Instead, the *Spirit* recommended a diverse list of books on the conflict, from writers both Northern and Southern.[151] Southerners were fully welcome back into the Union, and their views of war, slavery, and freedom were to be accorded equal airing.

The apotheosis of reunion came in 1883, when Ulysses S. Grant's body lay in state in New York's City Hall. Southerners had loathed him as their conqueror and joined with their Northern allies in attempting to unseat him, but now they bowed their heads in reverence. The casket, carried in procession from lower Manhattan to 125th Street, wound its way through huge crowds, attended by the official pallbearers, including Confederate generals Joseph E. Johnston and Simon Bolivar Buckner, along with Grant's Union comrades, William T. Sherman and Philip Sheridan.[152]

In the midst of the New Yorkers, standing with bared heads as the hero passed by for the last time, was the Virginia turfman Thomas W. Doswell, who had run Planet in Charleston during the secession winter. Doswell was in town for the races at Monmouth Park. He wrote to his wife from the Union Club at Fifth Avenue and 21st Street. He had been reluctant to stay to see the procession, but a friend had finally persuaded him. The two men watched the whole thing from a window overlooking the parade route. It was as if, he said, "the Lion and the Lamb had laid down together when you see Gens Johnston and Sherman riding together. . . . I have now spent a most enjoyable day, and a sight I should not have missed for a great deal." He closed hurriedly, anxious to catch the ferry back to New Jersey and the races.[153] The sight he had not particularly wanted to see had, in the end, moved Doswell deeply. He had seen his country knit together once again and felt his own part in it, watching from the windows of the Union Club surrounded by friends and on his way to Long Branch to mingle in the crowds on the rail, which Grant himself had loved to do. He had experienced racetrack reunion in a deeply personal form.

Racing men had helped to end Reconstruction, and they looked to a new national politics based on the belief that the wealthy must be allowed to rule, that black freedom must be constrained. At the racetrack, they saw in miniature the hierarchical world they wanted, its boundaries policed by violence and stories that defined the parameters of the possible. And they sought to model the United States on the world of the infield and the owner's box. But even as they tried to define what war and emancipation had meant, the black men on whom racing depended demonstrated how all-encompassing the consequences of freedom could be. Abe, in his grave at Ashland, could be enfolded in a reassuring web of narratives. But on

September 15, 1876, as Hayes and Tilden battled for the presidency while agreeing that Reconstruction must end, a fifteen year old named Isaac Burns won his first race on a filly named Glentina.[154] He would be as good as Abe Hawkins had ever been, as good as any rider ever. And his skill would confront the men of the racing world with a challenging vision of freedom and its multiple and far-reaching meanings.

6

I Ride to Win

T. Thomas Fortune seldom had time to go to the race-track. Editor of the *New York Age* and a vociferous voice for black rights, Fortune gloried in the epithet "Afro-American agitator."[1] He insisted on the necessity of political relentlessness, the indispensable importance of daily demonstrations of black dignity. In the summer of 1890, Fortune and his friend and attorney T. McCants Stewart were especially busy. That June, Fortune had entered a segregated New York hotel bar, asked to be served, and, when he was refused, sat in the bar until he was arrested. Represented by Stewart, he had sued the hotel, demanding equal access to public accommodations, and chronicled his case in his paper for a national audience. The two men would ultimately secure a favorable verdict and damages from the New York State Supreme Court, helping to pioneer legal and publicity strategies later used by generations of civil rights activists.[2]

Busy as they were, Fortune and Stewart made a point of going to the track a month after Fortune's arrest to see a match race that transfixed the whole nation.[3] Most of the crowd was fascinated with Salvator, the favorite of the day, who had already racked up great victories, including that year's Suburban Handicap. Born in 1886, Salvator was the son of imported stallion Prince Charlie. But from his mother, a daughter of Lexington, he had inherited the royal blood of nineteenth-century American racing.[4] A gleaming chestnut with a grim love for a hard-fought victory, Salvator was the cherished project of his trainer Matt Byrnes, who pointed out the horse's muscular jaw to reporters. "Oh, he's a bull dog," he told them affectionately. "It's his nature and his jaw shows it."[5] James Ben Ali Haggin, the horse's owner, had made a fortune in the gold rush, building a mining and real estate empire in California, where he located his 45,000-acre Rancho Del Paso Thoroughbred farm near Sacramento.[6] Many racing men already considered Salvator the dominant runner of his time. But one man was not convinced. J. T. Pulsifier, the owner of the impressive Tenny, thought his four year old, who had finished third in the Suburban, could beat the flashy chestnut. Pulsifier challenged Haggin to a match race.[7] A huge crowd turned out to see the contest at the Sheepshead Bay track, thronging into the grandstand and the infield, fighting for a view of the runners.

Fortune and Stewart had not come to see a horse, however famous. They wanted to see Salvator's jockey, a man at the apogee of his career. In 1890, Isaac Murphy was on the brink of thirty and already a legend. In the course of his career, Murphy's mounts won 44 percent of their races, still an unparalleled record.[8] Racing men of the 1880s turned to the great jockeys of the past to find a rider like him. The elderly Gilpatrick, decades after riding Lexington, saw Murphy take the notoriously stubborn Checkmate over a mile and three furlongs under a heavier weight than any of his competitors and win easily. One of the reporters at the rail spotted the old man, "and the look he gave Murphy as the latter dismounted spoke of a mind which, running far back down into the valley of time, was conjuring the shades of Abe and many of the old school of colored riders."[9] The immense crowd on the day of the match race, Fortune noted, included a large number of blacks, who had come to see the jockey and his mount. Women trained in a lifetime of decorum screamed and applauded as Murphy and Salvator took the track. The crowd roared again at the appearance of Tenny, ridden by the famous white jockey Snapper Garrison, equally well known for his bristling mustache and his panache in a close finish.

At the start, Murphy eased Salvator into the lead, letting the horse's tremendous strides gradually widen the distance between the two. The horses ran the quarter mile in twenty-five seconds, and then Salvator increased the pace, ticking off the half in a little over forty-nine seconds. Records fell one after another, as the two went the mile at the same clip. Tenny began to tire, and Salvator, now two lengths ahead, cut to the rail to save ground, looking like an easy winner. With only an eighth of a mile to go, Garrison urged his horse forward with "cyclonic fury," and Tenny bravely rushed the last hundred yards, coming up to challenge the leader. Murphy, as was his habit, had ridden the entire race using only the subtlest of signals, gently coaxing his horse to immense speed. Now he went to the whip, and Salvator barely held off his charging rival as the two horses went under the wire. It was, the *Spirit of the Times* recorded simply, "a race such as but very few if any of us had seen before and none of us may ever see again."[10]

After the race, Stewart introduced the thrilled Fortune to Murphy and his wife. At first, Fortune felt uncomfortably self-conscious about being a racetrack novice, but Murphy's soft-spoken and impeccable courtesy assuaged his uneasiness. Soon Fortune was asking probing questions with the zeal of a veteran reporter. Was it true that the jockey enjoyed cutting his margin of victory dangerously fine? Murphy looked at Fortune for a moment in silence, then broke into a smile and said four words. "I ride to win." For an instant, Murphy's steely determination flashed, and Fortune recognized a black man at the top of his profession, revealing himself to an equal. That kind of unflinching pursuit of excellence, that refusal to accept less, Fortune saw as integral to the struggle for full black citizenship. Accomplishments like Murphy's, Fortune hoped, could "make men lose, in measure, whatever they may possess of color prejudice."[11]

Fortune's hopes seemed justified that summer. The victory set off a public frenzy of adulation for both horse and rider. The prolific poetess Ella Wheeler Wilcox turned her well-documented facility for rhyme to the subject in a poem penned for the *Spirit of the Times*. Wilcox, a formidable literary comfort to millions of Victorian Americans, chose to adopt Murphy's perspective on the contest, chronicling the memories she imagined of the moment he and Salvator took the track. "The gate was thrown open, I rode out alone. / More proud than a monarch who sits on a throne. / I am but a jockey, but shout upon shout / Went up from the people who watched me ride out."[12] No one found it disturbing that Wheeler adopted a black man's voice in the periods of her strictly regimented verse. Nor did anyone suggest that depicting Murphy in such regal terms was inappropriate. Other writers would shortly do the same.

Only a few weeks later, Tenny and Salvator met again in the Champion Stakes. This time, Murphy let Garrison and Tenny take the lead and waited out his opponent. As the finish line approached, he turned Salvator loose, and the two came home in a canter ahead of the laboring Tenny. The easy victory confirmed Salvator's superiority beyond a doubt. Murphy had asked just enough of him to demonstrate his greatness, riding with exact timing. He had already had a chance to exercise his skills earlier in the day, when he took the Junior Champion Stakes with Strathmeath, coming from behind to best the leaders of a chaotic field of eighteen two year olds by a nose in a widely applauded display of horsemanship. He was grinning from ear to ear as he went to the winner's circle with Salvator, the *Spirit of the Times* reported, and it was no wonder: "He had won the Junior Champion and the Champion Stakes, but above all he had ridden the best horse of the decade, if not the century, on the American turf, in the race which was the supreme climax of a grand career."[13] The *Brooklyn Eagle* did not hesitate to call Salvator "the king of the turf." Track crowds surrounded him, trying to touch him. And if the horse were the king of racing, "Isaac Murphy is the prince of jockeys."[14]

After the victory, Salvator's trainer Matt Byrnes invited James Ben Ali Haggin, Murphy, and "half the judicial and political 'somebodies' of New York" to a celebratory clambake. Champagne flowed freely, the politicians made speeches, and the stage star DeWolf Hopper performed his famous recitation of "Casey at the Bat."[15] Several of the party guests posed for pictures against a fence, displaying their finery. Isaac Murphy, dressed in a frock coat, his bowler hat conservatively straight over his eyes, his walking stick held at a precisely casual angle against his light trousers, lounged carefully,

Isaac Murphy at the clambake celebrating Salvator with many of the luminaries of New York racing and politics. The clambake would later be cited as a
reason for Murphy's downfall. *Keeneland Library.*

his hand on the shoulder of the white man next to him. He was the
only black man in the group.

Isaac Burns was born a slave near Lexington, Kentucky, in 1861 to
America Murphy Burns.[16] When Isaac was three years old, his father
Jerry Burns enlisted in the 114th U.S. Colored Troops at Camp Nelson, Kentucky. Camp Nelson was one of the central recruiting
centers for black soldiers in the South. Men came there from all
directions, some bringing their families.[17] The 114th saw action in
some of the decisive fighting of early 1865, serving at the fall of Petersburg and in the Appomattox campaign. Jerry Burns may have
stood alongside his comrades and seen Robert E. Lee surrender his
sword to Ulysses S. Grant. Burns survived the war. But he did not
live to be mustered out. He died back at Camp Nelson in July 1865.
    America Burns and her son followed thousands of Kentucky blacks
into Lexington, the urban center of the Bluegrass. Between 1860

and 1870, the black population of Lexington shot up by 218 percent, much to the consternation of city authorities.[18] America Burns, like many single mothers, came to the city to try to make a better living for herself and her child. The records tell complicated stories about what young Isaac Burns would have been brought up to remember and believe about his father. No Jerry Burns enlisted at Camp Nelson, so historians have tried to piece together clues to his identity from army records.[19] When America Burns submitted a claim for her husband's pension, the clerks recorded on her application form that another widow and young son had come forward, identifying Jerry Burns as a man named Jerry Skillman.[20] Jerry Skillman enlisted at Camp Nelson in the summer of 1864. Jerry may have been one of the young male slaves belonging to the family of John W. Skillman, a farmer and stockbreeder in Bourbon County, in the hills east of Lexington. Charles Skillman, probably Jerry's brother, who enlisted with him, was a faithful member of veterans' organizations until his death and the first black person buried in Lexington's white cemetery.[21] Whether Jerry was trying to escape the attention of a former master or a former wife by changing his name remains uncertain, as does what he told America about himself. Friends later noted that America Burns had drawn her husband's army pension until her own death in 1879, suggesting that she proved her claim as a widow to official satisfaction. But whether she felt passion, loneliness, fear, anger, or disgust in widowhood, her emotions remain hers alone.[22]

The young mother's parents, Green and Anne Murphy, were established in Lexington, where Green Murphy worked in local auction houses. America Burns supported her son doing domestic work in white people's houses. By the spring of 1873, she had accumulated enough cash to open an account in Lexington's branch of the Freedman's Bank. She told the clerk to list Jerry, then eight years dead, as her husband and the twelve-year-old Isaac as her child. But the bank account was all her own. When the clerk asked, she specified, "No one to draw but myself." And she meticulously made her mark in the center of the signature line.[23] The traces America Murphy Burns left behind her are those of a woman implacably determined to make a respectable life for herself and her child, a woman who kept faith with the new institutions and hopes of

freedom. The poet Frank X. Walker has imagined her fear and sorrow and deep love for her son in verse: "An in case we meet so much
darkness / we think can't be no God, He puts somebody / in our
lives that allow us t' see God / in everything they do. I knowed
some dark days / but He sent me Isaac."[24] But she left no poetry. Her
only surviving words are the six on the bank application. What it
was like to be her son we do not know.

We do know that Isaac Burns grew up at the epicenter of influential and ugly disputes over the dimensions of freedom. A border
state never under a Reconstruction government, Kentucky divided
along bloody lines after the Civil War, with many former Unionists
gladly joining with old enemies to restrict black liberty. Only in
1870, with the passage of the Fifteenth Amendment, did Kentucky's
black men have a chance to vote. And in towns throughout the
Bluegrass white militias confronted the aspiring black voters who
had moved from the country to gain access to jobs and schools. By
1873, the city of Lexington had instituted a poll tax that disen-
franchised most blacks and withstood legal challenges. Cities and
states across the South took note of the Lexington model and the
Bluegrass precaution of mobilizing paramilitary groups to enforce
statutory restrictions on Election Day.[25] Isaac Burns was a young
teenager when the poll tax was established, old enough to attend to
men's conversations, to know what was going on and what it might
mean for his future.

But while he was exposed to those painful lessons about how hard
freedom would be to guarantee, Isaac was also learning a trade. To
give her son a start in a skilled profession, America Burns turned to
an old friend. She had been close to Eli Jordan and his wife since
Isaac's infancy, and when the boy was about twelve she sent him to
work for the older man, who trained the racing stables belonging to
the partnership of James Williams and Richard Owings at the Lexington track. Young Burns learned about horses from the ground
up. In exchange for room and board and a meager salary, he saddled,
unsaddled, and cleaned up after the stable's charges.[26] The first
racehorse he ever mounted threw him, and he wept because he was
afraid to get back on. But fear was not a luxury that boys in his new
profession could afford. He mustered his courage and climbed back

up. By 1875, when he was fourteen and weighed seventy pounds, his employers had decided he was competent enough to work fulltime as an exercise rider in the racing stable. He rode in his first race that year. In September 1876, he rode his first winner, the two-year-old mare Glentina, who carried eighty-seven pounds to victory. A few days later, he rode again at Louisville, winning on Williams and Owings's Springbranch, and this time the name that went into the record books was Isaac Murphy. America Burns, who died only three years later, may already have known that she did not have long to live. She asked her son to ride under her maiden name, in honor of his grandfather. Isaac and his mother had clung to the name Burns, to the past and respectability, but from now on he would be a Murphy, building his future from his mother's and grandfather's hopes and his own determination.[27]

Isaac Murphy was too young to remember slavery clearly, but he grew up in its shadow. He knew his future would be built on foundations laid in bondage. Once he left home, he spent most of his life learning from men who had absorbed their own first lessons in slavery.[28] Murphy worked for Eli Jordan for almost ten years; even after Jordan had encouraged him to seek more profitable jobs, they remained close friends. The jockey had known and trusted "the old man," as he affectionately called Jordan, since his childhood. But Jordan was also one of the best possible professional mentors for a young black horseman. First with Williams and Owings and then with the small but powerful stable of J. W. Hunt Reynolds of Fleetwood Farm, Jordan was a man to be reckoned with in Kentucky racing and sent likely contenders to the grand tracks of the East, where his name appeared beside his entries without reference to his race.[29] Jordan was part of a network of black men who had come of age and learned their way around a stable before emancipation. They had begun as grooms or jockeys; now they presided over strings of Thoroughbreds, training both horses and the young men who worked with them.

Murphy rode his first Kentucky Derby winner, Buchanan, under the direction of African American trainer William Bird, who had worked Prioress in England in the 1850s and Idlewild in New York during the Civil War and was still turning out champions. Owners paid for the upkeep of his charges, but Bird made the daily decisions about how and where they would compete, taking for granted the deference his long career had earned him.[30] Murphy would have heard from the older man the stories of the past, of the role that men of color, free and slave, had always played in American racing. The former slave Dudley Allen of Lexington, who owned and trained Kingman, Murphy's third Kentucky Derby winner, had served as a noncommissioned officer in the 5th U.S. Colored Cavalry. Allen would have known black men who had been murdered after they were taken prisoner by Confederates at the Battle of Saltville. From him Murphy could have heard the stories he had never heard from his own father, the stories of how black men had fought for their own freedom and the proud and dangerous role black horsemen like Allen had played in the emancipation of their people.[31]

Murphy would have learned valuable lessons as well from men only ten or fifteen years his senior, who had come simultaneously into freedom and adulthood. Murphy rode many winners trained by Albert Cooper, who had been born in Richmond in 1850 and had apprenticed with David McDaniel.[32] Cooper knew well that even his prestigious career was no protection from treatment similar to what black men endured in plantation stores throughout the postwar South. Cooper's employer, the mining king E. J. Baldwin, famously gave his trainer a raise and then, when it came time to pay him his salary, determined that Cooper owed him thirteen dollars. Cooper, who could not read or write, examined Baldwin's arithmetic and ultimately concluded, "Naught's a naught; figure's a figure; all's for the white man; nothing for the nigger."[33] That much math he knew, and he was fond of repeating the verse; he certainly would have wanted to remind the young jockey that, no matter how skilled he and Cooper were, they were still black men, and they had to be constantly alert to attempts at exploitation.

Murphy would have absorbed the great traditions he had inherited from his elders, and he would have had reinforced what he already knew about the caution necessary in freedom. But he also would have learned about liberty's unprecedented possibilities, not just its endemic injustices. He rode often for Ansel Williamson's protégé, Edward Brown. As an established trainer, Brown owned and worked a series of young horses that dominated Kentucky racing and then sold at hefty prices to Eastern owners. One of his most famous projects, Ben Brush, not only won the Kentucky Derby, the Suburban, and dozens of other races, but went on to found one of the great twentieth-century Thoroughbred families.[34] Holding out for high prices for his horses, Brown achieved personal wealth said in his lifetime to amount to $100,000 in cash, a stunning fortune for a man who had been sold on the auction block in Lexington as a youth.[35] Murphy could look at Brown, whom he must have run into daily around the tracks at Lexington and Louisville, and see that, in the profession he had entered, the heritage of slavery could be transmuted into proud independence and lucrative success. Murphy had good cause to remember one of Brown's early charges, Spendthrift, who went undefeated as a Kentucky two year old and continued to New York to test his mettle against the mightiest stables in America, the racing empire of George and Pierre Lorillard.

ANNIE MIDDLETON had grown up in Charleston society, and she had married Democratic powerbroker John Hunter, one of the shareholders in the track at Saratoga. She was accustomed to racing men's wealth, but the Lorillards still stunned her. "Goodness gracious me," she wrote to her mother, "they *are* rich—they must have more money in a day than we have in a year."[36] George and Pierre Lorillard inherited a tobacco fortune so immense that one witty observer imagined the family coat of arms as "a cuspidor couchant, with two cigars and a plug of tobacco rampant."[37] Between them, the two brothers dominated American racing in the second half of the 1870s and throughout the 1880s. Pierre's Iroquois became the first American-bred horse to win the Epsom Derby in 1881, bringing delirious joy to Jerome Park and Wall Street. Stable boys leapt into the air and shouted. Investors stopped trading on the floor of the stock exchange when the news came over the ticker.[38] Their rivals genially observed through gritted teeth that "the Northern turf must have been created for the special benefit of the Lorillards."[39]

But in 1878 rival turfmen believed Spendthrift was the horse they had been waiting for, the one capable of cracking the Lorillard monopoly on victory. His Kentucky owner Daniel Swigert wanted $15,000 for him, and racing men, seeking someone to pay his price,

Edward Brown as a successful and wealthy middle-aged man. Brown developed some of the best racehorses of the postbellum era and became part of a middle-class community of horsemen that caught the attention of the black press. *Keeneland Library.*

called on James R. Keene.[40] Keene was a hard-nosed businessman, whom even his own son usually thought of as "Mr. Keene." Doubtless, one racing historian dryly noted, "he was sometimes mentioned in less dignified terms in conversations of which he was not a part."[41] Born in England, Keene immigrated to America as a teenager and moved to San Francisco, where he made his first fortune speculating on the Bonanza Mines in Nevada. From there, Keene shot into public prominence, revealing an almost unparalleled skill at games of financial bluff and counterbluff. He transferred his base of operations to New York, where his particular talent for manipulating initial public offerings made him one of the dominant players on Wall Street.[42] So when turfmen began looking for a buyer for Spendthrift, they turned to Keene, who, though he had no previous connection with racing, certainly had the money to start one. They convinced Keene to purchase the young horse, who, as Keene's son Foxhall later recalled, "humbled the Lorillard pride and brought my father, at a single bound, to the forefront of American racing."[43]

Like most of Keene's investments, Spendthrift seemed like a sure thing. He reeled off wins in dashing style until the summer of his three-year-old year at Saratoga. There he encountered Falsetto, delicately built but with action "as regular as the piston-rod of an engine and as resistless as fate."[44] The property of Fleetwood Farm, Falsetto was one of Eli Jordan's charges, and his rider was Isaac Murphy. In the Travers Stakes, Murphy gave Falsetto his head in the stretch, and they soared past Spendthrift to win by almost three lengths. The victorious jockey gave an interview to the *Spirit of the Times*, detailing his strategy and revealing a remarkable ability to gauge not only his own horse's speed and stamina but those of several other animals around him with split-second precision. Rendering Murphy's remarks in meticulously correct English, the *Spirit* reporter left no doubt of his own opinion of the newcomer. "Murphy is one of the best jockeys in America," the writer concluded. "He is very observant (as the above conversation shows) during the progress of a race keeps a sharp lookout for danger, is quick to perceive the weak points of an adversary, and prompt to take advantage of them. He has a steady hand, a quick eye, a cool head, and a bold heart."[45] American racing had found a new hero.

Murphy and Falsetto took leading roles in a racing world that in the 1880s would help to foster the formation of a national and politically self-conscious upper class. Three months after Murphy's victory with Falsetto, the *New York Sportsman*, reporting from the race meeting at Baltimore, grandly proclaimed, "Now, as we have often pointed out, nothing can surpass the pleasure and beneficial effect of these re-unions between the able men of the North and South, East and West. . . . Narrow-minded blockheads, blind fanatics, and rapacious demagogues wilt upon the racecourse, and are virtually stricken dumb by the reverberations of the gallops on the track. The racehorse treads down into the dust the prejudices and passions which are base and bad."[46] The work of reunion seemed decidedly complete.

America's regions had assumed complementary roles in national racing. Southern turfmen grumbled that the richest fixtures remained firmly entrenched in the Northeast, while Northern racing men seldom brought their runners to the tracks at Louisville and New Orleans.[47] Chicago, which instituted its own rich slate of races at Washington Park in 1884, often drew Southern horses and became a secondary hub of high-class racing.[48] But the vast majority of Southerners continued to race their horses closer to home, saving only their best stock to bring to New York and Chicago. Kentucky and Tennessee farms produced the weanlings and yearlings, purchased by Eastern buyers, that would go on to make national and international reputations, like Spendthrift and Foxhall, the winner of the 1881 Grand Prix de Paris. In 1885, August Belmont began what became a standard practice for Eastern racing men, transferring his own breeding operation to the area around Lexington in central Kentucky.[49] Sanders and Benjamin Bruce, in addition to publishing *Turf, Field and Farm*, used their Bluegrass connections to pick up talented prospects at bargain prices for wealthy New Yorkers.[50] Many local breeders and trainers focused on developing horses for sale. Isaac Murphy rode frequently for "Black Jack" Chinn, the race starter and fiery Kentucky Democrat who founded an unparalleled dynasty of such horse traders.[51] Phil Chinn, his son, who worked well into the twentieth century, was fond of saying that his motto in sales was "Let the Yankee Beware." "In truth," he confessed circumspectly toward the end of his career, "I did not always reveal my full knowledge of the animal [to be sold]."[52] In the racing world, old regional elites and a rising class of specialized professionals made a tidy living by providing Southern raw materials for Eastern entrepreneurs. At tracks and in stables, a guiding principle of the New South—its underlying assumption that powerful men from both regions would extract Southern wealth for their own gain and that of their associates—worked in miniature. And turfmen saw in this formative aspect of their personal lives a reassuring indication of the proper path for national policy.

Racing thus became one of the institutions propelling the rise of a unified elite, composed of men who might live and make their money anywhere from Southern tobacco fields to Western mines but who rubbed shoulders in New York clubs, shook hands at the New York Stock Exchange, and ran their horses on New York tracks.[53] By the 1880s, many of them were affiliated as backers, stockholders, or business partners in that groundbreaking invention, the limited liability corporation, the institution that Columbia University president Nicholas Murray Butler called "the greatest single discovery of modern times." As these huge organizations extended their tentacles to bring all forms of production and supply under corporate control, they crushed their competitors and helped to expand the already evident gulf between owners and employees. Throughout the 1880s, there were more than 10,000 strikes and lockouts, as workers agitated for the minimal concession of an eight-hour day.[54] The persistence and vehemence of the protests further convinced corporate shareholders and owners that the nation must be governed in their interests, lest working-class radicalism carry the day. In the face of this perceived threat, Democrats and Republicans, previously tied to loyalties forged in wartime, came together in agreement about the necessity to protect the wealthy.[55]

Southern racing men and their affluent Northern peers still cherished old regional and party allegiances, but they valued their new loyalties as well. Elections were conducted in a new vocabulary, observed the *Spirit of the Times* with judicious approbation: "The term 'black republican' has not been heard in the land, and the word 'copperhead' has been as scarce as the snake it described."[56] New unities of interest were being formed among owners and propri-etors. In the 1880s and 1890s, Republican candidates toured the South speaking to local businessmen, hoping to woo them with the party's platform for the benefit of industry.[57] In 1887, William J. Minor's son Henry took a leading role in mobilizing militia and police against black sugarcane field workers striking under the aus-pices of the Knights of Labor. The violence culminated in slaugh-ter, with laborers mowed down by a Gatling gun mounted on the steps of the Terrebonne Parish courthouse. In the wake of the kill-ings, Minor ran for Congress as a Republican, calling for white votes, the protection of wealth, and the suppression of race and class un-rest.[58] A few years later, August Belmont assisted intransigent former Confederates in expanding their railroad interests.[59] Industries like the railroads and opponents like the Knights of Labor brought onetime rebels and former Unionists, Democrats and Republicans, firmly into a community of businessmen that transcended sectional lines.

Democrat Grover Cleveland, first elected president in 1884, hap-pily led this unified elite, in which party and sectional divides mat-tered less than shared interests and fears. A New Yorker, Cleveland represented for Southerners the assurance that their right to police black people within their borders would be held inviolate, and that their efforts to take a prominent place in a national economy fueled by Northern capital would be supported.[60] Cleveland proved as much a model of the values of intersectional cooperation as his sup-porters could have hoped, and he paid tribute to the importance of racing as a national institution in a country reunified in deference to wealth. He and his wife made a ceremonial visit to the famous Tennessee stud farm Belle Meade in 1887.

Black leaders knew that the emergence of this new consensus between Northern and Southern businessmen was an ominous de-velopment. As early as 1875, Frederick Douglass had warned pro-phetically, "If war among the whites brought peace and liberty to the blacks, what will peace among the whites bring? Has justice so deep a hold upon the nation, has reconstruction on the basis of lib-erty and equality become so strong that the rushing together of these mighty waves will not disturb its foundations? . . . Men are seeking new allies, and smiling in faces upon which they never smiled before since the war. A disposition is seen to shake off the negro and accept the old master's class."[61] Southern blacks did not need Douglass to tell them about the shifts they felt beneath their feet. Reports circulated that a Cleveland victory, the first by a Democrat since the Civil War, would mean a return to slavery.[62] But Republicans, to whom black voters had given electoral loyalty and to whom they looked for advocacy, seemed increasingly interested in the "new allies" Douglass feared in the South.

On his visit to Belle Meade, Cleveland shook hands with Bob Greene, the former slave who had supervised generations of the best breeding stock in the United States and some of the greatest champions of the 1880s. Cleveland would have been comfortable with the old man, a former slave whose public persona appealed to conservative Northern conceptions of loyal bondsmen, still in service to benevolent ex-masters. It was safe to shake hands with a man like that. Greene politely acknowledged the honor of the president's visit but said nothing else on the subject that survives.[63] In contrast, the year after he met Cleveland, he openly rejoiced when the home-bred Proctor Knott, ridden by the black jockey Pike Barnes, took the Futurity, then the richest fixture in American racing, over Salvator himself.[64] Greene had lived to see the rise of a class of free black horsemen and their achievements.

"The burden of our demand upon the American people," Frederick Douglass wrote, "shall simply be justice and fair play. We utterly repudiate all invidious distinctions, whether in favor or against us, and only ask for a fair field and no favor."[65] That fair field seemed to be found, in the 1880s, among those who worked on the backstretch, where, reporters noted, "darkies and whites mingle fraternally together, charmed into mutual happy sympathies by the inspiring influence of horse talk."[66] In that world, black jockeys competed against whites and won regularly, and, in that world, Isaac Murphy was the acknowledged star. In 1891, the official photograph of the jockeys at the Coney Island track showed a mixed group of black and white riders, posed to convey congenial professionalism. Isaac Murphy, kneeling in the second row, felt a white hand clasping his shoulder. He braced his own forearm on the back

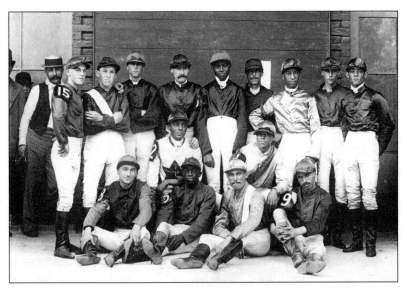

Group portrait of the jockeys at the 1891 race meeting at Coney Island. Isaac Murphy is in the middle row on the left. Anthony Hamilton sits directly in front of him. *Keeneland Library.*

of his best friend Tony Hamilton, sitting in front of him. He was almost smiling.

MURPHY WAS A PROMINENT MEMBER of the class of professional horsemen that the racing world of the 1880s required in order to function smoothly. Even as owners wrapped themselves firmly in their wealth and turned to the track to confirm their convictions, they depended on black and white skilled workers. Sam Hildreth, who had grown up around racehorses in Missouri and trained for some of the most prominent owners of the period, recalled his early surprise at his clients, "who hired people to do the work my father never would have entrusted to anybody else, except his own sons."[67] As racing grew ever larger, it demanded a substantial group of men who could handle, ride, and train Thoroughbreds for owners who were more comfortable on Wall Street than aboard a horse, however much they liked propping a foot on the backstretch rail and pointing out their runners to friends. Learning the trades of the track could be dangerous and difficult, but boys worked hard to do so, because they saw in racing both glamour and the possibility of economic and social mobility for themselves and their families. Young men, black and white, worked to become grooms and jockeys and hoped for big paydays and a good start on lucrative training careers when they grew to full adulthood.[68]

Preparation for a career as a jockey started early. In 1883, the *New York Sportsman* had to inform a youngster who had written to the paper asking about his prospects for entering the profession that he should consider another career. Fifteen was too old to begin learning the trade.[69] As being a jockey evolved into a more specialized line of work, it also became the province of smaller and lighter riders than ever before. The racetrack in the last two decades of the nineteenth century was increasingly a workplace for children and adolescents. Jockeys began learning the rudiments of racetrack life and work at the age of eight or nine.

American jockeys typically came from homes where the young had to work to help support their families or homes where no one cared how they supported themselves. In the North, they were often first-generation Americans, while in the South the job was passed down by former slaves to their sons. A boy turned up at the track or caught the eye of one of the horsemen who scoured orphanages and street corners for potential talent. If he were lightweight and diligent, he might be taken on by a trainer who needed an extra hand and was willing to teach him to ride, paying him or his parents a small salary plus room and board.

The apprenticeship process could be a brutal one for a boy. "Father Bill" Daly, the most famous developer of riding talent in the North, ruled his young charges, the children of urban poverty, with an iron fist. Jockey Winnie O'Connor, who attributed much of his later professional success to Daly's early lessons, suggested in his matter-of-fact recollection just how rough the teacher's pedagogy had been. Daly believed in taking a horse right to the lead, and, if O'Connor failed to do so, "I had to furnish a mighty good excuse or he would smack me without any apologies, right in front of the audience. Just imagine the chorus of modern sob sisters, now, if anything like that was pulled off today!"[70] O'Connor looked back equally, but young riders in training were often cheated or mistreated.[71] When boys entered into a contract, they guaranteed to maintain a very low weight, to allow their employers to dictate their friends and associates, and to work incredibly long hours. If they sought to leave their jobs, their names were broadcast around the tracks as contract violators, and other horsemen were forbidden to employ them.[72]

Young jockeys sometimes fought with their employers, but they battled their own bodies daily. As riders grew into manhood, they found it increasingly difficult to maintain the weights at which they had tipped the scales as boys. When racing ended for the year, an older jockey might gain as much as forty pounds, only to struggle frantically to take the weight off later on. Isaac Murphy regularly ballooned by twenty-five pounds in the off-season, and he became frighteningly proficient at losing weight in short order. On one occasion in 1883, he dropped his weight by thirteen pounds in thirty-six hours.[73] Throughout the late 1880s, the perils of jockeys' weight loss remained a constant topic in both the racing and the popular press. Murphy, whose sweaty schedule included Turkish baths and running in heavy clothes, combined with a starvation diet, was the most commonly cited victim of a health crisis that kept his profession in an iron grip throughout the whole of his career.[74] It was widely accepted that the iconic English jockey Fred Archer, who shot himself in 1886 at the age of twenty-nine, had been the victim of the punishing exigencies of weight loss, which had left him with no physical or mental resources to combat disease and depression. One American turfman took to the press to announce that he "should not be much surprised if one of America's foremost riders did not jump off Brooklyn Bridge some day," for much the same reasons Archer had shot himself.[75] More proximate health risks loomed as well. Job-related bulimia would have involved the potential inhalation of vomit, a factor that may have combined with immune system decline to produce the high incidence of dangerous lung infections among jockeys.[76]

But the job was no safer once the jockey boarded his mount. When his horse threw him into the fence at Washington Park in Chicago, the African American jockey Tom Britton survived but completely lost his memory. It took months for him to learn to read and write again and longer to get back into the saddle. Owners complained that whatever damage his brain had sustained had left him without ordinary prudential reflexes. The papers described his perilous exploits repeatedly, most extensively after he took another spill in St. Paul that threatened to cripple him for life.[77] Britton, however, was by comparison one of the lucky ones, as an adult who made a living for a time at the track. In 1885, sixteen-year-old first-generation American Paul Potter, whose parents lived in one of New York's immigrant enclaves, died on the track when several horses collided. Potter fell from his mount, and a horse thrown into the air by the collision came down on the boy's body and crushed his skull.[78]

At such times, successful jockeys closed ranks and acknowledged their responsibility to the youths they knew had wanted desperately to follow in their footsteps. Jimmy McLaughlin, perhaps the most famous white jockey of the day, who had grown up on New York's streets himself, brought his wife to the small house on West 36th Street to grieve with Potter's mother.[79] In 1887, when Edward West, a twenty-four-year-old African American jockey from Kentucky, died of injuries sustained in a fall at Saratoga, Isaac Murphy helped the young man's father collect his belongings and take them home.[80] Men like Murphy and McLaughlin, who had succeeded in a profession that was one of the few to promise wealth and status to young immigrant and black boys, understood that the danger would not dissuade other youths from trying to become like them. Shortly after Edward West's death, his sixteen-year-old brother, who weighed forty-five pounds, became a jockey. Another family lost a son in a fall at the track and lost his brother the same way the following year.[81]

Driving boys and their families on, despite gnawing fear, was dizzying hope, hope that came with a cash value. When asked, Isaac Murphy responded casually that he was not quite sure how much he stood to make in 1885, but he would not be surprised to better the $10,000 he had made the previous year by almost half as much again. (In today's dollars, that would mean an increase in annual earnings of about $120,000.) Not many men in America could have afforded to be offhand about those sums. Murphy made as much off taking individual mounts on a case-by-case basis as he did in salary from his regular stable. The total amounted to as much as the earnings of any member of the president's cabinet, the soft-spoken jockey asserted. No wonder Murphy was the center of a "circle of big-eyed dusky admirers" wherever he went.[82]

But Murphy was just the leading light of a whole cadre of black contemporaries who took significant roles in their profession and made good livings for themselves and their families. Even boys who were too cautious to dream of a salary like Murphy's could reasonably hope to elevate their families more quickly and surely than they could in other work open to them. When Lyman Weeks compiled his magisterial reference tome, *The American Turf*, in 1898, he included pages of photographs of bowler-hatted black men, staring with dignified composure into the camera.[83] Murphy, the South Carolina-born Anthony Hamilton who took New York by storm, Oliver Lewis, and other African American riders were to be found everywhere in the 1880s.[84] "Indeed," reported the *Spirit of the Times* in 1887, black jockeys "have almost monopolized the best mounts, and have been singularly successful, besides. . . . Let it once become known that Murphy, West, or Hamilton has been substituted in the saddle for some other jockey, and in a jiffy the betting figures are revolutionized, so quickly do the odds tumble. This may arise from the change bringing superior skill, or, perchance, from suspicion or distrust being turned into absolute confidence. . . . In either case it furnishes a striking commentary on the skill or integrity of the best of the colored jockeys."[85] One afternoon in the autumn of 1889, Murphy, Hamilton, Pike Barnes, and another prominent black rider, "Spider" Anderson, won every race on the card at the Gravesend track outside New York. "It was a field day for the dusky riders, and they forced their Caucasian counterparts to take positions in the background," reported the *New York Herald*.[86] First-generation freedmen had established themselves on the fastest tracks in America, and they seemed to have come to stay.

Behind them came a wave of boys, who had grown up idolizing the men of the freedom generation. Teenagers like James "Soup" Perkins and Alonzo "Lonnie" Clayton, who could maintain weights under ninety pounds and possessed the skills of adult professionals, commanded large paychecks and significant respect on the back-stretch.[87] Perkins, twenty years younger than Isaac Murphy, grew up in Lexington with his father John Jacob Perkins, who worked Standardbreds at the city's trotting track. Young James began galloping horses when he was ten. At thirteen, he was earning $4,000 a year under contract as the regular rider for a stable. By the time he was fifteen, he had nearly doubled his annual salary and ridden Halma to victory in the Kentucky Derby.[88] A year later, he had paid for a new, two-story, brick house for his family.[89] The financial obligations of youths like Perkins often extended beyond their families. Successful jockeys became, as Perkins's contemporary Lonnie Clayton once explained, the focal points of employment networks. At his professional peak, Clayton employed year-round a fulltime staff of four, a constant worry for someone with largely seasonal work.[90]

Horsemen formed firm bonds of friendship and patronage, assisting one another professionally whenever they could. Edward Brown made news when he struck a $1,000 deal with Isaac Murphy to ride one of his promising two year olds; the sum stipulated was the largest ever known to have changed hands between an African American owner and an African American jockey. Once he had accumulated a sufficient bankroll and registered his own official owner's colors, Murphy selected black jockeys for his horses, giving his backstretch colleague Pike Barnes the mount on his Barrister.[91] John Isaac Wesley Fisher, the former slave and blacksmith who shod all E. J. Baldwin's great runners with consummate skill, proudly remembered that Murphy had taken a hand with the young black men on the payroll at Baldwin's Santa Anita Ranch in California, teaching them the rudiments and complexities of race riding.[92]

BUT WHAT BLACK HORSEMEN WORKED to create was not merely economic security and professional advancement. Their success and stature fueled hopes of the coming of a racially integrated America, founded on the idea that equality was entailed in the freedom attained in emancipation. For many Americans both white and black in the 1880s, that was a nascent society that seemed embodied in Isaac Murphy. At the track, black audiences, keeping an eye peeled for a likely looking long shot in the paddock, could see Murphy standing with his usual quiet composure in a group of white trainers and owners.[93] When the *Spirit of the Times* printed posters for subscribers to frame in their homes and offices, they included pictures of Murphy in their gallery of great figures of the turf. An equestrian supplies dealer in Chicago used a portrait of him as an advertisement in the store's window.[94] Just as they had in earlier years, when Whig turfmen had named runners for Nicholas Biddle and Henry Clay, postbellum horsemen named their animals for men they admired. In 1884, Thoroughbred owner Edward Corrigan named one of his prize two year olds for Isaac Murphy.[95]

Even in famous company, Murphy's skill set him apart. In Murphy's career, he notched three Kentucky Derby wins, a record that stood until 1930, as well as victories in four American Derbys, five Latonia Derbys, and countless other stakes races.[96] His dominance, racing experts pointed out, was largely a result of uncanny precision. Jack Chinn, the boisterous Kentucky politician and horse trader, liked to remember the time he had asked Murphy to ride his horse Ban Fox in a race of three quarters of a mile. Weighing whether or not to take the mount, Murphy asked what time Ban Fox could do the distance in. A minute and fourteen and a half seconds, Chinn told him. That was an answer Murphy liked. He believed the heavily backed favorite couldn't match that pace. He pushed Ban Fox through the first two quarters of a mile in twenty four and a half seconds each and finished the race in precisely a minute fourteen and a half. When the leader flagged, Ban Fox caught him.

What Chinn remembered later was that, as he clicked his stopwatch at each quarter pole, the time was exactly what it should be, down to the half second. Even more clearly, he remembered Murphy's almost eerie stillness in the saddle.[97] A marvel of disciplined achievement, Murphy's accomplishments seemed so smoothly perfect that they inspired poetic effusions. "As he vaulted into the saddle of a great race horse on a great occasion, resplendent in silk or satin, and gathered his reins, he looked as handsome as Phaeton must have looked when he stepped into his chariot to guide the sun," one writer remembered him decades later.[98] American newspapers honored him with the nickname "the colored Archer," comparing him to Fred Archer, the legendary English jockey and the rider of Iroquois when he won the Epsom Derby. Archer was so famous that Englishmen used the phrase "Archer's up" as a later generation would use the thumbs-up sign.[99] Americans, still fascinated with British racing, could award no higher accolade to a homegrown jockey than to liken him to Archer. But the horseman Jack Joyner, who had taken his runners to England and studied both riders, insisted that "Archer should have been called 'the white Murphy.'"[100]

It was not just his silent skill with a horse that set Murphy apart among the prominent jockeys of his generation. That silence buttressed a superbly imposing dignity that even white turfmen noted. The *New York Sportsman* covered a revealing incident at the racetrack in Chicago. A young white gambler strolled up to Murphy, asked him about his mount, and began abusing the jockey when he received a polite but noncommittal response. Murphy "looked him full in the eye for a moment, and then turned calmly away from him, at the same time bisecting with a blow of his whip a fly that was crawling over his boot."[101] The paper reported that the black horsemen who saw the episode whooped triumphantly. They knew as well as Murphy did that he could not hit or talk back to a white man. He was bound by entrenched codes of racial deference and by his own reserve, which growing up with those codes had only compounded. But with a glance and a flick of the wrist, a display of coolly controlled and precise violence, he told everyone present that he was a man to be reckoned with and that his hapless tormentor was beneath his notice. Murphy showed a national audience what it would mean for a free black man to succeed against all comers in his profession and to demand civility as his due. Black horsemen recognized in that demand a sign of hope for their own struggles for dignity and the right to have their integrity respected, a model to emulate and admire. When a shady character approached the young black jockey Andrew Jackson with a payoff to throw a race, Jackson drew himself up proudly and refused, because he was "tryin' to rid' den fo' honor an' glory alike sech as Isaac Murphy."[102]

To be like Murphy was an evocative shorthand for making a new, free world, a political process enacted in daily work. In the 1880s, black men like Murphy ascended within the networks of professional patronage that had brought about their own rise, passing down skills and opportunities to boys who hoped to make lives at the track. They displayed to and for one another their security, even their affluence, and demonstrated their hopes for their own future and their children's. And, like the young Andrew Jackson, they asserted their own honor, their claim to glory as a right to be proudly preserved. The young Isaac Murphy had learned about the constraints on freedom as a boy in the streets of Lexington, but he and his colleagues pushed against those limitations. They exercised an amorphous but customary right of American citizenship, the right to imagine a hopeful and more just future, to believe that freedom could have profound consequences for their most private aspirations.

At the end of February 1878, Edward Brown had taken his old friend Henry Overton, the stallion supervisor at Woodburn Farm, with him to attend to buying a marriage license. Brown swore that there was no impediment to his marrying Lucy Gaines, pledging $100 as surety and signing his name with a confidently flourishing capital E. Overton, who had known Brown since childhood and slavery, signed to guarantee the bond with a sure and firm hand.[103] Brown had known who he wanted with him as he tendered his intention to make a family and a free and respectable life. As younger horsemen took the same steps, they turned to men like Brown, mentors and colleagues who knew their lives and hopes.

In the neighborhoods around racetracks, horsemen moved among clusters of prosperous black men who had set up households convenient to their work. A white reporter who visited the house of black trainer Bob Campbell professed himself taken aback at the furniture. "The regulation piano was there, and the embellishments were in keeping with those to be found in the house of a well-to-do merchant," he informed his readers. The house's amenities would not have surprised Pike Barnes and his fellow jockey Robert "Tiny" Williams, whom Campbell had entertained shortly beforehand, as he often did when they were in town.[104] They knew Campbell's house and those like it well. Black horsemen gathered in one another's homes to celebrate the events that marked the building of a community of free professionals.

Isaac Murphy and his wife Lucy hosted William Walker's wedding to Lexington's Hannah Estill. Only a few months later, Henry Overton's son William, who rode with great success under the nickname Monk, married Tom Britton's sister.[105] And Overton, Isaac Murphy, Dudley Allen, and several other solidly successful African American racing men stood by as Britton himself was married at Lexington's Fourth Street Colored Episcopal Church to neighborhood girl Pearl Jackson.[106] The Britton family and several other old friends, including local black activist Edward Chenault, attended when the Murphys threw a lavish party to celebrate Anthony Hamilton's wedding. The news made the front page of the *New York Times*, while newspapers all over America described the opulence of the ceremony and reception and enumerated the guests. The *Lexington Leader* initially expected that the event would "surpass anything in grandeur ever before attempted in colored society" but ultimately concluded that Murphy's reception for his friend "has seldom been equaled even in white circles."[107] When the Murphys celebrated their tenth wedding anniversary, their guests sat down to a seven-course meal, accompanied by musicians, and congratulated Lucy Murphy, who wore white silk and diamonds for the occasion.[108] In the security of a tightly knit community of colleagues and spouses, African American jockeys and trainers could enjoy their success and that of other black professionals and see in it hope for the future.

In the streets around Isaac Murphy's opulent home, black horsemen scrupulously kept up their properties and sent their children to school.[109] Fathers born in slavery had the satisfaction of seeing their backstretch lives give the next generation a start on security and respectability.[110] Tom Britton's sister Mary became the first African American woman to practice medicine in the state of Kentucky; his sister Julia moved to Memphis, where she taught music and joined the NAACP as a charter member in 1909.[111] Edward Brown's son Lee Lowell Brown would grow up to teach at the Eckstein Norton Normal School, serve as a vice-president of the Kentucky Negro Educational Association, and edit the *Louisville News*, writing up local politics for black newspapers around the country. His biography, meticulously detailed and including his memberships in a variety of fraternal orders, appeared regularly in African American *Who's Who* reference books.[112] His father had made him a child of the middle class who believed that black men must advance in intellectual and commercial life and that he had the capacity to effect change for himself and those around him.

It was no surprise that Lee Brown ultimately joined the black press. He grew up knowing men who frequented its pages. Black Americans subscribed to newspapers like T. Thomas Fortune's *New York Age* and smaller local publications, then passed copies to their friends and neighbors, read the columns aloud in barbershops, and told their children about the stories in the paper at the dinner table. Sections with headlines like "Doings of the Race" garnered particular attention, as they proudly recounted the careers and achievements of black politicians and professionals.[113] Horsemen regularly appeared in those columns, not only for their track victories but for their paychecks and parties.[114] African American newspapers covered Anthony Hamilton's wedding, so their readers could measure his affluence by the expensive jewels he reportedly showered on his bride.[115] But Isaac Murphy earned more column inches in the press than any black horseman in history. In July 1886, the *Cleveland Gazette* reported that Murphy earned $10,000 a year, and six months later the *New Orleans Weekly Pelican* added another $2,000 to his salary. The next year, they announced sweepingly that his personal fortune amounted to $125,000.[116]

Murphy—and to a lesser extent his colleagues—merited column inches because they earned immense sums. But both writers and readers knew that the money and the parties were notable precisely because they represented more than material wealth. Murphy did not just have money. He had poise, and he had unmistakable style both in and out of the saddle. And those qualities drew the attention and adulation of black audiences just as surely as his wealth or his success. Black conservatives, like their white Victorian counterparts, might find racing distasteful or denounce it as an occasion of sin. T. Thomas Fortune's *New York Age* acknowledged as much when it concluded a paean of praise to black jockeys by noting, "Somebody may say that this is beginning at the bottom round with a vengeance . . . but . . . I am one of those fellows who don't care much what it is if any man of the race is the best at it."[117] Moralizers might complain, but voices like Fortune's insisted that they must understand that black horsemen were too important to be ignored or diminished out of self-righteousness. Other African American newspapers, either adopting the *Age*'s position or responding to readers' demands, continued a steady flow of tidbits about black jockeys and trainers in their columns. Men who could not hope to become professionals, who saw the debates of politicians as far removed from their own lives, could see in Isaac Murphy a hero. Like him, they might come from war-damaged childhoods. They might have little or no formal education. But they saw that with an upbringing similar to their own and skills honed in barns and on farms like the ones many of them knew, Murphy, with rigorous training, talent, and luck, had made himself a symbol of unshakeable dignity and inspiring possibility. In daunting political, social, and economic circumstances, Murphy remained a symbol of the intangibles that were an integral part of the struggle for African American citizenship.

WHITE MEN WERE WELL AWARE of Murphy's charismatic gravitas. They saw the African American boys who dreamed of becoming Isaac Murphy. They caught glimpses of what that meant to black crowds and black families. John H. Davis remembered encountering a black mother in the stands at Churchill Downs and helping her find her son in the post parade. She had known, she said, when the child was only an infant, that he "war gwine ter make his mahk," so she had sent him to work in a racing stable. After a long period on the tracks of the East, he had come home, and she was eager to see him ride. She cheered when the boy brought the winner home and embraced him when he dismounted. "It would have broken her heart had he lost, and they mingled their tears in front of 6,000 people," Davis recalled.[118] Davis also sought to encapsulate his youthful feelings for Murphy himself: "From one end of the country to the other he was famous, and every little boy who took any interest in racing knew of and had an admiration for Isaac Murphy. He was black of skin, but his heart was as white as snow."[119] When white boys learned young a passion for the track, they learned about Murphy, his success and calm assurance, even as they had inculcated in them lessons about what black men were supposed to be like, their allegedly inevitable limitations.

Davis's syntactical choice to distinguish absolutely between Murphy's black skin and his white heart revealed the mental twists necessary to reconcile those early understandings. Men like Davis had to find ways to deal with the conflicts between their experience at the track and their belief in the necessary political and social subordination of free black men. Turfmen and journalists tendered gestures of respect and recognition to Murphy and his peers, but they remained deeply invested in that subordination and uneasy about its being undermined. Following in the footsteps of generations of white Thoroughbred owners and enthusiasts, they sought to acknowledge the special position of black horsemen in ways that would strengthen racial subordination, rather than imperiling it amid debate over the relationship of freedom and equality for African Americans.

Sometimes racing men took refuge in naked denial. Black men's independence and skill could not be politically or economically threatening because blacks were congenitally unsuited to self-directed effort. *Turf, Field and Farm*, citing its responsibility to the agricultural interests it served, insisted that free blacks were a "great incubus that is weighing down the material advancement" of much of its Southern circulation area. "As a class, with rare exceptions," the magazine pronounced, "they are idle and thriftless and live with no end in view, beyond getting enough for their daily wants. Their idea of freedom is plenty to eat and nothing to do."[120] Black people fundamentally misunderstood freedom and would misuse it, but they were truly too shiftless to be an imminent danger to white authority. But turfmen lived with the reality that the labor that supposedly drained the economy of its vitality largely powered the racing stables of the region and dominated the winners' circles at tracks all over the United States. Something had to be said about those "rare exceptions," the men who so consistently proved their industry, forethought, and acuity in the most testing circumstances on the backstretch, the men who turned these attributes to account for families, neighborhoods, and perhaps a whole people.

Some white turfmen assured themselves that the qualities that brought African Americans success and fame at the track were merely natural and innate ones, the instincts of primitives. U.S. Senator George Hearst of California, like his more famous son William Randolph Hearst, a talented fabricator of the sweeping and lurid generalization, announced that any black man possessed animal characteristics suited for horsemanship: "Put him astride a horse, and in riding a race he doesn't know what fear is."[121] But many white turfmen of the 1880s adopted a more sophisticated but time-tested strategy by stubbornly insisting that, while the black men they depended on were exceptional, their work had no revolutionary potential, that black horsemen were, indeed, faithful embodiments of racial hierarchy and limited freedom. Basil Duke, who had grown up at the Kentucky Association track to ride with John Hunt Morgan, judged that, while black riders were "not so intelligent and competent as their Caucasian successors in the same vocations, they were perhaps more trustworthy."[122] He located the source of that loyalty unhesitatingly in the mystical connection he touted between white master and black slave or former slave. Black horsemen of the 1880s could be painted in the same reassuring poses as the men who had worked Longfellow and Harry Bassett. It was unsurprising that Annie Porter's narrative of Charles Stewart appeared in the best years of Isaac Murphy's career. Stewart's aligning of himself with his masters, his incorrigible self-centeredness, would have been deeply appealing to white racing men of the 1880s.[123] Only a few weeks after the magazine hit newsstands, local authorities recovered sixteen bodies, the African American casualties of electoral violence, from Bayou Teche, near Charles Stewart's home.[124] The conjunction of story and murder revealed the tightly tied strategies deployed against African American efforts to expand freedom and demand equality. While elite turfmen built narratives of black men that rendered them harmlessly comic or staunchly faithful, the threat of violence remained omnipresent.

To fit all black horsemen into reassuring categories of loyalty and dependence required a flexible imagination. Boundaries of race that depended on generalization could be made stronger and more resilient if they encompassed the realities of individual difference. In a

fashion typical of a period often obsessed with the supposed meanings of skin tone, the *Spirit* distinguished in terms of color grada-
tion among the black jockeys that dominated racing: "some of them,
like Overton, Hollis and Britton, being very black, and some of
them, like Steppe, Williams and Allen, being bright mulattos."[125]
But the racetrack also brought a myriad of other distinctions based
on talent, position within a racing stable's employment structure,
degree of professional success, and manner of sitting on or talking
about a horse. A man like Isaac Murphy, the racing press reminded
its readers, was a world away from the reckless desperation of unknown grooms and exercise boys. He and a few white jockeys were
"men of mature minds, with families to look after, and as a rule they
are models of domestic propriety."[126] Murphy earned even more
laudatory mention as well. One *Spirit of the Times* reporter told his
readers, "I have seen men with valets—white men at that—who could
hardly claim more gentlemanly pretensions than . . . Isaac Murphy.
Well-behaved, courteous, decorous, without a suggestion of the
uncouth or depraved rough, he invites and deserves the esteem and
good-will of all."[127] The papers reported Murphy's five-figure purchase when he bought a home in Lexington, just as they noted his
white rival Jimmy McLaughlin's sale of his house in Brooklyn for a
substantial sum.[128] They described the "peachy blonde" attractions
of white jockey Snapper Garrison's new bride, but they also rhapsodized about the loveliness of "the beautiful octoroon" to whom Tony
Hamilton was said to be engaged.[129]

In acknowledging these differences and the skills and fame of
Murphy and his contemporaries, white turfmen bolstered the power
of their comfortable assertions of innate black character and preordained inferiority. In openly granting some of black horsemen's accomplishments, they strengthened their own assurance that those
accomplishments meant nothing. Jack Chinn, when telling stories
about Isaac Murphy, recounted their conversations in both his own
voice and a dialect of swallowed consonants and long vowels that he
attributed to the man he regarded as the best jockey of his generation. "You know how Isaac talks," he reminded his listeners and the
readers of the transcribed tale before launching in.[130] Most racegoers and newspaper readers, however, would never have heard

Murphy speak and would only have read his interviews, rendered in standard English. But Chinn's aside could assure them that they *did* know. They could safely imagine Murphy's words being spoken in the stock accents of minstrel show and caricature. They could insist to themselves that they knew how all black men talked, that there were unchanging markers of racial inferiority to which even the great Murphy was subject. And racing men kept a sharp eye out for opportunities to attribute Murphy's behavior to reassuring motives supposedly embedded in the essence of blackness. They celebrated Murphy's refusal of increasingly lucrative contracts to stay for many years with his employers at Fleetwood Farm, who had known him from childhood. One Kentucky turfman explained such behavior sagely, "When a nigger's bad, he's d—d bad; no doubt about it. But sir, when a nigger is attached to you and yours, all the money in New York couldn't make him sell you out."[131]

With such generalizations in mind, white turfmen could look to Murphy and his contemporaries as valuable correctives to other black men. Profiling South Carolina native Anthony Hamilton, the *New York Sportsman* drew a buffoonish picture of "many Afro-Charlestonians . . . who are now loafing around picking up a living by pilfering and raiding hen roosts, who might take a lesson" from the jockey.[132] Murphy himself was famously reputed to have schooled the young black rider John Stovall in the ethics of his profession. Cheating, he advised, did not pay, because "[a] jockey that'll sell out to one man will sell out to another. Just be honest, and you'll have no trouble and plenty of money."[133] The racing press celebrated the honesty of black jockeys as a class, bemoaning "that the same cannot be said of all white jockeys."[134] Black men may indeed have been more inclined toward honesty than their white counterparts, because they knew that prejudice might drive up the price they would pay for being found out.[135] But assumptions of black honesty also neatly accorded with white concerns about the rise in labor unrest, which the *Spirit of the Times* unhesitatingly attributed to "those large classes of uneducated foreigners, who are banded together in secret societies, and conscious of their strength, resist what they conceive to be wrong by violence."[136] The success of hardworking African Americans seemed to prove that blacks who agitated for the enforcement of constitutional rights and laborers of all races who demanded more extensive protections from the state were merely shirkers looking for special treatment and government handouts.[137]

Indeed, African American jockeys worked consistently within the bounds of free market contract, the pillar of conservative visions for postbellum American freedom. They began by announcing their qualifications and terms of service, as Isaac Murphy did in the *Kentucky Live Stock Record* as a jockey in his early twenties in 1883. Murphy succinctly noted, "I will make engagements to ride in the stakes for the coming racing season at Lexington, Louisville, Latonia, Chicago, and Saratoga. I will be able to ride at 110 (possibly 107) pounds."[138] This tender of services would have seemed the perfect first step in a negotiation on the free labor market to turfmen accustomed to seeing in the racetrack a prototype for the functioning of the nation. A qualified man presented himself to potential employers and entertained offers, with the state taking no hand in regulating the process. The papers followed Murphy's moves, starting in the 1880s, from employer to employer, working under increasingly remunerative contracts.[139] By the end of the decade, the mining king E. J. Baldwin, Murphy's employer, reported that the two had agreed in principle to a new contract, adding that Murphy was accumulating a stable of his own horses. The prize of the string was a highly touted Longfellow two year old.[140]

Here appeared to be proof that a talented and industrious man could succeed in the free market. He could move from being a salaried worker to owning the business in which he worked. Successful African American jockeys seemed to serve as models of the idealized form of free labor that wealthy men publicly embraced in the 1880s, denying in profoundly self-serving fashion how hard employers worked to exploit laborers and ensure their submission. In that sense, Murphy, Hamilton, and men like them could play a useful role in bolstering a view of the world in which inequality remained an entrenched verity. Murphy and his contemporaries could prove that, in extraordinary cases, black men could be accorded unusual privilege and recognition, because they modeled the success of key tenets of conservative political and economic thought. But they were never to understand themselves as people guaranteed certain types of treatment or to embrace Thomas Fortune's belief in them as symbols of the necessary coming of equality. Even L. P. Tarlton, a devoted Kentucky Republican, a litigator for black civil rights before the U.S. Supreme Court, and Murphy's longtime friend, who wrote an earnest and admiring obituary for the jockey, could think of no better epigraph for his article than Pope's couplet, "Honor and shame from no condition rise; / Act well your part, there all the honor lies."[141]

What happened when African American riders sought to use their skills as leverage in the marketplace or suggested that they wanted better guarantees of security and fairness than the benevolence of their employers?[142] Jockeys like Murphy, Hamilton, and Pike Barnes retained attorneys to comb through their contracts and did not scruple to threaten legal action when they felt they were unfairly treated.[143] As potentially litigious and demanding employees, who understood their rights and the market for their skills, African American jockeys could become symbols of the very efforts for equality and guaranteed rights that conservative turfmen feared.

White racing men did not hesitate to turn on black horsemen who provoked their fears. The *New York Sportsman* groused that legal intervention in contract negotiations was "one of the most regrettable things in connection with the seamy side of racing."[144] Putatively perfect representatives of the manifold benefits of unfettered contract labor and the fidelity of black workers, black riders paid the price of stepping out of the convenient narratives in which white turfmen had placed them. It was absurd to give "ignorant and uneducated" men the power that came with making five figures, voices on the backstretch chorused.[145] Anthony Hamilton, whose very dark skin had not prevented him from being held up as an example of industrious work to his supposedly shiftless contemporaries, could also be casually characterized as "densely ignorant," his manner labeled "brutish sullenness," his speech stigmatized as all but unintelligible.[146] Newspapers cried out over his white valet and suggested that having "white people dancing attendance" on him had ruined Hamilton.[147] Fears periodically flared up about "colored racing trusts," in which African American horsemen would supposedly conspire to enrich themselves at the expense of the bettors.[148]

In 1884, a reader complained in the *Milwaukee Sentinel* that he had seen Isaac Murphy drinking in the bar of a local hotel with a group of white men, though he "could not have bought a meal or a bed" there.[149] Just because Murphy was rich, the writer fumed, the hotel had made an exception to its policy of segregation. Whether Murphy was actually the man the enraged writer had seen hardly mattered. Murphy, who in 1884 became the only jockey ever to win the Kentucky Derby, the Kentucky Oaks, and the Clark Handicap in the same year, had become a symbol, his name shorthand for any black man who managed to get in someplace denied most African Americans, who staked a claim to equality by virtue of dignity and success.

Such tension between how successful black horsemen lived and how their patrons and employers wanted to see them could not continue indefinitely. Only a few days after Murphy's glorious victory with Salvator, the newspapers exploded when he rode the heavily favored mare Firenzi to an ignominious last place in the Monmouth Handicap and then, as he pulled the horse up, slid off into a heap on the track. He had clearly been drunk, most of the articles gasped, along with the racing stewards, who suspended him.[150] It was not the first time that Murphy had been accused of drinking before a race, but it was the first time it had affected his performance.[151] The jockey himself vehemently insisted that he had drunk nothing but a bottle of name-brand mineral water and that his disastrous performance was due to illness or poison administered by some anonymous enemy. Many newspapers were prepared to print his version of events. The gesture was not necessarily altruistic, since the controversy sold copies.[152]

A few supporters reminded the racing public that jockeys often drank champagne as a stimulant to combat the effects of self-starvation and that the root cause of the disgraceful episode was undoubtedly Murphy's grueling struggle to lose weight. If he had been drinking champagne, he had been using it in a well-established, quasi-medicinal fashion.[153] But shrill and vicious condemnations drowned them out. Racing officials should "make a salutary example of Isaac Murphy," one reporter trumpeted.[154] The compassion that had poured over Fred Archer after his suicide flowed in decidedly short supply. In part, the issue was one of proximity. Archer was thousands of miles away, a distance at which the deplorable can meld into tragedy or at least pathos. Americans had not lost money on Archer, as many had on Murphy. But it was more than that. Several reporters suggested Salvator's victory party, which had taken place several days earlier, as the real source of the problem. "The champagne ran in streams and rivers on that occasion," one writer assured his readers.[155] Murphy would have had to perform a truly astounding feat of prolonged intoxication for those showers of champagne to have affected his riding at Monmouth Park, and several credible witnesses insisted that he had seemed perfectly sober only a few minutes before the Monmouth Handicap went to the post. Cause and effect were not so simple. What had happened at the party, the racing correspondents vaguely suggested, had somehow ruined him in a more indirect and sinister way.

The acclaim that followed Murphy's victory with Salvator had taken him to unprecedented heights, and he paid the price for it. He had broken out of any possible narrative bounds that made his success seem safe and right to many of his white contemporaries. He had become a hero first and a black man second. And so in the whole disgraceful, complicated episode surrounding the Monmouth Handicap, in which malnutrition, illness, substance abuse, self-medication, or foul play combined for disaster, a single narrative emerged with rapid clarity. Murphy had been drunk and deserved to be punished. The sigh of relief, as he revealed a weakness, was all but audible.

For a few years, at least, Murphy retained some of his old charisma and authority. In 1893, the horsemen at Churchill Downs aired their confident opinions of his enduring prowess and agreed among themselves that he ought to have a chance to move up the ladder in his profession and shift from riding to training, as generations of black men before him had done.[156] That spring, the mare Jennie Treacy, a daughter of Falsetto, Murphy's first nationally famous mount, foaled a bay colt, fathered by the stallion Isaac Murphy.[157] His name still meant something. But the possibility of moving into a position like Eli Jordan's seemed increasingly unlikely.

Murphy never became a successful trainer. Like many virtuosos, he may have lacked the ability to pass on his skills and intuitions to less gifted protégés. He may quite simply have been a better jockey than a trainer. But trainers need customers, and white owners may have perceived Murphy as too controversial a figure to step into the shoes of Eli Jordan, Edward Brown, and Ansel Williamson. Questions of the parameters of black rights were in the air, and Murphy seemed to attract them. Despite well-publicized evidence to the contrary, turfmen had tried to convince themselves that Murphy's success and style had no effect on other African Americans. Murphy "mingles very little with his own race and spends his leisure hours reading and studying," the *Louisville Courier-Journal* reported after the jockey won the Kentucky Derby with Riley in 1890.[158] But they finally could not ignore what they saw with their own eyes. On one of the few occasions when track managers disciplined Murphy and substituted another jockey for him, "every negro on the track from the smallest pickaninny to the trainers espoused Murphy's cause as if it were their own." They hissed the man who had replaced him in the saddle for the occasion and cheered his defeat.[159] Murphy was one of theirs, a man who proved that their hopes need not be limited. And so, rather than getting the chance to train his own stable, Murphy was offered a job with a traveling stage show called "The Derby Winner," depicting some of his most famous victories as if they had happened long, long ago.[160] The Murphy era, it seemed, was safely over. The great man could be greeted with a nostalgic smile or a dismissive snicker. Murphy felt what had happened to his life so bitterly that he spoke to the *Spirit of the Times* with unprecedented openness: "When I won it was all right, but when I lost, and when not on the best horse, they would say, 'there, that nigger is drunk again.' "[161]

In February 1896, after five years of frustration, Murphy died at his home in Lexington of pneumonia and heart failure. He was thirty-five. The brothers of his fraternal order, the Lincoln Lodge of the Bethany Knights Commandery, marched with the casket, as did many of Murphy's colleagues. Several white turfmen attended, and former employers sent lavish floral arrangements. The coffin itself, trimmed in purple, was reputed to be a replica of the one in which Ulysses S. Grant rested.[162] It was an occasion of terrible sadness.

By any measure, 1896 was a watershed year. In the midst of the funeral coverage, Murphy's local paper reported a raucous battle in the Kentucky state capitol over a petty patronage appointment for a black man. Opponents "talked about 'Negro equality,' howled over the 'intermingling of races.' "[163] That spring, the United States Supreme Court handed down its decision in the case of *Plessy v. Ferguson*, finding that racial segregation was constitutionally permissible and that separate but equal facilities did not violate the spirit or letter of the Fourteenth Amendment. Justice John Marshall Harlan's was the only dissent.[164] Four years later, at a Brooklyn celebration of John Brown's hundredth birthday, Murphy's old admirer T. Thomas Fortune spoke bluntly about the future of constitutional protections for black Americans: "You want to organize and keep your powder dry, and be ready to demand an eye for an eye and a tooth for a tooth, for there is coming a great crisis for the negro in this country in which much blood may be shed."[165] Some African American leaders, like Booker T. Washington, protested Fortune's angry call to arms. But if his more conservative critics believed he spoke too soon, the crowds at Isaac Murphy's funeral would have known that Fortune issued his warning too late. As they huddled against the cold of February grief, it was clear that the crisis had already come.

7

I Have Got That Nigger Beat

SEASONED BETTORS FIGURED they knew where to put their money in the 1903 Kentucky Derby. In 1901, nineteen-year-old Jimmy Winkfield had piloted His Eminence to victory. By the end of the year, the young man had established himself as a rider of "good judgment and cold nerve."[1] In 1902, Winkfield used those qualities in his Derby ride aboard the fragile Alan-a-Dale, a product of the breeding program at Ashland, where the talented young black horseman Courtney Matthews started the colts.[2] Alan-a-Dale went to the lead early, and the other jockeys assumed the delicate-legged horse would fall back at the end. But Winkfield, intimately familiar with Churchill Downs from morning workouts, cagily kept his mount in the light footing along the inside rail, allowing stronger challengers to tire themselves in the deep sand in the middle of the track.[3] When horse and rider went under the wire, Winkfield became the first jockey to win two consecutive Kentucky Derbys since Isaac Murphy in 1890 and 1891, a feat unequalled until Ron Turcotte rode Riva Ridge in 1972 and Secretariat in 1973. By 1903, Winkfield had cemented his reputation on all the tracks in the Midwest and the South, from Chicago to New Orleans. When he sought an unprecedented third Derby win in three years, Louisville railbirds knew to watch his mount, Early, the property of veteran Midwestern horseman Patrick Dunne.

Jimmy Winkfield working Kentucky Derby winner Alan-a-Dale. Winkfield's experience exercising the fragile colt at Churchill Downs allowed him to craft the strategy that won the race. *Keeneland Library.*

Turning for home, Winkfield took Early to the lead but left space on the rail for the long shot Judge Himes, ridden by a first-time Derby competitor, the white jockey Henry Booker. When Judge Himes slipped through the hole, Early could not hold him off. After the race, Winkfield, surrounded by reporters, slumped against the wall of the jockeys' room and wept.[4] Booker, recounting his victory, told the newspapermen about the moment he had brought his horse up even with Early: "Winkfield turned around at me and laughed. It was then that I was sure I did not have a chance. That nigger, I was sure, was trying to make a sucker out of me." But Early did not have enough stamina to withstand the challenge, and Booker brought his horse surging to the lead. "I have got that nigger beat," Booker recalled his thoughts for the writers.[5] His grim satisfaction suffused his words. Jimmy Winkfield never rode in another Kentucky Derby, not because his skill had failed him, but because the track itself was changing profoundly, in ways that resounded in Booker's well-publicized bigotry.

THE YOUNGEST IN A FAMILY of seventeen children, Jimmy Winkfield grew up in the all-black hamlet of Chilesburg, Kentucky, a few miles east of Lexington. His father George, almost fifty when Jimmy was born, had joined up with the U.S. Colored Troops at Camp Nelson in 1865.[6] Jimmy was a member of the first free generation of his family. But Winkfield was still barely a teenager, doing odd jobs and hanging around the racetrack, when Isaac Murphy died in 1896. In 1897, he began his career as a rider, and by 1903 he had made his mark decisively, despite his disappointing Derby loss.[7]

The formidable John E. Madden, one of the nation's most successful owners, saw the rising young jockey at the New York tracks and gave Winkfield his seal of approval and a contract to ride his The Minute Man in the Futurity at Sheepshead Bay. Winkfield had come east to ride for Lexington horseman Bub May, but Madden's offer was a tempting ticket to the highest peak of his profession. As the jockey later told it, he took Madden's money and then accepted an additional $1,000 from May to stay with his original employer for the race. Enraged at being used, Madden informed the young man that he would never ride at top-class American tracks again.[8] Six months after his loss with Early, Winkfield signed a contract to ride in Europe in the 1904 season.[9] "They gave me a book so I could learn Polish," he remembered decades later, "and I rode two winners on opening day in Warsaw."[10] He was hardly the only American on the tracks of Poland, Russia, Germany, and France, where black and white riders from the United States migrated in search of higher weight limits and bigger paychecks.[11] But, even in cosmopolitan company, Winkfield stood out. In 1904, he captured the Warsaw Derby and began his ascent as one of Europe's premier jockeys.[12] Horsemen recognized talent when they saw it, and the bettors of eastern Europe put their money down on Winkfield's mounts, making "him a favorite even though he'd be riding a goat."[13]

Winkfield came home to Kentucky each winter, still trying to pick up a contract in the United States, near his family, including the wife he had left in Lexington. But he was fighting a rising tide of sentiment against black riders and trainers. "I know that just race prejudice keeps me out of my country," he told one African American newspaper in frustration.[14] The American racetrack that Jimmy Winkfield had seen as a teenager, the one on which Isaac Murphy had been a troubled hero, was inexorably changing. Ultimately, he gave up trying to find a place on it. By 1910, when he changed employers in Europe, boosting his contract by $2,000 annually, he no longer publicly expressed any desire to ride in the United States.[15] In 1911, his wife sued for divorce, citing abandonment. Testifying in the case, which Winkfield did not contest, his sister Maggie answered a lawyer's question about where her brother was. "He's with the horses," she answered simply. Generations of men before him had followed the animals and the opportunities they brought, but now staying with them meant leaving the United States behind.[16]

Winkfield's career soared, as European horsemen recognized his skills and accepted him as one of their own.[17] When the Russian Revolution broke out, he was living in an apartment opposite the Kremlin with a white valet, ensconced in luxury purchased with his princely salary. Escaping ahead of Bolsheviks unsympathetic to a man who made an opulent living piloting the playthings of the rich, Winkfield and a large group of horsemen took refuge in Odessa, where a track still operated. But he knew his safety was only temporary. "This ain't no longer a place," he recalled his thoughts on the subject, "for a small colored man from Chilesburg, Kentucky to be."[18] Packing up women, children, and 262 of the finest horses still to be found in war-torn Europe in 1919, Winkfield and his backstretch colleagues walked for three months through 1,100 miles of hostile territory to safety in Poland. It was an epic journey, on which only ten animals were lost, the lack of casualties a tribute to the skill and experience of the horsemen in charge.[19]

From Poland, Winkfield continued on to Paris, where he established himself as the darling of French tracks, known to adoring spectators as *le blackman*, the winner of some of the greatest races on the Gallic turf. After 1930, when he rode the last of more than 2,300 winners, he trained at his own stable in the equine colony of Maisons-Laffitte, where he resided in comfort with his Russian wife, their children, and his in-laws.[20] At the Winkfield home, African American expatriates and visitors always found a warm welcome. Josephine Baker and Bill "Bojangles" Robinson danced in the living room for parties of friends.[21] With the coming of the Nazi occupiers, the Winkfields quickly fled to the United States. Jimmy carried nine dollars in his pocket. They spent World War II in America, Winkfield wearing French suits to the track, concealing his connection with his white wife, and counseling patience to his son Robert, who was unaccustomed to American racial codes. In 1953, the family returned to France.[22]

In 1961, Winkfield came to the United States for an operation, explaining that if he were going to die, he wanted to die in Kentucky.[23] A *Sports Illustrated* reporter, catching wind of the visit, profiled the old man and drew national attention to him. Following successful surgery, the resurgent horseman decided to attend his first Kentucky Derby in nearly sixty years. *Sports Illustrated* invited Winkfield and his daughter Liliane to a dinner at Louisville's Brown Hotel during Derby week, but the two nearly missed the occasion, when the doorman, himself black, denied them entrance to the hotel because of their race. Winkfield, however, could not be kept away from the Derby, where he sat with his old friend, the white jockey Roscoe Goose, wearing a fedora, smoking a cigar, and watching the runners with a joyously knowing eye.[24] When the entries came on the track for the Derby to the strains of "My Old Kentucky Home," he wept openly.[25] Forty years later, Liliane Winkfield Casey explained the emotions that had welled up that day. "My father loved that song," she said. "To him, that was the national anthem."[26] It was the national anthem of an America of racetracks where a black man could comfortably support his family and know that his children could have the lives he wanted for them. But Jim Crow had changed that country beyond recognition.

IT WAS EASIER to go to Russia than to win a battle with John E. Madden. Jimmy Winkfield had learned the hard way that Madden usually won any fight he joined, a lesson that any racing man in America could have recited by heart in 1900. Madden, who had grown up in the rough-and-tumble world of second-class trotting tracks, brought his shrewdness to the Thoroughbred business and reaped tremendous success, which culminated when he bred Sir Barton, who became the first winner of the American Triple Crown in 1919. "Horsemen," the equine journalist Kent Hollingsworth explained, "quote Madden as a cadet quotes von Clausewitz, a lawyer cites Justice Holmes. . . ."[27] Madden often had to wade through crowds of Wall Street men, eager to purchase his latest prospect. "There's no trick to selling horses," Madden scoffed, "so long as you're selling good horses."[28]

One of the men to whom Madden sold in the late 1890s was William Collins Whitney, who had scaled back a lifetime of political and business interests and come "into racing . . . at an all-out gallop."[29] Whitney had married a sister of his Yale classmate Oliver Payne, the treasurer of Standard Oil, and used the gushers of cash that the conglomerate spouted to build a fortune that encompassed a dizzying array of businesses, including banking, tobacco, and mass transit.[30] Madden's consulting services helped to make Whitney one of the dominant Thoroughbred owners of the turn of the twentieth century. In 1901, his Volodyovski won the Epsom Derby, and Whitney, showing a talent for the magnificent gesture, telegraphed the news to the track at Sheepshead Bay and told the management to serve drinks to everyone on the grounds at his expense.[31] Henry Adams, who found Whitney's power and style repellent but perversely fascinating, summed up: "Whitney had . . . gratified every ambition, and swung the country almost at his will; he had thrown away the usual objects of political ambition like the ashes of smoked cigarettes; he had turned to other amusements . . . won every object that New York afforded . . . until New York no longer knew what most to envy, his horses or his houses."[32]

Whitney had been a lifelong conservative Democrat, and his tireless fund-raising efforts for Grover Cleveland had been rewarded with a post as secretary of the navy in 1884. But his relationship to Cleveland and the upper echelon of the party went far beyond official duties. In the White House, he and Cleveland regularly played poker, a game at which Whitney usually won. "Can you spend an evening here?" Cleveland once invited him. "I think I've got about ten dollars that I feel uncomfortable about."[33] Cleveland

and Whitney proudly identified themselves as Democrats, but they also feared shifts within their evolving party. They deplored party members who embraced the cause of farmers and industrial workers against big business, a movement embodied in the 1896 surge of support that made free silver advocate William Jennings Bryan the Democratic presidential candidate.[34] Cleveland despised the anger at big business that Bryan harnessed "as a sort of disease in the body politic."[35]

Powerful Northern political and economic conservatives like Whitney deplored the consequences of shaping national policy to protect farmers and laborers, of using government to ameliorate the ills of the poor and vulnerable. That, they believed as an article of faith, was not what government was for. Increasingly, they feared a conjunction of interests between black and white workers, the opening of a national debate about the nature of equality and its place in defining citizenship itself.[36] And these concerns had pressed closer to home than ever. Northern city dwellers found themselves with "much more than an academic interest in the Southern negro problem," as W. E. B. Du Bois observed dryly in his assessment of African Americans in the North in 1901.[37] As post-Reconstruction conditions in the South degenerated, black migration to New York City doubled in the 1890s, and the numbers leapt again after the turn of the century.[38] This exponentially increased proximity deeply troubled Northern conservatives.

Such men thus found themselves eager to align with their counterparts in the South and disinclined to interfere as cities, counties, and states implemented the minutely detailed proscriptions that came to be called Jim Crow laws.[39] Whitney counted among his allies former Confederate commander and staunch Lost Cause apologist John B. Gordon, with whom he did business in the South. Gordon proudly announced his intention to march "a larger army of Confederates than General Lee ever commanded" against striking workers in industrial cities if necessary.[40] These men were comrades standing shoulder to shoulder against the forces of unrest. And in order to ensure their success they were willing to cross boundaries even more sacrosanct than the Mason-Dixon line. They were willing in extremis to vote Republican.

Though W. C. Whitney sought first to challenge Bryan for the 1896 Democratic nomination himself, he ultimately became a staunch supporter of Republican nominee William McKinley. The Ohio politician had emerged as the candidate of a conservative coalition that transcended old divides. He had impressed white Southerners when they heard him on lecture tour, and they would have found reassuring Thomas Fortune's opinion of the candidate. As a fervent voice for black civil rights, Fortune saw nothing to admire in McKinley. "I despised Hayes," Fortune admitted freely, "but he was a Solomon compared to this modern thing that comes from Ohio."[41] Whitney and his allies recognized that McKinley would have to be their man. As a friend wrote to Whitney, bemoaning the necessity of crossing party lines, "It is a new revolution. It is not only silver coinage—it is the masses against the classes. This expression is in every mouth. McKinley is a bitter pill, but he must be taken to save the patient's life."[42] Whitney's fellow racing men, many of them of his political stripe, articulated similar feelings. Reporting his discussions with a bank president in Kentucky before the election, a *Spirit of the Times* reporter noted that his interlocutor was a Democrat, "but in his detestation of the principles represented by the Bryanites and the Silverites he threw party allegiance to the dogs, and was out-and-out for McKinley." The result, the paper predicted gleefully, was guaranteed. McKinley, in the parlance of the track, "would win in a walk."[43]

Men like Whitney found, as had generations before them, that the world of the Thoroughbred formed a valuable laboratory for observing in practice their ideas about who was to rule and how. They approved of McKinley's second-term vice president, Theodore Roosevelt, as a man who had proved himself in that arena. James R. Keene's son Foxhall, who rode to hounds regularly on Long Island, remembered a strenuous outing with Roosevelt, who was thrown from his horse and broke his arm but remounted and finished the hunt. "Never before or since have I seen a man do that, and from then on he commanded my highest admiration," Keene recalled.[44] Such episodes, racing men believed, constituted reliable guides to a man's fitness for executive authority.

Horses embodied the natural order of power, the purity and strength thought to prove white American superiority both at home

and in empire building abroad. The *Louisville Courier-Journal* rhapsodized in 1898, "the Kentuckian loves the thoroughbred . . . because the true Kentucky horse holds the qualities of pride . . . and
daring courage—that made Dewey smash the Dons, that send American volunteers today to Cuba."[45] The racehorse, like the stalwart
white American, seemed indisputable proof that the dominance of
particular powerful groups was evolutionarily preordained, that
such hierarchies were natural and right.[46] To W. C. Whitney, who
had asked his old college friend, the Social Darwinist William
Graham Sumner, to serve in his wedding, the world of breeding
Thoroughbreds seemed a corollary to his conviction that a chosen
few inherited the right to rule. He sighed contentedly to his wife
over the impeccable aristocracy of Thoroughbred bloodlines: "Colts
whose ancestors on both sides are known for a hundred years back
as famous for strength and speed, must certainly be good. Some of
them have pedigrees as long as those in the Old Testament."[47]
Whitney would not have been the first Thoroughbred enthusiast to
arrange a mating between two beautifully bred animals, only to end
up with a foal that, as horse trader Phil Chinn liked to say, "couldn't
outrun a fat man."[48] But Whitney never admitted that possibility,
because he saw in Thoroughbreds what he needed to see—the proof
that hierarchies were an immutable scientific fact, not to be disrupted by chance or change.

The turfman William Earl Dodge Stokes, much impressed with
the success of his breeding operation and that of his neighbor John
E. Madden, went a step further and enthusiastically suggested ap-
plying the lessons of horse breeding to the creation of a healthy,
well-adapted laboring class. Stokes pointed to jockeys as members
of a profession that demanded a very particular set of physical attributes and skills. The best solution for ensuring a continuous supply of such men would clearly be to create a jockey registry, which
would allow riders to select suitably pedigreed mates and pass on
their characteristics and profession to their sons. The success he
unquestioningly predicted for this process would then pave the way
for similar registries for any number of careers, creating perfect laborers through eugenics.[49] Such people were best regulated through
scientific systems previously reserved for animals; after all, Stokes

airily reminded his reader, "The mind of the negro gets its maturity at the end of the second or third or fourth grade, as the case may be. No system of teaching can correct it. It is due to the inherent fiber of the brain that only can be changed by a process of evolution which may take some thousands of years to accomplish."[50] Stokes advanced his reputation as a horse breeder to prove his right to make such generalizations. He was a man who knew what he was talking about, he reminded his readers with self-satisfaction, so they could safely follow his advice. "You do not build a great building without an expert master-mind to advise and direct you," he concluded.[51]

BUT THE REAL MASTERMIND behind the equine breeding program at Stokes's farm was a black man named Ed Willis.[52] Across Lexington's Winchester Pike at John E. Madden's farm, much of the operation depended on the shrewdness of the African American stable foreman Chuck Walker, who helped to supervise the young horses at home and at the track, riding alongside and monitoring their progress. "Do as I tell you in all things," the notoriously stern-willed and meticulous Madden told his employees, "unless Chuck Walker tells you different, then do as he says."[53] Men like Whitney and Stokes clung to their theories of hierarchy, but they depended on black men for the knowledge and skill that gave them the standing to proclaim that they had successfully used the world of the Thoroughbred to prove the inevitability of racial stratification.

In the wake of Isaac Murphy's death, the expertise of black horsemen sometimes moved out of public view to the breeding barn and the morning workout. Men like Willis and Walker did not catch the eye of afternoon race crowds. Marshall Lilly, perhaps the greatest exercise rider in history, learned his trade from Edward Brown and James Rowe as a boy and went on to work thirty years of twentieth-century racing stars, including Sysonby, Colin, Peter Pan, Regret, John P. Grier, Equipoise, and Twenty Grand, many of them Whitney family champions.[54] But only knowing railbirds recognized the quiet man in the bowler hat.

Black jockeys like Murphy, who attracted public attention, had certainly not disappeared, however. Arkansas's Lonnie Clayton,

who rode Azra to win the Kentucky Derby in 1892, used his earnings to buy his parents 160 acres of their own farmland and set himself up in a lavish Victorian home in Little Rock.[55] Reporters admir-
ingly chronicled the career of the Georgia-born Willie Simms both
at home and, when he took his saddle to England, abroad.[56] Simms's
fellow jockey Tod Sloan, a famous white rider from Indiana, used
the degrading racial epithets of the day to demean his black valet
but noted that he enjoyed Simms's company. The jockeys drank together after hours, borrowed clothes and cash from one another,
and shared the inconveniences and freedoms of an itinerant life.[57]
Sloan played a role in helping to convince Simms to try his luck in
1895 on English tracks, where Simms became the first jockey to
scandalize British racegoers by riding in the crouching position
over the horse's withers now employed at tracks all over the world.[58]
And in 1907, a new figure burst on the afternoon scene. The young
black jockey Jimmy Lee, the *Washington Post* informed its readers
sweepingly, was "the best young rider in America."[59]

Lee took the Kentucky tracks by storm, winning every race on
the card at Churchill Downs one day in June. As his final mount
turned for home, the screams were deafening. If the fences had not
held, one reporter wrote, the crowd would have burst through them
and carried him off on their shoulders. That summer Lee also captured the high-stakes Latonia Derby in a closely fought, muddy
contest. Afterward, "Lee was practically mobbed by men and even
women who wanted, more than anything in the world at this particular moment . . . to pat the back of this ignorant colored lad. . . . To
one who looked at it from afar off it appeared like the involuntary
expression of a crowd of people who love the turf for what it is, who
had suddenly become convinced that here was the best rider in the
land."[60] Lee was not merely a jockey that afternoon. He was a hero.

But only a few pages before the *Louisville Courier-Journal*'s account of his record-setting afternoon, the paper's headline writer
bemoaned "The Black Problem." The American economy would be
best served, the article's author insisted, if all black men could be
forcibly enlisted into a quasi-military forced labor system, in which
the army would supervise their work, dole out their pay in small
amounts, and house them in barracks. Only then would black men

be productive members of the community, rather than a menace that threatened economic and social order.[61] Men like Jimmy Lee were simply too dangerous to the complex system of legal, social, and cognitive codes that made up a Jim Crow world, an America that could propose such an arrangement because it categorized black men as brute manpower or as a collective threat.

The well-known Chicago turf writer Hugh Keough openly advanced in print the understandings that most white racing men left unspoken, even as they acted upon them. Most black jockeys, he admitted, knew better than to behave as if their success and skill commanded white respect: "They shed their halos when they doffed their colors, and they did not strut about the lawns to pre-empt the good seats in the grand stand or go about the resorts of white men flaunting loud stripes and checks and the fifteenth amendment." But their very existence, as his words suggested, inevitably reminded men like him of the mandates of equality now written into the Constitution. Men like Jimmy Lee continued to raise the same questions that Isaac Murphy had fifteen years earlier, and now they must be forced out of the world of racing, because, in Keough's estimation, they could not be "handled conveniently." Even if black horsemen themselves were carefully circumspect, they challenged the tenets of Jim Crow in the minds of their fellow African Americans. That challenge inevitably altered daily interactions between whites and blacks. "The praise that was bestowed upon the colored jockeys for their skill," Keough reflected disgustedly, "was accepted as a compliment to the entire race, and the porter that made up your berth took his share of it and assumed a perkiness that got on your nerves."[62] Since jobs as Pullman porters were highly valued and often depended on the ability to assume a posture of servility for the delectation of any white ticketholder, it seems highly unlikely that Keough actually saw real evidence that railroad porters' behavior changed depending on the performances of black horsemen.[63] But Keough believed that he saw it, because he was afraid that he might. And that was all that mattered.

A few years later, when the mighty Jack Johnson took boxing's heavyweight world title and then defended it against former champion Jim Jeffries in the so-called fight of the century in Reno, turf-

men and others could see clearly illustrated the connections between black athletic successes and the pride and pent-up anger of
African Americans. When Johnson hammered Jeffries, violence
broke out across the nation. In countless cases, ordinary black people
publicly expressed their exaltation, and vengeful whites responded
with lethal force.[64] The upheavals unnerved many politicians and
policymakers, but turfmen had an uneasily close view of Johnson's
success. James R. Keene's son Foxhall and W. C. Whitney's son
Payne had both watched the fight in Nevada and seen Jeffries go
down before the black man's combination of elusive agility and
powerful speed.[65] The victor, who was fond of giving interviews,
explained that his first plan for fame and fortune had been to become a jockey. He had groomed, ridden, and trained Thoroughbreds in Texas before he literally outgrew the sport, and Isaac Murphy was said to have been his boyhood hero.[66] Johnson proved in
disturbing fashion that black athletes who dominated interracial
competition posed a threat to racial subordination. And, while Johnson's looming figure bore no resemblance to a jockey's slight body,
it was black horsemen who had first inspired his dreams of supremacy, his demands to be accepted as a champion. Perhaps black
horsemen's success could not be safely channeled into the support of
white supremacy; perhaps decades of simultaneous acknowledgement of their talents and reaffirmation of their inferiority were not
enough to negate the meanings African Americans saw in their lives
and achievements. Perhaps Hugh Keough had been right and black
trainers and jockeys were dangerous. By 1910, black horsemen had
already begun to pay the price of such imaginings, as they were
forced from their jobs with methods both violent and subtle, with
strategies calibrated to the dangers they posed. The first and most
open of the developments that forced black jockeys out was a wave
of violence, followed by the rise of licensing procedures that cloaked
bigotry in bureaucracy.

The racetrack had never been a place for the faint of heart. But at
the turn of the century, its harshness took on a particular and ugly
edge for black men that exceeded the usual veiled hostility of endemic prejudice. In 1895, black jockey Jerry Chorn was called on
the carpet at the Latonia track in northern Kentucky for shouting

abuse at the starter before a race. When asked why he had done so, Chorn responded, "I would not have said a word but that he first shouted at me, 'Here, you d—d black nigger, why don't you move up?' That made me mad, and it wasn't the first time either."[67] Such anger must have mixed with anxiety for "Monk" Overton and fellow jockey "Tiny" Williams when they rode in front of almost empty stands one afternoon in Nashville in 1892 because the crowd had deserted the grounds to watch a lynching.[68] Black horsemen had faced down the daily perils of their work, the threats of white men anxious to assert their continuing authority, and decades of other fears. But at the turn of the century they faced a new danger— concerted campaigns to terrorize them.

At many of the major tracks, including the preeminent facilities at New York and Chicago, white jockeys combined to intimidate and defeat black riders. In the midst of a pack of flying horses on the backstretch, they tried to unseat black competitors, box them in, injure or kill them or scare them so badly that they quit racing.[69] Young Jimmy Winkfield, before he left for Europe, was involved in more than one incident in Chicago that left both him and his horse hurt. In 1900, he escaped with bruises, while the horse ended up with cracked ribs. Two years later, after his two Kentucky Derby victories, he and the well-regarded colt McChesney were forced into the fence and injured so badly that it took all summer for both to recover mobility.[70]

Jimmy Lee, a victim of similar tactics, took out his rage and frustration on one of his white competitors when the two men met on the steps of the St. Charles Hotel in New Orleans. Lee "grabbed him by the coat collar and told him that he would stand for no nonsense." It was a furious protest, cried out in a place that still echoed with planters' praise of Abe Hawkins's victories and the shouts of rival bidders in the slave auctions at the hotel bar. Lee had caught a fleeting glimpse of what that world, inherited from Abe Hawkins, could bring men like him, and he did not want to give it up without a fight. But he was doomed. One prominent white rider, questioned about the incident, summed up the opinion of his compatriots with chilling simplicity: "Lee was one of the greatest jockeys he had ever seen. . . . [b]ut . . . he and the other white boys did not like to have

The jockeys at the Westchester race meeting in 1908. Jimmy Lee is on the far left. While the jockeys of the 1891 photo are casually close, the white riders of 1908 pointedly touch each other and leave Lee isolated. The pictures suggest the changes that overtook the racetrack at the turn of the twentieth century. *Keeneland Library.*

the negro riding in the same races with them."[71] White jockeys said the same across the country.[72] In 1908, when the photographer John C. Hemment photographed the riders at the Westchester track's fall meeting, the white jockeys twined their arms around one another and left Lee a pointed distance apart. The group photographs of Isaac Murphy's time, with men resting hands and arms on each other with casual amicability, seemed very far away.

A mixture of straightforward desire to eliminate skilled competition and a supposedly natural racial disdain pervaded the sporting world. White riders bluntly informed owners and trainers that their expensive horses would not be safe if they persisted in hiring black men. In baseball, many white players and fans had already proven the efficacy of such complaints against successful black athletes like major leaguer Moses Fleetwood Walker and his black contemporaries in the minors. Even though the hard-bitten Tony Mullane, master of the brushback pitch, conceded that Walker was the greatest catcher ever to be his battery mate, he found playing with a black man deeply distasteful. Indeed, Mullane emphasized that Walker's talent was truly extraordinary because he never knew what pitch would be coming over the plate. Mullane refused to allow Walker to call his pitches because he could not bear to give a black catcher that kind of authority. Mullane's feelings were not unusual. Disgruntled players informed owners that they would leave for other teams or leagues if black players were not banned.[73] These were sentiments that would have been familiar to the white jockeys who rejected and ganged up on Jimmy Lee and Jimmy Winkfield.

But such demands—and the violent means of enforcing them—could not hope to succeed without the tacit consent of those who controlled white jockeys' paychecks. Their work was not done alone. "[T]hey were said," the New York Times acknowledged, "to be advised and upheld by certain horse owners and turfmen who have great influence in racing affairs."[74] In baseball, white owners were the ones who had the final authority to accept or reject their employees' demands to draw the color line. In 1887, the owners of the International League met and agreed not to extend contracts to African American players; though they would waver briefly in their commitment to lily-white baseball, Moses Walker quickly became the last black man in the minor leagues, retiring in 1889 to a job with the post office and an alcoholism that gnawed at him for life.[75] Black horsemen clung to their success longer because they were deeply entrenched in an old American sport and its customs, not rising stars in the nation's new pastime. But they depended on white owners for patronage and employment, and that made them vulnerable to those men's fears and insecurities, their influence and authority.

Influential racing men were better organized than ever before to control life and labor at the track. After a series of attempts to form a national governing body for the turf, fifty of racing's most powerful owners established the Jockey Club, which assumed authority over American tracks. First partnered with the American Turf Congress in the Midwest and then in solitary splendor, the Club took control of almost every aspect of racing's administration. Horses, owners, riders, and trainers that did not comply with its rules would be forbidden to race on its tracks, while facilities that chose not to enforce the regulations would be locked out of high-stakes competition. State authorities were content to leave the supervision of racing in the hands of men they knew and respected, so the Club and the state racing commissions that followed it, composed mostly of Club members, took on the weight of governmental power.[76] From the 1890s onward, jockeys and trainers who wished to ride on sanctioned tracks had to be licensed annually by an appropriate governing body, and their licenses—and thus their chance at sustained and lucrative employment—could be revoked without warning.[77] Arbitrary control of licensing meant that a conclave of racing owners controlled black men's access to employment not only in particular stables but in almost all stables. Jerry Chorn lost his license for years because it was said that he had developed an unsavory association with a gambler in San Francisco's Chinatown. The testimony that condemned the black jockey came from a disgruntled white colleague.[78] Experiences like Chorn's were the official and codified complement to the violence that racked the racing world at the turn of the century.[79]

But black jockeys suffered more insidious pressures as well. White Americans North and South enjoyed minstrel shows and coon songs that depicted black men whose diligence and moral compass had been eaten away by freedom, leaving their inferiority laughably apparent.[80] Among those typical entertainments were depictions of black horsemen. Minstrel routines featured blackface characters lurching around the stage in a pointedly pathetic facsimile of jockeys.[81] A popular series of Currier & Ives lithographs, devoted to the doings of an imaginary place called Darktown, included scenes from the racetrack, where African Americans clung to manes and tails by their fingernails, eyes rolling, limbs askew, unable to ride at all.[82] For every lithograph of Isaac Murphy or Pike Barnes winning a great stakes race, the famous printers produced one of ape-like black men jouncing ludicrously down the track toward disaster. One set of representations mirrored the reality, while the other depicted what many white Americans deeply wished the reality to

Currier & Ives lithograph of Pike Barnes winning the Futurity, the richest race in America, with Proctor Knott. The popular printmakers sold depictions of many black horsemen and their victories. *Library of Congress, Prints and Photographs Collection.*

be. A prospective purchaser could have whatever truth he wanted to buy. The men who administered racing wanted to see obsequious subordination and comical self-abnegation in the men who worked for them and responded happily when they found them. When one groom brought before the tribunal of the Jockey Club described himself as a "flat-footed, no-account loafer, an' a crap-shootin' son of a bitch," James R. Keene howled with laughter and elbowed his nephew and business associate with the command, "Buy me that nigger. . . . I like him."[83]

Keene spoke the language of the slave trade with self-satisfied fluency, secure in the knowledge that the minstrel shows, coon songs, and caricatures that abounded both on and off the track affirmed the brutish subordination of black men. But that security rubbed uncomfortably against the reality that many black horsemen refused to play the buffoonish character that so appealed to Keene and his friends. Black men jealous of their dignity, conscious of their professional status, did not routinely make jokes at their own expense for white men's benefit. So white turfmen and their peers embraced the broad caricatures of black men they found preferable

A CORINTHIAN RACE.
A High Toned Start.

Currier & Ives lithograph of the races in the fictional Darktown. Customers could purchase images like the print of Barnes and Proctor Knott or a Darktown print that depicted black men comically unable to ride. The contrast reveals white people's uneasiness with black horsemen's success and the strategies they used to assuage it. *Library of Congress, Prints and Photographs Collection.*

to the complex reality of dependence and acknowledged skill that defined their real-life relationships with black horsemen. They insisted that science itself dictated black men's inferiority in the world of the racetrack, just as it did in other spheres of life. And they mobilized their political and economic power to ignore or minimize the evidence of achievement that contradicted the demeaning stories they told about African American horsemen. They expelled black men from the jobs in which they had excelled, then insisted that their precipitous decline in employment was the product of an ineluctable evolutionary process, too far advanced to halt.

The drop in the number of black horsemen, one racing correspondent insisted, was decidedly not the result of bigotry. "A racing establishment," the reporter instructed his readers, "partakes somewhat of the features of a family. Its members are thrown closely together. As the two races will not mix in such close quarters, the head of the institution must have all one kind or the other. Under these circumstances the gradual exclusion of the Negro is inevitable."[84] The centuries-integrated world of the racetrack was an intolerable offense to the logic of Jim Crow, itself a response to deep-seated fears that black people might take advantage of the opportunities of freedom and the possibility of equality. So that complicated interracial history must be stamped out and the work of doing so concealed behind a façade of alleged Darwinian inevitability.

As the years wore on, the absence of black horsemen occasionally provoked comment. In 1922, the *Daily Racing Form* called it "as great a mystery as the total disappearance of the passenger pigeon."[85] Most publications were not quite so naïve. The *Blood-Horse* analyzed the alleged shortage of skilled jockeys and called for the return of African Americans riders as a relatively cheap and honest labor pool. Unrest among white jockeys had driven blacks out of their jobs, the magazine acknowledged, but increased track regulation could certainly fix that problem.[86] When journalists and racegoers searched for an explanation of the disappearance of black horsemen, they often settled on some personal, proximate version of what had happened over a period of months and years. Black men's decline in the racing world was an unfortunate result of a sordid set of practices common in the rough world of the backstretch, racing men sighed sagely. They ignored the fact that men who worked on salary would hardly have dared to threaten coworkers under the firm protection of powerful patrons. White jockeys had done the physical labor of eliminating black jockeys, but they had been tacitly allowed to do so, their efforts sustained by wealthy men deeply implicated in the creation of the world of Jim Crow. To suggest that a few white jockeys were the root of the problem was thus to ignore systemic inequality at work. But even that reductive explanation was typically given an added layer of comfortably dusty antiquity. Black horsemen's disappearance might be regrettable, but it was far too late to do anything about it now.

This trick of making conflicts barely a decade old seem distant and atavistic helped to entrench the inequalities that those battles painfully produced. "Superior intelligence" meant that white jockeys would always win out, the *Washington Post* informed its readers.

"So the white jockey is now crowding out the colored riders, as the paleface is pressing back the red man on the plains."[87] Black men had certainly proven their ability with Thoroughbreds, chimed in a St. Louis reporter, but their "gradual passing away . . . only marks the survival of the fittest."[88]

Charles Van Loan, who had matched his old friend Damon Runyon drink for drink in the bars around William Randolph Hearst's *New York Journal,* supported himself and his wife in modest comfort for a time in the years around 1915 with a series of stories in the *Saturday Evening Post* about a racetrack character named Old Man Curry. Van Loan's Curry was an eccentric, a small-time, old-fashioned horseman with a persistent ability to confound richer and more morally flexible competitors with his unfailing skill with a difficult horse. Part of Curry's anachronistic charm was his employment of the black jockey Moseby Jones, who wore loud checked suits and spoke in a dense dialect. Jones and Curry struggled throughout the stories with the problem of white jockeys. As Jones bitterly reminded his employer, when Curry ordered him to keep a particular horse off the rail, "Sutny will. Don't git me nothin' stickin' on 'at rail. 'Em white bu'glahs don't seem to crave me nohow, no time; 'ev just be tickled to death to put me . . . oveh 'e fence if we git clost 'nough to it."[89] But Van Loan cast Jones's difficulty as a curiosity that would soon no longer matter. When Curry protected an old black horseman named Uncle Gabe from the depredations of white gamblers, Van Loan described Gabe as "a real trainer of a school fast passing away," a former slave who represented the generations of skill that black horsemen had inherited. It was no coincidence that at the end of the story the old man thanked Curry, saying, "Mist' Curry, I'm quit hoss racin' now; but yo' the whites' man I met in all my life."[90] The integrity and dignity of black horsemen could be safely honored and the injustices they suffered deplored, as long as they were clearly retiring from the stage, their lines spoken with the inflections of the plantation minstrel.

BLACK ACTIVISTS AND JOURNALISTS never accepted such narratives of incompetence and inevitability. Why had black horsemen disappeared, the *Chicago Defender* asked? Because white owners and trainers "cannot take a colored jockey and mingle in the hotels with them."[91] The African American sociologist Kelly Miller warned blacks of the broader implications of a systematic effort to eliminate black horsemen from the track: "Let the Negro learn from the story of the jockey how he is being jockeyed out of his opportunity for jobs along all lines of endeavor."[92] They saw clearly that wealthy whites were using their control of jobs and of political influence to give credibility to the stories they told about black people's innate incompetence, their necessary subordination. They witnessed at the racetrack the overt and crude, the subtle and insidious workings of Jim Crow exposed.

Horsemen who had cherished both the vision and the reality of opportunity were forced to turn elsewhere. In 1906, Lonnie Clayton packed up the family he had made independent and prosperous in Arkansas and went to California, hoping to make a new life. A decade later, he died of pneumonia, leaving behind a job as a bellman at a Los Angeles hotel.[93] Sometimes, horsemen were literally expelled. In 1907, Willie Simms was actually escorted out of the Gravesend track on Long Island, where he had ridden many winners, accused of falsifying an admission badge to escape paying the price of an entrance ticket. A few years later, Simms ended up with a gunshot wound in a hospital in New Jersey, where he lived in a family that quarreled over small matters with the reflexive violence of desperation. In the end, he, too, died of pneumonia, a last, bitter legacy of his time as a jockey.[94] Former jockey Tommie Blevins did not live to die in bed. He tried to intervene in a late-night dispute, grabbing the arm of a white Lexington bartender who had pulled a gun on a patron. The bartender's nephew shot Blevins in the back of the head at point blank range, spattering brains and blood across the floor. The killer was acquitted of murder five months later, because the jury determined he had acted in self-defense.[95]

Some men raged against the closing of Jim Crow's walls around them. The great black trainer Frank Perkins grabbed any weapon that came to hand and smashed all the fixtures in a Cincinnati saloon one night, finally ending up in jail, where he had to be restrained for his own safety. "Monk" Overton, who had grown up in the security of Lexington's community of black horsemen, appeared in a police court in Chicago, experiencing similar symptoms of sudden and uncontrollable rage.[96] Overton's brother-in-law Tom Britton became so violently unpredictable that his wife Pearl divorced him, remarrying him a few years later.[97] James Perkins, Frank's brother, had known the pride of supporting his family in style as a teenager. By 1900, he was staring into a jobless future as one among millions of uneducated black men. Being the famous "Soup" Perkins no longer meant anything but embarrassment when he appeared on charges of disorderly conduct and his name made small headlines.[98] He supposedly sat alone and drank gin, perhaps because there seemed nothing else to do. "He was," one obituary writer summed up with unexpected grace, "awkward everywhere save on the horse." He lived only a few months beyond his thirty-third birthday.[99]

Perkins's obituarist commended the dead man for "never forgetting . . . that he was a Negro and never failing to act like one." This was the praise of a Jim Crow world, a world that many of Perkins's turf colleagues found they could not endure. The jockey Albert Isom went to a pawnshop, purchased a pistol and cartridges, loaded the gun at the counter, and shot himself in the head in front of the clerk.[100] Tom Britton, despondent because he could not find work, locked himself in a hotel room in Cincinnati and drank carbolic acid. In his suicide note, he told his wife Pearl good-bye forever. He would never see her again, he said, because he knew he would go to hell.[101]

Epilogue

He Didn't Go in No Back Doors!

In 1967, the quick-witted press agent Ted Worner, who boasted Ronald Reagan and Caesars Palace on his list of clients, was searching for a very particular publicity stunt. As he explained, he was "naturally looking for an angle for my Kentucky Club pipe tobacco" as the Kentucky Derby approached. At Worner's instigation, the tobacco company bankrolled a ceremonial reburial of Isaac Murphy, moving the jockey's casket from its resting place beside his wife in Lexington's black cemetery to a new grave next to Man o' War in a Lexington park. The greatest jockey in American history would now lie next to the greatest American racehorse. (Both horse and jockey were later moved to their present location near the entrance of the Kentucky Horse Park outside Lexington.) A few days before the Derby, in a small ceremony featuring representatives of Kentucky Club, Kentucky state officials, and the immortal Eddie Arcaro, winner of seventeen Triple Crown races, Murphy's body was reinterred.[1]

The event shared space in the newspapers with another notable set of Derby week developments. For months, fair housing advocates had been marching nightly into Louisville's segregated neighborhoods, demanding an open housing ordinance and facing menacing crowds of angry whites. The city government voted down such an ordinance in April, and the protests continued with redoubled energy. Both native son Muhammad Ali and Martin Luther King Jr. himself arrived in Louisville to support the call for fair housing, and Louisville's civil rights leaders announced that they intended to disrupt the Kentucky Derby in order to call attention to their cause. The comedian and activist Dick Gregory, who had also come to Louisville to assist, informed the press, "I ain't going to lay down in front of a horse myself, but there's a lot of cats that will. If it comes to closing the Derby up, we'll just have to close it up." In the days leading up to the Derby, a few young men, led by a Southern Christian Leadership Conference representative, were arrested for running in front of the horses during the course of a race.

In the end, movement leaders, including Martin Luther King, concluded that foregoing a racetrack protest would garner considerable municipal goodwill and increase the chances of an amicable settlement of housing issues. Some local activists protested the decision, but the Derby ran without incident.[2] City officials, however, had already made security arrangements for the occasion, and Proud Clarion won an upset victory on a track lined with grim-faced National Guardsmen. The black-owned *Louisville Defender*, a stalwart in previous city civil rights struggles, alternated in its pages descriptions of the protests and coverage of Isaac Murphy's reburial, along with photographs of Derby-winning black trainers and jockeys. Recalling the paper's long record in supporting battles for desegregation, the editors argued that Churchill Downs at Derby time was not an appropriate place to protest. The Derby, they wrote, "is a source of consuming pride because peoples of all origins and colors have helped to make it world famous." Black Americans had a stake in the Kentucky Derby, even if white Americans refused to acknowledge it.[3]

THE OCCASION OF MURPHY'S REBURIAL revealed how profoundly different white and black visions of the jockey and his compatriots were. Many white observers still sought to shape the famous black horseman into a supporter of their hierarchical visions of racial order. When Louisville reporter Frank Borries began his search for Murphy's original resting place in the 1950s, he first encountered an old story that claimed that Murphy had been buried in Mobile, Alabama, in the family plot of turfman William Cottrill, who allegedly wished to express his appreciation of Murphy's 1884 Kentucky Derby victory with Cottrill's Buchanan.[4] The story passed over Murphy's stormy relationship with Cottrill. Murphy had contracted to ride Buchanan in the Derby but later refused the mount, citing the horse's evil temper and tendency to bolt. Cottrill in turn refused to release the jockey from his contract, which meant that Murphy would be unable to ride in the race at all, and Murphy ultimately reconsidered. The newspapers at the time acknowledged that Murphy's steely brilliance had been responsible for bringing the recalcitrant animal home in front.[5] Later storytellers much preferred to elide the tense negotiation between employer and employee. They instead portrayed Murphy as a latter-day faithful slave, a loyal servant welcomed in death into the family with a gesture of condescending sentimentality.

When he could turn up no credible evidence to support the Alabama burial site, Borries directed his search elsewhere. He finally located a black man named Eugene Webster living in a housing project in Lexington. Webster remembered his father, an old friend of Murphy's, taking him regularly to visit the jockey's resting place. In 1909, as the grave's wooden marker had rotted away, a group of horsemen at the Lexington track had scraped together the cash to put up a homemade concrete marker over the grave, and they enlisted Webster's help to locate the appropriate site. There was no lettering, Webster explained to Borries when he brought him to the weed-choked, crumbling marker in the early 1960s. No one in the group had known how to engrave the surface, and they had not had the money to pay for it to be done. They had not needed words anyway. They knew who was buried there. "We were just a bunch of people that didn't want Ike's grave to get lost," Webster explained. "We wanted to do something for him."[6] He had, after all, done so much for them, even those who had never known him, purely by being who he was. They cherished his memory as a sacred trust.

Borries's quest for Murphy's body was a long and complex one because white and black people remembered the jockey and interpreted the meaning of his life so differently. And those divergences

continued well after his reburial. Many white racing fans and reporters were deeply uncomfortable with the political movements of
the 1960s, the calls for full black citizenship that surrounded the
Kentucky Derby of 1967 and surfaced again the following year. In
April 1968, when Derby hopeful Dancer's Image won the Governor's Gold Cup at the track in Bowie, Maryland, the colt's owner,
New Englander Peter Fuller, donated the purse to the recently wid-
owed Coretta Scott King. Racing split into factions over Fuller's
action, with some fans applauding his gesture and others insisting
that Fuller could have better donated the money to businessmen
who had suffered at the hands of inner-city rioters. A few weeks
later, Dancer's Image thundered to a come-from-behind win in the
1968 Kentucky Derby by a length and a half. After failing a disputed postrace drug test, the horse was stripped of his title, an act
that Fuller always regarded as punishment for his support of civil
rights.[7]

Many white reporters seized on Murphy as an antithesis to calls
for African Americans' admission into the full rights of citizenship.
Murphy had started life with few advantages, they pointed out,
but he had never been resentful or demanded a fairer chance.
"These are the things," proclaimed the *Lexington Leader,* "that make
the little fellow a giant object lesson in the American Way. It's
something to think about."[8] Murphy, they suggested, would never
have supported Martin Luther King and his allies; he would never
have contested systemic inequality, because to do so was fundamentally un-American. The *Thoroughbred Record* insisted that Murphy
would never have participated in the "anarchy and destruction" of
civil rights protest. With a rhetorical flourish, the *Record* concluded,
"If bones can feel and dust perceive, it would have been sheer cru-
elty to expose the bones and dust of Isaac Murphy to the events that
threaten Louisville on Derby Day. Bones and dust that once knew
dignity and distinction should not be asked to contemplate such
spectacles."[9]

But Murphy's bones had been exhumed into the air of the 1960s,
and they still had the power to inspire hope. Martin Brown, an African American horseman from south Louisiana, had resigned himself to a career as an exercise rider. But, in 1967, he came with the

trainer he worked for to Churchill Downs with a long shot for the Derby. There he met a reporter covering the Murphy reburial and learned for the first time about the jockey's storied career and the history of black riders. "I didn't know this," he recalled. The knowledge was part of what helped him decide, "Well, there's still hope for me."[10] Just as they had in T. Thomas Fortune's day, Murphy's success and stature fueled black people's determination that they be given the daily respect to which their humanity and their talents entitled them. Papa Jo Jones, the iconic drummer of Count Basie's orchestra, succinctly summed up what Murphy meant to him: "[H]e didn't go in no back doors!"[11]

THE BATTLES OVER MURPHY'S MEMORY and meaning occurred in the context of a racing world still living with the reality of white men's unabated fervor for the Thoroughbred and their dependence on skilled black men. In 1942, Harry Worcester Smith, whose Massachusetts textile mill fortune funded his lifelong devotion to horses, hatched the idea of giving a party in honor of turf historian John Hervey in New York. Smith broached the idea to the banker William Woodward, the chairman of the Jockey Club, and suggested that the event could be a definitive moment in the history of American sport. As he imagined the scene, the table would be laid with the trophies that Woodward's horses had won in both the United States and England, and around the board would be the great turfmen of the era: Arthur Hancock of Claiborne Farm, Man o' War's owner Samuel Riddle, and a select group of other luminaries. Smith urged Woodward to arrange for a photographer to commemorate the occasion. To round out the guest list, he finished, "There are your two sons-in-law and you would know their wish. It is a pity your boy is still young and now at Groton."[12] This dinner was the sort of event that a boy should experience, Smith believed. It would help to form him into the kind of man he should be.

Men like Woodward and Smith still believed that a passion for the Thoroughbred marked the man who was worthy to lead, so they worked to transmit that allegiance to their sons. Woodward published a memoir of his 1930 Triple Crown winner, the immortal Gallant Fox, including details of the horse's every physical characteristic down to the fraction of an inch. Woodward dedicated the book, "To My Son My Daughters and My Descendants So That in the Future They May Recall and Review the Quality and Deeds of Gallant Fox."[13] He bought little Billy Woodward a pony. Though the boy was never enthusiastic about riding, he grew up to own the temperamental champion Nashua. Harry Smith, who had always adored racing over fences on the steeplechase course and the hunting field, took equal care with the boys in his own family. Two years after he proposed the party for Hervey, he wrote to his grandson Tommy Smith, who was only six. "I write to say how happy I am that you love horses," the pleased grandfather told the child, "and I hope you will become as great a rider as your father, and that you will take my motto as yours: 'My line is the line of the foxes; my pace is the pace of the pack.'" His lessons took firm hold. In 1965, Tommy Smith traveled to England with his horse Jay Trump. The 100-6 long shot and his amateur jockey became the first American horse and rider to win the Grand National at Aintree.[14]

For Woodward and Smith, the lessons they were teaching were not only about horses but about how a man should behave, the things he should value, the skills he should hone to prove that he deserved authority and respect. But they depended on black men to help inculcate those invaluable lessons. At William Woodward's Belair Stud, even the master listened raptly to Andrew Jackson, the contemporary of Isaac Murphy who had once gone to Woodburn Farm and stood in a stall with Lexington, breathing the same air as the legendary stallion.[15] In his old age, Jackson taught Billy Woodward his first lessons with a horse.[16]

Harry Smith's horses were in the care of the African American trainer Dolph Wheeler. When Smith pulled off a difficult victory with The Cad in the Champion Steeplechase at Morris Park in 1900, he brought Wheeler along with him for a celebratory dinner at the Waldorf. And when the gentleman jockey grew into a proud father, Wheeler taught the Smith children to ride, passing on the skills that Harry Smith so valued and so loved to see exhibited in both his son and his grandson.[17] When Smith disbanded his stables, the two men kept in touch, and when Wheeler became fatally ill with diabetes, Smith paid for his hospital stay and visited regularly.

When the hospital called and informed Smith that Wheeler had died, he struggled to deal with the news. "I . . . just sat still . . . and thought how much he had been to me." He was one of the few white people to attend the funeral, held in a cold little chapel, and sat transfixed as a young girl sang "Nearer My God to Thee," her breath steaming out with the clear and perfect notes. "Never had I felt so lonely and sad," he remembered, and, when the minister invited him to speak, he stood awkwardly before the congregation, unable to account for why he was so tongue-tied, when "there were only black people present."

Smith had brought with him some of the most prestigious trophies his horses had won while in Wheeler's charge, and he laid them out around the coffin. He had been the famous one, he told the audience, but the credit for the victories in truth belonged to Wheeler. "There," he recalled telling them, "lay the true sportsman." It was the highest tribute in Smith's vocabulary. But when he sought to explain what he meant by that honorific, he could say in essence only that Wheeler "year after year, had revered me and my riding." Smith was pleased to see that the dead man had been dressed in an English-tailored hacking jacket that he had given to Wheeler from his own wardrobe after The Cad's victory in 1900, because the trainer so admired it. After the funeral ended, he paused to speak to the undertaker, passed him some cash, and instructed him to dress the body in another jacket and give him the coat. Smith sported the hardwearing garment for decades afterward at sporting events all over America. Wheeler, he insisted, would have wanted him to take the coat.[18]

Confronted with Wheeler as a person with his own life, in the midst of the obsequies, Smith had felt genuine sadness but also incomprehension. Perhaps that was what had momentarily made it so difficult to speak. His feelings were not original. Generations of white turfmen would have recognized in them the powerful bonds they had felt with black horsemen and the discomfort and even fear such men had inspired when they asserted their own autonomy and proved the transformative power of black aspiration.

MEN LIKE WHEELER were part of a community of black horsemen that shrank significantly but never entirely disappeared.[19] After the turn of the twentieth century, the percentage of black men licensed as jockeys and trainers dropped precipitously, as racetrack prejudice converged with black families' efforts to escape the strictures of segregation by leaving their native farms and towns. Bystanders reported that when two enormous stallions attacked one another on a Chicago street, a black woman calmly waded in and pried one's jaws off the other with a stick. She wasn't afraid of any horse alive, she said proudly, because her father, the greatest horseman she had ever seen, had taught her. She then collected her dumbfounded husband and left the scene.[20] She still remembered and valued old skills, but her children and grandchildren would be twentieth-century urbanites, unlikely to learn the skills that had made her father a man to be reckoned with. In fueling the Great Migration, Jim Crow substantially reduced the number of boys who hoped to become horsemen, indirectly as well as directly eating away at black men's racetrack employment. But black men continued to work, especially at smaller and less prestigious tracks, despite their dwindling numbers and the vehemence of bigotry that grew increasingly overt once African American horsemen were no longer an assumed presence in elite racing. Black horsemen remained repositories of skill and knowledge as they resolutely practiced their profession. Indeed, they played seldom-recognized but notable roles in the lives of some of the mightiest champions of the twentieth century.

When Man o' War started his career as a stallion at Faraway Farm, Will Harbut took over his care and shepherded countless tourists to the horse's stall, impressing on them that they were in the presence of greatness. The racing writer Joe Palmer quite seriously likened Harbut's lyrical account of the horse's victories to "Tennyson on the passing of Arthur."[21] Man and horse had been perfect together, Will Harbut's son Tom remembered. He recalled the bond between his father and the big animal, who died in 1947, less than a month after Harbut. "I was always enthralled by my father's knowledge of horses," Tom Harbut told a reporter more than fifty years later. "To remember it all and put it all in sequence like that. . . . I don't know whether he went to school at all." Will Harbut became part of the legend that he helped to create, but, when

Man o' War celebrated his twenty-first birthday with a party broadcast on national radio, Harbut was not invited to the banquet included in the festivities. Tom Harbut remembered that, too, and recalled that his mother had simply refused to attend an event at which the family was not truly welcome. The Harbuts loved Man o' War, but "we didn't feel like our family was special because of Man o' War. We always classified ourselves as a special family because we were family."[22]

Thirty years later, Secretariat became the only modern-day horse worthy to be mentioned in the same breath with Man o' War. Charlie Davis, his exercise rider, and Eddie Sweat, his groom, had already teamed up to take stablemate Riva Ridge to a win in the Kentucky Derby of 1972. The following year, they helped make Secretariat the Triple Crown champion, after his epic thirty-one-length victory in the Belmont Stakes. Both men had grown up in segregated South Carolina determined to work with Thoroughbreds. Eddie Sweat refused to discuss that part of his life with his children. But he knew he had found his vocation. He told his wife, "Before I met you I was with the horses and I'll still be doing it long after you're gone." His son described his father's relationship with Secretariat simply: "My father loved him as much as he loved me or my sisters."[23]

Charlie Davis also galloped Derby hopeful Silver Series for trainer Oscar Dishman Jr. before an injury took the colt off the path to the Run for the Roses. Dishman had learned his way around horses from his father, who worked with Thoroughbreds, and his grandfather, who kept his livestock in perfect order and his mouth tightly shut about the family's slave past. Dishman admitted that segregation cost him clients, since white trainers could eat and socialize with owners and try to influence them to take their horses away from black competitors. But Dishman's horses won many of the major fixtures in the Midwest, and grooms and exercise boys, he noted, always called him Mister Dishman. In the 1950s, he served as the lead plaintiff in the suit that desegregated the elementary schools in Scott County, Kentucky. All the Dishmans' children attended integrated schools and graduated from college.[24]

Men like Oscar Dishman made themselves professionals to be reckoned with. But black men were seldom granted access to the glittering opportunities for success and fame that their predecessors had enjoyed. Most had heard pseudoscientific arguments dinned into their ears for far too long, as white owners and reporters turned from discounting black intelligence to mourning the allegedly inexorable increase in black men's height and weight. African Americans were simply no longer biologically suited to being jockeys, pundits solemnly insisted. One groom interviewed in the early 1970s rolled his eyes, "Yeah, I know. We're all Wilt Chamberlains." The problem, he and his coworkers agreed, was that aspiring black riders were simply denied chances to move up in the business because powerful white owners refused to accord them opportunities commensurate with their talents.[25]

In 1953, the Jackie Robinson–edited magazine *Our Sports*, devoted to African American athletics, had circumspectly pointed out a basic part of the problem. Without more black trainers to support young black horsemen, hone their talents, and open up for them the possibility of professional advancement, there would never again be a competitive group of African American riders on the nation's tracks and in its newspapers.[26] Jim Crow had destroyed the extensive professional networks that had long given black men security and made them markers of hope and racial pride. When Hank Allen brought his own Northern Wolf to the Derby in 1989, he reflected on his status as the first African American trainer of record for a Derby horse in decades and asked a pointed question about the black grooms who had often played significant roles in bringing such horses to the post successfully: "Why didn't any of those grooms get the opportunity to become a trainer?" Allen had made enough money in professional baseball to bankroll himself. He was quick to say that there were older men more skillful than he was who had never gotten a chance to have a talent like Northern Wolf in their barns. He pointed to a friend of his, a jockey looking for rides, who had gotten several good mounts when owners and trainers had mistakenly thought he was Panamanian: "But when they found out he was from Detroit, all of a sudden he couldn't get any mounts. You tell me why."[27]

African American riders continued to experience similar job discrimination. Only in 2000 did Marlon St. Julien become the first

African American to ride in the Derby since 1921. It took more than a decade before another black rider, Kevin Krigger, rode to the Derby post aboard California speedster Goldencents. Though his mount faded badly and finished seventeenth, Krigger had already surmounted formidable odds to get into the race, as the Jockeys' Guild noted that only about 5 percent of riders in the United States in 2013 were black. But there will always be another Derby. Liliane Winkfield Casey, excited about Krigger's prospects, informed a reporter that her father would have said, "It's about time somebody else won."[28]

As the years have stretched on, black horsemen have preserved among themselves the memory of the time when men like them dominated the competition on the back turn. Edward Brown's son Lee Brown, long after he had established himself as an impeccably respectable correspondent for the black press, took an occasional break from covering politics and religion. When he filed an annual Kentucky Derby story, he ensured the preservation of his father's legacy. "The memory of him will never be forgotten by the followers of the turf," the younger Brown wrote. "The names of his horses have been handed down from generation to generation."[29] Lee Brown knew that his education, his profession, his security, his sense of who he was, he owed to his father. And his father had owed his own career to the kindly skill of Ansel Williamson, who had made him a jockey, and to Harry Lewis, who had first seen the greatness in Lexington and fostered the stallion who would father Asteroid, the horse that vaulted Brown to success at the age of fourteen. When Lee Brown memorialized his father, he also implicitly paid homage to his father's friends and to those who had come before them. Many black horsemen jealously guarded that legacy. In the 1970s, as the black jockey James Long hoped for a break on the New York tracks, he told a reporter how sad he was that he had not had the chance to meet Jimmy Winkfield before his death: "I really wanted to meet him for the same reason any kid who plays baseball would want to meet Babe Ruth. I don't want people to think we're new at this game. We've been at it a long time."[30] Throughout his run to the 2013 Derby, Kevin Krigger kept a photo of Winkfield in his locker, because the young jockey felt "proud to see him, the look in his eyes" every day. Winkfield, he explained, was telling him that he could win.[31]

Beginning in the 1990s, African American community activists seized on the stories and people that horsemen had spoken of among themselves and began to explore ways in which they could honor that past and demonstrate its relevance in an age in which very few people had ever seen a Thoroughbred in the flesh. The Project to Preserve African-American Turf History, a Louisville-based group, has been one of the organizations prominent in seeking to publicize African American contributions to the Kentucky Derby in particular. Their goal, in essence, is to tell the world that the *Louisville Defender* was right when it claimed the Derby as a proud achievement for black Americans. Leon Nichols, one of the activists prominent in the group, notes that the most common reaction, even in the black community, to the organization's work is, "I just didn't know that."[32] Successful TV actor Rodney Van Johnson knew that his grandmother's grandfather was named Oliver Lewis but never knew, until a researcher telephoned his mother, that Lewis had won the first Kentucky Derby. His mother urged him to go to the Kentucky Derby website to see for himself. "I remember seeing his face," Johnson said. "I saw it, and it brought tears to my eyes."[33] In 2011, the Project presented the first annual Isaac Murphy Derby Experience and Image Awards, an event to celebrate African American contributions to the Derby. The awards have since honored entertainers like Viola Davis, Danny Glover, and Angela Bassett. The ceremony presents the Derby as an event that should be accepted as part of a larger history of black achievement.

Kentucky communities have begun to memorialize black horsemen. Lexington named a new road Oliver Lewis Way, and the small town of Midway put up a historical marker honoring the life and achievements of Edward Brown.[34] The Isaac Murphy Memorial Art Garden will soon grow on a site now believed to be where the jockey's house once stood.[35] But many activists have pressed to bring the legacy of men like Lewis, Brown, and Murphy to life, to consider its contemporary meanings rather than merely commemorating it. As the Kentucky poet Frank X. Walker insists, "It can't be an exhibit in a museum. It can't be dead history."[36] In verse, Walker imagines that legacy as a broad charge: "Grab the reins of any and everything that makes your heart race. / Find your purpose. Find your purpose. / And hold on."[37] Answering that call, Walker has helped to found the Isaac Murphy Bicycle Club in Murphy's old neighborhood in the east end of Lexington. The club provides bicycle riding instruction, bikes, and mobile history lessons to local children who cannot afford the equipment and who often do not know about the nationally famous men who came from their own neighborhood. Walker has also spearheaded the Isaac Murphy Everybody Reads Project, in which students from kindergarten through twelfth grade in more than sixty Kentucky schools read his book about Murphy and explore together the questions it raises about community resources and achievement.[38] No wonder then, that, when the *Lexington Herald-Leader* covered a lecture former jockey James Long gave about the many horsemen buried in the city's black cemetery, the story generated response in the online comments section. One poster, an old friend of Long's from his days in New York racing, adjured him, "Keep telling the stories James."[39]

For decades, Ralph Ellison worked to craft a novel that would be a worthy successor to *Invisible Man*, leaving behind reams of manuscript at his death in 1994. In one of the last sections Ellison wrote, a character named McIntyre, a white reporter from Kentucky, finds himself in the opulent Washington, D.C., home of a murdered man. As the police begin the routine work of investigation, McIntyre wanders over the house and discovers a treasure trove of artifacts related to African American history. The unbroken line of objects, one after the other, forces McIntyre to consider uncomfortably what he believes about black Americans' place in the United States. *"Damn this room and the questions it raises,"* he complains, but he nevertheless stares at a cluster of pictures: a painting of John Brown, a photograph of Jack Johnson, and between them two lithographs, one of Pike Barnes winning the Futurity with Proctor Knott in 1888 and one of Isaac Murphy at Churchill Downs. It is in understanding such men, their lives, and their legacies, Ellison suggests, that we will come to grips with "our fractured democracy."[40] The ride, then, is nowhere near over.

Notes

Acknowledgments

Index

Notes

Prologue

1. "Sports and Sportsmen of the Olden Time," *American Turf Register,* Dec. 1831, 193.

2. John Hervey, *Racing in America, 1655–1865,* vol.1 (New York: Jockey Club, 1944), 24.

3. "Quarter Racing of the Olden Time," *American Turf Register,* May 1832, 450. This article, penned by Allen J. Davie, is the source of this account of the race.

4. On the ubiquity and importance of horses in earlier times and their relative neglect in historiography, see Ann Norton Greene, *Horses at Work: Harnessing Power in Industrial America* (Cambridge, MA: Harvard University Press, 2008), 5–23; Karen Raber and Treva J. Tucker, eds., *The Culture of the Horse: Status, Discipline, and Identity in the Early Modern World* (New York: Palgrave Macmillan, 2005), 2–3.

5. Hervey, *Racing in America, 1655–1865,* vol. 1, 74–77.

6. Kent Hollingsworth, *The Kentucky Thoroughbred* (Lexington: University Press of Kentucky, 1976), 16; Hervey, *Racing in America, 1655–1865,* vol. 1, 6–8, 64, 247–48.

7. John B. Irving, *The South Carolina Jockey Club* (Charleston: Russell and Jones, 1857), 14.

8. Hunter Dickinson Farish, ed., *The Journal and Letters of Philip Vickers Fithian: A Plantation Tutor of the Old Dominion, 1773–1774* (Williamsburg: Colonial Williamsburg, 1957), 177.

9. T.H. Breen, "Horses and Gentlemen: The Cultural Significance of Gambling among the Gentry of Virginia," *William & Mary Quarterly,* 3rd ser., 34.2 (1977): 239–57; Rhys Isaac, *The Transformation of Virginia, 1740–1790* (1982; Chapel Hill: University of North Carolina Press, 1999), 60, 99–120, 317.

10. Quoted in Keith Thomas, *Man and the Natural World: Changing Attitudes in England 1500–1800* (London: Penguin, 1983), 117.

11. For an examination of Jones's life and career, see Blackwell Pierce Robinson, "Willie Jones of Halifax," *North Carolina Historical Review* 18.1 (1941): 1–26, and 18.2 (1941): 133–70.

12. See Donna Landry, *Noble Brutes: How Eastern Horses Transformed English Culture* (Baltimore: Johns Hopkins University Press, 2009), 6–7, 139–63, on cross-class relationships in the eighteenth-century British equestrian world that influenced American views of slave horsemen and other stable subordinates.

13. Robin Law, *The Horse in West African History* (Oxford: Oxford University Press, 1980), 46–53.

14. Ibid., 64–76, 148.

15. Karol K. Weaver, *Medical Revolutionaries: The Enslaved Healers of Eighteenth-Century Saint Domingue* (Urbana: University of Illinois Press, 2006), 88–95.

16. William Cavendish, Duke of Newcastle, *A general system of horsemanship in all it's branches* (London: J. Brindley, 1743); Karen Raber, "A Horse of a Different Color: Nation and Race in Early Modern Horsemanship Treatises," in *Culture of the Horse*, ed. Raber and Tucker, 237; Kim F. Hall, *Things of Darkness: Economies of Race and Gender in Early Modern England* (Ithaca: Cornell University Press, 1995), 236–37.

17. Carlyle Brown, *Pure Confidence* (Alexandria, VA: Alexander Street Press, 2005), 9–11.

18. Robinson, "Willie Jones of Halifax," 8–9.

19. "Pedigree of Reality," *American Turf Register*, Aug. 1832, 594; Hervey, *Racing in America, 1655–1865*, vol.1, 157.

20. Allen J. Davie, "Marmaduke Johnson's Mare," *American Turf Register*, June 1833, 520.

21. Petition by Willie Jones to North Carolina General Assembly, 7 Dec. 1791, General Assembly Session Records, Dec. 1791–Jan. 1792, Box 1, North Carolina State Archives, Raleigh, NC.

22. For an example of discussion of the dynamics of this difficult choice, see Sylvia F. Frey, *Water from the Rock: Black Resistance in a Revolutionary Age* (Princeton: Princeton University Press, 1991), 53–80.

23. "Turf Register," *American Turf Register*, Nov. 1829, 163; Hervey, *Racing in America, 1655–1865*, vol.1, 125.

24. "Bill to liberate a Mulattoe Slave, named Austin Curtis, belonging to Willie Jones," 7 Dec 1791, General Assembly Session Records, Dec. 1791–Jan. 1792, Box 1, North Carolina State Archives, Raleigh, NC. See also William L. Byrd III, *In Full Force and Virtue: North Carolina Emancipation Records 1713–1860* (Bowie, MD: Heritage Books, 1999), 4.

25. William Faulkner, *The Hamlet* (New York: Vintage, 1991), 32–33.

26. Walter Johnson has cogently pointed out how crucial this kind of thought process was for the workings of slavery. See Walter Johnson, *River of Dark Dreams: Slavery and Empire in the Cotton Kingdom* (Cambridge, MA: Harvard University Press, 2013), 207.

27. Willie Jones Will, 1798, *Halifax County Wills, 1758–1824* vol. 3, 355–62, North Carolina State Archives.

28. Margaret M. Hofmann, *Genealogical Abstracts of Wills, 1758–1824 Halifax County, North Carolina* (Weldon, NC: Roanoke News, 1970), Ref #773; Paul Heinegg, *Free African Americans of North Carolina, Virginia, and South Carolina from the Colonial Period to about 1820*, 5th ed., vol. 1 (Baltimore: Clearfield, 2005), 383.

29. Arna Bontemps, *God Sends Sunday* (New York: Harcourt, Brace and Co., 1931; New York: Washington Square Press, 2005), 4, 20–21, 100–104, 129–30, 198.

30. Kirkland C. Jones, *Renaissance Man from Louisiana* (Westport, CT: Greenwood, 1992), 73.

31. Carole Case, *The Right Blood: America's Aristocrats in Thoroughbred Racing* (New Brunswick, NJ: Rutgers University Press, 2001), 52.

32. Joseph Durso, "Alfred Gwynne Vanderbilt, 87, Is Dead; Horseman from an Aristocratic Family," *New York Times*, 13 Nov. 1999, B11.

33. George Marshall death record, Illinois Deaths and Stillbirths Index, 1916–1947. Accessed through ancestry.com, 3 May 2013.

1. The Glory of the Four-Mile Horse

1. Charles E. Trevathan, *The American Thoroughbred* (New York: Macmillan, 1905), 148–50; Alexander Mackay-Smith, *The Race Horses of America, 1832 to 1872* (Saratoga Springs: National Museum of Racing, 1981), 18–19; Ephraim Conrad, *An Authentic History of the Celebrated Horse American Eclipse* (New York: 1823), Beinecke Rare Book and Manuscript Library, Yale University. The book is unpaginated.

2. Both challenge and response are quoted in full in Conrad, *An Authentic History*.

3. Conrad, *An Authentic History*; John Hervey, *Racing in America, 1655–1865*, vol. 1 (New York: Jockey Club, 1944), 261–62; Mackay-Smith, *Race Horses of America*, 42.

4. An Old Turfman, "The Great Match Race Between Eclipse and Sir Henry—Minutely Described by an Old Turfman," *American Turf Register*, Sept. 1830, 3. Old Turfman was the nom de plume of the New Yorker Cadwallader Colden.

5. Hervey, *Racing in America, 1655–1865*, vol. 1, 265; William H. P. Robertson, *The History of Thoroughbred Racing in America* (Englewood Cliffs, NJ: Prentice Hall, 1964), 53; Max Farrand, "The Great Race—Eclipse Against the World!" *Scribner's*, Oct. 1921, 460–61.

6. "Clear the Course," *National Advocate*, 27 May 1823. Variant spelling in the original.

7. Josiah Quincy Jr., *Figures of the Past from the Leaves of Old Journals* (Boston: Roberts Brothers, 1883), 96–97.

8. The two best accounts of the race, from which these quotes are drawn, are Old Turfman, "The Great Match Race Between Eclipse and Sir Henry," 3; Quincy, *Figures of the Past*, 97–100. A shorter account appears in Conrad, *An Authentic History*.

9. Quincy, *Figures of the Past*, 99–100; Farrand, "The Great Race," 464; Conrad, *An Authentic History*.

10. Elizabeth Amis Cameron Blanchard and Manly Wade Wellman, *The Life and Times of Sir Archie* (Chapel Hill: University of North Carolina Press, 1958), 104–5.

11. "Great Match Race," *National Advocate*, 30 May 1823.

12. Powhatan Bouldin, *Home Reminiscences of John Randolph of Roanoke* (Richmond: Clemmet & Jones, 1878), 18.

13. "Alderman Purdy and Mr. Randolph," *The Spirit of the Times*, 24 Dec. 1836, 358. Nonstandard capitalization in the original. See also James Douglas Anderson, *The Making of the American Thoroughbred, Especially in Tennessee, 1800–1845* (Norwood, MA: Plimpton Press, 1916), 162–63.

14. Robert Gage to James Gage, 15 April 1836, Folder 2, James M. Gage Papers #1812-z, Southern Historical Collection, The Wilson Library, University of North Carolina at Chapel Hill.

15. Hervey, *Racing in America, 1655–1865*, vol. 1, 247–48, and vol. 2, 102.

16. For a partial list of American racetracks in 1830, see "List of Race Courses in the United States, As far as ascertained," *American Turf Register*, Oct. 1830, 93.

17. Hervey, *Racing in America, 1655–1865*, vol. 1, 250–51, and vol. 2, 101–2.

18. For a sampling of jockey club rules, including all these common practices, see "Rules and Regulations for the Woodlawn Race Course Association, Louisville, Kentucky," (Louisville: Hull & Brother, 1859), Kentucky Historical Society, Frankfort, KY; "Rules and Regulations of the Metairie Jockey Club," *Sports in North America*, vol. 3, ed. George B. Kirsch (Gulf Breeze, FL: Academic International, 1992), 205–8; "Rules of the South-Carolina Jockey Club" (Charleston: A.E. Miller, 1853), South Carolina Historical Society, Charleston, SC; "Rules and Regulations of the Magnolia Jockey Club of the State of Alabama" (Mobile: Farrow and Dennett, 1860), South Carolina Historical Society; "Constitution of the Kentucky Association and Rules and Regulations for the Government of the Course" (Lexington: Kentucky Statesman Print, 1853), Margaret I. King Special Collections Library, University of Kentucky; "Constitution of the Adams County, Mississippi Jockey Club," William J. Minor Papers, Box 1, Folder 1, Louisiana and Lower Mississippi Valley Collections, Louisiana State University; "Norfolk Jockey Club Records" and "Richmond Jockey Club Records," Virginia Historical Society, Richmond, VA; "Rules and Regulations of the Savannah Jockey Club" (Savannah: John M. Cooper, 1856), Duke University Special Collections.

19. "Rules and Regulations for the Governing of the Woodlawn Race Course," Kentucky Historical Society; "Rules of the South-Carolina Jockey Club," South Carolina Historical Society.

20. Diary, 1845–54, and Diary, 1855–65, Thomas Porcher Ravenel Papers, 1810–1904, (1171.02.02), South Carolina Historical Society. The Pineville races typically took place in the second half of January, so yearly entries on the topic will be found in that date range.

21. Henry Ravenel Diary, 23 Oct. 1809, Henry Ravenel Family Papers, 1731–1867 (1171.02.01), South Carolina Historical Society.

22. Codicil to the will of Thomas W. Doswell, 25 July 1890, Series 6, Doswell Family Papers, Virginia Historical Society.

23. Rebecca Gustine Minor to "My dear Niece," 20 Aug. 1869, Box 1, Folder 7, Minor Family Papers, Mississippi Department of Archives and History, Jackson, MS.

24. John B. Irving, *The South Carolina Jockey Club* (Charleston: Russell & Jones, 1857), 210–12.

25. Ibid., 11–12, 209–10.

26. Christopher Olsen, *Political Culture and Secession in Mississippi* (New York: Oxford University Press, 2000), 24–26; Joanne Freeman, *Affairs of Honor* (New Haven: Yale University Press, 2001), xiii–xxiv.

27. See, on debt payment, W. Sinkler to Richard Singleton, 3 Feb. 1841, Box 1, Folder 22, Singleton Family Papers, South Caroliniana Library, University of South Carolina. For a discussion of the language of match race challenges, see Kenneth S. Greenberg, *Honor and Slavery* (Princeton: Princeton University Press, 1996), 138–39. On the necessary politeness when discussing pedigrees, see Panton, "Importance of Authentic Pedigrees," *American Turf Register*, April 1831, 362.

28. Bertram Wyatt-Brown, *Southern Honor: Ethics and Behavior in the Old South* (New York: Oxford University Press, 1982), 345–46.

29. William Cabell Bruce, *John Randolph of Roanoke*, vol. 1 (New York: G.P. Putnam's Sons, 1922), 130–31. Variant spelling in the original.

30. Michael O'Brien, *Conjectures of Order: Intellectual Life and the American South*, vol.1 (Chapel Hill: University of North Carolina Press, 2004), 669.

31. Greenberg, *Honor and Slavery*, 56–59.

32. Trevathan, *American Thoroughbred*, 185–87; Hervey, *Racing in America, 1655–1865*, vol.2, 70.

33. Bruce, *John Randolph of Roanoke*, vol.1, 549–50.

34. Irving, *South Carolina Jockey Club*, 29. The Biblical passages come from Job 39: 19–22.

35. Francis Blair to Andrew Jackson, 6 Oct. 1842, *Correspondence of Andrew Jackson*, vol. 6, ed. John Spencer Bassett (Washington, D.C.: Carnegie Institute, 1926–35), 173.

36. Irving, *South Carolina Jockey Club*, 29–30.

37. "Collectanea for the Historian of the American Thoroughbred Horse," comp. Fairfax Harrison, 1929, Small Special Collections Library, University of Virginia.

38. O'Brien, *Conjectures of Order*, vol. 1, 493.

39. J. H. Ingraham, *The South-West, By a Yankee*, vol. 2 (New York: Harper & Brothers, 1835), 78–79, 219–20.

40. C. W. Van Ranst to Richard Singleton, 17 April 1822, Box 1, Folder 5, Singleton Family Papers, South Caroliniana Library, University of South Carolina.

41. See, for a sample of Colden's network, Colden to W.J. Minor, 22 July 1833, 20 June 1835, 30 March 1836, Folder 5, William J. Minor Horse Racing Collection, Beinecke Rare Book and Manuscript Library, Yale University.

42. Hervey, *Racing in America, 1655–1865*, vol. 1, 247.

43. Glover Moore, *The Missouri Controversy 1819–1821* (Lexington: University of Kentucky Press, 1953), 55–58, 73–74; Robert Pierce Forbes, *The Missouri Compromise and Its Aftermath* (Chapel Hill: University of North Carolina Press, 2007), 7–13; Douglas R. Egerton, *He Shall Go Out Free* (Madison, WI: Madison House, 1999), 130–31, 209; Edward Bartlett Rugemer, *The Problem of Emancipation* (Baton Rouge: Louisiana State University Press, 2008), 79–81.

44. "Alderman Purdy and Mr. Randolph," 358.

45. A Native Born Marylander, "Turf Warfare Between the North and South," *American Turf Register*, Sept. 1834, 17 and "Turf Warfare Between the North and South—Explanation," *American Turf Register*, Nov. 1834, 130.

46. Quoted in T.J. Stiles, *The First Tycoon* (New York: Alfred A. Knopf, 2009), 58–59.

47. "Racing Calendar," *American Turf Register*, Dec, 1833, 205. T.J. Stiles, in his discussion of the incident, notes that Vanderbilt's horse was disqualified (see Stiles, *First Tycoon*, 89), but the abbreviation dis. in this case usually means distanced, which was a racing term in general use at the time. The distinction is an important one since a well-bred, expensive horse, owned by a respected competitor, could easily be distanced through poor racing luck or conditioning or any number of other factors known and dreaded by racing men. Disqualification, as Stiles suggests in his interpretation of the incident, implies that the horse and the owner do not belong in the competition at all, and that does not seem to have been the case.

48. Stiles, *First Tycoon*, 312–22.

49. Drew Gilpin Faust, *James Henry Hammond and the Old South* (Baton Rouge: Louisiana State University Press, 1982), 158–59.

50. Wade Hampton II to James Henry Hammond, 13 March 1840, *Family Letters of the Three Wade Hamptons*, ed. Charles E. Cauthen (Columbia: University of South Carolina Press, 1953), 30; Irving, *South Carolina Jockey Club*, 28–29.

51. J. C. Nott to James Gage, 8 Sept. 1838, Folder 3, James M. Gage Papers #1812-z, Southern Historical Collection, The Wilson Library, University of North Carolina at Chapel Hill.

52. Reginald Horseman, *Josiah Nott of Mobile: Southerner, Physician, and Racial Theorist* (Baton Rouge: Louisiana State University Press, 1987), 32, 42–43, 59–62.

53. J. C. Nott to James Gage, 5 Nov. 1836, Folder 2, James M. Gage Papers #1812-z, Southern Historical Collection, The Wilson Library, University of North Carolina at Chapel Hill.

54. J. C. Nott to James Gage, 8 Sept. 1838, Folder 3, James M. Gage Papers #1812-z, Southern Historical Collection, The Wilson Library, University of North Carolina at Chapel Hill.

55. "Blood Stock of Austin Woolfolk, Esq.," *Spirit of the Times*, 25 Sept. 1841, 354; William Calderhead, "The Role of the Professional Slave Trader in a Slave Economy: Austin Woolfolk, a Case Study," *Civil War History* 23.3 (1977): 197–206.

56. Steven Deyle, *Carry Me Back: The Domestic Slave Trade in American Life* (New York: Oxford University Press, 2005), 6–11. Walter Johnson has re-

cently coined the term "slave-racial capitalism" to describe the breadth of Southern slavery's economic and political implications. He has also valuably explicated the debates over whether slavery was technically "capitalist" or not. See Walter Johnson, *River of Dark Dreams: Slavery and Empire in the Cotton Kingdom* (Cambridge, MA: Harvard University Press, 2013), 14, 252–54.

57. Irving, *South Carolina Jockey Club*, 27.

58. Hervey, *Racing in America, 1655–1865*, vol. 1, 241–42.

59. See Stephanie McCurry, *Masters of Small Worlds: Yeoman Households, Gender Relations, and the Political Culture of the Antebellum South Carolina Low Country* (New York: Oxford University Press, 1995), 105–6. The world of the races was much like the world of the hunt in that respect. See Nicholas W. Proctor, *Bathed in Blood: Hunting and Mastery in the Old South* (Charlottesville: University of Virginia Press, 2002), 43–88.

60. McCurry, *Masters of Small Worlds*, 128–29.

61. Irving, *South Carolina Jockey Club*, 181.

62. McCurry, *Masters of Small Worlds*, 84–85, 92–93, 105.

63. Irving, *South Carolina Jockey Club*, 203–4; Charles Fraser, *Reminiscences of Charleston* (Charleston: J. Russell, 1854), 62–63.

64. Irving, *South Carolina Jockey Club*, 11.

65. Ibid., 11.

66. Mrs. St. Julien Ravenel, *Charleston: The Place and the People* (New York: Macmillan, 1912), 129. See, for a similar discussion, Irving, *South Carolina Jockey Club*, 11.

67. Irving, *South Carolina Jockey Club*, 14–15.

68. Ira Berlin has suggested the degree to which planters attempted to exert and entrench mastery by performing it in particular landscapes, including racetracks. See Ira Berlin, *Many Thousands Gone* (Cambridge, MA: Harvard University Press, 1998), 97–98.

69. William Ransom Hogan and Edwin Adams Davis, eds., *William Johnson's Natchez: The Antebellum Diary of a Free Negro* (1951; Baton Rouge: Louisiana State University Press, 1993), 81.

70. Edwin Adams Davis and William Ransom Hogan, *The Barber of Natchez* (Baton Rouge: Louisiana State University Press, 1954), 202–7.

71. Hogan and Davis, *William Johnson's Natchez*, 254, 509.

72. Ibid., 711. Variant spelling in original.

73. On Johnson's unusually long and close relationships with prominent Natchez white men, both turfmen and nonturfmen, see Davis and Hogan, *The Barber of Natchez*, 91–104.

74. "Slave Prisons—Flogging," *Western Citizen*, 5 Oct. 1847, 4.

75. James Stuart, *Three Years in North America*, 3rd rev. ed., vol. 2 (Edinburgh: Robert Caddell, 1833), 68. Variant spelling in original.

76. Isaac Weld, *Travels Through the States of North America and the Provinces of Upper and Lower Canada, During the Years 1795, 1796, and 1797*, 4th ed., vol. 1 (London: T. Gillett, 1807), 150.

77. Andrew Jackson to Major William B. Lewis, 5 Aug. 1828, vol. 3, *Correspondence of Andrew Jackson*, 418–19.

78. "Training Horses," *American Turf Register*, Aug. 1830, 593.

79. William J. Minor, "Short Rules for Training Two Year Olds" (New Orleans: Picayune, 1854), Box 1, Folder 2, William J. Minor Papers, Louisiana and Lower Mississippi Valley Collections, Louisiana State University.

80. Hervey, *Racing in America, 1655–1865,* vol. 1, 251–52.

81. Charles Alexander, *Battles and Victories of Allen Allensworth, A.M., Ph.D., Lieutenant-Colonel, Retired, U.S. Army* (Boston: Sherman, French & Co, 1914), 157, accessed through Documenting the American South, University Library, University of North Carolina at Chapel Hill, 2000, http://docsouth .unc.edu/neh/alexander/alexander.html.

82. "Sporting Intelligence," *American Turf Register,* March 1832, 357.

83. James Chesnut to Richard Singleton, 15 June 1841, Box 1, Folder 23, Singleton Family Papers, South Caroliniana Library, University of South Carolina.

84. Blanchard and Wellman, *Life and Times of Sir Archie,* 144–45; Franklin Reynolds, "A Man Obsessed with a Horse," *Thoroughbred Record,* 23 Dec. 1961, 48; J.M. Selden, "Age and True Parentage of Sir Archy," *American Turf Register,* Aug. 1834, 600.

85. Irving, *South Carolina Jockey Club,* 187–88.

86. Theodore Stewart interview, *The American Slave: A Composite Autobiography,* vol. 6, ed. George P. Rawick (Westport, CT: Greenwood, 1972), 357. Variant spelling in original.

87. William Green, *Narrative of Events in the Life of William Green (Formerly a Slave)* (Springfield: L.M. Guernsey, 1853), 3–5. Accessed through Documenting the American South, University Library, University of North Carolina at Chapel Hill, 2000, http://docsouth.unc.edu/neh/greenw/greenw .html.

88. Wade Hampton to Andrew Jackson, June 1810, *The Papers of Andrew Jackson,* vol. 2, ed. Harold D. Moser and Sharon Macpherson (Knoxville: University of Tennessee Press, 1985), 248.

89. Jacob Stroyer, *My Life in the South* (Salem: Salem Observer, 1885), 20–27. Accessed through Documenting the American South, University Library, University of North Carolina at Chapel Hill, 2001, http://docsouth.unc.edu /neh/stroyer85/stroyer85.html.

90. "On Training," *American Turf Register,* Dec. 1830, 160.

91. Walter Johnson has compellingly discussed the role of violence in forcing slave bodies to conform to white masters' expectations and fantasies. What happened to jockeys is the most explicit form of this set of practices I have seen. See Walter Johnson, *Soul by Soul: Life Inside the Antebellum Slave Market* (Cambridge, MA: Harvard University Press, 1999), 205–6.

92. On the realities, dynamics, and consequences of slave malnutrition, see Richard H. Steckel, "A Peculiar Population: The Nutrition, Health, and Mortality of American Slaves from Childhood to Maturity," *Journal of Economic History* 46.3 (1986): 732–41; Robert A. Margo and Richard H. Steckel, "The Heights of American Slaves: New Evidence on Slave Nutrition and Health," *Social Science History* 6.4 (1982): 525–30; Johnson, *River of Dark Dreams,* 179–87.

93. Mackay-Smith, *Race Horses of America,* 31.

94. "To Correspondents," *Porter's Spirit of the Times*, 28 May 1859, 200.

95. Frederick Douglass, *Narrative of the Life of Frederick Douglass*, ed. David W. Blight (Boston: Bedford/St. Martin's, 2003), 52–53.

96. Charles L. Wingfield, "The Sugar Plantations of William J. Minor, 1830–1860," MA thesis, Louisiana State University, 1950, 74.

97. The patterns of the correspondence between white horsemen suggest that horses (and written questions and answers about horses) were delivered by particular men, who could make sure a valuable animal arrived safely at its destination and could make judgments about horses they had seen. Such was the career of Richard Singleton's slave Levin, who was often on the road with horses and letters for other horsemen. For instance, see George Fryer to R. Singleton, 7 June 1842, Box 1, Folder 25, Singleton Family Papers, South Caroliniana Library, University of South Carolina. See Stephanie M. H. Camp, *Closer to Freedom* (Chapel Hill: University of North Carolina Press, 2004), 15–16, 30, for a discussion of the policing of mobility and its importance in slave men's lives.

98. John Randolph to George H. Burwell, 22 Feb. 1826, Stud Book of George H. Burwell, Marian Dupont Scott Papers, Small Special Collections Library, University of Virginia.

99. See, for an example of a horseman's pass, "Jesse Pass to Mr. Cottens in Georgia," 20 Nov. 1820, Box 14, Folder 314, Singleton Family Papers #668, Southern Historical Collection, The Wilson Library, University of North Carolina at Chapel Hill.

100. I have found no obituary notice for Cornelius and no mention of his death in the Singleton family collections I have examined. But by the early 1840s, Cornelius was evidently ready to pass his long-held responsibilities on to a younger man. The Singletons first hired the free black trainer Charles Sykes to take his place. See "Notes of the Month. January," *American Turf Register*, Jan. 1843, 52. See Hervey, *Racing in America, 1655–1865*, vol. 2, 109, on Merritt's importations.

101. A. T. B. Merritt to Richard Singleton, 27 Nov. 1845 and 27 Dec. 1845, Box 2, Folder 26, Singleton Family Papers, South Caroliniana Library, University of South Carolina.

102. Dylan C. Penningroth, "My People, My People: The Dynamics of Community in Southern Slavery," *New Studies in the History of American Slavery*, ed. Edward E. Baptist and Stephanie M. H. Camp (Athens: University of Georgia Press, 2006), 166–76.

103. See, for example, W. J. Minor's advertisement for his stallion Voucher, whose fee was forty dollars, along with a dollar for his groom. W. J. Minor Breeding Book, Box 2, Folder 37, William J. Minor Horse Racing Collection, Beinecke Rare Book and Manuscript Library, Yale University.

104. "R Singleton, Esq in a/t with B Taylor," Box 1, Folder 9, Singleton Family Papers, South Caroliniana Library, University of South Carolina.

105. A. T. B. Merritt to Richard Singleton, 13 April 1846, Box 7, Folder 142, Singleton Family Papers #668, Southern Historical Collection, The Wilson Library, University of North Carolina at Chapel Hill.

106. Account of Joseph Ingles for Richard Singleton 1849, Box 13, Folder 285, Singleton Family Papers #668, Southern Historical Collection, The Wilson Library, University of North Carolina at Chapel Hill.

107. A. T. B. Merritt to Richard Singleton, 27 Dec. 1845, Box 2, Folder 26, Singleton Family Papers #668, Southern Historical Collection, The Wilson Library, University of North Carolina at Chapel Hill.

108. A. T. B. Merritt to Matthew Singleton, 20 June 1847, Box 2, Folder 27, Singleton Family Papers, South Caroliniana Library, University of South Carolina.

109. Charles Redd to Richard Singleton, 5 June 1825, Box 1, Folder 6, Singleton Family Papers, South Caroliniana Library, University of South Carolina.

110. John Morris Morgan, *Recollections of a Rebel Reefer* (Boston: Houghton Mifflin, 1917), 6–7. Accessed through Documenting the American South, University Library, University of North Carolina at Chapel Hill, 1999, http://docsouth.unc.edu/fpn/morganjames/morgan.html.

111. Jonathan Martin, *Divided Mastery* (Cambridge, MA: Harvard University Press, 2004), 118.

112. A. T. B. Merritt to Matthew Singleton, 23 March 1847, Box 2, Folder 27, Singleton Family Papers, South Caroliniana Library, University of South Carolina. It may have been particularly important to keep Hark away from areas prone to malaria outbreaks because he already had the disease. Merritt says that his hiring fee is so low because Hark is now prone to bouts of a chronic illness.

113. "Notes of the Month. February," *American Turf Register*, Feb. 1843, 100; Martin, *Divided Mastery*, 109.

114. N., "Suggestions to Breeders and Turfmen," *Spirit of the Times*, 9 June 1838, 133. His biographers have identified N. as Josiah Nott.

115. Horseman, *Josiah Nott*, 110, 125–26, 300; Joan Cashin, *A Family Venture: Men and Women on the Southern Frontier* (New York: Oxford University Press, 1991), 112.

116. N., "N. of Arkansas in the East," *Spirit of the Times*, 19 June 1841, 181. N. and N. of Arkansas were two different correspondents.

117. Pierce Butler to Francis W. Pickens, 12 March 1834, Francis W. Pickens Papers, South Caroliniana Library, University of South Carolina.

118. Johnson, *Soul by Soul*, 205–6.

119. Irving compared to Cornelius a black groom belonging to Mr. Sinkler. He didn't name the groom, but he was probably talking about Hercules, who became famous as the winning trainer of the Albine-Planet match race in 1861. See Irving, *South Carolina Jockey Club*, 187–88.

120. Ravenel, *Charleston*, 392.

121. A. T. B. Merritt to Richard Singleton, 31 Dec. 1847, Box 7, Folder 146, Singleton Family Papers #668, Southern Historical Collection, The Wilson Library, University of North Carolina at Chapel Hill; A. T. B. Merritt to Matthew Singleton, 23 April 1847, Box 2, Folder 27, Singleton Family Papers, South Caroliniana Library, University of South Carolina.

122. James Chesnut to Richard Singleton, 9 Dec. 1840, Box 1, Folder 22, Singleton Family Papers, South Caroliniana Library, University of South Carolina.

123. John James Audubon and John Bachman, *The Quadrupeds of North America* (New York: V.G. Audubon, 1849), 8–9. See, for a discussion of similar relationships on the plantation, Proctor, *Bathed in Blood*, 119–25, and Annette Gordon-Reed, *The Hemingses of Monticello* (New York: W. W. Norton, 2008), 575.

124. Stroyer, *My Life in the South*, 31.

125. Bouldin, *Home Reminiscences*, 101.

126. Bruce, *John Randolph of Roanoke*, vol. 1, 43–44; vol. 2, 695–96.

127. Michael Tadman, *Speculators and Slaves* (1989; Madison, WI: University of Wisconsin Press, 1996), xix–xxxii; Deyle, *Carry Me Back*, 208–23.

128. Johnson, *Soul by Soul*, 22–23.

129. See, on the danger of assuming that slave owners would have had to view slaves as less than human to treat them as they did, Johnson, *River of Dark Dreams*, 206.

130. Stroyer, *My Life in the South*, 32.

131. Stroyer, *My Life in the South*, 27–28, 20–21.

132. Johnson, *Soul by Soul*, 21; Camp, *Closer to Freedom*, 62–68.

133. See James Sidbury, *Ploughshares into Swords: Race, Rebellion, and Identity in Gabriel's Virginia, 1730–1810* (Cambridge: Cambridge University Press, 1997), 65–66, for the role of the horse in intersecting Atlantic ideologies of power. See, on the powerful feelings of pride slaves took in their own resilience and skilled labor, Johnson, *River of Dark Dreams*, 164–65.

134. See, for example, the note from Richard Singleton's business agents about their search for the escaped slave Levin. Goodman and Miller to Richard Singleton, 8 Feb. 1831, Box 4, Folder 97, Singleton Family Papers #668, Southern Historical Collection, The Wilson Library, University of North Carolina at Chapel Hill.

135. Henry Clay Bruce, *The New Man* (York, PA: Anstadt and Sons, 1895), 43–45. Accessed through Documenting the American South, University Library, University of North Carolina Chapel Hill, 1997, http://docsouth.unc.edu/fpn/bruce/bruce.html.

136. Johnson, *River of Dark Dreams*, 222–24.

137. A. T. B. Merritt to Richard Singleton, 20 April 1847, Box 2, Folder 27, Singleton Family Papers, South Caroliniana Library, University of South Carolina.

138. On the historiography of the relationship between the authority vested in privileged male slaves by white men and the power those men had in the slave community, see Robert L. Paquette, "The Drivers Shall Lead Them: Image and Reality in Slave Resistance," *Slavery, Secession, and Southern History*, ed. Robert L. Paquette and Louis L. Ferleger (Charlottesville: University of Virginia Press, 2000), 31–58.

2. Knowed a Horse When He Seed Him

1. See E. Leverich to Mrs. James Porter, 12 April 1870, Annie Porter to Henry Leverich, 21 Oct. 1879, Alexander Porter Papers, Louisiana and Lower Mississippi Valley Collections, Louisiana State University.

2. All quotations within Charles Stewart's narrative, unless otherwise noted, come from Annie Porter, "My Life as a Slave," *Harper's New Monthly Magazine*, Oct. 1884, 730–38. Variant spelling in original.

3. The prominent racing historian Alexander Mackay-Smith was the first to recognize that Stewart's clothes as described in Porter's article closely correspond to the formal clothes worn by black horsemen in portraits of the period. See Alexander Mackay-Smith, "Ante-bellum Black Trainers and Jockeys," National Sporting Library newsletter, Dec. 1979, 4.

4. Melvin Patrick Ely, *Israel on the Appomattox* (New York: Alfred A. Knopf, 2004), 152–74.

5. John Hervey, *Racing in America, 1655–1865* (New York: Jockey Club, 1944), vol.2, 31.

6. Alexander Mackay-Smith, *The Race Horses of America, 1832–1872* (Saratoga Springs: National Museum of Racing, 1981), 10; Mackay-Smith, "Ante-bellum Black Trainers and Jockeys," 3.

7. R.R. Beasley to J.E. Hutchinson, 30 Aug. 1841, Alexander Porter Papers, Louisiana and Lower Mississippi Valley Collections, Louisiana State University.

8. Brenda E. Stevenson, *Life in Black and White: Family and Community in the Slave South* (New York: Oxford University Press, 1996), 255; Emily West, *Chains of Love: Slave Couples in Antebellum South Carolina* (Urbana: University of Illinois Press, 2004), 60–67.

9. Dylan C. Penningroth, "My People, My People: The Dynamic of Community in Southern Slavery," in *New Studies in the History of American Slavery*, ed. Edward E. Baptist and Stephanie M.H. Camp (Athens: University of Georgia Press, 2006), 168–69. On the importance to a slave society of allowing slaves to own other slaves, see Orlando Patterson, *Slavery and Social Death* (Cambridge, MA: Harvard University Press, 1982), 184.

10. See description of Charles signed by William R. Johnson, 23 Aug. 1839, in R.R. Beasley to J.E. Hutchinson, 30 Aug. 1841, Alexander Porter Papers, Louisiana and Lower Mississippi Valley Collections, Louisiana State University.

11. Stewart's situation thus bolsters William Dusinberre's argument that there was no such thing as a slave elite, only particular privileged slaves whose position had very little effect on their families and friends. See William Dusinberre, *Them Dark Days: Slavery in the American Rice Swamps* (New York: Oxford University Press, 1996), 179.

12. On Johnson's financial disaster, see Peter S. Carmichael, *Lee's Young Artillerist* (Charlottesville: University of Virginia Press, 1995), 17, 179n22. For the evidence of his debts, see Series 5 and 6, Johnson Family Papers, Virginia Historical Society.

13. Thoroughbred breeders have traditionally treated sire lines as more important than the contributions of mares, and the stallion's name rather than the dam's identifies foals. But racing breeders have long unofficially understood that mares have a crucial part to play in producing a great horse. Relatively new research indicates that the gene for an abnormally large and efficient heart is inherited from the mother.

14. Albion, "Reminiscences of the Turf," *Spirit of the Times*, 24 Nov. 1877, 439.

15. "Editorial Reminiscences. Old Boston's Early Life," *Spirit of the Times*, 19 Nov. 1859, 486; "On Dits in Sporting Circles," *Spirit of the Times*, 7 May 1842, 114; Kent Hollingsworth, *The Great Ones* (Lexington: The Blood Horse, 1970), 39.

16. Ricardo, "Arab Gone To Tennessee," *American Turf Register*, Nov. 1829, 116. Variant spelling in original.

17. James David Miller, *South by Southwest* (Charlottesville: University of Virginia Press, 2002), 11; Joan Cashin, *A Family Venture: Men and Women on the Southern Frontier* (New York: Oxford University Press, 1991), 20.

18. Melvin L. Adelman, "The First Modern Sport in America: Harness Racing in New York City, 1825–1870," in *Sport in America*, ed. David K. Wiggins (Champaign, IL: Human Kinetics, 1995), 100–113.

19. Melvin L. Adelman, *A Sporting Time: New York City and the Rise of Modern Athletics* (Urbana: University of Illinois Press, 1986), 42–48; Hervey, *Racing in America, 1655–1865*, vol. 2, 155–56; Peter L. Rousseau, "Jacksonian Monetary Policy, Specie Flows, and the Panic of 1837," *Journal of Economic History* 62.2 (2002): 473–86; Peter Temin, *The Jacksonian Economy* (New York: W. W. Norton, 1969), 92, 148.

20. "Imported Stock at the South," *Spirit of the Times*, 21 July 1838, 180.

21. "The Great Peyton Stake," *Spirit of the Times*, 28 Oct. 1843, 411.

22. See, for the only scholarly discussion of this breeding network, Arvilla Taylor, "Horse Racing in the Lower Mississippi Valley Prior to 1860," MA thesis, University of Texas, 1953, 32. For an example of how these networks were arranged, see Thomas Alderson to W. J. Minor, 20 April 1850, Box 1, Folder 1, William J. Minor Horse Racing Collection, Beinecke Rare Book and Manuscript Library, Yale University, and "Recollections, The Federal Raid Upon Ashland Plantation in July 1862," Rosella Kenner Brent Papers, Louisiana and Lower Mississippi Valley Collections, Louisiana State University, 14.

23. "On Dits in Sporting Circles," *Spirit of the Times*, 5 June 1841, 162; James Douglas Anderson, *Making the American Thoroughbred, Especially in Tennessee, 1800–1845* (Norwood, MA: Plimpton Press, 1916), 7.

24. "Subscription list," ms., 1840–1842 Folder; W. D. Lancaster to the Secretary of the Lexington Jockey Club, 31 Dec. 1850, 1850–1859 Folder; A. L. Bingaman and H. P. McGrath to Charles Wheatley, 17 Dec. 1859, 1850–1859 Folder, Kentucky Association for the Improvement of the Breeds of Stock records, Margaret I. King Special Collections Library, University of Kentucky.

25. Taylor, "Horse Racing in the Lower Mississippi Valley," 130–31.

26. Martha Ann Peters, "The St. Charles Hotel, New Orleans Social Center, 1837–1860," *Louisiana History* 1.3 (1960): 196–99; "Notes of the Month. February," *American Turf Register*, Feb. 1843, 100.

27. "Notes of the Month. March," *American Turf Register*, March 1842, 168.

28. Hervey, *Racing in America, 1655–1865*, vol. 2, 196.

29. Richard Tattersall to W. J. Minor, 10 Feb. 1837, Box 1, Folder 24, William J. Minor Horse Racing Collection, Beinecke Rare Book and Manuscript Library, Yale University. Variant spelling in the original.

30. W.J. Minor to Rebecca Gustine, 3 Dec. 1828, Box 1, Folder 9, William J. Minor and Family Papers, Louisiana and Lower Mississippi Valley Collections, Louisiana State University. The Minor and Family papers are distinct from the William J. Minor Papers, also in the Louisiana and Lower Mississippi Valley Collections at LSU.

31. "Agreement," ms., Box 1, Folder 39, William J. Minor Horse Racing Collection, Beinecke Rare Book and Manuscript Library, Yale University; Purdy to W.J. Minor, 27 May 1850 and "Account for John Purdy, 1852," Box 2E547, Folder 13, James Campbell Wilkins Papers, Dolph Briscoe Center for American History, University of Texas.

32. Charles L. Wingfield, "The Sugar Plantations of William J. Minor, 1830–1860," MA thesis, Louisiana State University, 1950, 12.

33. "The Late New Orleans Races," *Spirit of the Times*, 10 Feb. 1849, 606.

34. "Capt. Minor and His Stable," *Spirit of the Times*, 22 Jan. 1848, 567.

35. Mark A. Keller, "Horse Racing Madness in the Old South: The Sporting Epistles of William J. Minor of Natchez (1837–1860)," *Journal of Mississippi History* 47.3 (1985): 171–72.

36. See Michael O'Brien, *Conjectures of Order: Intellectual Life and the American South, 1810–1860* (Chapel Hill: University of North Carolina Press, 2004), vol. 1, 553–56, for a discussion of the significance of pseudonyms in Southern magazine writing.

37. Hervey, *Racing in America, 1655–1865*, vol. 2, 197–98.

38. See, for a comparable association of personal honor with disputes in the world of the sporting press, Gideon Smith to Richard Singleton, Dec. 21 1834, Richard Singleton Papers, 1826–1835, (43/4) South Carolina Historical Society. On Minor's career as a sporting correspondent, see Keller, "Horse Racing Madness in the Old South," 165–85; Kenneth S. Greenberg, *Honor and Slavery* (Princeton: Princeton University Press, 1996), 139.

39. Ann Norton Greene, *Horses at Work: Harnessing Power in Industrial America* (Cambridge, MA: Harvard University Press, 2008), 130.

40. "The Mouth of Pryor," *Porter's Spirit of the Times*, 4 Oct. 1856, 76.

41. On the Pryor controversy, see "The Age of the Race-Horse Pryor," *Spirit of the Times*, 6 Sept. 1856, 354; "The Age of Pryor," *Spirit of the Times*, 4 Oct. 1856, 403; untitled rough drafts of correspondence and magazine articles in Box 2, Folder 41, William J. Minor Horse Racing Collection, Beinecke Rare Book and Manuscript Library, Yale University.

42. Cadwallader Colden to W.J. Minor, 22 July 1833, Box 1, Folder 5, William J. Minor Horse Racing Collection, Beinecke Rare Book and Manuscript Library, Yale University.

43. Benjamin Perley Poore, *Biographical Sketch of John Stuart Skinner*, ed. John L. O'Connor (New York: 1924), 3–28.

44. Francis Brinley, *The Life of William T. Porter* (New York: D. Appleton and Company, 1860; New York: Arno, 1970), 32–33; Norris Wilson Yates, *William T. Porter and the Spirit of the Times* (Baton Rouge: Louisiana State University Press, 1957), 4–9.

45. See Hervey, *Racing in America, 1655–1865*, vol. 2, 93–94.

46. Brinley, *Life of William T. Porter*, 62–63.

47. Yates, *William T. Porter and the Spirit of the Times*, 31; Mackay-Smith, *Race Horses of America*, 132.

48. Norris Yates, "The *Spirit of the Times:* Its Early History and Some of Its Contributors," *The Papers of the Bibliographical Society of America* 48.2 (1954): 148.

49. Edwin Adams Davis, ed., *Plantation Life in the Florida Parishes of Louisiana, 1836–1846, as Reflected in the Diary of Bennet H. Barrow* (New York: AMS Press, 1967), 413.

50. William Ransom Hogan and Edwin Adams Davis, eds., *William Johnson's Natchez: The Antebellum Diary of a Free Negro* (1951; Baton Rouge: Louisiana State University Press, 1993), 166.

51. Lees and Waller to R.A. Alexander, 21 July and 29 July 1856, Box 8, Folder 25, Alexander Family Papers: Woodburn Farm Series, Kentucky Historical Society.

52. "Sporting Epistle from the West," *Spirit of the Times*, 1 Oct. 1836, 261.

53. Quoted in Brinley, *Life of William T. Porter*, 81–82.

54. Yates, *William T. Porter and the Spirit of the Times*, 22.

55. Brinley, *Life of William T. Porter*, 83–87; Mackay-Smith, *Race Horses of America*, 136–37; Eugene Current-Garcia, " 'York's Tall Son' and His Southern Correspondents," *American Quarterly* 7.4 (1955): 380–81.

56. Quoted in Brinley, *Life of William T. Porter*, 186–87.

57. O'Brien, *Conjectures of Order*, vol. 1, 758–59; John Mayfield, *Counterfeit Gentlemen: Manhood and Humor in the Old South* (Gainesville: University Press of Florida, 2009), 51.

58. See Yates, *William T. Porter and the Spirit of the Times*, 88, on Southwest humor as a confirmation for readers of Southern distinctiveness. For an example of the best of the magazine's humorous pieces, including Porter's use of "universal Yankee nation," see *A Quarter Race in Kentucky and Other Tales*, ed. W.T. Porter (Philadelphia: Carey & Hart, 1846).

59. Viator, "Night Funeral of a Slave," *Spirit of the Times*, 14 April 1849, 89.

60. On Stewart's appearance in the Troye portrait and the portrait's publication in the *Turf Register*, see "Medley," *American Turf Register*, May 1833, 437; Mackay-Smith, *Race Horses of America*, 9.

61. John Michael Vlach, *The Planter's Prospect: Privilege and Slavery in Plantation Paintings* (Chapel Hill: University of North Carolina Press, 2002), 2–7.

62. Mackay-Smith, *Race Horses of America*, 371–72.

63. See, on some slaves' pride in their own labor and expertise, Walter Johnson, *River of Dark Dreams: Slavery and Empire in the Cotton Kingdom* (Cambridge, MA: Harvard University Press, 2013), 164–65.

64. John Stauffer, "Frederick Douglass and the Aesthetics of Freedom," *Raritan* 25.1 (Summer 2005): 115.

65. *Obituary Addresses on the Occasion of the Death of the Hon. Henry Clay, A Senator of the United States from the State of Kentucky, Delivered in the Senate and in the House of Representatives of the United States, June 30, 1852, and the Funeral Sermon of the Rev. C. M. Butler, Chaplain of the Senate, Preached in the Senate, July 1, 1852* (Washington, D.C.: Robert Armstrong, 1852), 127.

66. Horace Greeley, *Recollections of a Busy Life* (New York: J.B. Ford and Company, 1868), 166.

67. "New Orleans Jockey Club Races," *Spirit of the Times*, 15 April 1843, 84.

68. Jeff Meyer, "Henry Clay's Legacy to Horse Breeding and Racing," *Register of the Kentucky Historical Society* 100.4 (2002): 477.

69. Henry Clay to Nicholas Biddle, 12 Sept. 1838, *The Papers of Henry Clay*, v. 9, ed. Robert Seager II (Lexington: University Press of Kentucky, 1984), 227.

70. Henry Clay to Nicholas Biddle, 1 Oct. 1838, *Papers of Henry Clay*, v. 9, 234.

71. Wade Hampton to Henry Clay, 3 June 1845, Clay-Russell Family Papers, Margaret I. King Special Collections Library, University of Kentucky.

72. William Newton Mercer to Henry Clay, 24 Nov. 1845, *Papers of Henry Clay*, v. 10, ed. Melba Porter Hay (Lexington: University Press of Kentucky, 1991), 251.

73. Meyer, "Henry Clay's Legacy," 473; Kent Hollingsworth, *The Kentucky Thoroughbred* (Lexington: University Press of Kentucky, 1976), 159–60.

74. "'Uncle Ned' and Eclipse," *Spirit of the Times*, 12 June 1841, 7.

75. *Spirit of the Times*, 7 May 1836, 96.

76. Jacob Swigert to R. A. Alexander, 26 July 1842, Box 8, Folder 9, Alexander Family Papers: Woodburn Farm Series, Kentucky Historical Society.

77. For more extensive discussion of Peyton's politics and turf exploits, see Walter T. Durham, *Balie Peyton of Tennessee: Nineteenth Century Politics and Thoroughbreds* (Franklin, TN: Hillsboro Press, 2004), ix, 12, 61–62.

78. Balie Peyton, "Mr. Peyton's Colt Livingston," *Spirit of the Times*, 25 Feb. 1837, 12.

79. "Report From St. Catherine's," 29 Dec. 1830, Box 58, Folder 1, Surget-McKittrick-MacNeil Papers, Mississippi Department of Archives and History; "On Dits in Sporting Circles," *Spirit of the Times*, 29 Feb. 1840, 618.

80. Hogan and Davis, *William Johnson's Natchez*, 287. For a discussion of Whig electoral strategy and the log cabin motif in 1840, see Michael F. Holt, *The Rise and Fall of the American Whig Party* (New York: Oxford University Press, 1999), 105–6.

81. Cecilia M. Shulman, "The Bingamans of Natchez," *Journal of Mississippi History* 63 (2001): 305–6; Stephen Duncan to Henry Clay, Jan. 9, 1838, *Papers of Henry Clay*, v. 9, 123.

82. "Col. W. J. Minor," *Natchez Courier*, 26 Aug. 1852.

83. "On Dits in Sporting Circles," *Spirit of the Times*, 15 May 1841, 126; "On Dits in Sporting Circles," *Spirit of the Times*, 21 Jan. 1843, 560.

84. Wendell Holmes Stephenson, *Alexander Porter Whig Planter of Old Louisiana* (Baton Rouge: Louisiana State University Press, 1934), 117–18.

85. Alexander Porter to Dr. John Ker, 3 April 1836, Box 2, Folder 17, Ker Family Papers #4656, Southern Historical Collection, The Wilson Library, University of North Carolina at Chapel Hill.

86. Thomas Brown, *Politics and Statesmanship: Essays on the American Whig Party* (New Haven: Yale University Press, 1985), 125.

87. William Kauffman Scarborough, *Masters of the Big House: Elite Slaveholders of the Mid-Nineteenth Century South* (Baton Rouge: Louisiana State University Press, 2003), 30; Morton Rothstein, "The Natchez Nabobs: Kinship

and Friendship in an Economic Elite," *Toward a New View of America: Essays in Honor of Arthur C. Cole*, ed. Hans L. Trefousse (New York: Burt Franklin and Co., 1977), 105–7.

88. John M. Sacher, *A Perfect War of Politics: Parties, Politicians, and Democracy in Louisiana, 1824–1861* (Baton Rouge: Louisiana State University Press, 2003), 51–52.

89. See Richard Follett, *The Sugar Masters* (Baton Rouge: Louisiana State University Press, 2005), 104–5, for a discussion of the entrance of steam engines into the cane fields and Kenner's particular innovations in that regard.

90. Rothstein, "Natchez Nabobs," 103–6.

91. Quoted in Scarborough, *Masters of the Big House*, 256–57.

92. O'Brien, *Conjectures of Order*, vol. 2, 914–15.

93. David S. Heidler and Jeanne T. Heidler, *Henry Clay, The Essential American* (New York: Random House, 2010), 53.

94. Merrill D. Peterson, *The Great Triumvirate* (New York: Oxford University Press, 1987), 373; Heidler and Heidler, *Henry Clay*, 398.

95. John Ashworth, *"Agrarians" and "Aristocrats": Party Political Ideology in the United States, 1837–1846* (London: Royal Historical Society, 1983), 69.

96. See, on Clay's personal financial dealings and the appeal of his programs to Southerners with similar backgrounds, Daniel Walker Howe, *The Political Culture of the American Whigs* (Chicago: University of Chicago Press, 1979), 130–31.

97. My discussion in this section is indebted to Howe, *Political Culture of the American Whigs*, 21–32, and Eric Stoykovich, "In the National Interest: Improving Domestic Animals and the Making of the United States, 1815–1870," PhD diss., University of Virginia, 2009, 149–54.

98. Quoted in Heidler and Heidler, *Henry Clay*, 36.

99. Heidler and Heidler, *Henry Clay*, 35, 131–32, 372–74, 447–48.

100. Lacy K. Ford, *Deliver Us from Evil: The Slavery Question in the Old South* (New York: Oxford University Press, 2009), 300–301; Heidler and Heidler, *Henry Clay*, 131.

101. Ford, *Deliver Us From Evil*, 326; Heidler and Heidler, *Henry Clay*, 299–300.

102. Howe, *Political Culture of the American Whigs*, 134–37; D. Clayton James, *Antebellum Natchez* (Baton Rouge: Louisiana State University Press, 1968), 152–53; Morton Rothstein, "The Changing Social Networks and Investment Behavior of a Slaveholding Elite in the Antebellum South: Some Natchez 'Nabobs,' 1800–1860," *Entrepreneurs in Cultural Context*, ed. Sidney M. Greenfield, Arnold Strickon, and Robert T. Aubey (Albuquerque: University of New Mexico Press, 1979), 79; Shulman, "Bingamans of Natchez," 308–9.

103. See Ford, *Deliver Us from Evil*, 327–28, for an assessment of Clay's ideas about the ultimately adversarial nature of slavery and his embrace of certain forms of paternalism in his own dealings with some slaves.

104. "Address of Nicholas Biddle, Esq., to the Agricultural Society of Philadelphia County, on the 8th Oct. 1840," *Spirit of the Times*, 7 Nov. 1840, 428. On Biddle's passion for agricultural improvement and his belief that setting an

example for farmers was his social responsibility, see Thomas Payne Govan, *Nicholas Biddle: Nationalist and Public Banker 1786–1844* (Chicago: University of Chicago Press, 1959), 58–59.

105. Mackay-Smith, *Race Horses of America*, 9.

106. "Letter from a Virginia Turfman," *Spirit of the Times*, 24 June 1837, 149.

107. "Daniel Webster," *Spirit of the Times*, 18 May 1839, 121; "Mr. Webster's Farm," *Spirit of the Times*, 21 Jan. 1843, 563. On Webster's career as a farmer and his love for agricultural pursuits, see Rexford B. Sherman, "Daniel Webster, Gentleman Farmer," *Agricultural History* 53.2 (1979): 475–86.

108. Edward Bartlett Rugemer, *The Problem of Emancipation: The Caribbean Roots of the American Civil War* (Baton Rouge: Louisiana State University Press, 2009), 8–9.

109. Alexander Porter to Josiah Johnston, 15 April 1832, Josiah Stoddard Johnston Papers, Historical Society of Pennsylvania, Reel 8, microfilm ed.

3. A Storm Is Approaching

1. J.M., "The Kentucky Stables," *Spirit of the Times*, 23 May 1846, 151.

2. "Sixth Day Great Four Mile Race," 1838–39 folder, Kentucky Association for the Improvement of the Breeds of Stock records, Margaret I. King Special Collections Library, University of Kentucky.

3. John Hervey, *Racing in America 1655–1865* (New York: Jockey Club, 1944), vol. 1, 230; William H. P. Robertson, *The History of Thoroughbred Racing in America* (Englewood Cliffs, NJ: Prentice Hall, 1964), 67; Kent Hollingsworth, *The Great Ones* (Lexington: The Blood Horse, 1970), 169; Kent Hollingsworth, *The Kentucky Thoroughbred* (Lexington: University Press of Kentucky, 1976), 21.

4. Hervey, *Racing in America, 1655–1865*, vol. 2, 281. For another instance of the distinction between possession of a horse and possession of his racing qualities, see "Racing in Tennessee," *Porter's Spirit of the Times*, 8 Oct. 1859, 91.

5. Hervey, *Racing in America, 1655–1865*, vol. 2, 281–86; Hollingsworth, *Kentucky Thoroughbred*, 24–26; Robertson, *History of Thoroughbred Racing*, 68–69; Hollingsworth, *Great Ones*, 170–71; Willa Viley personal copy, "Constitution of the Kentucky Association and Rules and Regulations for the Government of the Course" (Lexington: Kentucky Statesman Print, 1853), Margaret I. King Special Collections Library, University of Kentucky.

6. Eliza Ripley, *Social Life in Old New Orleans: Being Recollections of My Girlhood* (New York: D. Appleton, 1912), 245.

7. "The Great Post Stake. Kentucky Victorious!," *Spirit of the Times*, 15 April 1854, 103. My account of the race, unless otherwise noted, is taken from this article.

8. Ripley, *Social Life in Old New Orleans*, 248.

9. Ibid., 246.

10. Hervey, *Racing in America, 1655–1865*, vol. 2, 288–29; Alexander Mackay-Smith, *The Race Horses of America, 1832–1872* (Saratoga Springs, NY: National Museum of Racing, 1981), 214; Hollingsworth, *Great Ones*, 166.

11. Hollingsworth, *Great Ones*, 165; Mackay-Smith, *Race Horses of America*, 263; G. M. G. Stafford, *The Wells Family of Louisiana and Allied Families* (Alexandria, LA: Standard Printing, 1942), 92.

12. Untitled ms., Box 2, Folder 40, William J. Minor Horse Racing Collection, Beinecke Rare Book and Manuscript Library, Yale University.

13. A Young Turfman, "Lexington and Lecomte Again," *Spirit of the Times*, 17 Nov. 1855, 474; Untitled ms., Box 2, Folder 40, William J. Minor Horse Racing Collection, Beinecke Rare Book and Manuscript Library, Yale University.

14. "Metairie Jockey Club Races," *New Orleans Daily Picayune*, 8 April 1853, 2.

15. "On Dits in Sporting Circles," *Spirit of the Times*, 27 Jan. 1855, 594.

16. A Young Turfman, "Lexington's Great Time Match," *Spirit of the Times*, 24 March 1855, 67.

17. "Metairie Jockey Club Meeting," *Spirit of the Times*, 22 April 1854, 115; Larkin, "Lexington and Lecomte's Great Race," *Spirit of the Times*, 10 June 1854, 199.

18. Hervey, *Racing in America, 1655–1865*, vol. 2, 291–94; for a sampling of their challenges and attacks on one another, see "Sporting Challenges," *New Orleans Daily Picayune*, 11 June 1854, 3; "The Turf," *New Orleans Daily Picayune*, 21 June 1854, 1; "The Challenge From Lexington," *Spirit of the Times*, 8 July 1854, 246; "On Dits in Sporting Circles," *Spirit of the Times*, 14 Aug. 1854, 318.

19. For an indication of Gilpatrick's national standing as a contract rider, see "On Dits in Sporting Circles," *Spirit of the Times*, 2 Sept. 1848, 330.

20. "Nine Cheers for Lexington," *Spirit of the Times*, 7 April 1855, 90.

21. "The Great Four Mile Race," *Spirit of the Times*, 28 April 1855, 126.

22. Walter McGehee Lowrey, "The Political Career of James Madison Wells," *Louisiana Historical Quarterly* 31.4 (1948): 1000.

23. A Young Turfman, "Lexington and Lecomte Again," *Spirit of the Times*, 17 Nov. 1855, 474.

24. W. J. Minor to T. J. Wells, 1 Sept. 1854, Box 1, Folder 3, William J. Minor Papers, Louisiana and Lower Mississippi Valley Collections, Louisiana State University; untitled ms. Box 2, Folder 40, William J. Minor Horse Racing Collection, Beinecke Rare Book and Manuscript Library, Yale University.

25. For a discussion of Lecomte's difficulties leading up to the race and the drugging allegations, see untitled ms., Box 2, Folder 40, William J. Minor Horse Racing Collection, Beinecke Rare Book and Manuscript Library, Yale University. For the details of the race itself, see Hollingsworth, *Great Ones*, 167.

26. See for recent scientific examination of the cause of the horse's blindness, "One Hundred Sixty Years After His Birth A Racehorse's Bones Return to Lexington," *Smithsonian Science*, 17 Nov. 2010. Accessed 28 Oct. 2013, http://smithsonianscience.org/2010/11/after-160-years-racehorse-lexingtons -bones-returned-to-the-town-of-his-birth/.

27. Jonelle Fisher, *For All Times: The Story of Lucas Brodhead* (N.P.: St. Crispian Press, 2002), 16–17.

28. "Lexington's Bones," *New York Sportsman*, 20 Nov. 1875, 305.

29. Charles E. Trevathan, *The American Thoroughbred* (New York: Macmillan, 1905), 305.

30. Craig A. Bauer, *A Leader among Peers: The Life and Times of Duncan Farrar Kenner* (Lafayette: Center for Louisiana Studies, 1993), 49–50.

31. Slave lists, Series 1, Box 1, Folder 3, Duncan Kenner Papers, Louisiana and Lower Mississippi Valley Collections, Louisiana State University.

32. "The Turf and Turfmen," *Spirit of the Times*, 23 July 1853, 271.

33. Nowhere have I seen a case that more clearly illustrates Walter Johnson's formulation that slavery, in its simplest form, was "a person with a price." See Walter Johnson, *Soul by Soul: Life Inside the Antebellum Slave Market* (Cambridge, MA: Harvard University Press, 1999), 2.

34. Daniel Walker Howe, *What Hath God Wrought: The Transformation of America, 1815–1848* (New York: Oxford University Press, 2007), 690–98.

35. "The Lexington Races," *Porter's Spirit of the Times*, 11 June 1859, 234.

36. "Sporting Epistle from 'A Young Turfman,'" *Spirit of the Times*, 16 April 1853, 102.

37. Harry Worcester Smith, "The Sportsman's Bookshelf," *Thoroughbred Record*, 8 Aug. 1925, 67; "Metairie (N.O.) Jockey Club Races," *Porter's Spirit of the Times*, 18 April 1857, 108.

38. "Metairie Jockey Club Races," *New Orleans Daily Picayune*, 3 April 1861, 1; "Great Day on the Metairie," *New York Tribune*, 18 April 1861, 7.

39. For an example of Abe's name in a racing summary in which he rode the winner, see "New Orleans Races," *Porter's Spirit of the Times*, 21 Jan 1860, 331. For a complimentary discussion of one of his defeats, see "Metairie Jockey Club Races," *Spirit of the Times*, 14 April 1860, 114.

40. "The New Orleans Races on the Old Metairie—Winter Meeting of 1860," *Porter's Spirit of the Times*, 21 Jan. 1860, 328; "New Orleans Races," *Porter's Spirit of the Times*, 21 Jan. 1860, 331.

41. "Lexington and Lecomte: The Great Turf Events of the Past Season," *Spirit of the Times*, 8 Sept. 1855, 355; "New Orleans Spring Races," *Spirit of the Times*, 19 April 1856, 115; "Metairie Jockey Club Races," *Spirit of the Times*, 28 July 1860, 607.

42. "How Lexington Was Saved to the Turf," *Turf, Field and Farm*, 1 Feb. 1884, 75. The story is told of Robert Burbridge, though it is unconfirmed, and Burbridge did not die until well after Harry himself had changed ownership.

43. See on Duncan Kenner's collection of equine paintings, Rosella Kenner Brent, "Recollections, The Federal Raid Upon Ashland Plantation in July 1862," 21, Rosella Kenner Brent Papers, Louisiana and Lower Mississippi Valley Collections, Louisiana State University.

44. For a discussion of Hark's reaction to the situation, see W. J. Minor to T. J. Wells, 9 Oct. 1855, Box 1, Folder 4, William J. Minor Papers, Louisiana and Lower Mississippi Valley Collections, Louisiana State University.

45. W. J. Minor to T. J. Wells, 12 May 1855, Box 1, Folder 4, William J. Minor Papers, Louisiana and Lower Mississippi Valley Collections, Louisiana State University.

46. For a call to think more seriously about the role of informers in the slave community, see Walter Johnson, "On Agency," *Journal of Social History* 37.1 (2003): 116.

47. Historians have only recently begun to analyze how slaves understood white masters' fears and assumptions and used their knowledge to craft the stories they told. See, for example, James Sidbury, "Plausible Stories and Varnished Truths," *William and Mary Quarterly*, 3rd ser., 59.1 (2002): 182–84.

48. For a summary of the conflicting evidence, see W.J. Minor to T.J. Wells, 12 Sept. 1855, Box 1, Folder 4, William J. Minor Papers, Louisiana and Lower Mississippi Valley Collections, Louisiana State University.

49. Lyman Horace Weeks, *The American Turf: An Historical Account of Racing in the United States with Biographical Sketches of Turf Celebrities* (New York: Historical Company, 1898), 370; Americus, "Sale of Lecomte, Etc.," *Spirit of the Times*, 17 May 1856, 162.

50. Hervey, *Racing in America*, vol. 2, 301–2.

51. W.J. Minor to T.J. Wells, 15 June 1854, Box 2, Folder 16, William J. Minor and Family Papers, Louisiana and Lower Mississippi Valley Collections, Louisiana State University.

52. "Newmarket Second October Meeting," *Bell's Life in London and Sporting Chronicle*, 18 Oct. 1857, 4.

53. John H. Davis, *The American Turf* (New York: John Polhemus, 1907), 33–34; Roger Longrigg, *The History of Horse Racing* (New York: Stein and Day, 1972), 216.

54. Quoted in Herbert M. Casson, *Cyrus Hall McCormick: His Life and Work* (Chicago: A.C. McClurg & Co., 1909), 126–31; Robert F. Dalzell Jr., "American Participation in the Great Exhibition of 1851" (Amherst, MA: Amherst College Press, 1960), 47–57.

55. "The Races at Havana," *Spirit of the Times*, 15 April 1843, 78.

56. A Young Turfman, "Racing Prospects in Louisiana and Mississippi," *Spirit of the Times*, 8 Nov. 1851, 450.

57. "English Writers on American Horses," *Porter's Spirit of the Times*, 23 May 1857, 184. Variant spelling in the original.

58. R.J.M. Blackett, *Building an Antislavery Wall: Black Americans in the Atlantic Abolitionist Movement* (Baton Rouge: Louisiana State University Press, 1983), 161, 197–98; Matthew Mason, "Keeping Up Appearances: The International Politics of Slave Trade Abolition in the Nineteenth-Century Atlantic World," *William and Mary Quarterly*, 3rd ser., 66.4 (2009): 820–31.

59. Privateer, "William Bird, Trainer for Gov. Bowie," *New York Sportsman*, 4 Aug. 1883, 120.

60. "Engagements of Mr. Ten Broeck's and Mr. Harlan's Horses in England," *Porter's Spirit of the Times*, 1 Oct. 1859, 76.

61. "Mr. Harlan," *Porter's Spirit of the Times*, 1 Oct. 1859, 72. On the question of whether Robert Harlan was the son or brother of James Harlan, see Loren P. Beth, *John Marshall Harlan: The Last Whig Justice* (Lexington: University Press of Kentucky, 1992), 12–13.

62. Malvina Shanklin Harlan, *Some Memories of a Long Life, 1854–1911* (New York: Random House, 2002), 43.

63. William J. Simmons, *Men of Mark: Eminent, Progressive and Rising* (Cleveland: George M. Rewell, 1887), 613–14. Accessed through Documenting the American South, University Library, University of North Carolina at Chapel Hill, 2000, http://docsouth.unc.edu/neh/simmons/simmons.html; Beth, *John Marshall Harlan*, 12–13; Linda Przybyszewski, *The Republic according to John Marshall Harlan* (Chapel Hill: University of North Carolina Press, 1999), 23. James Gordon has compiled the most comprehensive assessment available of Robert Harlan's relationship to the James Harlan family. See James W. Gordon, "Did the First Justice Harlan Have a Black Brother?" *Western New England Law Review* 15.2 (1993): 159–238.

64. "On Dits in Sporting Circles," *Spirit of the Times*, 4 Dec. 1858, 510.

65. "Mr. Harlan," *Porter's Spirit of the Times*, 1 Oct. 1859, 72.

66. Mackay-Smith, *Race Horses of America*, 237; Eugene Current-Garcia, "'York's Tall Son' and his Southern Correspondents," *American Quarterly* 7.4 (1955): 375n; "The Wars of the 'Spirits,'" *Spirit of the Times*, 24 Sept. 1859, 390; "The Truth, the Whole Truth, and Nothing but the Truth," *Porter's Spirit of the Times*, 10 Sept. 1859, 25.

67. Patricia Cline Cohen, Timothy J. Gilfoyle, and Helen Lefkowitz Horowitz, *The Flash Press: Sporting Male Weeklies in 1840s New York* (Chicago: University of Chicago Press, 2008), 41–43. Wilkes and his milieu are also illuminated in Patricia Cline Cohen, *The Murder of Helen Jewett* (New York: Random House, 1998), 218.

68. George Wilkes, *The Mysteries of the Tombs* (New York: 1844), Beinecke Rare Book and Manuscript Library, Yale University.

69. Cohen, Gilfoyle, and Horowitz, *Flash Press*, 44; David S. Reynolds, *Beneath the American Renaissance* (New York: Alfred A. Knopf, 1988), 177; Alexander Saxton, "George Wilkes: The Transformation of a Radical Ideology," *American Quarterly* 33.4 (1981): 439–40.

70. Yates, *William T. Porter and the Spirit of the Times*, 195; Cohen, *Murder of Helen Jewett*, 16–19.

71. Quoted in Reynolds, *Beneath the American Renaissance*, 174.

72. "The Libel on Porter's 'Spirit of the Times,'" *Porter's Spirit of the Times*, 14 Aug. 1858, 377.

73. Alexander Saxton, *The Rise and Fall of the White Republic* (London: Verso, 1990), 212.

74. David A. Williams, *David C. Broderick: A Political Portrait* (San Marino, CA: Henry E. Huntington Library and Art Gallery, 1969), 6; Richard J. Purcell, "Senator David C. Broderick of California," *Studies: An Irish Quarterly Review* 28.111 (1939): 417; Donald E. Hargis, "Straight toward His Heart: George Wilkes's Eulogy of David C. Broderick," *California Historical Society Quarterly* 38.3 (1959): 197.

75. Williams, *David C. Broderick*, 70n, 81, 85–86.

76. Saxton, *Rise and Fall of the White Republic*, 210.

77. Drew Gilpin Faust, *James Henry Hammond and the Old South* (Baton Rouge: Louisiana State University Press, 1982), 346–47.

78. *Speech of the Honorable D.C. Broderick of California Against the Admission of Kansas Under the Lecompton Constitution, delivered in the Senate of the United States, March 22, 1858* (Washington D.C.: Lemuel Towers, 1858), 13.

79. Ibid., 3.

80. "David C. Broderick," *Wilkes's Spirit of the Times*, 22 Oct. 1859, 97; Saxton, *Rise and Fall of the White Republic*, 212.

81. *The Answer of John F. Chamberlin to the Complaint of George Wilkes, In an Action to Recover Damages for Defamation of Character* (New York: William J. Read, 1873), 4–5.

82. David A. Williams, "The Forgery of the Broderick Will," *California Historical Society Quarterly* 40.3 (1961): 209.

83. "Cordial Greetings," *Spirit of the Times*, 26 Feb. 1859, 25.

84. "Kansas and the Championship," *Porter's Spirit of the Times*, 20 Feb. 1858, 393; "Twelve Hours in the Gallery of the Senate on Kansas Day," *Porter's Spirit of the Times*, 10 April 1858, 83.

85. David M. Potter, *The Impending Crisis 1848–1861* (New York: Harper & Row, 1976), 90–120.

86. For recent discussion of Douglas's leadership role in the passage of the Compromise, see Robert V. Remini, *At the Edge of the Precipice: Henry Clay and the Compromise That Saved the Union* (New York: Basic Books, 2010), 143–49; Fergus M. Bordewich, *America's Great Debate: Henry Clay, Stephen A. Douglas, and the Compromise That Preserved the Union* (New York: Simon and Schuster, 2012), 303–16.

87. Hervey, *Racing in America, 1655–1865*, vol. 2, 258.

88. Henry Clay to John Morrison Clay, 7 March 1851, *Papers of Henry Clay*, vol. 10, ed. Melba Porter Hay (Lexington: University Press of Kentucky, 1991), 881.

89. Will of Henry Clay, *Papers of Henry Clay*, vol. 10, 901–2.

90. "Natchez (Miss.) Races," *Spirit of the Times*, 20 Dec. 1851, 523.

91. "Col. W.J. Minor," *Natchez Courier*, 26 Aug. 1852. On Southern misgivings about the Scott candidacy in 1852, see Michael F. Holt, *The Rise and Fall of the American Whig Party* (New York: Oxford University Press, 1999), 674–75.

92. Quoted in William Stanley Hoole, *Alias Simon Suggs: The Life and Times of Johnson Jones Hooper* (1952; Tuscaloosa: University of Alabama Press, 2006), 80.

93. Holt, *Rise and Fall of the Whig Party*, 927.

94. Hoole, *Alias Simon Suggs*, 89.

95. The overlap between Whigs and Know Nothings varied in different areas. For example, in Louisiana the Know Nothings included some Whigs but also picked up supporters from other portions of the political spectrum, while in Virginia the Know Nothings were far more clearly a refuge for former Whigs. See John M. Sacher, *A Perfect War of Politics: Parties, Politicians, and Democracy in Louisiana, 1824–1861* (Baton Rouge: Louisiana State University Press, 2003), 240; William A. Link, *Roots of Secession: Slavery and Politics in Antebellum Virginia* (Chapel Hill: University of North Carolina Press, 2003), 123.

96. For the importance of Fillmore's visit to New Orleans, see William H. Adams, *The Whig Party of Louisiana* (Lafayette: University of Southwestern Louisiana, 1973), 261–62. For the admiration for Fillmore's role in the compromise, particularly among Deep Southern Whigs, see Sacher, *Perfect War of Politics*, 250–51; Adams, *Whig Party of Louisiana*, 227–28.

97. See W.J. Minor to T.J. Wells, 15 July 1855, Box 1, Folder 4, and W.J. Minor to T.J. Wells, 29 Sept. 1856, Box 1, Folder 5, William J. Minor Papers, Louisiana and Lower Mississippi Valley Collections, Louisiana State University. Emphasis in original.

98. Holt, *Rise and Fall of the Whig Party*, 358.

99. Link, *Roots of Secession*, 145–146.

100. *Letters of John Minor Botts, of Virginia, on the Nebraska Question* (Washington, D.C.: John T. and Lem. Towers, 1853), 6, 15, Beinecke Rare Book and Manuscript Library, Yale University; see also *Speech of Hon. John M. Botts, on the Political Issues of the Day, Delivered at the African Church in the City of Richmond, August 8, 1856* (Richmond: National American, 1856), Virginia Historical Society.

101. "On Dits in Sporting Circles," *Spirit of the Times*, 14 Aug. 1858, 318.

102. Cliquot, "Progress of the American Turf," *Porter's Spirit of the Times*, 7 Aug. 1858, 359.

103. "Letter from 'Vindex,'" *Spirit of the Times*, 5 Nov. 1859, 464.

104. "THE CELEBRATED BLOOD-HORSE BORDER RUFFIAN," *Porter's Spirit of the Times*, 13 Nov. 1858, 161.

105. Lees and Waller to Robert Alexander, 22 Nov. 1856, Box 9, Folder 54, Alexander Family Papers: Woodburn Farm Series, Kentucky Historical Society; Fisher, *For All Times*, 17; "On Dits in Sporting Circles," *Spirit of the Times*, 22 Nov. 1856, 486; "The Stallion Scythian," *Porter's Spirit of the Times*, 29 Nov. 1856, 208.

106. "On Dits in Sporting Circles," *Spirit of the Times*, 27 Aug. 1859, 342.

107. Charles Emery Stevens, *Anthony Burns A History* (Boston: John P. Jowett, 1856), 198–99. Accessed through Documenting the American South, University Library, University of North Carolina at Chapel Hill, 1999, http://docsouth.unc.edu/neh/stevens/stevens.html; Albert J. Von Frank, *The Trials of Anthony Burns* (Cambridge, MA: Harvard University Press, 1998), 288–90.

108. "On Dits in Sporting Circles," *Spirit of the Times*, 18 May 1839, 126; "On Dits in Sporting Circles," *Spirit of the Times*, 15 June 1839, 174; "On Dits in Sporting Circles," *Spirit of the Times*, 7 Dec. 1839, 474; "Notes of the Month: February," *American Turf Register*, Feb. 1840, 93; "On Dits in Sporting Circles," *Spirit of the Times*, 1 Feb. 1840, 570; Receipts, 1857–1858 folder, Pineville Jockey Club records, Galliard Family Papers, 1758–1901, (1033.00), South Carolina Historical Society.

109. John Minor Botts to unknown, 8 Jan. 1857, Box 1, Folder 5, Merritt Family Papers, Special Collections Research Center, Swem Library, College of William and Mary; "The Late Col. McDaniel," *New York Sportsman*, 7 Feb. 1885, 101.

110. Stevens, *Anthony Burns*, 199–201.

111. Ibid., 210–13.

112. The pieces from the *Tribune* were the work of Mortimer Thomson, who wrote them under the obvious pseudonym Q.K. Philander Doesticks. His pieces were later compiled into a pamphlet. See Q.K. Philander Doesticks, "What Became of the Slaves on a Georgia Plantation?" (1863), Daniel Murray Pamphlet Collection, Library of Congress. Accessed at http://memory

.loc.gov/cgi-bin/query/r?ammem/murray:@field(DOCID+@lit(lcrbmrpt2305)).
For background on Doesticks, the Butler family, and the sale, see Catherine Clinton, *Fanny Kemble's Civil Wars* (New York: Simon and Schuster, 2000), 161.

113. Lurton D. Ingersoll, *The Life of Horace Greeley* (Chicago: Union, 1873; New York: Beekman, 1974), 58–59.

114. Ralph Ray Fahrney, *Horace Greeley and the* Tribune *in the Civil War* (Cedar Rapids, IA: Torch Press, 1936), 1–2; Robert C. Williams, *Horace Greeley: Champion of Whig Freedom* (New York: New York University Press, 2006), 61.

115. John Minor Botts, "Union or Disunion: The Union Cannot and Shall Not be Dissolved. Mr. Lincoln Not an Abolitionist. Speech of the Hon. John Minor Botts at Holcombe Hall in Lynchburg, Virginia, on Thursday Evening, October 15, 1860" (Lynchburg, 1860), 16, 23, Virginia Historical Society.

116. John Minor Botts, *The Great Rebellion: Its Secret History, Rise, Progress, and Disastrous Failure* (New York: Harper & Brothers, 1866), 196.

117. "The American Horses in England," *Wilkes's Spirit of the Times*, 28 Jan. 1860, 324.

4. These Are the Verities

1. Alexander Mackay-Smith, *The Race Horses of America 1832–1872* (Saratoga Springs: National Museum of Racing, 1981), 247; "Death of Nina," *New York Sportsman*, 27 Sept. 1879, 151.

2. Albion, "Reminiscences of the Turf," *Spirit of the Times*, 26 Jan. 1878, 682.

3. "To Correspondents," *Porter's Spirit of the Times*, 21 Aug. 1860, 408.

4. "Daniel Boone," *Spirit of the Times*, 20 Nov. 1875, 345.

5. Quotes and information about the trophy are taken from "Complimentary Plate Worth $2200. Planet and Daniel Boone," *Spirit of the Times*, 2 June 1860, 193.

6. "The Coming Match Between Planet and Daniel Boone," *Spirit of the Times*, 9 June 1860, 233.

7. "Great Race Between Planet and Congaree," *Porter's Spirit of the Times*, 25 Sept. 1860, 73.

8. "South Carolina Jockey Club," *Porter's Spirit of the Times*, 9 Feb. 1861, 360.

9. Edward Cantey, *Sketch of the Racing Mare Albine* (Columbia, SC: The State Company, 1913), 5–7, South Caroliniana Library, University of South Carolina.

10. DuBose Heyward, *Peter Ashley* (New York: Farrar & Rinehart, 1932), 139.

11. For a discussion of Heyward's efforts at historical accuracy in the novel and his intent to use the race episode to say something serious about living with the inescapable legacy of a slaveholding past, see James M. Hutchisson, *DuBose Heyward: A Charleston Gentleman and the World of Porgy and Bess* (Jackson: University Press of Mississippi, 2000), 109–10.

12. Heyward, *Peter Ashley*, 136–37.

13. Ibid., 250–51.

14. Cantey, *Albine*, 8–10.

15. Ibid., 10–11; Randy J. Sparks, "Gentleman's Sport: Horse Racing in Antebellum Charleston," *South Carolina Historical Magazine* 93.1 (1992): 29. Sparks's article is the best discussion of the role of racing in the antebellum culture of Charleston.

16. Heyward, *Peter Ashley*, 309.

17. Walter McGehee Lowrey, "The Political Career of James Madison Wells," *Louisiana Historical Quarterly* 31.4 (1948): 1003.

18. "A Memorial to the Senate and House of Representatives in the Congress of the United States," Box 10, Folder 78, Alexander Family Papers, Kentucky Historical Society. See for Crittenden as a turfman, Wendell Holmes Stephenson, *Alexander Porter Whig Planter of Old Louisiana* (Baton Rouge: Louisiana State University Press, 1934), 126–7.

19. "I Am an American Citizen," *Porter's Spirit of the Times*, 4 Dec. 1860, 233.

20. "Races to Come," *Porter's Spirit of the Times*, 8 Jan. 1861, 313.

21. "'Boots' on the Crisis," *Spirit of the Times*, 2 March 1861, 52.

22. "Spirit of the Week," *Porter's Spirit of the Times*, 27 Nov. 1860, 216.

23. John S. Ryan to A. F. Giraud, 20 Dec. 1860, John S. Ryan Papers, South Caroliniana Library, University of South Carolina.

24. "Third Day of the Metairie," *New York Tribune*, 10 April 1861, 3.

25. Louis Bringier to Stella Bringier, 6 April 1861, Box 2, Folder 17, Louis A. Bringier and Family Papers, Louisiana and Lower Mississippi Valley Collections, Louisiana State University.

26. William A. Link, *Roots of Secession: Slavery and Politics in Antebellum Virginia* (Chapel Hill: University of North Carolina Press, 2003), 247.

27. "Spirit of the Week," *Porter's Spirit of the Times*, 16 April 1861, 120. Clay's birthday was on the twelfth, the day the first shots were fired.

28. William Stanley Hoole, *Alias Simon Suggs: The Life and Times of Johnson Jones Hooper* (1952; Tuscaloosa: University of Alabama Press, 2006), 152–54.

29. Walter T. Durham, *Balie Peyton of Tennessee: Nineteenth Century Politics and Thoroughbreds* (Franklin, TN: Hillsboro Press, 2004), 198.

30. John Minor Botts, *The Great Rebellion: Its Secret History, Rise, Progress, and Disastrous Failure* (New York: Harper & Brothers, 1866), 226.

31. Hamilton Busbey, "The Running Turf in America," *Harper's New Monthly Magazine*, July 1870, 249; John Minor Botts to unknown, 8 Jan. and 29 March 1857, Box 1, Folder 5, Merritt Family Papers, Special Collections Research Center, Swem Library, College of William and Mary; Clyde C. Webster, "John Minor Botts, Anti-Secessionist," *Richmond College Historical Papers* 1.1 (1915): 29–30; Mackay-Smith, *Race Horses of America*, 162.

32. George Wilkes, "Letters from the War," *Wilkes's Spirit of the Times*, 11 May 1861, 147.

33. George Wilkes, *The Great Battle, fought at Manassas, between the federal forces, under General McDowell, and the Rebels, under Gen. Beauregard, Sunday, July 21, 1861. From notes taken on the spot* (New York: Brown & Ryan, 1861), 29–30.

34. "A Turfman on the Battle Field," *Porter's Spirit of the Times*, 21 Sept. 1861, 54.

35. W.J. Minor to T.J. Wells, 19 Nov. 1861, Box 2, Folder 18, William J. Minor and Family Papers, Louisiana and Lower Mississippi Valley Collections, Louisiana State University.

36. "The South Carolina Jockey Club," *Charleston Daily Courier*, 5 Feb. 1862, 1.

37. Michael O'Brien, *Conjectures of Order: Intellectual Life and the American South* (Chapel Hill: University of North Carolina Press, 2004), vol. 1, 388; Ann Norton Greene, *Horses at Work: Harnessing Power in Industrial America* (Cambridge, MA: Harvard University Press, 2008), 88–89.

38. Peter S. Carmichael, *Lee's Young Artillerist: William R. J. Pegram* (Charlottesville: University of Virginia Press, 1995), 12.

39. Quoted in Gary Gallagher, *The Confederate War* (Cambridge, MA: Harvard University Press, 1997), 107. Gallagher argues persuasively that young men like Pegram, raised in a political world increasingly divided on sectional lines, gave particularly staunch loyalty to the Confederacy. Part of that political education for Southerners of Pegram's class and age would have been conducted at the track, where, increasingly, Southern champions competed solely among themselves.

40. Peter S. Carmichael, *The Last Generation: Young Virginians in Peace, War, and Reunion* (Chapel Hill: University of North Carolina Press, 2005), 203.

41. Edward L. Bowen, *Masters of the Turf* (Lexington: The Blood Horse, 2007), 222.

42. Greene, *Horses at Work*, 88.

43. Mackay-Smith, *Race Horses of America*, 316.

44. Avery Craven, ed., *"To Markie": The Letters of Robert E. Lee to Martha Custis Williams from the originals in the Huntington Library* (Cambridge, MA: Harvard University Press, 1933; Ann Arbor: University Microfilms International, 1979), 73–75.

45. "Great War Horses Traveller and Copenhagen," typescript, Box 1, Folder 7, Elizabeth Amis Cameron Blanchard Papers #3367, Southern Historical Collection, The Wilson Library, University of North Carolina at Chapel Hill. Other breeds of horse, like the American Saddlebred, would later claim Traveller as well.

46. Lyman Horace Weeks, *The American Turf: An Historical Account of Racing in the United States with Biographical Sketches of Turf Celebrities* (New York: The Historical Company, 1898), 29.

47. Alden Hatch and Foxhall Keene, *Full Tilt: The Sporting Memoirs of Foxhall Keene* (New York: Derrydale, 1938), 52–53.

48. H.W. Harris to W.J. Minor, 31 Dec. 1863, Box 1, Folder 8, and Henry C. Minor to W.J. Minor, 23 Nov. 1863, Box 1, Folder 15, William J. Minor Horse Racing Collection, Beinecke Rare Book and Manuscript Library, Yale University; Mackay-Smith, *Race Horses of America*, 226.

49. Edward E. Leslie, *The Devil Knows How to Ride: The True Story of William Clarke Quantrill and His Confederate Raiders* (New York: Random House, 1996), 343–54.

50. William Preston Mangum, II, *A Kingdom for the Horse* (Prospect, KY: Harmony House, 1999), 79–80.

51. John Hervey, *Racing in America, 1655–1865* (New York: Jockey Club, 1944), vol. 2, 345.

52. Ridley Wills II, *The History of Belle Meade* (Nashville: Vanderbilt University Press, 1991), 106.

53. Cantey, *Albine*, 11–12.

54. "The Thorough-bred Horses Coming North," *Spirit of the Times*, 3 Jan. 1863, 284; "SALE OF THOROUGH-BRED STOCK AT NEW ORLEANS," *Spirit of the Times*, 24 Jan. 1863, 333; "Sales of Confiscated Blood-Horses at New Orleans," *Harper's New Monthly Magazine*, 4 April 1863, 221–22; "Thorough-bred Horses From the South," *Spirit of the Times*, 11 April 1863, 93.

55. "Sherwood (S.C.) Races," *Wilkes's Spirit of the Times*, 23 Feb. 1861, 395.

56. See, for extended discussion of slaves' understanding of war news and its implications for them, Steven Hahn, *A Nation under Our Feet: Black Political Struggles in the Rural South from Slavery to the Great Migration* (Cambridge, MA: Harvard University Press, 2003), 13–115.

57. Winthrop D. Jordan, *Tumult and Silence at Second Creek: An Inquiry into a Civil War Slave Conspiracy* (Baton Rouge: Louisiana State University Press, 1993), 217.

58. Frank Wysor Klingberg, "The Case of the Minors: A Unionist Family within the Confederacy," *Journal of Southern History* 13.1 (1947): 35–36; Jordan, *Tumult and Silence at Second Creek*, 208–9, 257–58.

59. Jordan, *Tumult and Silence at Second Creek*, 328–39.

60. Ibid., 314, 323.

61. "On-Dits in Sporting Circles," *Spirit of the Times*, 17 March 1860, 66.

62. J. Carlyle Sitterson, "The Transition from Slave to Free Economy on the William J. Minor Plantations," *Agricultural History* 17.4 (1943): 217. Rosella Kenner Brent remembered that Whale had been so badly behaved that the Federals had not taken him, but he is advertised in the confiscation sale with the other horses. See "Sale of Thorough-bred Stock at New Orleans," *Wilkes's Spirit of the Times*, 24 Jan. 1863, 333.

63. Within her narrative, Rosella Kenner Brent left two distinct accounts of the raid and detailed descriptions of some of the men involved, including Henry Hammond. See Rosella Kenner Brent, "Recollections, The Federal Raid Upon Ashland Plantation in July 1862," Rosella Kenner Brent Papers, Louisiana and Lower Mississippi Valley Collections, Louisiana State University.

64. Curtis Parker Flowers, "Thoroughbred Horses at Muscle Shoals," *Alabama Heritage* (Spring 2006): 33.

65. In delivering the two horses, Durastus made a significant contribution to American equine history. Gaines's Denmark became one of the formative sires of the American Saddlebred breed, and Mambrino Chief helped to shape both the Standardbred and the Tennessee Walking Horse. See, for indications of his movements, Mary E. Wharton and Elizabeth Williams, eds., *Peach Leather and Rebel Gray: Bluegrass Life and the War, 1860–1865* (Lexington, KY: Halicon, 1986), 152; Mangum, *Kingdom for the Horse*, 50–51.

66. "The New York Races," *Spirit of the Times,* 12 July 1862, 297; Dan M. Bowmar, *Giants of the Turf* (Lexington: The Blood Horse, 1960), 14.

67. Privateer, "William Bird, Trainer for Gov. Bowie," *New York Sportsman,* 4 Aug. 1883, 120.

68. *Famous Horses of America* (Philadelphia: Porter and Coates, 1877), 25.

69. Charles E. Trevathan, *The American Thoroughbred* (New York: Macmillan, 1905), 315–16.

70. Ed. James, *The Life and Battles of John Morrissey: with Portraits from the Life of John Morrissey, John C. Heenan, Yankee Sullivan and Bill Poole* (New York: 1879), 3–4.

71. Richard K. Fox, *Prize Ring Heroes* (New York: Richard K. Fox, 1889), 34–35; James, *Life and Battles of John Morrissey,* 4–5. On Rynders's long political career, see Tyler Anbinder, "Isaiah Rynders and the Ironies of Popular Democracy in Antebellum New York," *Contested Democracy: Freedom, Race, and Power in American History,* ed. Manisha Sinha and Penny von Eschen (New York: Columbia University Press, 2007), 31–48.

72. Edwin G. Burrows and Mike Wallace, *Gotham: A History of New York City to 1898* (New York: Oxford University Press, 1999), 635, 823; Elliott J. Gorn, *The Manly Art: Bare-Knuckle Prize Fighting in America* (Ithaca: Cornell University Press, 1986), 109.

73. Jon Bartels, *Saratoga Stories: Gangsters, Gamblers & Racing Legends* (Lexington: Eclipse Press, 2007), 17–21.

74. Steven A. Riess, *City Games: The Evolution of American Urban Society and the Rise of Sports* (Urbana: University of Illinois Press, 1989), 19–20; Gorn, *Manly Art,* 125, 141–42. On Morrissey's long-standing rivalry with and hatred for Poole, see James, *Life and Battles of John Morrissey,* 12–13; Fox, *Prize Ring Heroes,* 48–51; Bartels, *Saratoga Stories,* 19–21.

75. Landon Manning, *The Noble Animals: Tales of the Saratoga Turf* (Saratoga, 1973), 140; James, *Life and Battles of John Morrissey,* 5; Bartels, *Saratoga Stories,* 16; Riess, *City Games,* 15.

76. "Letter from John Morrissey," *Wilkes's Spirit of the Times,* 21 April 1860, 99.

77. Edward Hotaling, *They're Off! Horse Racing at Saratoga* (Syracuse: Syracuse University Press, 1995), 40.

78. Ibid., 48.

79. Ibid., 51–52; Carl Sandburg, *Abraham Lincoln,* vol. 3 (New York: Harcourt, Brace & Co., 1939), 332.

80. Hotaling, *They're Off!,* 48; Perry Belmont, *An American Democrat* (New York: Columbia University Press, 1940), 623n.

81. T.J. Stiles, *The First Tycoon* (New York: Alfred A. Knopf, 2009), 398–99.

82. "Letter from Larkin," *Wilkes's Spirit of the Times,* 28 Jan. 1865, 342.

83. Mary Simmerson Cunningham Logan, *Reminiscences of a Soldier's Wife* (New York: Charles Scribner's Sons, 1913), 201–2.

84. "The Races at St. Louis," *Wilkes's Spirit of the Times,* 28 May 1864, 204.

85. "Some Old Time Racing," *Thoroughbred Record,* 17 Aug. 1901, 79.

86. "Metairie Jockey Club Races," *Spirit of the Times,* 13 April 1861, 153.

87. "The Paterson Races," *Wilkes's Spirit of the Times,* 18 June 1864, 244.

88. "The American Turf," *Wilkes's Spirit of the Times*, 17 June 1865, 252; "The St. Louis Races," *Wilkes's Spirit of the Times*, 5 Nov. 1864, 153. Variant spelling in the original.

89. "The Paterson Races," *Wilkes's Spirit of the Times*, 18 June 1864, 244; "Hoboken Spring Meeting," *Wilkes's Spirit of the Times*, 30 June 1866, 276; Hotaling, *They're Off!*, 44; Edward Hotaling, *The Great Black Jockeys* (Rocklin, CA: Forum, 1999), 177.

90. Hotaling, *Great Black Jockeys*, 182.

91. "From Saratoga," *New York Tribune*, 11 Aug. 1865, 1.

92. "The Democratic 'Union,'" *Daily Saratogian*, 28 July 1864, 2.

5. The Only Practical Means of Reunion

1. Walter S. Vosburgh, *Racing in America, 1866–1921* (New York: Jockey Club, 1922), 86; "Longfellow," *Spirit of the Times and Sportsman*, 11 Nov. 1893, 521–22.

2. W.S., "The Blue-Grass Country," *Spirit of the Times*, 17 Dec. 1870, 275.

3. Kent Hollingsworth, *The Great Ones* (Lexington: The Blood Horse, 1970), 137, 153.

4. Edward Bowen, *Masters of the Turf* (Lexington: The Blood Horse, 2007), 9–10.

5. "Nomad in the Blue Grass Country—The Famous Breeding Studs," *Turf, Field and Farm*, 1 Dec. 1871, 337–38. The piece is more readily found in a compilation of Custer's articles for the magazine. See Brian W. Dippie, ed., *Nomad: George A. Custer in* Turf, Field and Farm (Austin: University of Texas Press, 1980), 82. Variant spelling in the original.

6. Jeff Meyer, "Henry Clay's Legacy to Horse Breeding and Racing," *Register of the Kentucky Historical Society* 100.4 (2002): 483.

7. Dippie, *Nomad*, 76–77.

8. "Monmouth Park," *New York Times*, 29 Jan. 1872, 5.

9. Maryjean Wall, *How Kentucky Became Southern* (Lexington: University Press of Kentucky, 2010), 99–103.

10. "Longfellow's Complete Victory," *Spirit of the Times*, 6 July 1872, 329.

11. "The Late Colonel McDaniel," *New York Sportsman*, 7 Feb. 1885, 101.

12. See, on McDaniel's stables and the prevalence of black horsemen in Northern racetrack towns like Saratoga, Myra B. Young Armstead, *Lord, Please Don't Take Me in August: African Americans in Newport and Saratoga Springs, 1870–1930* (Urbana: University of Illinois Press, 1999), 71–72.

13. "Racing Matters," *Daily Saratogian*, 17 April 1873, 3.

14. Melville D. Landon, *Saratoga in 1901* (New York: Sheldon and Co., 1872), 13. Variant spelling in the original.

15. Alison Leigh Cowan, "Scrawled in the Margins, Signs of Twain as a Critic," *New York Times*, 18 April 2010, A17.

16. "The Racing Season at Long Branch," *Spirit of the Times*, 22 June 1872, 297.

17. "The Great Race," *New York Times*, 3 July 1872, 5.

18. "Longfellow's Complete Victory," *Spirit of the Times*, 6 July 1872, 329.

19. "The Racing Season at Long Branch," *Spirit of the Times*, 22 June 1872, 297.

20. "Longfellow and His Rider," *Turf, Field and Farm*, 19 July 1872, 85.

21. *Live Stock Record*, 29 Sept. 1894, 203.

22. "The Great Race," *New York Times*, 3 July 1872, 5.

23. "Longfellow," *Spirit of the Times and Sportsman*, 1 Nov. 1893, 521–22.

24. "Saratoga: The Greatest Contest in American Turf History," *New York Times*, 17 July 1872, 5.

25. "The Saratoga Cup," *Spirit of the Times*, 14 Sept. 1872, 65.

26. Charles E. Trevathan, *The American Thoroughbred* (New York: Macmillan, 1905), 344–45.

27. William Woodward, *Memoir of Andrew Jackson, Africanus* (New York: Derrydale, 1938), 31–32.

28. Falcon, "The Next Racing Season," *Louisville Courier-Journal*, 24 Feb. 1874, 3.

29. "Horse Talk," *New York Times*, 1 March 1874, 5.

30. Samuel Hildreth, *The Spell of the Turf* (Philadelphia: J.B. Lippincott, 1926), 31–33.

31. Alexander Mackay-Smith, *The Race Horses of America* (Saratoga Springs: National Museum of Racing, 1981), 277; William H.P. Robertson, *The History of Thoroughbred Racing in America* (Englewood Cliffs, NJ: Prentice Hall, 1964), 103; Charles B. Parmer, *For Gold and Glory: The Story of Thoroughbred Racing in America* (New York: Carrick and Evans, 1939), 124; Edwin G. Burrows and Mike Wallace, *Gotham: A History of New York City to 1898* (New York: Oxford University Press, 1999), 954; Vosburgh, *Racing in America, 1866–1921*, 10.

32. Robertson, *History of Thoroughbred Racing*, 105–6; Parmer, *For Gold and Glory*, 125–26.

33. Bernard Livingston, *Their Turf* (New York: Arbor House, 1973), 234.

34. "Racing in the South," *Turf, Field and Farm*, 11 Nov. 1865, 232. See also "The Turf in the South," *Turf, Field and Farm*, 4 Nov. 1865, 217.

35. Petition and letter to the President and Members of the South Carolina Jockey Club, 12 Oct. 1870, Records of the South Carolina Jockey Club, 1842–1900, microfilm, South Carolina Historical Society.

36. Dale A. Somers, *The Rise of Sports in New Orleans, 1850–1900* (Baton Rouge: Louisiana State University Press, 1972), 92–93; "Sale of the Metairie Course," *Spirit of the Times*, 11 May 1872, 201; "The Metairie Jockey Club," *Spirit of the Times*, 15 June 1872, 280; Robertson, *History of Thoroughbred Racing*, 88.

37. "The Turf in St. Louis," *Wilkes's Spirit of the Times*, 27 May 1865, 201. Minor is identified incorrectly as W.L. Minor in the story.

38. See typescript copy of Minor's obituary in *Turf, Field and Farm*, 22 Oct. 1869, 265, Box 2, Folder 43, William J. Minor Horse Racing Collection, Beinecke Rare Book and Manuscript Library, Yale University.

39. William Kauffman Scarborough, *Masters of the Big House: Elite Slaveholders of the Mid-Nineteenth Century South* (Baton Rouge: Louisiana State University Press), 398; Harry Worcester Smith, "The Sportsman's Bookshelf,"

Thoroughbred Record, 8 Aug. 1925, 68; Mackay-Smith, *Race Horses of America*, 315.

40. Vosburgh, *Racing in America, 1866–1921*, 5–6; Fairfax Harrison, *The Background of the American Stud Book* (Richmond: Old Dominion Press, 1933), 81–82.

41. Melvin L. Adelman, "Quantification and Sport: The American Jockey Club, 1866–1867; A Collective Biography," *Sport in America: New Historical Perspectives*, ed. Donald Spivey (Westport, CT: Greenwood Press, 1985), 54–57; Vosburgh, *Racing in America, 1866–1921*, 5.

42. "The American Jockey Club," *New York Sportsman*, 5 June 1875, 20.

43. *List of Members and Rules of the American Jockey Club* (New York: 1880), 19–61, Fairman Rogers Collection, Rare Book and Manuscript Library, University of Pennsylvania.

44. Matthew Hale Smith, *Twenty Years Among the Bulls and Bears of Wall Street* (Hartford: J.B. Burr and Co., 1870), 258.

45. Dan M. Bowmar, *Giants of the Turf* (Lexington: The Blood Horse, 1960), 51.

46. Vosburgh, *Racing in America 1866–1921*, 6.

47. Burrows and Wallace, *Gotham*, 714; Niall Ferguson, *The House of Rothschild* (New York: Viking 1998), vol. 1, 370–73; vol. 2, 66–67.

48. Steven A. Riess, *City Games: The Evolution of American Urban Society and the Rise of Sports* (Urbana: University of Illinois Press, 1989), 25; Steven A. Riess, "Sports and Machine Politics in New York City, 1870–1920," *Sport in America*, ed. David K. Wiggins (Champaign, IL: Human Kinetics, 1995), 171–72.

49. "Long Branch Races," *New York Times*, 8 July 1871, 8; Alexander B. Callow, *The Tweed Ring* (New York: Oxford University Press, 1965), 107–8.

50. "King Tweed and His Subjects," *New York Times*, 28 Sept. 1870, 4.

51. Anita Leslie, *The Remarkable Mr. Jerome* (New York: Henry Holt and Co., 1954), 19–49. Leslie was Jerome's great-great niece, and her biography draws significantly on family materials.

52. William Worthington Fowler, *Twenty Years of Inside Life in Wall Street* (New York: Orange Judd, 1880; Westport, CT: Greenwood, 1968), 178–79.

53. Leslie, *Remarkable Mr. Jerome*, 78–81.

54. Ibid., 8.

55. "American Jockey Club," *New York Tribune*, 26 Sept. 1866, 8.

56. Joshua Lawrence Chamberlain, *The Passing of the Armies* (New York: G.P. Putnam's Sons, 1915), 358–59.

57. Ibid., 229.

58. Captain Robert Edward Lee, *Recollections and Letters of General Robert E. Lee* (New York: Doubleday, Page, 1905), 193.

59. Quoted in Kirk Savage, *Standing Soldiers, Kneeling Slaves: Race, War, and Monument in Nineteenth-Century America* (Princeton: Princeton University Press, 1997), 144.

60. Ibid., 133–35.

61. Ulysses S. Grant, *Personal Memoirs of U.S. Grant* (New York: C.L. Webster and Co., 1886), 85–86.

62. James Grant Wilson, "War-Horses of Famous Generals," *Century Magazine*, May 1913, 52; Horace Porter, "Lincoln and Grant," *Century Illustrated Magazine*, Oct. 1885, 939.

63. Clyde C. Webster, "John Minor Botts, Anti-Secessionist," *Richmond College Historical Papers* 1.1 (1915): 36.

64. William J. Simmons, *Men of Mark: Eminent, Progressive and Rising* (Cleveland: George M. Rewell & Co., 1887), 614–15. Accessed through Documenting the American South. University Library, University of North Carolina at Chapel Hill, 2000, http://docsouth.unc.edu/neh/simmons/simmons .html.

65. William J. Minor to Stephen Duncan, 16 Sept. 1865, Stephen Duncan Correspondence, Box 1, Folder 1a, Louisiana and Lower Mississippi Valley Collections, Louisiana State University.

66. D. R. Riley to E. E. Eagle, 20 May 1867, 1860–1885 Folder, Kentucky Association for the Improvement of the Breeds of Stock records, Margaret I. King Special Collections Library, University of Kentucky. Emphasis in original.

67. David W. Blight, *Race and Reunion* (Cambridge, MA: Harvard University Press, 2001), 68–70.

68. "Public Privileges," *Weekly Louisianian*, 2 May 1874, 2; Somers, *Rise of Sports in New Orleans*, 96–97.

69. "The Politicians Against the People," *Spirit of the Times*, 12 Sept. 1868, 56.

70. Robertson, *History of Thoroughbred Racing*, 87–88.

71. Harrison, *Background of the American Stud Book*, 54–55; Wall, *How Kentucky Became Southern*, 71; Mackay-Smith, *Race Horses of America*, 277–78; Jonelle Fisher, *For All Times: The Story of Lucas Brodhead* (N.P.: St. Crispian Press, 2002), 108–9.

72. "The Five Races of Man," *Turf, Field and Farm*, 21 Dec. 1867, 392.

73. "The Confederate B.'s," *Spirit of the Times*, 4 Oct. 1873, 180.

74. "'Stonewall' Jackson," *Turf, Field and Farm*, 3 Feb. 1866, 72.

75. Blight, *Race and Reunion*, 160–62.

76. Phil., "Letter from Mobile," *Kentucky Live Stock Record* 9 April 1881, 227.

77. S. D. Bruce, *The American Stud Book*, vol.1 (Chicago: E.B. Myers and Company, 1868), 478, Fairman Rogers Collection, Rare Book and Manuscript Library, University of Pennsylvania.

78. Hamilton Busbey, "The Running Turf in America," *Harper's New Monthly Magazine*, July 1870, 251.

79. "The Turf as a Means of Restoring Cordial Relations," *Spirit of the Times*, 13 June 1868, 210.

80. John B. Irving, *The American Jockey Club: Jerome Park: introductory* (New York: Thitchener & Glastaeter, 1866), 12–13, Fairman Rogers Collection, Rare Book and Manuscript Library, University of Pennsylvania.

81. Heather Cox Richardson, *West from Appomattox: The Reconstruction of America after the Civil War* (New Haven: Yale University Press, 2007), 131. My discussion of these developments in American economic and social life is

informed by Richardson, *West from Appomattox*, 64–66, 100–101; Alan Trachtenberg, *The Incorporation of America* (1982; New York: Hill and Wang, 2007), 42–87; Sven Beckert, *The Monied Metropolis: New York City and the Consolidation of the American Bourgeoisie, 1850–1896* (Cambridge: Cambridge University Press, 1993), 177–207.

82. On the increasing importance of the idea of contract and varying viewpoints on it, see Amy Dru Stanley, *From Bondage to Contract: Wage Labor, Marriage, and the Market in the Age of Slave Emancipation* (Cambridge: Cambridge University Press, 1998), 75–93.

83. For the push to bring white Southerners back into the national Democratic fold, see Irving Katz, *August Belmont: A Political Biography* (New York: Columbia University Press, 1968), 169. For insightful discussion into the vision of the labor problem as national and interracial, see Heather Cox Richardson, *The Death of Reconstruction: Race, Labor, and Politics in the Post-Civil War North, 1865–1901* (Cambridge, MA: Harvard University Press, 2001), xiii–xv, 57–89; Stanley, *From Bondage to Contract*, 61; Richardson, *West from Appomattox*, 47–61, 141.

84. Blight, *Race and Reunion*, 123, 138.

85. "THE DEATH PENALTY," *New York Herald*, 15 July 1871, 7.

86. For the political role of wealthy men's recreations in this period, see Beckert, *Monied Metropolis*, 3–9, 154.

87. Henry James, *Collected Travel Writings: Great Britain and America*, ed. Richard Howard (New York: Library of America, 1993), 752–53.

88. John Hope Franklin, *A Southern Odyssey: Travelers in the Antebellum North* (Baton Rouge: Louisiana State University Press, 1976), 269–71.

89. Fowler, *Twenty Years of Inside Life*, 243.

90. For a description of the Jerome Park clubhouse and its décor, see W. S. Vosburgh, *Cherry and Black: The Career of Mr. Pierre Lorillard on the Turf* (N.P.: Printed for P. Lorillard, 1916), 4.

91. Irving Katz, "Investment Bankers in American Government and Politics," PhD diss., New York University, 1965, 37–40.

92. William H. Seward to August Belmont, 19 May 1863, and Daniel Sickles to August Belmont, October 1870, Belmont Family Papers, Columbia University; Katz, "Investment Bankers," 51–52; Katz, *August Belmont*, 98–103.

93. Allan Nevins and Milton Halsey Thomas, eds., *The Diary of George Templeton Strong* (New York: Macmillan, 1952), vol. 3, 510; Ferguson, *House of Rothschild*, vol. 2, 115.

94. Beckert, *Monied Metropolis*, 84–89, 144–50, 163–71. On the power of what Iver Bernstein has termed the "Belmont circle" and its postwar unity with Republican industrialists in the face of working-class agitation, see Iver Bernstein, *The New York City Draft Riots* (New York: Oxford University Press, 1990), 130–31, 238–39.

95. *The American Jockey Club* (New York: Thitchener & Glastaeter, 1867), 66–67, Keeneland Library, Lexington, Kentucky.

96. Parmer, *For Gold and Glory*, 136; T. J. Stiles, *The First Tycoon* (New York: Alfred A. Knopf, 2009), 549.

97. Melvin L. Adelman, *A Sporting Time: New York City and the Rise of Modern Athletics, 1820–1870* (Urbana: University of Illinois Press, 1986), 88.

98. Vosburgh, *Cherry and Black*, 9.

99. Vosburgh, *Racing in America, 1866–1921*, 78–79.

100. " 'Larkin' Again in Harness," *Spirit of the Times*, 4 March 1871, 42.

101. Edward Spencer, *An Outline of the Public Life and Services of Thomas F. Bayard, Senator of the United States From the State of Delaware, 1869–1880* (New York: D. Appleton and Co., 1880), 161–64.

102. Charles Callan Tansill, *The Congressional Career of Thomas Francis Bayard 1869–1885* (Washington, D.C.: Georgetown University Press, 1946), 52; Blight, *Race and Reunion*, 117–22; David Black, *King of Fifth Avenue* (New York: Dial Press, 1981), 383–386.

103. Tansill, *Congressional Career of Thomas Francis Bayard*, 66–67.

104. Ibid., 102–14.

105. Eric Homberger, *Mrs. Astor's New York: Money and Social Power in a Gilded Age* (New Haven: Yale University Press, 2002), 178–86.

106. Blight, *Race and Reunion*, 124–25; Katz, *August Belmont*, 197–204; Jerome Mushkat, *The Reconstruction of the New York Democracy, 1861–1874* (Rutherford, NJ: Fairleigh Dickinson University Press, 1981), 193–204.

107. "The Democratic Conventions," *Spirit of the Times*, 15 June 1872, 281.

108. "The New Era," *Spirit of the Times*, 18 May 1872, 217.

109. Philip M. Katz, *From Appomattox to Montmartre: Americans and the Paris Commune* (Cambridge, MA: Harvard University Press, 1998), 56–58, 127–28.

110. Alexander Saxton, "George Wilkes: The Transformation of a Radical Ideology," *American Quarterly* 33.4 (1981): 438. The point is discussed further in Alexander Saxton, *The Rise and Fall of the White Republic* (London: Verso, 1990), 205.

111. "Mr. Murphy Can Be Accommodated," *Spirit of the Times*, 20 July 1872, 360.

112. "Racing for the South," *Spirit of the Times*, 31 Aug 1872, 41.

113. For example, Duncan Kenner's former jockey Henry Hammond became a powerbroker in Reconstruction-era Ascension Parish and very comfortably made deals with white planters. See James D. Wilson Jr., "The Donaldsonville Incident of 1870: A Story of Local Party Dissension and Republican Infighting in Reconstruction Louisiana," *Louisiana History* 38.3 (1997): 333–35.

114. See Blight, *Race and Reunion*, 311, for an evocative discussion of the emotional ties between the past in slavery and the future of freedpeople. See Susan Eva O'Donovan, *Becoming Free in the Cotton South* (Cambridge, MA: Harvard University Press, 2007), 53–54, 129–32, for a discussion of how particular job skills and situations in slavery, particularly for men, shaped the experience of and opportunities available in free labor.

115. "The Stables at Saratoga," *Turf, Field and Farm*, 5 Aug. 1865, 11; "Racing Prospects," *Turf, Field and Farm*, 5 Aug. 1865, 9.

116. "The Saratoga Summer Meeting," *Spirit of the Times*, 7 Aug. 1869, 388; "The Turf at Mobile," *Turf, Field and Farm*, 17 March 1866, 168.

117. Untitled ms., Box 2, Folder 40, William J. Minor Horse Racing Collection, Beinecke Rare Book and Manuscript Library, Yale University.

118. "Twenty Years' Turf Reminiscences," *New York Sportsman*, 8 March 1884, 173.

119. James Robert Saunders and Monica Renae Saunders, *Black Winning Jockeys in the Kentucky Derby* (Jefferson, NC: McFarland, 2003), 6, 12–13; Philip Von Borries, *Racelines* (Chicago: Masters Press, 1999), 170–73.

120. William Preston Mangum, *A Kingdom for the Horse* (Prospect, KY: Harmony House, 1999), 120; Mackay-Smith, *Race Horses of America*, 224.

121. "Stables at Jerome Park," *New York Sportsman*, 29 May 1875, 11.

122. The earliest mention of Abe's last name comes from Harry Worcester Smith, "The Sportsman's Bookshelf," *Thoroughbred Record*, 8 Aug. 1925, 66–67. Smith's information came from Rosella Kenner Brent and her son, who had firsthand knowledge.

123. "The American Turf," *Wilkes's Spirit of the Times*, 16 June 1866, 243.

124. "Answers to Correspondents," *Spirit of the Times*, 21 July 1866, 326; "Answers to Correspondents," *Spirit of the Times*, 4 Aug. 1866, 361; "Answers to Correspondents," *Spirit of the Times*, 15 Sept. 1866, 37.

125. Ben H. Weaver, "The Passing of 'Uncle Bill,'" *Turf and Sport Digest*, Dec. 1933, 38.

126. "A Losing Book," *New York Sportsman*, 19 June 1875, 42.

127. John H. Davis, *The American Turf* (New York: John Polhemus, 1907), 85.

128. Red Smith, "The Belmont Starts with George," *To the Swift: Classic Triple Crown Horses and Their Race for Glory*, ed. Joe Drape (New York: St. Martin's, 2008), 26–27.

129. "Echoes of the Week," *New York Sportsman*, 16 June 1888, 574.

130. Saunders and Saunders, *Black Winning Jockeys*, 19; Jonelle Fisher, *Nantura, 1795–1905* (N.P.: St. Crispian Press, 2004), 103.

131. Wall, *How Kentucky Became Southern*, 104.

132. "The Four-Mile Heat Race," *New York Sportsman*, 20 July 1878, 25; "The Ten-Broeck-Mollie M'Carthy Match," *Kentucky Live Stock Record*, 13 July 1878, 24.

133. "An Interview with F. B. Harper—Some Inconsistencies Worth Noting," *Kentucky Live Stock Record*, 3 Aug. 1878, 72–73.

134. Nina Silber, *The Romance of Reunion* (Chapel Hill: University of North Carolina Press, 1993), 108–9.

135. Harvey Argyle, "A Horse-Race For a Wife in the Days of Slavery," *As I Saw It* (San Francisco: Home Publishing 1902), 212–63.

136. "Hoboken Spring Meeting," *Spirit of the Times*, 30 June 1866, 27; "Twenty Years' Turf Reminiscences," *New York Sportsman*, 19 April 1884, 293.

137. "Racehorses for Mr. Jerome," *New York Sportsman*, 10 July 1880, 19.

138. "Death of Abe the Jockey," *Spirit of the Times*, 11 May 1865, 173; "Death of Old Abe," *Turf, Field and Farm*, 4 May 1867, 280.

139. Harry Worcester Smith, "Sportsman's Bookshelf," *Thoroughbred Record*, 8 Aug. 1925, 66–67. Again, Smith's information came from Rosella Kenner Brent, so he was probably repeating a long-told family story. A similar ac-

count also appears in "Over and Under the Turf," *New York Tribune*, 23 Dec. 1889, 4.

140. "A Race Rider Reads his Obituary and Is Delighted," *Turf, Field and Farm*, 1 June 1867, 339; "Death of an Old Jockey," *Natchez Courier*, 14 May 1867; "Over and Under the Turf," *New York Tribune*, 23 Dec. 1889, 4.

141. "Spring Races—First Day," *New Orleans Times*, 12 April 1866, 2.

142. See, for a discussion of the evolution of opinion, K. Stephen Prince, "Legitimacy and Interventionism: Northern Republicans, the 'Terrible Carpetbagger,' and the Retreat from Reconstruction," *Journal of the Civil War Era* 2.4 (2012): 548–53.

143. Robert Harlan to John Marshall Harlan, 1 June 1877, microfilm reel 4, John Marshall Harlan Papers, Library of Congress.

144. C. Vann Woodward, *Reunion and Reaction: The Compromise of 1877 and the End of Reconstruction* (Boston: Little, Brown, 1951), 24–25; Michael F. Holt, *By One Vote: The Disputed Election of 1876* (Lawrence: University Press of Kansas, 2008), 121.

145. Holt, *By One Vote*, 156.

146. Walter McGehee Lowrey, "The Political Career of James Madison Wells," *Louisiana Historical Quarterly* 31.4 (1948): 1107; Testimony of Duncan F. Kenner Before the Select Committee on the Privileges, Powers, and Duties of the House of Representatives in Counting the Votes for President and Vice-President of the U.S., 44th Congress, *Congressional Record*, House Miscellaneous Documents, 44–42, 376–87.

147. Kenner testimony, 384–85.

148. G. M. G. Stafford, *The Wells Family of Louisiana and Allied Families* (Alexandria, LA: Standard Printing, 1942), 100.

149. "Tilden and Morrissey," *New York Times*, 18 Oct. 1878, 1. The accusation here is less direct, but it does suggest Morrissey's potential role in possible deals for Louisiana's votes.

150. Edward O. Frantz, *The Door of Hope: Republican Presidents and the First Southern Strategy, 1877–1933* (Gainesville: University Press of Florida, 2011), 32.

151. "A Decision Reserved," *Spirit of the Times*, 29 Sept. 1877, 23.

152. Blight, *Race and Reunion*, 215–16.

153. Thomas W. Doswell to Frances Anne Sutton Doswell, undated, Series 4, Doswell Family Papers, Virginia Historical Society.

154. L. P. Tarlton, "A Memorial," *Thoroughbred Record*, 21 March 1896, 136.

6. I Ride to Win

1. Emma Lou Thornbrough, *T. Thomas Fortune: Militant Journalist* (Chicago: University of Chicago Press, 1972), 110–11.

2. Shawn Leigh Alexander, *An Army of Lions: The Civil Rights Struggle before the NAACP* (Philadelphia: University of Pennsylvania Press, 2012), 39–53.

3. The account of Stewart and Fortune's day at the race is taken from T. Thomas Fortune, "The Prince of Jockeys, Isaac Murphy of Kentucky In and Out of the Saddle," *New York Age*, 5 July 1890, 1.

4. William H. P. Robertson, *The History of Thoroughbred Racing in America* (Englewood Cliffs, NJ: Prentice Hall, 1964), 138.

5. "Post and Paddock," *Spirit of the Times*, 7 June 1890, 878.

6. Walter S. Vosburgh, *Racing in America, 1866–1921* (New York: Jockey Club, 1922), 147; Robertson, *History of Thoroughbred Racing*, 143.

7. Vosburgh, *Racing in America, 1866–1921*, 148.

8. James Robert Saunders and Monica Renae Saunders, *Black Winning Jockeys in the Kentucky Derby* (Jefferson, NC: McFarland, 2003), 51. Eddie Arcaro, the winner of five Kentucky Derbys, won 22 percent of his races, and the great Willie Shoemaker won 24 percent of the time. Since 1995, the National Turf Writers Association has given the annual Isaac Murphy Award to the jockey in American racing with the best winning percentage in a minimum of 500 races.

9. Vigilant, "The Metropolitan Meeting," *Spirit of the Times*, 15 Oct. 1881, 303.

10. This account of the race is drawn from "Post and Paddock," *Spirit of the Times*, 28 June 1890, 1014.

11. "Sports and Sportsmen," *New York Age*, 18 April 1891, 4.

12. The entire poem appears in Ella Wheeler Wilcox, "How Salvator Won," *Spirit of the Times*, 12 July 1890, 1082.

13. "Post and Paddock," *Spirit of the Times*, 16 Aug. 1890, 142–43.

14. "He Is King," *Brooklyn Daily Eagle*, 29 Aug. 1890, 4; "Poor Tenny," *Brooklyn Daily Eagle*, 13 Aug. 1890, 2.

15. "Post and Paddock," *Spirit of the Times*, 30 Aug. 1890, 226.

16. Pellom McDaniels III, *The Prince of Jockeys: The Life of Isaac Burns Murphy* (Lexington: University Press of Kentucky, 2013), 43.

17. For Murphy's father's enlistment in the army at Camp Nelson, see L. P. Tarlton, "A Memorial," *Thoroughbred Record*, 21 March 1896, 136. Tarlton had known Murphy from boyhood and was later both his employer and his attorney, so his word on the subject of Murphy's family history is the closest thing we have to a first-person account. Many of the details of Murphy's early biography are taken from this lengthy obituary. On black enlistment at Camp Nelson, see Victor B. Howard, *Black Liberation in Kentucky* (Lexington: University Press of Kentucky, 1983), 79; John David Smith, "The Recruitment of Negro Soldiers in Kentucky, 1863–1865," *Register of the Kentucky Historical Society* 72.4 (1974): 384; Richard D. Sears, *Camp Nelson, Kentucky* (Lexington: University Press of Kentucky, 2002), xxxviii–xxxix.

18. Howard, *Black Liberation in Kentucky*, 100.

19. For an example of some of the more recent detective work on the subject using these records, see McDaniels, *Prince of Jockeys*, 56–8.

20. Civil War Pension Index, 1861–1934, Record for Jerry Burns/Jerry Skillman, pension application # 174318. Accessed through ancestry.com, 12 Jan. 2011.

21. "G.A.R. Internment," *Lexington Morning Transcript*, 19 April 1888, 4.

22. The woman who contested America Burns's claim to Jerry Skillman's pension was named Caroline Skillman, which was also the name of Charles Skillman's second wife. So what looks like bigamy may, in fact, have been a

clerical error. See Roster, 114th U.S. Colored Troops Infantry Regiment, American Civil War Research Database. Accessed 11 Nov. 2011; Civil War Pension Index, 1861–1934, Record for Charles Skillman, pension application # 398818. Accessed through ancestry.com, 11 Nov. 2011; Slave schedules, United States Census 1860, entry for J. W. Skillman, Eastern Division of Bourbon County, Kentucky. Family friend L. P. Tarlton wrote in his obituary for Isaac Murphy that America Murphy Burns had received her husband's pension until her death. Tarlton, "A Memorial," 136.

23. Freedman's Bank Records, #1479, entry for America Burns. Accessed through ancestry.com, 12 Jan. 2011.

24. Frank X. Walker, "Healing Songs," *Isaac Murphy: I Dedicate This Ride* (Lexington: Old Cove Press, 2010), 63.

25. Patrick A. Lewis, "The Democratic Partisan Militias and the Black Peril: The Kentucky Militia, Racial Violence, and the Fifteenth Amendment, 1870–1873," *Civil War History* 56.2 (2010): 145–71.

26. See, for a perceptive discussion of the potentially daunting aspects of this employment for a young boy, Maryjean Wall, "Kentucky's Isaac Murphy: A Legacy Interrupted, the Intersection of Race and the Horse Industry in the Bluegrass," MA thesis, University of Kentucky, 2003, 19–32.

27. Betty Earle Borries, *Isaac Murphy: Kentucky's Record Jockey* (Berea: Kentucke Imprints, 1988), 1–22; Wall, "Isaac Murphy," 36–37; L. P. Tarlton, "A Memorial," 136; "Louisville Races," *New York Sportsman*, 30 Sept. 1876, 470. For James T. Williams's account of Murphy's first tearful ride (and a suggestion that America Burns may already have been chronically ill in Murphy's youth), see "Freeland's Famous Jockey," *New York Times*, 20 Aug. 1885, 3. For Eli Jordan's account of his acquaintance with America Burns and his role in Isaac Murphy's training, see "Ike Murphy's Real Name," *Lexington Leader*, 29 July 1891, 7. For Murphy's own brief account of his beginnings, see "Isaac Murphy," *Kentucky Leader*, 20 March 1889, 3.

28. See, for a discussion of the importance of the expertise of men born in slavery for shaping postwar racing, Wall, "Isaac Murphy," 121.

29. L. P. Tarlton, "A Memorial," 136; "Horses at Saratoga," *Spirit of the Times*, 28 June 1877, 717; "Prospects of the Running Turf: Horses in Training, New York," *Spirit of the Times*, 7 Feb. 1880, 1; "Breeding Farms in Kentucky," *Kentucky Live Stock Record*, 28 Feb. 1885, 136.

30. "Nashville Notes," *New York Sportsman*, 26 May 1883, 408; William Woodward, *Memoir of Andrew Jackson, Africanus* (New York: Derrydale, 1938), 21–28.

31. "KINGMAN," *Louisville Courier-Journal*, 14 May 1891, 6. For Allen's service, see Civil War Pension Index, 1861–1934, Record for Dudley Allen, pension application #1210136. Accessed through ancestry.com, 13 Nov. 2011. For a brief assessment of the Saltville atrocities, see Thomas D. Mays, "The Battle of Saltville," *Black Soldiers in Blue: African American Troops in the Civil War Era*, ed. John David Smith (Chapel Hill: University of North Carolina Press, 2002), 200–226.

32. For a brief biographical sketch of Cooper, see Lyman Horace Weeks, *The American Turf: An Historical Account of Racing in the United States with*

Biographical Sketches of Turf Celebrities (New York: The Historical Company, 1898), 356.

33. "Echoes of the Day," *New York Sportsman*, 6 March 1886, 172; Alden Hatch and Foxhall Keene, *Full Tilt: The Sporting Memoirs of Foxhall Keene* (New York: Derrydale, 1938), 25.

34. "'Brown Dick' Owner of Ben Brush," *Thoroughbred Record*, 18 May 1895, 310; Vosburgh, *Racing in America, 1866–1921*, 166–67; Alexander Mackay-Smith, *The Race Horses of America, 1832–1872* (Saratoga Springs, NY: National Museum of Racing, 1981), 224.

35. "Miscellaneous Turf Gossip," *Thoroughbred Record*, 18 May 1895, 313.

36. Annie Hunter to Harriott Middleton, 23 Sept. 1883, Harriott Middleton Family Papers, 1861–1905 (1168.02.08), South Carolina Historical Society. Emphasis in original.

37. Hugh Bradley, *Such Was Saratoga* (New York: Doubleday, Doran, 1940), 186.

38. Robertson, *History of Thoroughbred Racing*, 127–30; Woodward, *Memoir of Andrew Jackson*, 17; W. S. Vosburgh, *Cherry and Black: The Career of Mr. Pierre Lorillard on the Turf* (N.P.: Printed for P. Lorillard, 1916), 43–44; Roger Longrigg, *The History of Horse Racing* (New York: Stein and Day, 1972), 226; Henry Clay Simpson Jr., *Josephine Clay, Pioneer Horsewoman of the Bluegrass* (Louisville: Harmony House, 2005), 61.

39. Weeks, *American Turf*, 278.

40. Robertson, *History of Thoroughbred Racing*, 130.

41. Hatch and Keene, *Full Tilt*, 6; Robertson, *History of Thoroughbred Racing*, 157.

42. Hatch and Keene, *Full Tilt*, 7–9; Edward Bowen, *Masters of the Turf* (Lexington: The Blood Horse, 2007), 9; William Worthington Fowler, *Twenty Years of Inside Life in Wall Street* (New York: Orange Judd, 1880; Westport, CT: Greenwood, 1968), 554; Dan M. Bowmar, *Giants of the Turf* (Lexington: The Blood Horse, 1960), 123–25.

43. Vosburgh, *Racing in America, 1865–1921*, 108; Hatch and Keene, *Full Tilt*, 10.

44. Vosburgh, *Cherry and Black*, 68.

45. "Saratoga," *Spirit of the Times*, 26 July 1879, 624. Variant punctuation in original. See also Ranger, "Saratoga Summer Meeting," *New York Sportsman*, 26 July 1879, 37.

46. "The Running at Baltimore," *New York Sportsman*, 1 Nov. 1879, 210.

47. Albion, "Baltimore," *Spirit of the Times*, 3 Nov. 1877, 364.

48. Vosburgh, *Racing in America, 1865–1921*, 59.

49. The best work on this shift in Kentucky's role and on the evolution of this class of professionals can be found in Maryjean Wall, *How Kentucky Became Southern* (Lexington: University Press of Kentucky, 2010), 69–70, 155–69.

50. Wall, *How Kentucky Became Southern*, 69–70, 84.

51. Thomas D. Clark, "The People, William Goebel, and the Kentucky Railroads," *Journal of Southern History* 5.1 (1939): 41–42; "Latonia," *Spirit of the Times*, 13 Oct. 1888, 433.

52. R. Gerald Alvey, *Kentucky Bluegrass Country* (Jackson: University Press of Mississippi, 1992), 138–40.

53. Sven Beckert, *The Monied Metropolis: New York City and the Consolidation of the American Bourgeoisie, 1850–1896* (Cambridge: Cambridge University Press, 1993), 238–58.

54. Alan Trachtenberg, *The Incorporation of America: Culture and Society in the Gilded Age* (1982; New York: Hill and Wang, 2007), 79–91.

55. Beckert, *Monied Metropolis*, 292–313.

56. "Spirit of the Times," *Spirit of the Times*, 30 Oct. 1880, 344.

57. Edward O. Frantz, *The Door of Hope: Republican Presidents and the First Southern Strategy, 1877–1933* (Gainesville: University Press of Florida, 2011), 66.

58. Rebecca J. Scott, *Degrees of Freedom: Louisiana and Cuba after Slavery* (Cambridge, MA: Harvard University Press, 2005), 55–56, 80–86.

59. E. P. Alexander to August Belmont, 23 Oct. 1888, Belmont Family Papers, Columbia University.

60. Charles W. Calhoun, *Minority Victory: Gilded Age Politics and the Front Porch Campaign of 1888* (Lawrence: University Press of Kansas, 2008), 154.

61. Frederick Douglass, "The Color Question," 5 July 1875, typescript, 4. Speech, Article, and Book File, Frederick Douglass Papers, Library of Congress. Accessed through American Memory Project, http://memory.loc.gov /ammem/doughtml/dougFolder5.html.

62. Richard Watson Gilder, *Grover Cleveland: A Record of Friendship* (New York: Century Company, 1910), 217–18.

63. "Distinguished Visitors at Belle Meade," *New York Sportsman*, 29 Oct. 1887, 396.

64. "Proctor Knott's Futurity," *New York Sportsman*, 15 Sept. 1888, 236; "Echoes of the Week," *New York Sportsman*, 15 Sept. 1888, 234.

65. Douglass, "Color Question," 7.

66. "Fallen Favorites: First Day at the Louisiana Jockey Club Fall Meeting," *New Orleans Times*, 14 Dec. 1873, 10.

67. Samuel Hildreth, *The Spell of the Turf* (Philadelphia: J.B. Lippincott, 1926), 46.

68. "A Jockey's Trials and Successes," *Live Stock Record*, 5 Jan. 1895, 11.

69. "To Correspondents," *New York Sportsman*, 27 Jan. 1883, 50.

70. Winnie O'Connor, *Jockeys, Crooks and Kings* (New York: Jonathan Cape and Harrison Smith, 1930), 5–9; Robertson, *History of Thoroughbred Racing*, 168.

71. John Dizikes, *Yankee Doodle Dandy: The Life and Times of Tod Sloan* (New Haven: Yale University Press, 2000), 35–39.

72. See, for example, "WANTED," *New York Sportsman*, 19 Nov. 1881, 335; "Warning to Employers," *New York Sportsman*, 21 May 1887, 495.

73. "Racing," *New York Sportsman*, 12 Jan. 1889, 32; "How a Jockey Lives," *Frank Leslie's Illustrated Newspaper*, 22 Aug. 1885, 14; "The Turf," *New York Sportsman*, 30 June 1883, 512.

74. For an example of the many stories about Murphy's suffering to make weight, see "Echoes of the Day," *New York Sportsman*, 17 Oct. 1885, 314.

75. "Echoes of the Day," *New York Sportsman*, 8 Jan. 1887, 36; Laura Thompson, *Newmarket: From James I to the Present Day* (London: Virgin, 2000), 222.

76. Edward Hotaling, *The Great Black Jockeys* (Rocklin, CA: Forum, 1999), 271; Lynn S. Renau, *Racing around Kentucky* (Louisville: N.P., 1995), 137.

77. "Tom Britton Injured," *Lexington Leader*, 8 Aug. 1892, 2; "Latonia," *Spirit of the Times and Sportsman*, 11 July 1896, 834.

78. "The Tattler's Tattle," *New York Sportsman*, 7 Nov. 1885, 377.

79. "Little Paul Potter Buried," *New York Times*, 3 Nov. 1885, 8; Schedule 1, Supervisor's District 1, Enumeration District 400, 1880 United States Census, 30.

80. "Racing," *New York Sportsman*, 17 Sept. 1887, 266; "Turf and Training Notes," *New York Sportsman*, 1 Oct. 1887, 313.

81. "Killed on the Race Track," *New York Sportsman*, 14 July 1877, 22.

82. "A Jockey's Life," *Chicago Tribune*, 10 July 1885, 2; "Isaac Murphy," *Kentucky Leader*, 20 March 1889, 3.

83. Weeks, *American Turf*, 357–66.

84. Weeks, *American Turf*, 395; "Hamilton, The Jockey," *Live Stock Record*, 7 July 1894, 7.

85. "St. Louis," *Spirit of the Times*, 25 June 1887, 729.

86. "Colored Jockeys Show the Way," *New York Herald*, 20 Sept. 1889, 8; "Five Favorites First," *New York Herald*, 20 Sept. 1889, 3; "Turf Notes in Brief," *New York Sportsman*, 28 Sept. 1889, 301.

87. "Western Light-Weight Jockeys," *Live Stock Record*, 25 Aug. 1894, 117.

88. Borries, *Isaac Murphy*, 15–16; Weeks, *American Turf*, 386; Steve Thomas, "Link to 1895," *The Blood-Horse*, 19 April 1986, 2813; "Local Turf News," *Live Stock Record*, 4 Nov. 1893, 296; "Local Turf News," *Live Stock Record*, 29 Sept. 1894, 198; "Western Racing," *Spirit of the Times and Sportsman*, 26 Nov. 1892, 688; "What the Jockeys Say," *Louisville Courier-Journal*, 7 May 1895, 2.

89. "Racing Notes," *Turf, Field and Farm*, 21 March 1896, 276.

90. "Die Poor," *Lexington Leader*, 12 Feb. 1898, 7. Maryjean Wall comments on the significance of jockeys as, in effect, the owners of small businesses. See Wall, "Isaac Murphy," 105.

91. "Horse Gossip," *Turf, Field and Farm*, 18 March 1892, 382; "Colors Claimed," *New York Sportsman*, 28 April 1888, 396; "Lexington," *New York Sportsman*, 19 May 1888, 464.

92. C.B. Glasscock, *Lucky Baldwin* (Indianapolis: Bobbs-Merrill, 1933), 237–38. Murphy would not necessarily have had to go to California to ride Baldwin's horses, since the best runners would have been brought east for the major fixtures of the day, but the jockey did spend time at Santa Anita, which helps to substantiate Fisher's recollection. See "Echoes of the Day," *New York Sportsman*, 3 April 1886, 246.

93. See, for example, "Echoes of the Week," *New York Sportsman*, 17 Aug. 1889, 145–46; A.J. Liebling, *Back Where I Came From* (San Francisco: North Point Press, 1990), 38.

94. "The Spirit Picture Gallery," *Spirit of the Times*, 29 Aug. 1885, 144; "Spirit of the Times," *Spirit of the Times*, 26 Sept. 1885, 284.

95. "Post and Paddock," *Spirit of the Times*, 29 Nov. 1884, 557.

96. Hotaling, *Great Black Jockeys*, 269; Robertson, *History of Thoroughbred Racing*, 166.

97. "The Colored Archer," *Louisville Courier-Journal*, 15 May 1890, 2.

98. "Famous American Jockeys," *Thoroughbred Record*, 6 March 1920, Isaac Murphy File, Keeneland Library.

99. Thompson, *Newmarket*, 222; Vosburgh, *Racing in America, 1865–1921*, 122.

100. Borries, *Isaac Murphy*, 113.

101. "The Tattler's Tattle," *New York Sportsman*, 22 Aug. 1885, 152.

102. Woodward, *Memoir of Andrew Jackson*, 11. Variant spelling in the original.

103. Edward Dudley Brown subject file, Woodford County Historical Society, Versailles, Kentucky; "Passing of Venerable Horseman," *Thoroughbred Record*, 18 Sept. 1926, 154.

104. "Western Turf Notes," *Spirit of the Times*, 2 Jan. 1892, 904.

105. "Colored Social Events: A Celebrated Jockey Married and an Entertainment Given the Bride and Groom," *Lexington Leader*, 10 June 1891, 2; "Jockey Will Overton to Marry a Sister of Jockey Tom Britton Tomorrow," *Lexington Leader*, 21 Sept. 1891, 5.

106. "Britton-Jackson, The Noted Colored Jockey, Thos. Britton, Is United," *Lexington Transcript*, 6 May 1891, 1; Wall, "Isaac Murphy," 13.

107. "Jockey Hamilton To Be Married," *New York Times*, 12 Jan. 1891, 1; "Jockey Hamilton," *Lexington Leader*, 12 Jan. 1891, 5; "Murphy Entertains," *Lexington Leader*, 25 Jan. 1891, 5; "Grand Reception Given by Isaac Murphy and Wife, to Anthony Hamilton and Bride," *Lexington Transcript*, 25 Jan. 1891, 5.

108. "Jockey Isaac Murphy," *Lexington Leader*, 24 Jan. 1893, 5; "Won Fame as a Jockey," *Lexington Leader*, 31 Jan. 1893, 2. For another example of the elegance of Murphy family entertaining, see the coverage of the wedding of Murphy's cousin Julia Robinson, "Colored Society," *Lexington Leader*, 17 April 1892, 5.

109. Nancy O'Malley, "The Pursuit of Freedom: The Evolution of Kinkeadtown, An African American Post-Civil War Neighborhood in Lexington, Kentucky," *Winterthur Portfolio* 37.4 (2002): 204–16; Wall, "Isaac Murphy," 97–98; "Isaac Murphy's New House," *New York Times*, 13 June 1887, 1.

110. Wall, "Isaac Murphy," 7, 52, 68.

111. McDaniels, *Prince of Jockeys*, 131–32; "Killed Herself," *Lexington Leader* 1 June 1891, 4.

112. "Brown Dick," *Louisville Courier-Journal*, 12 May 1906, 4; *Proceedings of the Kentucky Negro Educational Association*, 53rd Annual Session, 17–20 April 1929, 4, 13. Accessed through Kentuckiana Digital Library, 31 Dec. 2011, http://kdl.kyvl.org/catalog/xt7n028pcp8j_1; Frank Lincoln Mather, ed., *Who's Who of the Colored Race* (Chicago: N.P., 1915), vol. 1, 43; Thomas Yenser, ed., *Who's Who in Colored America*, 4th ed. (Brooklyn: T. Yenser, 1933–37), 601. See for a discussion of similar patterns in neighborhoods in which black horsemen lived, O'Malley, "Pursuit of Freedom," 216.

113. Patrick S. Washburn, *The African American Newspaper: Voice of Freedom* (Evanston, IL: Northwestern University Press, 2006), 49–51.

114. See, for example, "Doings of the Race," *Cleveland Gazette*, 10 April 1886, 1; "Doings of the Race," *Cleveland Gazette*, 10 July 1886, 1.

115. "Annie and Anthony," *Huntsville Gazette*, 17 Jan. 1891, 1; "The Future Great," *Indianapolis Freeman*, 24 Jan. 1891, 5.

116. "Doings of the Race . . . The Best Jockey a Colored Gentleman," *Cleveland Gazette*, 10 July 1886, 1; "People and Events," *New Orleans Weekly Pelican*, 4 Dec. 1886, 4; "Personal Mention," *New Orleans Weekly Pelican*, 19 March 1887, 3.

117. "Sports and Sportsmen," *New York Age*, 18 April 1891, 4.

118. John H. Davis, *The American Turf* (New York: John Polhemus, 1907), 122–24. Variant spelling in the original.

119. Davis, *American Turf*, 102–3. Davis's conferring whiteness on Murphy to validate his own feelings of respect suggests how complex white racing men's relationship to many black riders and particularly to Murphy was. David Wiggins, who has worked extensively on Murphy's career, significantly underestimates the complicated power of this confusion of emotions when he sweepingly asserts that African American jockeys were thought to work in a job inherited from slavery and thus one that was ill-suited to white workers or to white admiration. See David K. Wiggins, "Isaac Murphy, Black Hero in Nineteenth Century American Sport, 1861–1896," *Canadian Journal of the History of Sport and Physical Education* 10.1 (1979): 31.

120. "The Great Need of Kentucky," *Turf, Field and Farm*, 23 July 1881, 56.

121. "Turf Notes in Brief," *New York Sportsman*, 10 Aug. 1889, 129.

122. Basil W. Duke, *The Civil War Reminiscences of Basil W. Duke, C.S.A.* (New York: Cooper Square Press, 2001), 29.

123. For discussion of the political agenda behind the increasing popularity of narratives about loyal slaves, see Micki McElya, *Clinging to Mammy: The Faithful Slave in Twentieth-Century America* (Cambridge, MA: Harvard University Press, 2007), 5–11. See also Nina Silber, *The Romance of Reunion* (Chapel Hill: University of North Carolina Press, 1993), 113–33; David W. Blight, *Race and Reunion* (Cambridge, MA: Harvard University Press, 2001), 217–27.

124. C. Vann Woodward, *Origins of the New South 1877–1913* (1951; Baton Rouge: Louisiana State University Press, 1971), 57.

125. "Racing in the West," *Spirit of the Times*, 7 June 1890, 861.

126. "A Hint to Our Friends, the Middleweight Jockeys," *New York Sportsman*, 24 Nov. 1882, 408.

127. "New Orleans," *Spirit of the Times*, 8 May 1886, 456.

128. "Turf and Training Notes," *New York Sportsman*, 18 June 1887, 568; "Jumbled Little Bits," *New York Sportsman*, 9 Feb. 1889, 134.

129. "The Tattler's Tattle," *New York Sportsman*, 6 March 1886, 173; "Jumbled Little Bits," *New York Sportsman*, 17 Aug. 1889, 146.

130. "Post and Paddock," *Spirit of the Times*, 18 Aug. 1883, 84.

131. "Post and Paddock," *Spirit of the Times*, 15 Dec. 1883, 592.

132. "Echoes of the Day," *New York Sportsman*, 5 Feb. 1887, 122.

133. "Miscellaneous Turf Gossip," *Thoroughbred Record*, 29 Feb. 1896, 100.

134. "Southern Racing," *Spirit of the Times*, 29 March 1890, 413.

135. For a discussion of this possibility, see Wiggins, "Isaac Murphy," 20–21.

136. "The Great Strike," *Spirit of the Times*, 4 Aug. 1877, 750.

137. See, for a discussion of the importance of the figure of the economically successful African American in these debates, Heather Cox Richardson, *The Death of Reconstruction: Race, Labor, and Politics in the Post-Civil War North, 1865–1901* (Cambridge, MA: Harvard University Press, 2001), 183–216.

138. "First-Class Jockey," *Kentucky Live Stock Record*, 24 March 1883, 170. The advertisement turned out to be unnecessary. In the notes column of the same issue of the magazine, Murphy reported that, at press time he had more job offers than he could handle. See "Isaac Murphy," *Kentucky Live Stock Record*, 24 March 1883, 180.

139. "Saratoga," *Spirit of the Times*, 5 Sept. 1885, 169–70; "Chicago," *Spirit of the Times*, 17 July 1886, 785; "Isaac Murphy," *Kentucky Leader*, 20 March 1889, 3; "Jumbled Little Bits," *New York Sportsman*, 23 March 1889, 262; "Jumbled Little Bits," *New York Sportsman*, 6 April 1889, 310.

140. "Lexington, Ky.," *Spirit of the Times*, 24 Dec. 1887, 733.

141. Tarlton, "A Memorial," 136. For Tarlton's political commitment, see "Latonia," *Spirit of the Times and Sportsman*, 4 June 1892, 819; McDaniels, *Prince of Jockeys*, 156.

142. David Wiggins posits that, as Isaac Murphy became increasingly successful, he realized his own value as a marketable commodity and began to negotiate more selectively for employment. See David K. Wiggins, *Glory Bound: Black Athletes in a White America* (Syracuse: Syracuse University Press, 1997), 25–26.

143. See, for example, "Racing Notes," *New York Times*, 9 Oct. 1889, 3; "Post and Paddock," *Spirit of the Times and Sportsman*, 29 Oct. 1892, 539.

144. "Is the Laborer Worthy of His Hire?," *New York Sportsman*, 29 Nov. 1884, 456.

145. "Jockey Fees," *Spirit of the Times*, 23 June 1888, 392.

146. "Some Famous Jocks," *Lexington Leader*, 14 July 1892, 3; "Post and Paddock," *Spirit of the Times*, 21 Sept. 1889, 342; "Echoes of the Week," *New York Sportsman*, 19 Jan. 1889, 45.

147. "Hamilton's Poor Riding," *Brooklyn Daily Eagle*, 17 Aug. 1890, 3.

148. See, for one example, "Jumbled Little Bits," *New York Sportsman*, 19 Oct. 1889, 365.

149. "A Wealthy Negro Horse Jockey," *Milwaukee Sentinel*, 6 Jan. 1884, 9.

150. Borries, *Isaac Murphy*, 89–90; "Murphy Suspended," *Lexington Leader*, 29 Aug. 1890, 1; "Horse Gossip," *Turf, Field and Farm*, 5 Sept. 1890, 277; "Murphy Was Drunk," *Lexington Leader*, 27 Aug. 1890, 1; "Isaac Murphy's Mistake," *Lexington Leader*, 29 Aug. 1890, 3; "Murphy Lost Them $100,000," *New York World*, 27 Aug. 1890, 1.

151. Borries, *Isaac Murphy*, 99–100; "Post and Paddock," *Spirit of the Times*, 3 Sept 1887, 201; Longfellow, "Racing at Latonia," *Spirit of the Times and Sportsman*, 2 June 1894, 337.

152. See "Apolinaris Natural Mineral Water," *Kentucky Live Stock Record*, 24 Nov. 1877, 330; "Was Isaac Murphy Poisoned?" *Live Stock Record*, 22 Nov. 1890, 329; "Isaac Murphy Ill," *Lexington Leader*, 22 Nov. 1890, 1; "Isaac Murphy Harshly Judged," *Lexington Leader*, 9 Jan. 1891, 4; "Drunk or Drugged," *Brooklyn Daily Eagle*, 27 Aug. 1890, 2; "Isaac Murphy's Fall," *Cleveland Gazette*, 30 Aug. 1890, 2; "A Strange Illness," *Detroit Plaindealer*, 5 Sept. 1890, 1.

153. "Turf and Training Notes," *New York Sportsman*, 27 Aug. 1887, 204; "Post and Paddock," *Spirit of the Times*, 30 Aug. 1890, 226; "The Old-Time Jockeys," *Thoroughbred Record*, 1 May 1897, 209.

154. "A Grave Turf Scandal," *Brooklyn Daily Eagle*, 28 Aug. 1890, 1.

155. "Post and Paddock," *Spirit of the Times*, 30 Aug. 1890, 226. See also "A Monmouth Sensation," *New York Times*, 27 Aug. 1890, 3.

156. Longfellow, "Out at Churchill Downs," *Live Stock Record*, 18 Feb. 1893, 109.

157. "Post and Paddock," *Spirit of the Times and Sportsman*, 11 March 1893, 307.

158. "The Colored Archer," *Louisville Courier-Journal*, 15 May 1890, 2. See, for similar language on the subject, "KINGMAN," *Louisville Courier-Journal*, 14 May 1891, 6.

159. "Echoes of the Day," *New York Sportsman*, 7 Jan. 1888, 4.

160. Longfellow, "Racing at Latonia," *Spirit of the Times and Sportsman*, 2 June 1894, 338; "Western Racing," *Spirit of the Times and Sportsman*, 1 Dec. 1894, 670.

161. "New Orleans," *Spirit of the Times and Sportsman*, 22 Feb. 1896, 156. For a similar opinion, see "Kentucky In Front," *Spirit of the Times and Sportsman*, 20 Nov. 1895, 646.

162. "Isaac Murphy Buried," *New York Times*, 18 Feb. 1896, 6; "Post and Paddock," *Spirit of the Times and Sportsman*, 15 Feb. 1896, 135; "Isaac Murphy's Death," *Thoroughbred Record*, 15 Feb. 1896, 79; "Local Turf News," *Thoroughbred Record*, 14 March 1896, 126; "ISAAC MURPHY," *Lexington Leader*, 12 Feb. 1896, 4; "Noted Jockeys to Act as Pall Bearers at Isaac Murphy's Funeral," *Lexington Leader*, 14 Feb. 1896, 8; "LAST RITES," *Lexington Leader*, 16 Feb. 1896, 1; "Laid to Rest," *Lexington Leader*, 17 Feb. 1896, 5; "Wills Probated," *Lexington Leader*, 9 March 1896, 7; "Isaac Murphy: Lincoln Lodge of Masons Adopts Resolutions on His Death," *Lexington Leader*, 16 March 1896, 7. See, for discussion of the funeral, Wall, "Isaac Murphy," 114.

163. "A Knock Out," *Lexington Leader*, 16 Feb. 1896, 5.

164. For one analysis of the roots of Harlan's dissent, see Linda Przybyszewski, *The Republic according to John Marshal Harlan* (Chapel Hill: University of North Carolina Press, 1999), 95–99.

165. "Crisis for Negro Race," *New York Times*, 4 June 1900, 6; Rayford W. Logan, *The Betrayal of the Negro: From Rutherford B. Hayes to Woodrow Wilson* (1954; Cambridge, MA: Da Capo Press, 1997), 312–13.

7. I Have Got That Nigger Beat

1. "Winkfield's Success as a Jockey," *Louisville Courier-Journal*, 4 May 1902, sec. 3, 2.

2. Brownie Leach, "Major McDowell's Courtney," *The Blood-Horse*, 29 Jan. 1938, 218–19; Janet Patton, "Lexington House Offers Clues into Life of Little-Known Yet Acclaimed Black Horse Trainer," *Lexington Herald Leader*, 24 July 2011.

3. "Winkfield Tells How Alan-a-Dale Won," *Louisville Courier-Journal*, 4 May 1902, sec. 3, 2; Roy Terrell, "Around the World in Eighty Years," *Sports Illustrated*, 8 May 1961, 73–74.

4. "Winkfield Heartbroken," *Louisville Courier-Journal*, 3 May 1903, sec. 3, 4; "Pat Dunne Does Not Kick; He Only Complains," *Louisville Courier-Journal*, 3 May 1903, sec. 3, 4.

5. "Booker Thinks His Ride Won the Race," *Louisville Courier-Journal*, 3 May 1903, sec.3, 3.

6. Roster, 124th Infantry, U.S. Colored Troops, Accessed through Civil War Research Database; Joe Drape, *Black Maestro: The Epic Life of an American Legend* (New York: William Morrow, 2006), 5.

7. See, for example, "Close at New Orleans," *Spirit of the Times and Sportsman*, 31 March 1900, 230–31; "Chicago Racing," *Spirit of the Times and Sportsman*, 11 Aug. 1900, 83; Susan Hamburger, "Jimmy Winkfield: The 'Black Maestro' of African American Athletes," in *Out of the Shadows: A Biographical History of African American Athletes*, ed. David K. Wiggins (Fayetteville: University of Arkansas Press, 2006), 8–9; Drape, *Black Maestro*, 5–38.

8. Ed Hotaling, *Wink* (Camden, ME: McGraw-Hill, 2005), 76–79; Terrell, "Around the World," 79–80.

9. "Horse World," *Lexington Leader*, 12 Nov. 1903, 3; "Papers Signed," *Lexington Leader*, 15 Nov. 1903, 1.

10. Terrell, "Around the World," 80–81.

11. "Yankee Jockeys Abroad," *New York Times*, 25 Feb. 1901, 8; "Our Jockeys for Austria," *New York World*, 23 Feb. 1901, 4; "Colored Notes," *Lexington Leader*, 3 Sept. 1911, 5; "Jockey Thomas Sold to Russia," *Lexington Leader*, 23 Aug. 1911, 1.

12. Terrell, "Around the World," 80–81; "Horse Gossip," *Lexington Leader*, 7 June 1904, 7.

13. "Jockey Winkfield Did Well in Russia This Year," *Louisville Courier-Journal*, 11 Dec. 1904, sec. 3, 6.

14. "Jimmy Winkfield," *Cleveland Gazette*, 4 March 1905, 2. See also "Jimmy Winkfield," *Lexington Leader*, 1 Dec. 1904, 8.

15. "Winkfield," *Lexington Leader*, 7 March 1910, 1.

16. "Wants Divorce," *Lexington Leader*, 15 May 1911, 7; Drape, *Black Maestro*, 148.

17. For a discussion of the eastern European horse culture in which Winkfield flourished for more than fifteen years after he left the United States, see Drape, *Black Maestro*, 122–30; Hotaling, *Wink*, 135.

18. Terrell, "Around the World," 71.

19. The best discussion of the journey comes from Drape, *Black Maestro*, 188–98. See also Hotaling, *Wink*, 165–66; Hamburger, "Jimmy Winkfield," 15.

20. "Jockey Winkfield Now a Landlord," *Cleveland Gazette*, 6 June 1925, 2; Terrell, "Around the World," 71; Hotaling, *Wink*, 175–83; Drape, *Black Maestro*, 206–15.

21. Drape, *Black Maestro*, 229; Hotaling, *Wink*, 241–43.

22. "Those Germans Didn't Even Leave Him 'An Oat,' Declares Jockey-Trainer Jimmy Winkfield On His Return From France," *Lexington Leader*, 1 June 1941, 13; Terrell, "Around the World," 87; Hotaling, *Wink*, 274–80; Hamburger, "Jimmy Winkfield," 17; Drape, *Black Maestro*, 236–47.

23. Terrell, "Around the World," 88.

24. Hotaling, *Wink*, 291–92.

25. Drape, *Black Maestro*, 253.

26. William C. Rhoden, "The Long Ride to Redemption," *New York Times*, 28 April 2002, sports sec., 11.

27. Kent Hollingsworth, *The Wizard of the Turf: John E. Madden of Hamburg Place* (Lexington, KY: N.P., 1965), 2, 11–23.

28. Kent Hollingsworth, *The Kentucky Thoroughbred* (Lexington: University Press of Kentucky, 1976), 102–3.

29. William H. P. Robertson, *The History of Thoroughbred Racing in America* (Englewood Cliffs, NJ: Prentice Hall, 1964), 181.

30. W. A. Swanberg, *Whitney Father, Whitney Heiress* (New York: Charles Scribner's Sons, 1980), 168.

31. Ibid., 184; Bernard Livingston, *Their Turf* (New York: Arbor House, 1973), 50.

32. Henry Adams, *The Education of Henry Adams* (1918; Boston: Houghton Mifflin, 2000), 347–48.

33. Mark D. Hirsch, *W. C. Whitney: Modern Warwick* (Binghamton, NY: Vail-Ballou, 1948), 238–39; Dan M. Bowmar, *Giants of the Turf* (Lexington: The Blood Horse, 1960), 155; Swanberg, *Whitney Father, Whitney Heiress*, 16.

34. Elizabeth Sanders, *Roots of Reform: Farmers, Workers, and the American State, 1877–1917* (Chicago: University of Chicago Press, 1999), 410–11.

35. Richard Watson Gilder, *Grover Cleveland: A Record of Friendship* (New York: Century, 1910), 212–13.

36. Omar H. Ali, *In the Lion's Mouth: Black Populism in the New South, 1886–1900* (Jackson: University Press of Mississippi, 2010), 4–10.

37. W. E. Burghardt Du Bois, *The Black North in 1901* (New York: Arno Press, 1969), 5.

38. Marcy S. Sacks, *Before Harlem: The Black Experience in New York City before World War I* (Philadelphia: University of Pennsylvania Press, 2006), 9.

39. For discussion of the system's significance in the politics of both race and class in the South, see Glenda Elizabeth Gilmore, *Gender and Jim Crow: Women and the Politics of White Supremacy in North Carolina* (Chapel Hill: University of North Carolina Press, 1996), 61–62; Kevin K. Gaines, *Uplifting the Race: Black Leadership, Politics, and Culture in the Twentieth Century* (Chapel Hill: University of North Carolina Press, 1996), 30–31. For a brief overview of the creation of the complex of codes that made up Jim Crow, see C. Vann Woodward, *The Strange Career of Jim Crow*, rev. ed. (London: Oxford University Press, 1966), 97–108.

40. John B. Gordon to W. C. Whitney, 27 Nov. 1897, Container 94, Harry Payne Whitney Collection of William Collins Whitney Correspondence, Library of Congress.

41. Quoted in Edward O. Frantz, *The Door of Hope: Republican Presidents and the First Southern Strategy, 1877–1933* (Gainesville: University Press of Florida, 2011), 110–11. See also Frantz, *Door of Hope*, 62–63, 76–77, 107. For an admiring description of McKinley's Southern lecture tour, see "A New Era," *Kentucky Leader*, 23 Aug. 1888, 1.

42. Quoted in Hirsch, *W. C. Whitney*, 507. For an account of Whitney's efforts to avert the dangers of Bryanism, see Hirsch, *W. C. Whitney*, 477–507.

43. "Racing at Newport," *Spirit of the Times and Sportsman*, 22 Aug. 1896, 162.

44. Alden Hatch and Foxhall Keene, *Full Tilt: The Sporting Memoirs of Foxhall Keene* (New York: Derrydale, 1938), 102.

45. "Kentucky Conquers," *Louisville Courier-Journal*, 5 May 1898, 6.

46. Matthew Frye Jacobson, *Barbarian Virtues: The United States Encounters Foreign Peoples at Home and Abroad, 1876–1917* (New York: Hill and Wang, 2000), 139–72.

47. Hirsch, *W. C. Whitney*, 585. Swanberg, *Whitney Father, Whitney Heiress*, 44. See, for a discussion of the connection between a fascination for Thoroughbreds and a nineteenth-century passion for allegedly scientifically sanctioned social hierarchy, Ann Norton Greene, *Horses at Work: Harnessing Power in Industrial America* (Cambridge, MA: Harvard University Press, 2008), 235–36.

48. R. Gerald Alvey, *Kentucky Bluegrass Country* (Jackson: University Press of Mississippi, 1992), 138–39.

49. W. E. D. Stokes, *The Right to be Well Born* (New York: C.J. O'Brien, 1917), 83–87, 160–61.

50. Ibid., 101.

51. Ibid., 29.

52. Maryjean Wall, "Isaac Murphy: A Legacy Interrupted, The Intersection of Race and the Horse Industry in the Bluegrass," MA thesis, University of Kentucky, 2003, 139–40.

53. Lynn S. Renau, *Racing around Kentucky* (Louisville: N.P., 1995), 146.

54. Kent Hollingsworth, "A Man Who Knew Champions," *The Blood-Horse*, 24 Nov. 1975, 5153–54; Edward Bowen, *Masters of the Turf* (Lexington: The Blood Horse, 2007), 15.

55. "'Lonnie' Clayton," *Thoroughbred Record*, 7 March 1896, 113; Broad Church, "New Orleans," *Spirit of the Times and Sportsman*, 6 March 1897, 212; "Like Finding It," *Arkansas Gazette*, 6 April 1895, 1; "Jockey Clayton Will Ride Again," *Arkansas Democrat*, 24 March 1904, 6; Lonnie Clayton Subject File, North Little Rock History Commission.

56. "Jockey Simms Will Ride for Dwyer," *New York World*, 3 April 1903, 12; "How Simms was Discovered," *Thoroughbred Record*, 9 Feb. 1895, 87.

57. James Forman Sloan, *Tod Sloan, by Himself*, ed. A. Dick Luckman (New York: Brentano's, 1915), 84–85.

58. "Ike Thompson's Views," *New York Sun*, 5 May 1895, 8; "Foul Starts Turf Feud," *New York Times*, 3 Sept. 1900, 4; "Jockey Sims a Winner," *New York Sun*, 3 Dec. 1900, 8; C.C. Champine, "Musings Without Method," *Thoroughbred Record*, 12 Dec. 1936, 340. Newspapers and magazines occasionally spelled Simms's name as Sims.

59. "Better Than Miller," *Washington Post*, 13 June 1907, 9.

60. "'The Abbot' Wins the Latonia Derby in Mud," *Louisville Courier-Journal*, 11 June 1907, Dale Austin file, Jim Bolus Collections, Kentucky Derby Museum, Louisville, Kentucky. See also "Rides Six Winners," *Indianapolis Freeman*, 15 June 1907, 7; "Wonderful Record Made by Jockey Lee," *Louisville Courier-Journal*, 6 June 1907, 8; "The Abbot Wins Latonia Derby," *Thoroughbred Record*, 15 June 1907, 381; "Jockey J. Lee, the 'Black Demon' of the Turf," *Louisville Courier-Journal*, 6 June 1907, 8; "Chat of the Course," *Louisville Courier-Journal*, 6 June 1907, 8.

61. "The Black Problem," *Louisville Courier-Journal*, 6 June 1907, 6.

62. "Horse World," *Lexington Leader*, 14 Jan. 1902, 7.

63. Beth Tompkins Bates, *Pullman Porters and the Rise of Protest Politics in Black America, 1925–1945* (Chapel Hill: University of North Carolina Press, 2001), 17–22; Larry Tye, *Rising from the Rails* (New York: Henry Holt and Co., 2004), 23–35.

64. Thomas R. Hietala, *The Fight of the Century: Jack Johnson, Joe Louis, and the Struggle for Racial Equality* (Armonk, NY: M. E. Sharpe, 2002), 40–45.

65. Randy Roberts, "Year of the Comet: Jack Johnson versus Jim Jeffries, July 4, 1910," in *Sport and the Color Line*, ed. Patrick B. Miller and David K. Wiggins (New York: Routledge, 2004), 57.

66. *Jack Johnson, My Life and Battles*, ed. and trans. Christopher Rivers (Westport, CT: Praeger, 2007), 16–17; Geoffrey C. Ward, *Unforgivable Blackness: The Rise and Fall of Jack Johnson* (New York: Alfred A. Knopf, 2004), 13.

67. "A Popular Meeting," *Spirit of the Times and Sportsman*, 19 Oct. 1895, 455.

68. Broad Church, "Nashville," *Spirit of the Times and Sportsman*, 7 May 1892, 640.

69. See, for an acknowledgement of these tactics, "Few Negro Jockeys Left," *Washington Post*, 11 Jan. 1907, 8. See also Charles B. Parmer, *For Gold and Glory: The Story of Thoroughbred Racing in America* (New York: Carrick and Evans, 1939), 150.

70. "Jockey War at Chicago," *Thoroughbred Record*, 18 Aug. 1900, 77; "Hawthorne's Close," *Spirit of the Times and Sportsman*, 4 Oct. 1902, 243.

71. "Gossip of the Racetrack," *New York Sun*, 23 May 1908, 5.

72. See, for example, "Jockeys Draw the Line on Color," *Atlanta Constitution*, 5 Nov. 1904, 9.

73. Mark Ribowsky, *A Complete History of The Negro Leagues 1884 to 1955* (New York: Birch Lane, 1995), 18–19; David W. Zang, *Fleet Walker's Divided Heart: The Life of Baseball's First Black Major Leaguer* (Lincoln: University of Nebraska Press, 1995), 37–44, 54–55.

74. "Negro Jockeys Shut Out," *New York Times*, 29 July 1900, 14. The successful black cyclist Major Taylor, a sports celebrity of the same period, had his American career curtailed by a similar complicity of the white authorities of his sport in the violent attacks of his white competitors. See Andrew Ritchie, "The League of American Wheelmen, Major Taylor and the 'Color Question' in the United States in the 1890s," *Ethnicity, Sport, Identity: Struggles for Status*, ed. J.A. Mangan and Andrew Ritchie (London: Frank Cass, 2004), 15–30; Andrew Ritchie, *Major Taylor: The Extraordinary Career of a Champion Bicycle Racer* (Baltimore: Johns Hopkins University Press, 1988), 83.

75. Ribowsky, *Negro Leagues*, 32–34; Zang, *Divided Heart*, 47–58.

76. "State Racing Commission," *Spirit of the Times and Sportsman*, 9 April 1898, 363; Carole Case, *The Right Blood: America's Aristocrats in Thoroughbred Racing* (New Brunswick, NJ: Rutgers University Press, 2001), 19–20; John Dizikes, *Yankee Doodle Dandy: The Life and Times of Tod Sloan* (New Haven: Yale University Press, 2000), 81–82; Edward Hotaling, *The Great Black Jockeys* (Rocklin, CA: Forum, 1999), 302–3; Robertson, *History of Thoroughbred Racing*, 175; Lyman Horace Weeks, *The American Turf: An Historical Account of Racing in the United States with Biographical Sketches of Turf Celebrities* (New York: The Historical Company, 1898), 144.

77. "The Licensing of Jockeys," *Spirit of the Times and Sportsman*, 4 March 1893, 251; "To Trainers and Jockeys," *Spirit of the Times and Sportsman*, 31 March 1894, 370; "New Orleans," *Spirit of the Times and Sportsman*, 7 April 1894, 412.

78. *San Francisco Chronicle*, 28 March 1896, 11; "Post and Paddock," *Spirit of the Times and Sportsman*, 4 April 1896, 352; "Jockey Chorn's Mount First," *New York Times*, 9 Dec. 1902, 6.

79. William C. Rhoden has termed the process of altering the rules of a sport to deny black athletes opportunities the Jockey Syndrome, a phenomenon he traces through the twentieth century. See William C. Rhoden, *$40 Million Slaves: The Rise, Fall, and Redemption of the Black Athlete* (New York: Crown, 2006), 67–68. See, on the same topic, James Robert Saunders and Monica Renae Saunders, *Black Winning Jockeys* (Jefferson, NC: McFarland, 2003), 104–5.

80. George M. Frederickson, *The Black Image in the White Mind: The Debate on Afro-American Character and Destiny, 1817–1914* (New York: Harper & Row, 1971), 260–62; Gaines, *Uplifting the Race*, 68; Sacks, *Before Harlem*, 7–9, 42–56; Nina Silber, *The Romance of Reunion* (Chapel Hill: University of North Carolina Press, 1993), 133–39.

81. Frank Dumont, *Burnt Cork or the Amateur Minstrel* (New York: De Witt, 1881), 74.

82. Sacks, *Before Harlem*, 49–56; Wall, "Isaac Murphy," 81–82; Bryan F. Le Beau, *Currier and Ives: America Imagined* (Washington, D.C.: Smithsonian Institution, 2001), 233–34.

83. Hatch and Keene, *Full Tilt*, 33–34.

84. "Horse World," *Lexington Leader*, 14 Jan. 1902, 7.

85. "Negro Riders of Renown," *Daily Racing Form*, 17 Feb. 1922, 1.

86. "Negro Jockeys," *The Blood-Horse*, 27 July 1929, 5.

87. "Negro Rider on Wane, White Jockeys' Superior Intelligence Supersedes," *Washington Post*, 20 Aug. 1905, sports sec., 3.

88. "Is the Black Jockey Doomed?" *Topeka Plaindealer*, 27 July 1906, 1.

89. Charles E. Van Loan, *Old Man Curry* (New York: George H. Doran, 1917), 18. Variant spelling in original. For a biting sketch of Van Loan, see Jimmy Breslin, *Damon Runyon* (New York: Laurel, 1991), 59–75.

90. Van Loan, *Old Man Curry*, 251–76. Variant spelling in original.

91. "Passing of the Colored Jockeys," *Chicago Defender*, 10 Feb. 1912, 4.

92. Kelly Miller, "'Jockeyed' Out of Jobs," *Amsterdam News*, 22 Feb. 1928, 20.

93. Lonnie Clayton Subject File, North Little Rock History Commission.

94. "Ex-Jockey Simms Ejected," *New York Times*, 22 Sept. 1907, sec. 4, 1; "Ex-Jockey Sims Shot," *Amsterdam News*, 6 June 1923, 1; "Final Rites for Noted Ex-Jockey," *Amsterdam News*, 2 March 1927, 1.

95. "Tommie Blevins Former Well Known Jockey Killed in a Saloon Fight," *Lexington Leader*, 30 Sept. 1900, 1; "Goes Free," *Lexington Leader*, 8 March 1901, 5.

96. "Frank Perkins," *Lexington Leader*, 9 Oct. 1897, 5; "Jockey 'Monk' Overton is Insane," *Thoroughbred Record*, 30 April 1910, 211.

97. "Jock'y Britton's Wife," *Lexington Leader*, 15 May 1894, 6; "Tom Britton Remarries," *Lexington Leader*, 10 July 1900, 7.

98. Robert S. Nevill, "The Thoroughbred," *Turf, Field and Farm*, 14 Sept. 1900, 1053; "'Soup' Perkins Fined," *Lexington Leader*, 25 Sept. 1900, 5; "'Soup' Perkins Practically Penniless," *Indianapolis Freeman*, 29 Sept. 1900, 7.

99. "'Soup' Perkins Last Noted Negro Rider," *Lexington Leader*, 12 Sept. 1911, 10; "'Soup' Perkins," *Lexington Leader*, 17 Aug. 1911, 1; "Colored Notes," *Lexington Leader*, 21 Aug. 1911, 7.

100. "Attempt Failed," *Lexington Leader*, 12 Aug. 1899, 7. Isom lost the sight of the eye the bullet had plowed through.

101. "Took His Own Life," *Lexington Leader*, 20 May 1901, 7; "Lost $50 on a Race," *Lexington Leader*, 20 May 1901, 7.

Epilogue

1. E.J. Kahn, "Worner Revisited," *New Yorker*, 13 April 1981, 32–33.

2. David J. Garrow, *Bearing the Cross: Martin Luther King, Jr., and the Southern Christian Leadership Conference* (New York: William Morrow, 1986), 560–61; Luther Adams, *Way Up North in Louisville: African American Migration in the Urban South, 1930–1970* (Chapel Hill: University of North Carolina Press, 2010), 174–80; Tracy E. K'Meyer, *Civil Rights in the Gateway to the South: Louisville, Kentucky, 1945–1980* (Lexington: University Press of Kentucky, 2009), 129–36.

3. "Derby Demonstrations Neither Helpful Nor Prudent," *Louisville Defender*, 4 May 1967, 6. See also "Isaac Murphy Gets New Resting Place," *Louisville Defender*, 4 May 1967, 1; "Demonstrators 'Prep' for Derby Effort;

Carmichael Due Here," *Louisville Defender*, 4 May 1967, 1; "Negro Jockeys Once Prominent in Ky. Derby," *Louisville Defender*, 4 May 1967, 1; "Long Shot Wins 93rd Derby as Threat of Disturbances Looms," *Louisville Defender*, 11 May 1967, 1; Taylor Ballew, "Isaac Murphy Is Restored to Place of Honor at Lexington," *Louisville Defender*, 11 May 1967, 11; John Alexander, "Isaac Murphy Honored Again," *Lexington Leader*, 4 May 1967, 1; Kent Hollingsworth, "A Misty 93rd Kentucky Derby," *The Blood-Horse*, 13 May 1967, 1208.

4. *Mobile Press* clipping, Isaac Murphy File, Keeneland Library; Betty Earle Borries, *Isaac Murphy: Kentucky's Record Jockey* (Berea, KY: Kentucke Imprints, 1988), 105.

5. "Louisville," *Spirit of the Times*, 24 May 1884, 516.

6. Frank Borries, "Ike Murphy's Grave," *Courier-Journal Magazine*, 7 May 1961, 14–16; Borries, *Isaac Murphy*, 106–7.

7. Robert J. Clark, "Tiger Blood," *Thoroughbred Record*, 27 April 1967, 1130; Linda J. Greenhouse, "Questions the Question," *Thoroughbred Record*, 11 May 1968, 1220; William Robertson, "Pick Up the Pieces and Hold Up Your Head," *Thoroughbred Record*, 18 May 1968, 1297; Douglas Martin, "Peter D. Fuller Dies at 89; Had to Return Derby Purse," *New York Times*, 19 May 2012, A22.

8. John Alexander, "Isaac Murphy Now Legend to Thoroughbred Racing," *Lexington Leader*, 4 May 1967, 11.

9. David Alexander, "Delayed Honors," *Thoroughbred Record*, 6 May 1967, 1176.

10. Ed McNamara, *Cajun Racing* (New York: DRF Press, 2008), 135.

11. Paul Devlin, ed., *Rifftide: The Life and Opinions of Papa Jo Jones as Told to Albert Murray* (Minneapolis: University of Minnesota Press, 2011), 80.

12. Harry Worcester Smith to William Woodward, 11 Sept. 1942, Box 1, Folder 8, Elizabeth Amis Cameron Blanchard Papers #3367, Southern Historical Collection, The Wilson Library, University of North Carolina at Chapel Hill.

13. William Woodward, *Gallant Fox: A Memoir* (New York: Derrydale Press, 1931), 97–103.

14. "Grandfather's Advice," *National Sporting Library Newsletter* 34 (June 1992): 2.

15. William Woodward, *Memoir of Andrew Jackson, Africanus* (New York: Derrydale, 1938), 33.

16. Susan Braudy, *This Crazy Thing Called Love: The Golden World and Fatal Marriage of Ann and Billy Woodward* (New York: Alfred A. Knopf, 1992), 69–70.

17. Harry Worcester Smith, "Steeplechasing," 43–44, Folder 1, Sporting Reminiscences, 1939, n.d., Accession #12652, Special Collections, University of Virginia Library.

18. Harry Worcester Smith, "The Death of Wheeler," 4–10; "The Tautz Coat," unpaginated, Folder 2, Sporting Reminiscences, 1939, n.d., Accession #12652, Special Collections, University of Virginia Library.

19. Debra Barbezat and James Hughes have done the most detailed work on the decline in black horsemen's numbers and the causes of that decline in their paper "Finding the Lost Jockeys." An unpublished copy is in the author's possession.

20. "A Battle Between Stallions," *Live Stock Record*, 8 July 1893, 25.

21. Joe H. Palmer, *This Was Racing*, ed. Red Smith (New York: A.S. Barnes, 1953), 80–81. See also on Harbut as a shaper of Man o' War's career, Dorothy Ours, *Man o' War: A Legend Like Lightning* (New York: St. Martin's, 2006), 269–70.

22. Maryjean Wall, "In Their Own Words," *Lexington Herald-Leader*, 26 Aug. 2001, K1.

23. Lawrence Scanlan, *The Horse That God Built* (New York: Thomas Dunne, 2007), 13, 121–25.

24. "Oscar Dishman Jr., Thoroughbred Horse Trainer for More Than 40 Years, Dies at 77," *Lexington Herald-Leader*, 3 October 2000; Interview with Oscar Dishman Jr., 16 Sept. 1986, Blacks in Lexington Oral History Project, Louie B. Nunn Center for Oral History, University of Kentucky Libraries.

25. Bernard Livingston, *Their Turf* (New York: Arbor House, 1973), 258–59. For a similar summing up of the situation from the perspective of a man born in the nineteenth century, see Nate Cantrell, interview with Jim Bolus, 4 March 1975, typescript, Jim Bolus Collections, Kentucky Derby Museum, Louisville, Kentucky.

26. Ted Carroll, "What Happened to the Negro Jockey?" *Our Sports*, July 1953, 71.

27. Rick Cushing, "In Recent Years, Derby Hasn't Been Mixed Race," *Louisville Courier-Journal*, 30 April 1990, Black Jockeys File, Keeneland Library.

28. Melissa Hoppert, "Jockey. Period," *New York Times*, 29 April 2013, D1.

29. Lee L. Brown, "Memory of Turf King Recalled As Classic Kentucky Derby Looms," *Pittsburgh Courier*, 18 May 1929, B4.

30. "New Era for black jockeys," *Louisville Courier-Journal*, 16 July 1974, B11.

31. Nick Rousso, "The Right Man at the Right Time: Kevin Krigger Chases the Derby Dream," kentuckyderby.com, accessed 6 May 2013, http://www.kentuckyderby.com/news/2013/05/03/right-man-right-time-kevin-krigger-chases-derby-dream.

32. Leon Nichols, telephone interview with the author, 14 Nov. 2011.

33. Larry Muhammad, "Oliver Lewis and His Ride into Derby History," *Louisville Courier-Journal*, 25 April 2004, H1.

34. Karla Ward, "Newtown Pike Extension to Be Renamed Oliver Lewis Way," *Lexington Herald-Leader*, 31 Aug. 2010; Edward Dudley Brown subject file, Woodford County Historical Society, Versailles, Kentucky.

35. Merlene Davis, "Bring Your Shovel to the Isaac Murphy Art Garden, *Lexington Herald-Leader*, 10 May 2011.

36. Frank X. Walker, telephone interview with the author, 23 Nov. 2011.

37. Frank X. Walker, "Healing Songs," *Isaac Murphy: I Dedicate This Ride* (Lexington: Old Cove Press, 2010), 65–66.

38. Frank X. Walker interview; Tom Eblen, "Isaac Murphy Bicycle Club Seeks to Get Kids on Path to Fitness, Fun," *Lexington Herald-Leader,* 29 Aug. 2011.

39. Jill13, comment, John Cheves, "Jockey Discovers History of Black Horsemen at Local Cemetery," *Lexington Herald-Leader,* 19 June 2011.

40. Ralph Ellison, *Three Days before the Shooting,* ed. John F. Callahan and Adam Bradley (New York: Modern Library, 2010), 933–38.

Acknowledgments

This project would never have been completed without the extraordinary generosity of a tremendous number of people. My first research on this topic was conducted at the Keeneland Library in Lexington, Kentucky, where Cathy Schenck and her staff provided an invaluable and comfortable place to work, as well as rare sources and illustrations key to the project. All historians should be lucky enough to work at Keeneland. I owe deep thanks to all the repositories I visited in Kentucky, including the University of Kentucky Library, the Kentucky Historical Society, the Kentucky Derby Museum at Churchill Downs, the Lexington Public Library (particularly the admirably efficient folks in the Kentucky Room), and the Woodford County Historical Society.

I also owe a large debt to the staffs at the Louisiana and Lower Mississippi Valley Collections at Louisiana State University, the Southern Historical Collection at the University of North Carolina, and the South Caroliniana Library at the University of South Carolina. Special thanks are due to Graham Duncan of the South Caroliniana Library, who introduced me to collections that I had not dared to hope existed. I also wish to thank the stunningly efficient staff of the Virginia Historical Society, Mary Jo Fairchild and everyone at the South Carolina Historical Society, and the unfailingly helpful archivists at the Mississippi Department of Archives and History. The Dolph Briscoe Center for American History at the University of Texas, the Swem Library at the College of William

& Mary, the National Sporting Library, and the Special Collections Department at Duke University also provided valuable assistance.

As I completed early research in the Northeast, I was fortunate enough to benefit from the collections and expertise of the staff at a number of archives, including the Rare Book and Manuscript Library at the University of Pennsylvania, the Rare Book and Manuscript Library at Columbia University, the National Museum of Racing, and the Saratoga Historical Society. The Saratoga Springs Public Library is a model for institutions of its kind. My greatest debt is to the Beinecke Library at Yale, where I was fortunate enough to find unparalleled resources and librarians who set a standard that spoils the researcher.

In the final months of my research, the North Carolina State Archives, the Benson Ford Research Center of the Henry Ford Museum, and the North Little Rock History Commission kindly and quickly provided me with crucial information. A week spent at the Library of Congress and the Small Special Collections Library at the University of Virginia shaped my ultimate vision of the project's trajectory. And as I finished up final details, the interlibrary loan staffs at Loyola University New Orleans and Washington University in St. Louis rapidly secured me necessary materials. In the field of interlibrary loan, very special thanks are due to the staff at the East Bank Regional Branch of the Jefferson Parish Public Library. They worked for months and successfully located a succession of obscure titles for a patron they came to know by name, and they were always models of friendly professionalism. Finally, Leon Nichols, James Long, and Frank X. Walker all kindly consented to grant me telephone interviews as I finished up the manuscript. Particular thanks are due to Anna Currance, who urged me to go to the Virginia Museum of Fine Arts and see paintings she thought might be relevant to my work, an outing that changed the course of this project. The VMFA has courteously allowed the reproduction of some of those paintings in this book. A very special thank you to Catherine Woodford Clay, who allowed me to reproduce her marvelous Troye painting of Medley and Charles Stewart, and to Mary Rezny, who patiently worked with me to create a marvelous image to give my readers an idea of the painting's remarkable impact.

A John F. Enders Fellowship from Yale and a fellowship from the Gilder Lehrman Center for the Study of Slavery, Resistance, and Abolition helped to fund my research. I am also very grateful to the friends who have supported me through the research process. Without Liz Westin, this project would have been nearly impossible. She gave me a place to come home to during my long research trips to Lexington, and her intelligence and wit made the whole experience delightful. And, at the very end, she made it possible for me to find my favorite illustration in the book. Monica Westin has kept me sane and sanguine about my life and this project for more than a decade. Tia Subramanian, Lincoln Mayer, and Tess Senderowicz all hosted me at various times and deserve huge thanks, since putting up with a historian in the hours between archive visits must be a frustrating experience. There is no better person to take a research trip with than Amanda Behm, and I hope we do it again soon. Jenny Lambe, Lauren Pearlman, Jeff Gonda, and Sigma Colon have been great friends and patient and insightful listeners to my concerns about this project. Marcy Kaufman made the history department at Yale an efficient and cheerful place to work through the force of her own kindness and intelligence. Tim Retzloff and Rick Yuille have been dear in friendship and formidable in research expertise. Joe Yannielli's unfailing kindness about other people's work and his intellectual creativity are both inspirational. Harold Baquet graciously contributed his artistic talent to the project and encouraged me to keep thinking about difficult historical questions, because they still matter. Jan Bradshaw has been an inspiring example of wit and resilience. I am proud to call her my friend. Ryan, Carl, Jessika, Glenda, and all the Brasseauxs have treated me like one of their own since my first day of graduate school, for which I cannot thank them enough. I could not have found a better place to spend two years than the American Culture Studies program at Washington University. Iver Bernstein ought to give lessons in how to be a supportive colleague, and Randy Calvert, Noah Cohan, Ben Cooper, Kate Fama, Jennifer Gallinat, Heidi Kolk, and Tina Marti did their best to make sure that writing a book did not drive me any further around the bend than I was before.

I particularly want to thank my teachers. Barbara Beachler gave me the gift of passion for African American history and literature, for which I cannot thank her enough. Francis Couvares was the first person to show me the kind of historian and teacher I wanted to be. Kevin Sweeney has always given me invaluable and witty advice on topics that span the university and the racetrack. I have benefited immensely from Clark Dougan's wisdom and kindness. Kim Townsend has been my dear friend for more than a decade, and both his friendship and his sensitive reading of this manuscript are deeply important to me. I also owe many thanks to my students, who continue to convince me that all this is worth doing. Joe Geylin and Kathryn Olivarius have earned extra thanks, since they both read these pages with their usual insight.

Joanne Freeman has been a source of excellent and much-appreciated advice. Edward Rugemer has been a sympathetic and meticulous critic and mentor. I am very grateful to both of them for their support of me and of this project. My biggest thanks must go to David Blight, who has known me since before I wanted to be a historian and who has been unfailingly kind to me and supportive of my work ever since. He has been a discerning reader, an inspiring mentor, and a good friend.

It has been a great pleasure to work with Joyce Seltzer throughout this process. I am grateful for her belief that this project was interesting and important, and I feel lucky to have benefitted from her skill, her kindness, and her patience. I have always admired Brian Distelberg's intelligence and dry wit, and I have been pleased to have him play such an important role in bringing the manuscript to completion. My thanks are also due to Fitzhugh Brundage and an anonymous reader, both of whom made suggestions that improved the manuscript a great deal. Edward Wade and John Raymond helped to put the final touches on the project with swift professionalism.

I have saved my thanks to my family for last, since what I have to thank them for is the most complicated to put into words. The horses drew me to this project in the beginning, and they have seen me through it. Anne Dunn and Morris and Adin Caffery have taken care of me throughout, as they always do. My mother understood the tough spots better than anyone and helped me through them as no one else could. My father and I have shared this process from the beginning. He has read every word of these pages many times and has served as a consultant on matters big and small. He and Al and I worked on this project every day, and now that it is at an end, I'm so glad we did it together.

Index